A heartfelt story which
a powerful teaching tool…this
lead by examp

Benjamin Breaking Barriers is a compelling read, coming at a time when 1 in every 88 children is being diagnosed with autism. This story appeals to heart and mind alike, taking the reader through the fascinating process of autism therapy while also revealing the psyche and philosophies of Benjamin's mother. A valuable resource for anyone involved in working with an autistic individual; parents and therapists alike will find inspiration in the creative ideas put forth by the author.

Synopsis: Benjamin is diagnosed with autism at the age of two, and his symptoms fit textbook descriptions. He is completely nonverbal and has withdrawn from the world; he has disappeared into the devastating isolation of autism and is taken over by the strange, repetitive behaviors that accompany the condition. Through the loving and determined intervention of his mother, and with the help of a caring community of family members, friends, therapists, and consultants, Benjamin eventually develops speech and begins to know the joys of interacting with the people and the environment around him. He is revealed to have an essentially sunny and loving nature, although the problems caused by his autism are often heart wrenching and can subvert his personality.

Over the course of years, virtually all of Benjamin's waking hours are spent in therapeutic activity and engagement; he is continually guided by the creativity and energy of his mother. She refuses to lower her standards and "be reasonable". Instead, she continually reaches for the stars in hopes that Benjamin will one day move beyond his autism and lead a life of normalcy. Meanwhile, she struggles to maintain her own sense of self, burning the midnight oil in pursuit of her professional life as a musician and a writer. The deep spiritual relationship that exists between mother and son allows them to grow into a team; together, they achieve goals that few would have dreamed possible.

Now it is 2013, the present. Benjamin is in high school and, with the aid of his mother, has embarked on the path of becoming a compelling public speaker. He has already moved audiences to both laughter and tears with his forty-five-minute presentation on autism titled, *Breaking Through Barriers,* and is making an impact on his peers and the larger community, encouraging people in all walks of life to meet their own challenges. He has a website, a blog, and a Facebook page, and is being recognized as an exceptional role model.

Benjamin's life story is inseparable from the storyline of his mother's dedication to helping him, and the two intertwined histories provide an inspiring narrative—the underlying message is one of hope and perseverance. The author recognizes that the storm clouds of life can have a silver lining and that unexpected gifts may be reaped from this recognition. She finds ways to meet the daily challenges that arise from her son's autism and detects the hand of destiny in the process. Thus, the story of Benjamin is punctuated by moments of elation and celebration that will uplift the reader's spirit.

Google *Benjamin Breaking Barriers* to locate our website, blog, YouTube channel, and Facebook page.

Advance Praise for Malva Freymuth Tarasewicz's
Benjamin Breaking Barriers: Autism — A Journey of Hope

"Full of deep emotion, raw edges, and heart-lifting moments...both a love story and a guidebook. At the heart is the relationship between mother and son and how the bond has given Benjamin wings to show the world who he is: a young man with autism who has built a life on his interests, passions, skills, and—most of all—relationships. Get ready to fall in love!"

Anna Stewart—author of *Mother Blessings: Honoring Women Becoming Mothers*

"Truly inspiring and engaging. I recommend that any parent whose child has special needs or any professional who works with these families read this book. It will give them hope and perspective on what is possible."

Dr. Robert Melillo—chiropractic neurologist and bestselling author of *Disconnected Kids*; *Reconnected Kids; Autism: The Scientific Truth;* co–founder of *Brain Balance Achievement Centers*

"Remarkably intimate and heartfelt...encourages and inspires. A brilliant memoir that is also a teaching tool, providing a wealth of insight and education for families who are facing autism. The dance that Malva has created weaves traditional and alternative therapies with pure, unconditional love and positive regard. The beauty of her love will help Benjamin continue on his journey, as well as many others who are able to learn from their story."

Patti Ashley, Ph.D.— psychotherapist and author of *Living in the Shadow of the Too-Good Mother Archetype*

"An inspirational, hopeful, and concrete roadmap for how parents can help children with autism to reach their full potential. It is also a testament to the perseverance and love of a parent who is determined to help her child come into his own."

Rosalind Wiseman—New York Times bestselling author of *Queen Bees and Wannabes*; *Masterminds and Wingmen*

"*Benjamin Breaking Barriers* touches the core. That the arts may bring forth speech and are expressive of the human being that playfully engages and learns, is this book's discovery. That we make ourselves through art is its revelation. In her choice of artistic activities that bring forth Benjamin's personality and through which he develops his capacities, Malva works with that which is intrinsic to us as human beings, that human ground between play and discipline, the loving interest that awakens as it engages in what it discovers. This book breaks boundaries for us readers too."

Glenda Monasch—eurythmy therapist and co-founder of *Sound Circle Eurythmy*

"A gifted writer, a gifted parent, and a patient, caring mom. Others can learn and benefit from Malva's experiences and considerable wisdom. She provides abundant examples of hope which show that many of the myths of autism can be challenged and even overcome. There are many distinctions that set giftedness and autism apart, but there are also many parallels, and Benjamin displays many of these commonalities. This "twice exceptionality" (having areas of extreme strength and areas of extreme limitations) is often hard for others to accept and understand. Benjamin required much therapeutic intervention, but *all* children benefit from guidance, modeling, role playing, direct instruction, and self-reflection. All children need someone who believes in them. For the reader's benefit, various therapeutic practices are shared, along with explanations."

Terry Bradley, M.A.— Gifted and Talented specialist, president-elect of the *Colorado Association of Gifted and Talented*

For further endorsements/reviews, please visit
www.benjaminbreakingbarriers.com

Benjamin Breaking Barriers
Autism — A Journey of Hope

Malva Freymuth Tarasewicz

*to Elise and Judy —
with very best wishes,
Jan 2014
Malva*

*Dear Elise,
I feel so lucky to have you as
a friend! Enjoy my close-
up!
— Benjamin*

*This book presents the experiences and opinions of the author. It is not
intended to be a substitute for consultation with professional clinicians.
The publisher and the author disclaim responsibility for any adverse effects
resulting directly or indirectly from information contained in this book.*

Front and back cover photos: Janet Folsom
Cover & book layout: Eric May
Printed in the United States

Publisher's Cataloging-In-Publication Data

Tarasewicz, Malva Freymuth.
Benjamin Breaking Barriers: Autism—A Journey of Hope / Malva Freymuth
Tarasewicz. – 1st ed.
1. Autistic children—United States—Biography.
2. Parents of autistic children—United States—Biography.
3. Autism in children—Treatment—Case studies.
4. Autism in adolescence—Treatment—Case studies.
5. Tarasewicz, Benjamin.
6. Tarasewicz, Malva.
I. Title.

Library of Congress PCN: 2013920100
ISBN 978-0-9670027-4-3 (soft cover)

Dedication

For Benjamin—
the son and angel who has shaped my life…

For my husband, Rick—
whose loving support has made it possible to follow my inner voice…

And for Peter and Karin, my parents—
who have been a help and influence throughout…

I love you all.

Table of Contents

Part I: The Window of Greatest Opportunity
Birth to Age Five

1999

Part II: Keep Reaching for the Stars
Age Five to Young Adulthood, and Beyond

Appendix

NOTE: In the interest of protecting privacy, most individuals in this account appear under a pseudonym.

Part I

The Window of
Greatest Opportunity

Birth to Age Five

Prologue

Imagine—you have a child, a beautiful child, of golden heart and loving manner, blue-eyed, blond-haired, and with the face of an angel…of ready smiles that light the world, of laughter and joy shared generously, making all around smile and laugh in response…

Imagine—that child begins to talk and to communicate with you, and then…gradually, you find that the blue eyes aren't looking at you anymore… you realize that you haven't heard the babbling and the first words in a while… you find that your child is withdrawing into a world all its own, far away from yours, rocking in the mindless rhythm of those children you just saw on TV— in the program that featured the neglected children of Rumanian orphanages, starved for touch and human contact…

But *your* child has always been loved, and hugged, and talked to. You have given up your career aspirations for a while, putting them on ice so you can fully enjoy the new experience of parenthood. You have long been desirous of this most important job on the planet: that of cultivating a caring, compassionate human being whose life will touch others, whose life will be fulfilling and meaningful…

Imagine—you are now handed a diagnosis. *Autism.* You are shocked to read phrases like *"lifelong disability…intensive, ongoing therapy offers some chance for improvement…a lifetime of support and accommodation likely…is occurring with increasing frequency…cause(s) as yet unknown…"*

Now what?

If you are like me, you get to work. You don't waste time. Every hour of delay means that your child is one hour more down that inexorable path towards isolation. Every day that you lose will allow your child's diverted brain to move farther down that lonely path, away from the fullness of life and love, away from the vigorous world of *"us,"* of *"we,"* of the *community.*

You try to deal with your confusion of feelings—the frantic desire to deny reality, the painful paroxysms of grief, the flaring fire of anger—and you push past the initial paralysis of being overwhelmed. You dive into therapeutic interventions, and you find your way into gradual acceptance while working to recover your shining star-of-a-child from the deep, dark clouds that have obscured its light.

You also find yourself writing in a personal journal, creating a daily log detailing the process that you and your child are going through.

That is how it was for me seventeen years ago. Upon realizing that my son Benjamin had autism, I immediately began therapeutic work with him. Every evening, I sat down and wrote about what we had done, about what Benjamin had achieved (or hadn't), about how I was feeling and what I thought might be done to help him the next day.

By the time Benjamin was seven years old and had entered first grade in a public school, I had already generated several-thousand pages of single-spaced, finely typed journal entries filled with the creative ideas that were helping Benjamin. The joys and the heartaches that accompanied our journey were in there too. And while I cut back my journaling somewhat after Benjamin became elementary school age, I did continue to record the meaningful aspects of his life and mine. These materials have allowed me to tell our story, up to the present, in all its fullness.

I have been an intuitive writer since childhood. I am also a professional musician; my primary instrument is the violin. Since my early teens, my mind has been preoccupied with questions such as: How can I best build this particular skill? How can I make it more efficient? How can I make it part of something beautiful and meaningful?

It is no surprise then, that when Benjamin was diagnosed, I already possessed the necessary analytical and creative skills to begin working with him in a therapeutic manner. And oh, how much I have learned from Benjamin along the way! When you are dealing with autism, you learn to take nothing for granted; every little thing that might naturally be expected to develop in a child becomes something that must be worked at, triggered, developed, created. What a miracle then, what a cause for celebration, when a new neural pathway springs into life or an oft repeated drill becomes an integrated skill.

But, when you are in the midst of toiling, not knowing whether anything will come of it, you find that the real challenge is maintaining the capacity for hope and renewed determination. You realize that you need the help and support of two kinds of angels: the unseen kind, as well as the kind embodied in the people who share their love and talents with you.

This is the story of how, with ongoing help, Benjamin has grown from being a lost and silent toddler to being a bright, social young adult who loves his friends and gives inspiring educational presentations, in spite of the fact that he still has to deal with autism challenges on a daily basis.

1997

1

Where It All Began: San Diego, California
January 1997

A stiff ocean breeze whipped my hair as I jogged alongside the ocean, comfortable in a light sweat shirt and thin running tights. It was January and, just as I did each morning come rain or shine, I was out exercising, pushing our blue baby-jogger with its large wheels and fat tires. Benjamin—two-and-a-quarter years old and big for his age—was nestled in the canvas seat with a woolly blanket tucked around his legs. As his comfortable carriage rolled along, he gazed silently out across the grey waters of the Pacific Ocean, watching the rhythmic ebb and flow of small waves breaking close to shore, contemplating the white fizz that ran up the beach and then disappeared, soaking into fine beige sand. The early morning fog was lifting. Blue patches of sky were already visible, and rays of sunshine were beginning to dapple the uneven sand, creating a play of light and shadow across the generous beach.

On returning home from our morning outing, I parked the jogger behind the quaint cottage we had rented for the past two-and-a-half years, lifted Benjamin out of his seat, and watched him climb the two stairs that led to our back door. We went inside, and Benjamin made a beeline for his box of wooden blocks. He plunked down and began building a tall tower, carefully balancing narrow blocks, one on top of another. Soon, the tower was nearly as tall as he was. Tensing his body and breathing rapidly with excitement, Benjamin stopped to survey his creation with an intent and serious look on his face, his arms outstretched and his hands rotating rapidly in an odd twirling-flapping motion. Then he picked up another block and very carefully placed it on top of the previous one.

I held my breath, watching. Slowly, the tower swayed and then toppled with a crash. Benjamin crowed with excitement, standing rigidly on tiptoe and giggling wildly as his hands danced and twirled. Then he immediately began the process all over again, seemingly oblivious to my presence, completely absorbed by his activity.

I sighed, feeling excluded. Benjamin rarely showed interest when I tried to engage him in playing with me, and if I interrupted his repetitive games, he would give shrill, high pitched shrieks, agitated and distressed at my intrusion. At other times, Benjamin would have a vacant look in his eyes, and I was repeatedly struck by how withdrawn and dejected my beautiful, golden little boy seemed. How could this be? Benjamin had once been such a happy, bubbly child...

I had been voicing my growing concerns to our pediatrician, to no avail. Frustrated, I thought back to our most recent "well baby" appointment. The intake nurse had brought us to one of the little examination rooms, and Benjamin had immediately begun twirling the seat of the round office stool. The shiny vinyl seat had whirled smoothly, inches away from Benjamin's eyes as he tottered tensely on his tiptoes, mechanically jackknifing his torso forward, flapping and twirling his hands on straight, rigidly outstretched arms. Benjamin had practically choked with tense excitement as I exclaimed, "Doesn't this strike you as strange behavior?" Looking disconcerted, the nurse had nodded hesitantly and then called out into the hallway.

"Doctor, could you please come take a look at this?"

He had walked in, a friendly comfortable man who had been in practice for many years and whose own children were nearly grown. "Oh, Benjamin's probably just going through a stage, I wouldn't worry. Let's wait and see if he grows out of it."

After the doctor left, the nurse had whispered to me, "I don't think I would wait." But, not being the doctor, she really couldn't say anything more.

My husband, Rick, was a Navy pilot, and our current tour-of-duty in San Diego was nearly over. Within the next month, we would be transferring to a military base overseas, and I was currently on my own with Benjamin, getting things ready for the move. Rick had already departed well before the Thanksgiving holidays for special flight training, preparing for his new assignment with an aircraft squadron in Rota, Spain. Now, with Benjamin acting so withdrawn, I was becoming apprehensive about our upcoming adventure abroad.

I stepped out onto the patio, picked a ripe tomato, snipped a few leaves of basil from one of my garden planters, and then returned to the kitchen where Benjamin was ignoring the slices of fruit I had previously set before him. "He almost always waits for me to feed him," I thought, wondering once again why hunger didn't seem to motivate Benjamin into eating on his own as most children his age did. He would rather pick up his spoon and flip it up and down in front of his face.

I contemplated Benjamin as I offered him little bites of food. "He's so silent. And he doesn't point at things the way other children do when they want something." My mind wandered back to the time well over a year ago when Benjamin had been fifteen months old. He had begun trying to talk and had actually spoken a few words over the span of about three weeks. I had been over the moon with delight when his first two words came out as *"Geige"* (violin) and *"Buch"* (book). I had been talking and singing in German, wanting Benjamin to grow up bilingually as I had done, and these first words had uncannily reflected my own passion for music and reading.

Two more meaningful sounds had emerged: *"Ja"* (yes), and *"nam-nam"* to indicate that something tasted yummy. But then, Benjamin's four lovely words had simply faded away. They hadn't even been replaced by nonsense sounds or experimental vocalizations. Not once had Benjamin tried saying anything close to "Mama" or "Dada," although I distinctly remembered him babbling the syllables "ma" and "da" as a little baby, just five months old.

Now, prompted by an undefinable angst and feeling desperate for input, I phoned one of my closest friends in San Diego. "Abby, I need to get a handle on what I'm observing in Benjamin," I told her. "Our pediatrician isn't giving me anything to go on, but I *know* that something isn't right."

After listening to my concerns, Abby cautiously asked me, "Could Benjamin have autism?"

"Autism?" I echoed vaguely. "I've heard the term, but don't have a clue about what it means."

Abby told me that autism could cause social disconnection, lack of eye contact, and problems with language. Someone with autism would also tend to have odd, repetitive movement patterns. This description fitted Benjamin perfectly, and an unexpected wave of relief flooded me. With a diagnostic term to work with, I could take action instead of spinning my wheels, worrying.

I wrapped up the conversation and called another friend. "Do you know anything about autism, Polly?"

"Funny that you should ask," she said. "I once looked up autism in one of my baby books. That was after I stopped by your house and saw Benjamin rocking like crazy in his highchair."

"I remember that time," I told her. Benjamin had been about fourteen months old, and Polly had seen him slamming his body to and fro, giggling insanely as he made the wiggly highchair screech in protest. We had laughed together as Benjamin's delight filled the room, his athletic efforts propelling the chair across the smooth kitchen floor, inch by inch.

Polly continued. "I didn't mention my concern to you because Benjamin's eye contact was so good when I saw him. I thought I must be mistaken; lots of children like to rock vigorously. Hang on for a second, let me grab that book and tell you what it says." I heard the clunk of the receiver and then the sound of pages being rifled.

"Here..." Polly had picked up the receiver again. She read me a description that essentially matched Abby's, and then continued, "'...*may display self-injurious behavior such as head banging.*' Benjamin doesn't do that, does he?"

I felt a bit faint, remembering. "Actually, Benjamin went through a five-month phase where he purposefully banged his forehead on the ground, almost like he was trying to punish himself. It scared me because it was so deliberate, but it faded away after I took him for some cranio-sacral therapy; we were in Colorado, visiting my parents." Polly listened as I described the therapy session.

I recalled the practitioner's gentle hands resting on Benjamin's head as I cradled him in my arms. We were silent as Benjamin's lashes began fluttering; he seemed to be on the verge of sleep. Then, a sudden rush of color appeared; Benjamin's left ear began flaming bright red, and then his chubby cheeks too flushed feverishly. His eyes flew open as if with shock, and he began to cry with heart wrenching sobs. Within an instant, I too was crying, dissolving with no conscious thought. Instead, I felt a wrenching ache in my gut, as if the painful separation of body from body at birth were flooding through me again. As I sobbed, I was put in mind of the trauma that had attended Benjamin's birth.

While I had been in labor at the hospital, Benjamin's vital signs had weakened alarmingly with each contraction, and I had been filled with fear for my baby's life as I struggled to push him out of my womb and into the world. He was born just in the nick of time and, as the midwife cradled him in her hands, the cause of the problem became apparent. Benjamin's umbilical cord had been triple-wrapped, becoming tightly twisted around his torso, his neck, and his right arm, cutting off his circulation and slowing his heartbeat, threatening his survival. Now the emotional imprint of this experience was being dredged up from some deep, subconscious place, and as we cried together, both Benjamin and I were releasing the stored burden.

"I'd heard of people responding emotionally to bodywork, but hadn't ever experienced such a thing," I told Polly. "At that moment, I felt that Benjamin and I were inextricably linked—like one mind, one soul, reliving the same experience... The important result, though, was that Benjamin stopped his head banging, and he even began vocalizing, breaking his silence for just a few days."

That afternoon, I went to the local library with Benjamin and collected a small stack of books on autism. "Buy a copy of *Son Rise,* by B. Kaufman," the librarian recommended, looking concerned. "It's an amazing story that will surely inspire you."

On arriving home, I saw our phone message-machine blinking, its indicator light flashing red. Rick had phoned responding to my request that he do some internet research. "I couldn't find much information on how to deal with autism." Rick's voice crackled on the machine. "The internet is still fairly new and so its usefulness for research is limited. However, I did find mention that birth trauma might be a contributing cause. Also, it's likely there's a genetic component. Apparently, in many cases of autism, the parents are talented in areas such as music, math, computers, and engineering. We certainly fit that profile." Rick went on to say that his squadron was heading out on a mission, and that he wouldn't be able to call me back for the next several days. I would have to take the next steps on my own.

Later that evening, with Benjamin fast asleep, snuggly tucked under his covers, I cracked open the library books. I skimmed through the already familiar descriptions of the diagnosis and felt sweat beading on my forehead as I repeatedly read phrases like, "*...life-long condition... incurable... involves social isolation and limited speech development... institutionalization may be required...*"

I slowed down and began reading more carefully when case histories were presented. The hairs on my body prickled, and by the time I had gotten to descriptions of teen difficulties with sexual issues and stories about the grossly inappropriate advances that a "hormonal autistic" might make, I was retching and howling through a flood of tears streaming down my face; I was near to vomiting from the emotional pain that scorched my being. It was well past midnight and, as I read on, one horrifying nightmare after another was being conjured.

Meanwhile, in the next room, my little angel lay sleeping peacefully, his bright blond hair and rosy cheeks straight out of a Boticelli painting. I muffled my anguished cries with a pillow, feeling tortured, my heart cramping, stabbed by needles of fear, my gut twisting with snakes. With tears blinding me and snot running faster than my cloth hankies could handle, I threw the books down in a heap upon the floor, clutched the eiderdown comforter around myself, and rocked, unable to fathom the idea of my beautiful child growing up to embody this hideous future. Sleep eluded me for the rest of that night.

The next morning, just after breakfast, I settled Benjamin in his stroller and shakily walked over to a nearby book shop. Yes, they had a copy of *Son Rise.* I stood amongst the bookshelves and began thumbing through the book, skipping to the parts where the parents described strategies that they had used in helping their child.

As I read, I felt a lifeline of hope being extended to me. I paid for the book, wheeled Benjamin to a nearby park, and continued reading, skimming the chapters until it became clear that intense and ongoing therapeutic intervention had allowed the child to recover from autism by the time he was five years old. I looked up into the trees and thought, "That's us. That's what we are going to do. We are going to beat autism, and I will do whatever it takes."

The child in *Son Rise* had shown considerably more severe symptoms than what I was observing in Benjamin. The parents had tirelessly interacted with their son, finding ways to engage him and to stimulate his brain in order that memory, speech, and a myriad of physical skills might be developed. Eventually, they had put together a team consisting of the child's siblings, assorted family friends, and students of various ages, all committed to interacting with the autistic boy. They had recorded their son's progress in a daily log, and this had become the basis for their book.

"If they managed all that, then I can do it too," I thought, feeling empowered to act rather than to cry. As I looked back at the volume in my hand, I meditated on the three core values that had allowed the family to maintain a healthy attitude towards their therapeutic work: *unconditional love, acceptance of the present, and hope for the future.*

The parents had decided that they would unconditionally love their child for who he was, even as they attempted to foster growth and change. If the child couldn't progress as much as they hoped, they would still love and accept him rather than considering him a failure. The parents also chose to keep recognizing the miraculous in the mundane, and this had kept them appreciating the steps of progress their child made, even if these steps were infinitesimally small. And throughout, they determinedly kept up a positive attitude, maintaining a sense of hope in spite of the challenges.

Now I was determined to follow the path this family had forged, thinking that I would be able to manage—even overseas, even without family or friends to support me. Little did I know...

2

Barely In Time
February, 1997

There wasn't a moment to lose, and I scrambled to get a diagnosis for Benjamin. On hearing of our impending move, the schedulers at Children's Hospital in San Diego arranged an appointment for the following week. In the meantime, I didn't sit around and wait. I jumped into action, following my intuition, and started by making changes to Benjamin's diet. Knowing that food sensitivities could cause a variety of behavioral symptoms, I decided to eliminate likely suspects: high-gluten grains were common allergens, and Benjamin had already experienced trouble with milk products.

Fortunately, I wouldn't have to overhaul my kitchen like the family in *Son Rise* had done; I was an avid label reader and nothing with artificial ingredients or additives ever made it into my reusable canvas grocery bags. This vigilance stemmed from a lifetime of eating organically grown produce, much of it coming from the large vegetable garden that my parents tended in their back yard. Their example had taught me about the importance of avoiding pesticides, hormones, and other chemical influences commonly found in commercially produced foods.

The next thing I did was to regularly brush Benjamin's body with a very soft hairbrush, thus stimulating his skin and heightening his body awareness. I also started massaging Benjamin several times per day, thinking that this might aid in releasing some of the physical tension he so frequently displayed. Too, the loving intention I put into my hands might awaken him to our connection which, in turn, might motivate Benjamin to try communicating with me, even if he couldn't yet speak.

I thought back to the blissful time before Benjamin had become so distant. I had held him incessantly, snuggling him, feeling I could never get enough of his sweet baby scent, his velvety soft skin, and the sensation of "aliveness" that radiated from his solid little body. I remembered sitting on a friend's porch, visiting with her and another mom while our little ones played nearby on the floor. Benjamin had sat alone like a little Buddha, content and self-contained, happily absorbing the atmosphere without interacting with the other children. I had felt compelled to pick him up and cuddle him, in spite of my friend's surprised exclamation. "Don't you ever put that child down? You could probably use a break…"

Hmmm. Perhaps I had subconsciously sensed the beginning of Benjamin's autistic withdrawnness, long before it had become so obvious.

The most important change I made during those first days of revelation was to tune in to Benjamin's subtle communications—little things I had been missing but that had surely been there before. I began describing these precious rays of light in the baby journal I had begun directly after Benjamin's birth. I had wanted to capture the magic of having a baby and of watching him grow, and now my propensity for journaling had me recording the steps taken towards rescuing Benjamin from what was surely autism.

I feel like I'm learning telepathy, I now wrote. *This afternoon, I had a picture book on my lap, and Benjamin reached over to lightly touch the drawing of an owl. It occurred to me that he might want to hear its sound, so I hooted, "Whoo-whoo..." He seemed interested, inching closer and closer until he was leaning against me. Then I noticed him touching the owl in different ways. I thought, "It's like he's playing the piano." So when he touched softly, I "whoo-whooed" softly, and when he touched firmly, I "whooed" loudly. This went back and forth, turning into a little game. It was thrilling because for the past many months, my overtures to play with Benjamin have seemingly been rebuffed. Then, this evening, when I was putting Benjamin to bed, he tentatively placed his hands on my shoulders as if to say, "Stay here." I wonder: how often has Benjamin tried to tell me something? How often have I missed the communication because it was so subtle?*

Benjamin's delicate communications were certainly being picked up by the cranio-sacral therapist I had contacted. Natasha, a young woman close to my age, had responded immediately to my pleas of help. "I'll be happy to make house calls, and we can start tomorrow afternoon," she had told me upon hearing I had no vehicle available to me; our car was already aboard a ship, on its way overseas.

Benjamin was in a miserable state on the day of our first appointment. I told Natasha, "I think he's picking up on my distress and reflecting it back to me. Two nights ago, I read a bunch of clinical descriptions of life with autism. Since then, I've been feeling ill with grief. My mind feels poisoned by the information, and Benjamin has vomited a few times since then. He isn't showing any other symptoms, and I don't think he's coming down with an illness. I really sense that his symptoms are emotional, a mirroring of my feelings."

Natasha nodded understandingly, and then kneeled down to gently lay her hands on Benjamin as he twiddled and twirled his toys around. He ignored her presence but, as she kept her hands quietly resting on him, he became calm and peaceful, no longer caught up in repetitive motions.

As the minutes passed and Natasha's hands moved gradually down from

Benjamin's head to his torso, I could feel his increasing sense of peace stealing into my heart. I watched, amazed, as Benjamin gradually took up eye contact with Natasha, his face beginning to show signs of happiness. By the end of the half-hour session, Benjamin was making little humming sounds and seemed almost playful. I was amazed at the shift in his demeanor; he had been miserable all day long but now seemed quite content.

We'd already had a second session with Natasha before arriving at Children's Hospital for Benjamin's diagnostic appointment. I parked the car that a friend had lent me and walked across the parking lot with Benjamin hopping alongside me, his hand tightly clutched in mine. I sang to him, feeling encouraged by the subtle interplay of communication that had developed between us throughout the past week. Upon entering the building, we were introduced to the friendly, motherly psychologist who would be assessing Benjamin. "What a handsome little boy," she commented, admiring Benjamin's long golden hair and kneeling down to look at his sky-blue eyes. She led us down a hallway to the "play room," and my nose wrinkled from the lingering smell of disinfectant.

I sat down, telling the psychologist, "Even when Benjamin was only six months old, I was already noticing odd little behaviors…" I went through a list of notes and observations I had prepared, and then the psychologist started in on a lengthy assessment questionnaire. Soon, my head was aching from the fluorescent lighting and from the strain of feeling my tenuous connection with Benjamin evaporating; he was off in a corner, looking distinctly lost. If this space was making *me* feel so poorly, what might it be doing to *him*? The overwhelming smells, the harsh lighting, and the garish colors of cheap plastic toys grated on my nerves, and I asked the psychologist if we might finish the questionnaire later. "I can't stand seeing Benjamin like this. I feel like I've begun 'reaching' him in the past week and would like to show you…"

I gave Benjamin a little tickle and encouraged him to play a game of "Row, row, row your boat." Sitting on the floor with Benjamin facing me, his legs straddled over mine, I grasped his arms and sang, vigorously rocking his body back and forth in time to the music. Benjamin couldn't help looking up at me, and then he began smiling as the game engaged him. Once I released him however, he tripped aimlessly around the room, at a loss for what to do with any of the toys except to toss them about—that is, until he found a car with wheels that he could spin. As he settled down to obsess on the wheels, I sat down protectively behind Benjamin.

I explained. "If you ask him to give up the toy, he'll probably resist. If you insist on taking it, he'll throw himself vigorously backwards with ear-piercing shrieks. I worry that he'll get a brain injury from slamming into the floor, and so I place myself strategically when I anticipate this behavior happening." The psychologist nodded and then tried to gain Benjamin's attention. She wanted him to carry out a few simple tasks involving toys, but Benjamin didn't understand what she wanted. She asked me to try cajoling him, and I made an attempt but told her, "Benjamin has never done any of these things. Actually, I didn't realize he should be able to."

She confirmed that a typically developing child would have no problem manipulating toys and playing with them in the way she had demonstrated. "Children naturally imitate, that is how they learn. But I take it your boy doesn't copy anything you do?" I shook my head no, my heart sinking. Benjamin must be even farther behind than I realized. After a bit more discussion, the psychologist confirmed my fears: Benjamin was indeed suffering from autism.

I nodded mutely, feeling empty and numb. I had already convinced myself of this, but now I realized that, subconsciously, I must have been hoping—against all odds—that the expert would tell me I had been wrong, that things really weren't that bad, that Benjamin would be fine. But no, Benjamin was a textbook case of regressive autism, no question about it.

Time was nearly up. Our overseas move to Spain was imminent, but I had scheduled two sessions of play therapy at the hospital. As Benjamin and I made our way up a flight of stairs to the therapist's playroom, I talked continually, expressing enthusiasm and encouragement. "You're so big and strong. Look at you, climbing all these stairs. What a big boy you are." Overnight, I had become a motor mouth, talking and singing to Benjamin in both English and German, thinking that perhaps I had been too quiet with him in the past. "If I increase his exposure to language, maybe he'll be more encouraged to try talking," was my overriding thought.

Now we were in the playroom, and the therapist was giving me some strategies for teaching the pivotal behavior of turn-taking. She kept emphasizing the importance of getting eye contact. Blowing soap bubbles through a wand held in front of her face, she enticed Benjamin to look at her. "Give very specific praise," she corrected me when I attempted to imitate her style. I was trying to get Benjamin's attention and was chattering to him.

"Rather than talking a lot, say 'nice quiet,' 'nice waiting,' 'good looking,' 'good turn-taking,' and so on," she instructed. "Language acquisition is one of the primary problems for someone with autism. Speech needs to be taught in small, basic units, and there needs to be much repetition of the same vocabulary until it has been learned. Focus on the most important words in a sentence, i.e. the nouns and verbs, and leave out the rest until Benjamin clearly starts to understand you."

I expressed surprise. "I thought I hadn't been speaking enough around Benjamin." The therapist quickly set me straight. Based on her explanations, I could now imagine what the world might sound like to Benjamin: "*blah blah* Benjamin *blah blah blah* Mommy *blah blah blah* apple...*blah*...banana." The many words of a complex sentence would be a form of sound clutter, obscuring the few basic words that Benjamin was familiar with.

"When Benjamin begins responding consistently to a minimalist version of speech, you can add in more words," the therapist reassured me.

"And what shall I do about his shrieking and backwards body slamming?" I asked, knowing that I needed expert advice. "I've seen other children throwing tantrums, and I have read parenting books that explain how to handle them effectively, but nothing I've tried with Benjamin has worked."

The therapist explained that Benjamin's hyper-reactivity was not normal, and that it was linked to his autism. "You'll have to accept that tantrums will be a part of your work with him; Benjamin's autism will automatically cause him to resist interaction and change. Even though you know that Benjamin might tantrum when you initiate a particular interaction, you can work through it and gradually shape his behavior so he isn't so reactive."

She continued her explanation. "For example, if Benjamin is obsessed on spinning a toy like he is right now, you might try taking it—in a nice manner, of course—and then return it immediately. The next time you take it, wait just a moment longer before you give it back. Gradually make your turn with the toy longer and longer, and try to get some eye contact in exchange for returning the toy."

Reaching out to demonstrate, she touched the wooden block that Benjamin was engrossed in manipulating. Benjamin instantly shrieked and threw himself backwards, and I dived towards him, barely managing to keep his head from thumping on the carpet. The therapist patiently went through the process of turn-taking, just as she had described, and I was soon on the verge of tears, watching helplessly as Benjamin screeched and wildly threw himself backwards every time the toy left his fingers. "We'll try that again the day after tomorrow and see how it goes," the therapist told me as I carried my sobbing child out of the room. "Trust me, he *can* learn that tantrums won't work anymore."

When we returned two days later, I could see that she was right. Benjamin's reactivity to the therapist's "interference" was already less immediate, and he seemed to understand that the toy would be given back to him within a few short moments if he didn't start screaming. "You'll need to be patient," she reminded me. "Keep stretching his tolerance. Remember, you can take advantage of Benjamin's obsession with a toy. Since he is motivated to get the toy back, you can start pushing him for more eye contact or even some other communication before rewarding him with the object."

Motivation. Rewards. Simple communication and much repetition. These would be the basic building blocks for helping Benjamin to learn.

Benjamin was responding to my experimental tries at teaching him about pointing. Knowing that he adored strawberries, I put several of the luscious, ruby fruits on the kitchen counter, just out of reach. Kneeling down by Benjamin, I pointed. "Mm, yummy strawberries." Placing his hand on my wrist, I slowly moved my pointer finger towards the berries until I touched them. "Want strawberry?" Popping the fruit into Benjamin's mouth, I repeated the process until all the berries were gone.

After a few days of teamwork, Benjamin began grabbing my wrist at various times. When this happened, I immediately knelt down, shaping my hand into a pointer and asking whether there was something he wanted. "Show me, sweetheart. Point." Benjamin was learning that I could be useful to him, and I felt encouraged, seeing that my idea was working.

The chaos of moving was upon us, and eventually the last boxes disappeared into shipping containers, good-byes were said, and we were on our way to Spain. En route, though, Benjamin and I were spending a week visiting my parents in Boulder, Colorado.

On our first morning there, we woke up to world of sparkling white; more than twelve inches of snow had fallen overnight. After a leisurely breakfast together, my parents, Benjamin, and I embarked on a walk around their neighborhood of old brick houses and large back yards. This was Benjamin's first time experiencing snow. After returning indoors, I saw the blinking light on my parents' message machine, and when I pressed the "play" button, I heard Rick's voice. His words were nearly obscured by the hissing sound of static. An overseas call. "Malva, I urgently need to talk to you. I'll try calling again in an hour. Please stay near the phone."

My heart began to pound. What might be wrong? Throughout our years of intermittent separation due to military deployments (Rick's squadron would fly in obscure locations around the world for up to nine months at a time), I had always feared getting a call notifying me of a crash or some other disastrous news. From the sound of Rick's voice, something big had happened. I tried to remain calm but jumped nevertheless when my parents' phone eventually rang.

Rick was on the line. "Malva, I'm at the base in Rota, Spain. We're on a long-distance training mission, and my crew chose Rota as the destination. What luck. I've had a little time to look around and talk to key people. I have concluded that we can't possibly go through with moving here, now that we know about Benjamin's autism."

I sat stunned, hearing Rick's words and trying to grasp what they implied. He continued. "Rota is small, it's isolated, and there is the language barrier to contend with. There is simply no support system here for us."

"But, your military orders...your training...all our stuff..." I trailed off.

"I've talked with the commanding officer of the squadron. Because of the seriousness of Benjamin's diagnosis, he will support a request to have my orders changed."

"Wow." I sat down, my knees going weak. Military orders were only changed in dire circumstances. Had I been deluded by ignorance, thinking I could adequately provide therapy for Benjamin without any outside assistance? How much support would we need? Trembling a little, I remained quiet, thinking about the *Son Rise* story and how it had taken a village to raise a child out of autism. Rick's voice broke into my silence.

"I'll be getting transferred to the squadron in Whidbey Island, in Washington. It's the only other choice available to me at this juncture."

"What? Whidbey Island?" I reeled with shock. "But... Whidbey is isolated too; you've told me before that it's one-and-a-half hour's drive from Seattle."

"I know." I could hear the upset in Rick's voice. "However, it's my only option outside of Rota. At least it's stateside and within reach of a big city."

I tried to picture the situation and then said, "Can you imagine Benjamin being locked into a car seat for hours just in order to have a therapy session in Seattle? And what about all that rain?" I knew that living in a place with so much precipitation, clouds, and then darkness throughout long winter months would be disastrous for me. With my tendency towards depression, I absolutely needed enough sunshine to keep from falling into my own internal abyss.

As we talked, a solution began to form. "We've so often discussed moving back to Boulder," I reminded Rick. "Maybe this is the time to do that. Boulder is filled with alternative-type therapists, and there are lots of great health food stores. If I need expert help with Benjamin, I know I'll be able to find it. Plus, my parents are here, more than willing to help, and I have old friends here as well."

I could hear the pain in Rick's voice as he thought out loud. "Malva, I cannot get out of this tour of duty. However, we could make it an 'unaccompanied' tour: you and Benjamin could stay in Boulder, and I would live in the bachelor officer's quarters at the Whidbey naval base."

I pictured this scenario, and my heart ached at the thought of three years of separation, of three years without a Daddy around for Benjamin. We had been married for nearly ten years, and roughly a third of those years had already involved maintaining a long-distance relationship: first for Rick's flight training while I completed my doctoral degree, then for a short term college teaching opportunity for me, and finally for several lengthy overseas squadron deployments. Could we face separation yet again?

The stability of our time in San Diego had been wonderful, and Benjamin had been growing up in an ideal situation. Now I felt breathless, sinking under the weight of change and responsibility. As wrenching as the thought of separation was, nothing else made sense. We would have to live apart once again. "It's now or never," I said, summoning up all my strength. "From what I understand, the next few years are Benjamin's 'window of opportunity' for recovering from autism. If we don't give it everything we've got right now, we'll regret it for the rest of our lives."

3

Settling in Boulder, Colorado
Late-February, 1997

So it was decided. Benjamin and I would stay in Boulder and, for now, would live with my parents in the same old brick house that held all my childhood memories. Then, in June, we would move into a house of our own that was currently being rented out. Years ago, my parents, Rick, and I had pooled resources and, with careful planning, had risked buying the house from a friend's neighbor. Even as Rick had embarked on his military career and I had made do with establishing a private music studio in each new location we moved to, we had been certain that Boulder would one day be our permanent home.

Now my head was whirling with the combined sentiments of distress and gratitude as I began making phone calls, locating public resources such as the Developmental Disabilities Center (a non-profit agency funded by state and federal revenues), getting in contact with other parents of children with autism, and setting up appointments for Benjamin.

We would continue with cranio-sacral therapy since Benjamin had responded so positively to Natasha's work in San Diego. Indeed, during one session, there had been a magical few moments of intense connection where Natasha had been face-to-face with Benjamin, her hands resting lightly on him. She had started making sounds, saying, "Mm... Mm.... Mama..." and Benjamin had copied her. Then she had tried saying, "Nnn. Nana. D, Dada," and he had echoed these syllables too, even trying the smacking sound of a kiss and attempting the explosive consonant "p-p-p." The moments of imitation had been singular and fleeting. I hadn't been able to get intentional sounds out of Benjamin since then, but he had nevertheless progressed out of his silence and was making an increasing number of spontaneous vocalizations.

Homeopathy was another safe and gentle therapy I was looking into. In spite of his autism, Benjamin was clearly sensitive to emotional energies, and homeopathy was an approach that might bring about increased balance and harmony within him. I started off my search for a practitioner by talking to parents whose children attended the local Waldorf school. (As an aside: the Waldorf philosophy focuses on making the fine arts an integral part of every learning activity; even reading, writing, and arithmetic are enlivened by creativity and artistry. Furthermore, Waldorf teachers are trained to consciously nurture the soul and spirit of every student. Because of my affinity for this approach, I had always been quick to locate the "Waldorf community" in every new place that Rick's work had taken us, and in this way, had invariably connected with people who were "on my wavelength.")

Now, as I chatted with parents, I kept hearing about a homeopath named Julie and decided to make an appointment with her. Within the week, Benjamin and I were in Julie's office, sunshine streaming in through enormous windows. I liked her immediately. Her dark hair, quick smile, and lively, intelligent eyes over a strong nose made me think of a keenly observant hawk.

"Tell me about this boy," she said, watching Benjamin as he wandered around inspecting the round knobs attached to closet, cupboard, and door. My story spilled out as Benjamin became hyper-stimulated by the sight of the round objects; he twirly-flapped his hands and hopped stiffly on his tip-toes. Julie continued observing Benjamin, listening intently to my narrative and taking copious notes.

Eventually she asked, "What tastes good to him?"

I was surprised. "That's relevant?"

Other surprising questions came. By now, Benjamin had been sitting for a while, spinning the wheels of a large wooden truck.

"Look at his ears, they're bright red," Julie pointed out. "And his right cheek is red too, but the other one not so much. All these little idiosyncrasies can help me hone in on a remedy appropriate to the situation." Opening a closet door, she revealed shelves of small, dark, glass bottles, all meticulously labeled and alphabetically arranged. Julie picked out a remedy, got a tiny paper cup of filtered water, and added a few drops from the little bottle. She handed the cup to me, and I carefully dribbled the mixture into Benjamin's mouth.

"Don't let him eat or drink anything for half an hour, and avoid products containing mint or camphor," she cautioned. "They can neutralize the remedy."

I laughed with surprise. "This is like handling a magic spell."

Benjamin was becoming increasingly energized, and this newly discovered vigor was expressing itself through both his voice and his actions. He had learned that I would respond to any hint of desire coming from him and was now approaching me with great intention, grabbing my hand and pulling me around, reaching for things himself, and sometimes even using his pointer finger to touch things.

I had been diligently working with the concepts learned from the play therapist back in San Diego and, by now, Benjamin was beginning to understand the concept of turn-taking. I found that turn-taking practice was particularly easy when Benjamin was seated in the safety swings at the playground. I would give him a nice firm push and, once the swing got going, I would hand Benjamin a hair ribbon or something else that he liked, giving it to him just at the moment when he swung closest to me. As he held the object, he would be swinging backwards and then, when he traveled forwards again, I would take the object back. The next time the swing carried him towards me, I would again give the bauble to him, and so on. Benjamin was catching on to the game and was now eager to give and take various toys and objects in turns.

The last days of February were upon us, and I had just received a packet of information from the Autism Research Institute. As I looked through the sheaf of papers, I found an information sheet on sensory integration. Apparently, this therapy could be very helpful for someone with autism. "I know just the person to help me," I thought.

The next day, I took Benjamin with me to visit Maggie, a friend of mine and a leading physical therapist in Boulder. Maggie was a petite young woman of great intelligence, and her small physical frame encompassed a boundless reserve of enthusiasm and energy. I quickly filled her in on our situation and told her I had already begun massaging Benjamin regularly, as well as body-brushing him daily.

"That's great," Maggie enthused. "You need to add joint compressions to that. Here, let me show you." She took my arm, one of her hands above my elbow and the other hand below, and then she pushed the bones of my upper arm and forearm together, causing a compression in my elbow joint. "You can hold the pressure for five seconds, or you can push and release in a rhythmic fashion," she said, demonstrating a pulsing pattern of compressions. "Do this daily, addressing all the major joints of arms and legs. You can take care of the spine by rhythmically pushing down on Benjamin's shoulders, next to his neck, while he's sitting."

We moved over to a large gym mat where balls and foam rollers of various sizes lay waiting. "You'll want to do lots of bouncing, rolling, and rocking too," Maggie told me as she coaxed Benjamin onto a big, blue gymno-ball. Benjamin responded to her smiling enthusiasm, allowing Maggie to bounce him vigorously up and down in a sitting position. His hair flew, his head bobbed, and he started giggling as his eyes flickered around the room. Then Maggie showed me how to roll him around on the ball, especially on his tummy, challenging his sense of balance. Fright showed on Benjamin's face as he felt like he might fall; he didn't trust Maggie to keep hold of him.

"How about this: I'll sing a little song while moving Benjamin around—it might help him relax," I suggested, taking over the exercise so that Maggie could coach me on important details.

"Great idea," Maggie affirmed. "You'll be simultaneously stimulating Benjamin's brain with movement, musical sound, and language. That is, of course, integrating."

As I slowly manipulated Benjamin on the big ball, rolling him around in rhythm to my singing, his look of fear gave way to a tentative smile, and he briefly glanced up at me. I praised him, saying, "Good looking," and then lifted him back into a sitting position, bouncing him and reciting a traditional German horse-riding-poem that I remembered from my childhood.

I had often jolted along at a brisk trot on my dad's knees while hearing these same words and had started giving Benjamin such "horsey-rides" as soon as he was old enough to sit up without support. Now Benjamin's gaze was directed at my face; he definitely recognized this poem. "I can use these exercises to get more eye contact," I exclaimed to Maggie, my mind percolating with ideas for transforming the growing list of exercises into fun games.

Next, Maggie brought out a little blue-and-red child's trampoline with a handle for Benjamin to hold on to as he jumped. "You can take this home with you, I haven't been using it," she offered generously. "Benjamin should spend lots of time jumping. That will stimulate his vestibular system and give him lots of sensory feedback through his joints and muscles."

Now Maggie had Benjamin climb up onto a round office chair and sit comfortably while she spun him rapidly around his vertical axis. Then she stopped him abruptly, peering closely at his eyes. "Benjamin doesn't have a normal level of nystagmus; that's the side-to-side flickering that normally occurs right after you stop spinning and your brain processes the change in your body's momentum. So, you'll want to do a lot of spinning with him as well. The easiest way is to use one of these hammocks." Maggie seated Benjamin in a finely knit hammock-chair that hung suspended from a rope attached to a hook-and-swivel unit in the ceiling. Maggie pulled the sides of the hammock snuggly around Benjamin so that he was enclosed, as if in a cocoon.

"You can swing him, or spin him, or both," she said, demonstrating. "And work on eye contact and language skills at the same time."

I reached towards the hammock saying, "Here, let me try something. I have an idea for getting eye contact." I swung Benjamin and began to sing. He looked up at me, obviously enjoying the sensation of swinging while being firmly cradled. I watched his eyes closely; the moment he shifted his gaze away from me, I stopped singing. His eyes moved back up to me, expressing mild puzzlement. I immediately started singing again but as soon as his attention wandered, I broke off. His eyes came back to mine. I hugged Maggie, delightedly exclaiming, "This is going to work. Benjamin has figured out that

I'll only sing if he is looking at me."

By now, Maggie's next patient was waiting. As I ushered Benjamin out of the therapy space, Maggie called after me, "Remember to visit the lumber yard for some 4 x 4's to create a balance beam. And find some manipulative toys for eye/hand coordination."

I nodded and waved; I was already planning my next stop. I would be visiting my parents' neighbors who had generously offered to loan me a variety of toys. They had four older children, and had amassed an astounding collection of playthings over the years.

Once Benjamin was engaged in eating lunch with my parents, I walked across the alley behind their house. The neighbors welcomed me in and helped fill a large bin with the high-quality toys they had invested in for their own children. Wooden train sets, hand-carved pull-toys, interesting puzzles with tastefully colored pieces; a variety of manipulative toys made their way into the bin. Clearly, the neighbors were of the same opinion as I: aesthetically pleasing, high-quality toys can make a positive difference in a child's development.

"Keep them as long as you need, our kids aren't playing with them anymore," they assured me, and I hugged them thankfully.

"Our own belongings are taking an unaccompanied vacation to Europe," I said jokingly. "It'll be several months before they make it back to the United States and then to Boulder. I'm glad to be home, even without our stuff."

4

Spring Has Sprung
March, 1997

A veritable carpet of snowdrops was blooming along the fence in my parents' front yard, and the promising green tips of crocuses and daffodils were peeking through mulched leaves. The mild March weather was conducive to playing outdoors, and I was gently guiding Benjamin through the playground skills that most children pick up on their own. Now Benjamin was learning to do somersaults and was finding delight in games of chase, giggling with anticipation as I came running after him to sweep him off his feet into a whirling twirl.

My parents watched as I helped Benjamin reach up and hold on to the "trapeze" that was part of our newly purchased swing set. "I'd like to get a dog for Benjamin," I told them. "Benjamin has no siblings to intrude on his space, and having a big animal around will help liven things up, particularly once we've moved into our own house." Within days, I had brought home a sweet-natured black Labrador from our local Humane Society, and was regularly holding Benjamin's hands in mine, making him stroke "Walker's" soft fur.

One evening, shortly after Walker had joined our family, I tucked Benjamin into bed and, despite exhaustion, roused myself to write about our progress. I headed for the kitchen, pushed open the door, and found my nostrils crinkling as they were assailed by the rank aroma of feces. Our new dog lay sprawled on the tiled kitchen floor, pink tongue lolling happily, his tail furiously wagging, thumping the floor.

"What have you done?" I demanded furiously, surveying the white, fluffy mess spread out over the kitchen floor, interspersed with lumpy streaks of brown smeared across russet tiling. Walker rolled over playfully, using a paw to scrape at the white stuff on his nose. If his timing hadn't been so poor, I might have laughed at his antics. But the capacity for finding humor in the situation eluded me just now. "You're disgusting. That's Benjamin's poopy diaper." Walker had retrieved it from the open trashcan and had proceeded to have a field day with it.

"Out," I shouted, cleaning off his nose and paws, and then shoving him into the next room. I mopped up the mess, took everything outside, and came back in to do my journaling. Walker awaited me in the living room where he had chewed my brand new pair of Walkman headphones to ribbons. I had left him unsupervised just a few minutes too long.

After my initial flash of anger, I sat down and cried with weariness. In addition to actively engaging Benjamin all day, I had been getting up before dawn in order to practice violin, unable to give up on this one activity which for years had defined my essence. "This is crazy," I thought now. "I can't keep fighting my new reality. The violin has simply got to take a rest."

I sprawled across an armchair and took stock. For now, Benjamin would be getting cranio-sacral therapy once each week, and the plan was to eventually cut back, going to every other week, and then to once per month. He would also be getting homeopathic treatment once per month on average, more frequently if needed. Already, we were doing sensory integration activities daily, and I was working continuously on engaging Benjamin, trying to build up a basis for communication.

Now I was ready to add therapies for speech and behavior development. I had learned that our insurance plan classified autism as a mental illness rather than a medical condition and that, therefore, speech and behavioral therapies would not be covered. We would have to manage these costs on our own. Deeply frustrated, I had consulted the parents of another child with autism, and they had recommended talking to a young woman named Rhea.

I phoned Rhea the next morning, and she asked me to read *Let Me Hear Your Voice,* by Catherine Maurice. "I want you to know what you'll be getting into," she explained. "Then you can decide whether you want to pursue behavioral therapy. It's not everyone's cup of tea, in spite of its effectiveness."

I went to the library, found the book, and started reading about how two siblings (both diagnosed with autism) had been cured of their condition through intensive behavioral intervention. The eloquently written story made me realize that there was more to teaching language and behavioral skills than I had initially thought, and I was relieved to find an outline for systematically building these skills in the appendices.

The book also provided important details on "applied behavioral analysis" (ABA therapy). Researcher Dr. O. Ivar Lovaas had already worked with many autistic children by 1993 (when *Let Me Hear Your Voice* was published), and he had achieved astonishingly good results with about half his clients, using the principles of behavior modification. The other half of patients had also made gains in their functioning, although not to the same high level. However, the data collected by Lovaas showed that behavioral therapy was the driving force behind the observed improvements.

When I phoned Rhea to set up a therapy session, I told her, "I've been experimenting, trying to copy some of what's described in the book, but I really need to see this approach in action; I feel unsure of what I'm doing. Also, do I absolutely need to tally skill repetitions and numerically chart Benjamin's progress as is described in the book? I appreciate the organized structure that behavioral therapy will provide, but at the same time, I'm concerned about dampening my creativity and spontaneity when interacting with Benjamin."

"I know what you mean," Rhea answered. "I also dislike the tallying process although I do it quite often. Basically, I tailor the 'strictness' of my approach to the needs and desires of my clients. The question is whether you feel ready to commit. Behavioral therapy is very directive, and not everyone can work in that way."

"I am used to discipline," I told Rhea. "And I can appreciate the need for building up skills by analyzing them and breaking them down into manageable components. That's precisely what I do when teaching young children to play the violin." Now I summarized what I was already doing with Benjamin.

"It sounds like you've gotten a good start," Rhea said appreciatively. "I'll show you how structured 'table work' can supplement your naturalistic approach. You'll also want to get going on some sign language."

5

Beginning with Behavioral Therapy
Mid-March, 1997

The morning that Rhea was to come over, Benjamin and I were on a "wake-up walk." Benjamin had run down the sidewalk to a neighbor's house, wanting to inspect a brass doorknob, and I was tickling him, trying to distract and turn him around without causing a tantrum. I caught sight of a lithe, dark-haired young woman watching us. She smiled broadly, her face radiating enthusiasm. "I'm Rhea," she said, walking over to meet us. "And this must be Benjamin."

Kneeling down, she looked into Benjamin's beautiful sky-blue eyes. He was regarding her quizzically, and Rhea exclaimed, "The two of you are amazing together—I see so much love. And Benjamin's face isn't as blank as I sometimes see in children with autism. I'm excited."

Benjamin's rosy cheeks were glowing from exercise, and his golden hair glinted in the morning sun as he resumed running, no longer interested in the newcomer. The three of us navigated the short distance back to my parents' house, and Rhea hauled two trunks filled with toys into an uncluttered room where I had set up a low square table and a little child's chair for Benjamin.

Rhea opened the trunks to reveal a jumble of toys such as puzzles, shape-sorters, dolls, whistles, and lots of "spinny" toys: the kind where you push a button and something starts to turn, or flash, or go up and down. My heart sank momentarily as the garish colors of the hard plastics knocked me in the eyes, but I put the feeling aside.

"What do you like, Benjamin? Oh, the spinny things, huh?" Rhea asked as Benjamin reached for one of them, drawn as if by a magnet. Within moments, he had figured out how to make the thing revolve dizzyingly and had reacted with a frenzy of hand flapping, belly tensing, and rigid, tiptoe hopping. My stomach began churning with anxiety as I watched Benjamin getting sucked into the toy and becoming disconnected from the people around him.

"Okay, those can be his rewards, the things he works for," Rhea explained, disentangling Benjamin from the toy while I tickled him to prevent an explosion of screeching protest. "Now, here we go. Sit down," Rhea said to Benjamin.

Using a firm but friendly tone, she repeated the command several more times as I helped her to maneuver Benjamin into the little chair. To me, she said, "We need to work on eye contact, and we need to teach him how to imitate because that's the most basic way that people learn things: through watching and copying others. We'll start with a follow-the-leader exercise."

Rhea knelt down, facing Benjamin as he sat on his little chair. She swung her arms up saying "copy me" in an enthusiastic tone.

Benjamin was looking past her, his eyes resting on the bin where the spinny toy had disappeared. "Copy me, arms up," Rhea exclaimed, demonstrating again, then taking Benjamin's hands, swinging his arms up while repeating the command.

Benjamin's gaze floated to her, but he looked blank. Rhea guided him through the motion several more times, but Benjamin remained limp and uncomprehending. I fidgeted, not wanting to interfere, yet quickly recognizing that something was missing. After another few repetitions, I spoke up and offered a suggestion. "Benjamin loves music," I said. "How about using a fun sound to get him interested? Like, 'Copy me, *wheeee...*'"

I sang out the *wheeee* with a swooping, happy sound, and Benjamin perked up. Encouraged by this subtle but immediate response, I felt I should offer further assistance and so asked, "How about if I kneel behind Benjamin and help him move his arms while you act as the leader? I'll be manipulating him like a puppet, but it might get the idea across..."

"This is great," Rhea exclaimed as we synchronized our actions. "It's obvious that you're a teacher, and I can see you'll be able to help me as I work with Benjamin."

After several more repetitions of "copy me, *wheeee*," Rhea moved on to demonstrate clapping, with me continuing to animate Benjamin's arms from my position behind him. As we copied Rhea's rhythmic clapping, I began singing a German patty-cake song that Benjamin loved. My sense was that we should create a genuine reason for clapping rather than just clapping for the sake of imitation. The atmosphere in the room brightened as the song brought an element of playful joy into the exercise.

"Good copying. Good clapping," Rhea praised, beaming at Benjamin.

"We want to teach some sign language too," Rhea now explained. "That way, Benjamin will have a means of communication while we figure out how to get some speech out of him." She tapped both index fingers together while her other fingers remained curled into a loose fist. "This means 'more'," she told me and reached for the little bowl of dried fruits I had prepared; she had explained that we might be using food rewards to motivate Benjamin's cooperation. Rhea took a few raisins and popped them into Benjamin's mouth.

"More," she said, demonstrating the sign. Then she took Benjamin's hands in hers and made his fingertips touch in a little tapping motion. "More. Good saying 'more'," she exclaimed, popping another raisin into Benjamin's mouth. To me, she clarified, "We can work on refining the sign and getting it more correct later on. For now, he just needs to get the basic idea."

Rhea repeated the process several times, rewarding Benjamin with raisins after each repetition. Then she patted the tabletop twice with both hands, palms down, saying, "All done." She took Benjamin's hands and made him pat the table too, again saying, "All done."

Benjamin was beginning to sag and fade, not comprehending what was going on. Rhea pulled out the spinny toy that had attracted his attention earlier and waved it in front of his face. Instantly, Benjamin was galvanized, reaching eagerly for the toy. Rhea spoke quickly to me. "Make him pat his left arm with his right hand," she said. "That means 'help'." I followed through, and Rhea handed Benjamin the toy, laughing.

"Good saying 'help'," she praised. Benjamin made the toy spin wildly, lapsing back into his typical self-stimulatory behaviors, flapping and tensing. Rhea gently took the toy away, and then, before Benjamin could begin to scream in protest, I took his hand in mine and made him sign, "Help." Immediately, Rhea rewarded Benjamin with the toy.

After several more trials, I glanced meaningfully at Rhea and guided Benjamin to pat the table with both hands, saying, "All done." It was time to get him out of that chair and to let him move around.

My mom had been present throughout the session, quietly watching from a corner. Now she took Benjamin onto her lap, distracting him from the garish toys while I looked through Rhea's bins and listened to her explanation of how Benjamin would be "learning how to learn."

I responded by summarizing my understanding of the situation. "So, the brain of a child with autism isn't wired to assimilate language and respond to social cues in the way that a typical child's brain does. We are trying to restructure Benjamin's brain by providing appropriate, therapeutic stimulation, and hopefully, this will cause his brain to generate new or alternate neural pathways that can compensate for the impairments associated with autism." Rhea nodded, agreeing with my interpretation.

By now, I had gotten to the bottom of the bins and had found some toys that were aesthetically pleasing to me while still having a mechanical component that might attract Benjamin's attention: a cute little wind-up owl that would waddle drunkenly across the table; a whistle that was shaped like a row-boat—it had a flag that would spin, activated by airflow while you tooted; another whistle, this one shaped like a bird's cage where the bird would flutter and bob when you blew, making a chirruping sound. "These would be nice to use as motivators," I told Rhea, holding up the toys. "I really don't want Benjamin to become so hyper-stimulated from playing with 'spinny' toys and gadgets; he gets too lost in them."

Rhea expressed understanding. "You can use whatever toys you like, as long as they catch Benjamin's interest enough to motivate him to work."

I asked where I might purchase intriguing toys like the ones I was holding, and then we scheduled a second therapy session, tentatively planning to meet twice per week.

The next day, Benjamin surprised me by energetically pointing across my parents' long, European-style kitchen at an avocado sitting high upon a shelf. My heart leaped. Six weeks had passed since I had begun working on pointing skills, and now Benjamin was demonstrating that he had truly made the connection.

"Good pointing," I exclaimed, rushing to slice open the ripe fruit, rewarding Benjamin with a spoonful of delicious, creamy green. I seated him at the kitchen table and waved the spoon with another bite of avocado near my face, attracting Benjamin's eye contact and requesting, "Benjamin, say 'more'." After demonstrating the sign for "more," I shaped Benjamin's hands, helping him to make the sign. "Good saying 'more'," I praised.

Now, with every ensuing bite of avocado, Benjamin had to make the sign for "more." I was taking advantage of the natural setting, showing Benjamin that his new skill didn't only apply in the structure of his "work space."

On the last day of March, we had our fourth session with Rhea. We settled Benjamin into his little chair and started off with enthusiastic rehearsals of "copy me: *wheeee*, arms up…" Just as I had been doing during each of our previous three sessions, I helped Benjamin to raise his arms in response to Rhea's example.

After a few trials however, I sensed an energy shift in Benjamin, as if he had suddenly lighted up from inside. Following my intuition, I refrained from pushing Benjamin's arms up as Rhea continued playing the leader. Lo and behold, Benjamin tentatively followed Rhea's motion *on his own*, slowly lifting his arms up towards the ceiling.

"Yes," I whispered, a grin splitting my face. Then I began whooping, and both Rhea and my mom broke into applause. Startled, Benjamin looked around and, seeing joy beaming from our faces, he broke into a delighted smile himself.

"Let's try that again," Rhea exclaimed. "Copy me." Again Benjamin lifted his arms slowly, imitating without any help. My heart sang as I watched Benjamin gaining confidence with each successive repetition. New neural connections were being formed before my very eyes.

Then it was time to work on play skills. Rhea brought out a little train and placed it on the table. As if magnetized, Benjamin was immediately drawn to the wheels, wanting to spin them, but Rhea was quick. She grasped the locomotive saying, *"Choo-choo-oo,"* and making the train chug around the table top. Benjamin stared at the wheels in fascination, twirling his hands on outstretched arms and tightening his belly. Rhea took his right hand, placed it under hers, and helped him to push the train. Benjamin tipped his head sideways and continued watching the wheels, going limp under Rhea's guiding hand. At least he was interested even though his focus wasn't where we wanted it.

Rhea exchanged the train for a colorful ball. "Roll," she exclaimed, propelling the ball into Benjamin's lap. He giggled. "More," Rhea said as she formed his hands to make the appropriate sign for asking.

"Roll." "More." "Roll." Benjamin awkwardly grabbed at the ball and tried to roll it. The ball veered off the table and bounced on the floor, and Benjamin followed it with his eyes. This was becoming fun. Soon however, Benjamin started looking fatigued, and it seemed like a good opportunity to help him sign, "All done." I lifted him off his chair and enfolded him in an enormous bear-hug, rocking him back and forth, telling him how proud I was.

6

The Energy Connection
April 1997

Benjamin's learning curve had been gathering momentum, and I marveled at the many little miracles that were happening. Even before starting therapy with Rhea, Benjamin had begun spontaneously imitating some of my gestures and actions; however, his motions had been generally tentative, only hinting at the full movement he was attempting to copy. In contrast, the day after our breakthrough session with the "arms up" command, Benjamin eagerly began copying when I sang our German baking song. He clapped the steady rhythm right along with me, and at the end of the song, assertively imitated my broad gestures of shoving a big cake into an oven.

Tears of joy gathered in my eyes as I beamed at Benjamin and started the song all over again, not wanting to slow our momentum; it seemed too good to be true. Benjamin maintained his engagement for another round of the song before I stopped, hugging and bouncing him around, making him giggle. "Good copying, honey-bun!"

Within another few days, Benjamin was independently, albeit tentatively, waving "hello" and "good-bye" in response to my own arm gesture as I sang the "waving song" that Rhea had taught me. We had been practicing this motion daily since our second therapy session and again, the combination of movement with music seemed to facilitate Benjamin's comprehension.

Benjamin was hypersensitive about the feel of various materials and textures on his skin, particularly on the palms of his hands. "Young children learn so much about the world through touch," I thought, recognizing that Benjamin's autism-driven tactile sensitivity needed work. He had already rejected Play-Doh, refusing to touch it after discovering how it felt, and now I had found a much more pleasant, moldable material with a silky texture, beautiful color, and natural fragrance as a replacement. I began by gently mushing a ball of this material into Benjamin's palm, and he began screeching with protest. I refused to take the dough away, recalling what the play therapist in San Diego had said about overcoming resistance. Soon, I was wrestling a kicking, screaming, flailing little monster, and doubts were swirling through me.

Was this really the right thing to do? What about the love and joy that I was trying to maintain? What if I backed off? What if Benjamin didn't stop his resistance? How long should I keep going? I struggled with my child and my internal quandary, and after what seemed like an eternity, Benjamin's thrashing finally eased, and his screaming subsided into tearful sobs.

We cried together then, as I held Benjamin against me, rocking him and humming a melody, still keeping the dough firmly squashed between his hands. After a long time, Benjamin's tension and upset drained away. Hugging his warm, solid little body to me, I prayed that we wouldn't have to go through this again.

Thankfully, when I brought out the moldable material the next day, Benjamin refrained from screaming and, although he *did* show some resistance, I soon had his hands pressed into the mass of soft stuff, making him knead and squeeze it. Now, with each successive try, Benjamin was adapting more easily and quickly to the squishy sensation. Our struggle had been worthwhile.

Benjamin was beginning to sign on his own. "All done" was the easiest signal, and he had begun spontaneously tapping his open palms on the table after completing a puzzle and after we had eaten a snack or meal. Now he was even patting his chest to indicate "Benjamin's turn" while making aggressive vocalizations. "It's as if he's struggling to say something, but the only thing that will come out is *'lallallal'*," I told Rhea when she came for our next therapy session.

We had been experimenting with getting Benjamin to imitate mouth shapes and sounds. So far, he could only manage to follow my lead when I opened my mouth wide to take in a deep breath and then closed it to hum, making an "mmm" sound. For some reason, he couldn't copy any other sounds at will, even though these might be the same sounds he would produce when spontaneously babbling.

I thought back to the magical moment in our Coronado cottage when Natasha had been intensely tuned in to Benjamin, and he had purposely echoed her sounds. "I hope researchers figure out how autism blocks the brain from following its normal developmental progression," I said musingly to Rhea. "Maybe Benjamin's current language issues wouldn't have developed if we had started speech therapy when he first began losing his words." Rhea looked at me, shrugging helplessly. "I know, there's no use crying over spilled milk," I said. "I just can't help wondering since I noticed so many autism indicators early on. If we had gotten a more prompt diagnosis, we could have intervened before things got this far off track."

We had discovered that Benjamin couldn't blow on the many intriguing whistles that we tempted him with. It also seemed that he couldn't stick out his tongue on purpose, although I wasn't sure whether this stemmed from his overall difficulties with imitation or whether Benjamin was actually incapable of directing his tongue to make that movement.

"He doesn't have any trouble closing his mouth on his 'sippy-cup'," I told Rhea. "We've been practicing drinking from an ordinary glass, and Benjamin is learning to play with his juice, blowing bubbles into it instead of drinking. However, it seems like the concept of closing his mouth around a small opening and blowing rather than sucking is completely eluding him."

"There is something called 'oral apraxia'," Rhea told me. "It's when the language center of the brain isn't interfacing with those muscles that control the mouth and tongue, and therefore voluntary speech isn't possible."

I thought this through. "It sounds like he's got to grow some new neural pathways."

Rhea nodded agreement, saying, "You'll have to keep working on Benjamin's communication through signing. All this therapy you're doing will keep his brain stimulated, and we'll just keep motivating him to try copying your mouth. Hopefully the right connections will develop." Rhea now ventured a guess. "My feeling is that once Benjamin figures out how to blow, he'll have gained enough control over his mouth to begin copying sounds."

With this in mind, I decided to buy a variety of drinking containers with attached straws of different sizes and shapes. I figured that Benjamin would surely become adept at forming his mouth into the required "O" shape in order to suck up his juice through these. Then, perhaps the ability to blow bubbles through a straw would emerge as well.

Benjamin's eye/hand coordination was quite good, and he was learning to string enormous wooden beads onto a thick cord. He was also catching on to manipulating a peg-board with fat solid-colored pegs in every color of the rainbow. "Put in. Pull apart. Match color." We had been practicing these skills repeatedly, and Benjamin's understanding was increasing noticeably.

I had added colorful wooden puzzle-templates with outlines of large numbers and letters engraved into them; correlating shapes would fit perfectly into the flat template. While Benjamin was quickly gaining skill in putting the correct numbers and letters into their places, he was having considerable difficulty with the shape-sorters that Rhea had lent us. These were puzzles where various large, solid, geometrically shaped forms needed to be fitted through correlating openings in a flat surface. I was surprised that Benjamin seemed stymied by the addition of a depth dimension since he wasn't having trouble with the flat puzzles.

Rhea was again working with Benjamin, and as I watched, I had the growing sense that Rhea wasn't fully present; something about her energy felt subdued and perhaps a little depressed. She was praising Benjamin, her voice whooping up to show her pleasure, but somehow she sounded hollow to me. She was making funny faces to get Benjamin's attention, but I felt that her heart wasn't in it. Benjamin seemed to feel it too; he remained unengaged and looked almost tearful by the end of their time together. "Benjamin is picking up on her vibes, just like I am," I thought, amazed that he could be so sensitive in spite of his autism.

After weeks of great progress, Benjamin was becoming withdrawn, and I was compensating by putting out much extra energy, buoying him up with my joyful gusto. The ongoing effort was wearing me out, and one morning, I momentarily snapped under the strain of working against Benjamin's introverted reluctance.

I had been trying to get a more definitive response to the command, "Look at me," and was mentally comparing Benjamin's spotty responses to the ideal outcomes described in *Let Me Hear Your Voice*. The goal was for Benjamin to respond within five seconds of hearing the command, and we were nowhere close to that. Using a drill format didn't seem to be helping, and the motivational power of food rewards was wearing thin; Benjamin simply wasn't responding. My inclination was to work on the command in a naturalistic way, finding real-life reasons for commanding eye contact, but this wasn't working either. Currently, nothing seemed enticing enough to warrant Benjamin's attention.

"Look at me," I suddenly yelled, overcome by a frustrated anger unlike anything I had ever felt towards my beloved child. "Look at me!" I moved towards Benjamin and tried to force him to turn his head towards me. He resisted, making his body rigid, and I felt myself crumbling with shame at my loss of self-control. I stood up and turned away, then paced back and forth trying to blow off steam. "We're both worn out, we've both been working hard," I mumbled to myself. "Just stop, take a break. Don't let yourself become motivated by fear and worry. Remember the loving, '*Son Rise* attitude'; focus on finding the intrinsic joy of things…"

I thought about Benjamin's recently increased compulsion to spin objects and the fact that he now tried to hide this activity when he saw me coming. I had been getting stricter about limiting his self-stimulatory behaviors, and this approach seemed to be backfiring. Also, Benjamin had just started banging his head on the ground again, a behavior that had been absent for over half a year.

I decided that we both needed a nap. As I lay in bed, eyes closed, I meditated on the idea of maintaining inner clarity and positive intentions. Then I took Benjamin outside for a walk around the neighborhood. I cleared my mind of the strict learning program that I had so intensively focused on for the past weeks and became aware of the invigorating spring scents that surrounded us.

"Mmm, smell the violets." I picked a small bouquet and held it under Benjamin's nose. We walked on and when we reached a stone garden wall, I picked Benjamin up, setting him on his feet atop the wall and guiding him to walk along it in order to work on his balancing skills. I looked up at the peaceful blue sky and imagined soaking in its calm aspect. I could feel my inner equilibrium being restored and, by the time we finished our walk, I had regained a positive outlook.

"I need to focus on loving interaction rather than forcefully pushing for progress," I reminded myself, pulling out a storybook to read with Benjamin. He sat in my lap willingly, looking at the pictures. One page showed a little girl sitting on the ground, leaning back, holding her teddy-bear's arms as he sat on her tummy. Seeing this, Benjamin promptly stood up. He took my hand, placed it on his head, and then used *his* hands to manipulate *mine* so that *his* head could be made to nod "yes." He hadn't yet figured out how to nod "yes" on his own, and was depending on me to make the motion happen. Now I gaped, incredulous, reading Benjamin's intentions.

"Yes, darling, they are playing 'Row, row, row your boat' just like we do...and you want to play too." Benjamin's face was bright as he clambered onto my lap, knowing that I would rock him and sing our rowing song. The positive shift I had made in my intentions and energy was definitely having a harmonizing effect on both of us.

This incident made me ponder the role of emotions and spiritual energy, and to think about their influence on the communications between people. Even though Benjamin's autism was disrupting his capacity for interpreting the world around him, he certainly wasn't impervious to the underlying currents of human interaction. I thought back to how Benjamin had mirrored my feelings of deep distress when I had first read about autism a few months earlier. I also recalled how Natasha's sensitivity and inner calm had been healing to both of us. And I thought about what might be happening just now with Rhea.

"Benjamin can't buffer someone's energy if it happens to be negative. I'll give Rhea a call and share my thoughts with her; we both need to strive for a genuinely positive attitude when working with Benjamin. What a tall order. I'll be spending my lifetime on that one."

My heart was heavy with missing Rick. Already, six months had passed since we had been together as a family, and my grief was a palpable pain residing in my chest. A longtime family friend, recognizing my burden, offered to do a bit of art therapy with me. "You need something healing for yourself," she counseled. "Otherwise, you won't be able to sustain your work with Benjamin."

Grateful, I began a series of evening visits to Ursula's whimsical art-and-sculpture-filled house. As I stroked watercolor paints onto thick paper, Ursula made suggestions that helped me to relax my intellect and to become centered in my emotions. Entering a meditative state, I painted abstract shapes and swirls of color.

I began acknowledging the heaviness of the challenges that now lay upon me. During the daytime, when I was working with Benjamin, I needed to shut the door on these feelings otherwise I wouldn't be able to function. At night though, after I had tucked Benjamin into bed, the pain often flooded over me, and now I looked forward to my time at Ursula's, knowing that the peaceful act of painting would gently feed my soul.

I had spoken to Rhea, asking her to shift from a drill-style format to a more playful approach. "We need to keep motivating Benjamin with a feeling of joy. I see him shutting down in response to the drilling."

When Rhea opened up her toy bins, she pulled out something that I hadn't seen before: a coppery metal bowl about six inches across, accompanied by a short wooden dowel with a carved handle. Balancing the bowl on her outstretched palm, she turned to Benjamin and exclaimed, "Look at me," while tapping the bowl. It made a wonderful bell-like sound. Then Rhea began sliding the wooden dowel firmly around the rim of the bowl, and the room reverberated with an enchanting, unearthly tone.

Benjamin had been rocking mindlessly, paying Rhea no heed, but now he stopped and turned, staring at the bowl in fascination. He remained entranced as the sound continued filling the room. Finally, Rhea raised the dowel with a flourish, announcing, "Benjamin's turn." As she took his hands in hers, Rhea told me, "This is a Tibetan singing bowl. I used to work at a Buddhist preschool and they had these in various sizes, using different tones to mark transitions between activities. I fell in love with the sound."

"It *is* magical," I agreed and then asked where I might purchase one.

"There's a Tibetan import store downtown," Rhea told me.

After letting Benjamin experiment with the bowl, Rhea began showering him with iridescent soap bubbles. "Blow," she encouraged as Benjamin smiled up into the floating bubbles. He still didn't understand about blowing, but at least he was now showing contentment in Rhea's presence. Then, for the remainder of the session, Rhea worked on turn-taking using a tub of water with a small water-wheel placed in its center. She showed Benjamin how to pour a stream of water in order to spin the wheel, and he responded quite happily. Rhea's more playful approach was clearly motivating him to keep interacting.

At our next session some days later, Rhea pulled out a doll, a comb, and some powder. "I think Benjamin is ready to work on some symbolic play skills," she explained. "We want him to learn the actions that can lead to imaginary play."

Benjamin obviously enjoyed the feel of the talcum powder, and he willingly allowed Rhea to guide his hands as she made him rub the doll's tummy with powder. Running the comb through the doll's hair was a considerably more difficult task for Benjamin, and after a few tries, Rhea moved on, placing a miniature playground slide about six inches long on the table.

"*Whee*," she exclaimed, making the doll glide down the incline of the toy slide.

Benjamin gazed at the slide for a few moments, and then his hands began twirling in excitement. He quickly climbed up onto the table and stood with his legs straddled over the toy. Slowly, Benjamin lowered his bottom, bending over to check whether he was sitting on the slide yet. A terribly puzzled look crossed his face. I knew that he must be thinking something like, "How strange. I can't go down this slide even though it looks just like the big one out in the yard." Tears of laughter slid down my cheeks at the sweetness of the moment. Rhea laughed too, but somehow, I was again struck by the impression that she wasn't her usual self.

The second week of April had begun when Rhea came for our eighth therapy appointment. She again focused on symbolic play using a doll. First, she reviewed combing the doll's hair and then helped Benjamin to rub powder on its body. Then she showed him how the doll could be dressed in miniature clothing and how he could pretend to feed the doll. Benjamin was clearly nonplussed by these activities, and as Rhea attempted to get him engaged and participating, there was a palpable damper on her emotions. The atmosphere in the room seemed devoid of happiness, and after a while, Benjamin began to cry with no apparent reason.

"Rhea is definitely feeling depressed," I thought. "And Benjamin is reflecting her inner state." I intervened, snuggling Benjamin until his tears dried up. Then I asked my mom to take him out into the garden. As I talked with Rhea, she admitted to having some serious difficulties in her own life; she needed a break from her work. Sympathizing, I expressed my appreciation for what she had taught me. "Please don't worry about letting us down," I reassured her while erasing several scheduled sessions from my planner. "I can manage. Now that I've watched behavioral therapy in action, I feel more confident about striking out on my own." We said good-bye then, and I later heard that Rhea had moved out of state.

Benjamin's cranio-sacral therapist was suggesting that we cut back our sessions to twice per month. "Most of Benjamin's tight areas have become more consistently pliable," Cheryl explained. "There is a particular area located near the speech center of the brain which tends to hold tremendous tension, but I felt a good release in there today."

Shortly after this appointment, Benjamin came down with a high fever but showed no other symptoms of illness, and after a few days spent recuperating without any demands placed on him, he had recovered and seemed ready to get back to work.

We sat down at his little table, and he eagerly completed his number puzzle and half of his alphabet puzzle without any assistance, copying my excited applause with vigorous clapping of his own. "Yay, Benjamin," I cheered again and again, and Benjamin beamed at me each time, relishing the praise. Later, after drinking some juice, he handed me his empty cup and very deliberately signed "more" instead of crying and throwing the cup to the floor as he had become accustomed to doing. Later on, he pointed at several distant objects, attempting to nod "yes," and when I handed him the desired objects, he swung his arms up as if to sign, "*Whee!*" Benjamin was clearly indicating happiness.

"This is remarkable," I exclaimed to my mom. "My intuition tells me that Cheryl's work released a lot of stress in Benjamin, and that this triggered the feverish reaction. He was progressing steadily for so long that his body enforced a break—a time for assimilation. That's like me when I've been holding up under a lot of sustained pressure; as soon as I relax, *boom*, I get sick. But what often takes me by surprise is the rearrangement of priorities and the feeling of renewal that can follow illness."

Now I returned to playing piano with Benjamin, just as we had been doing each day before he had gotten sick. I had been assisting him in picking out a few simple songs, encouraging him to use all his fingers rather than just his pointers. Now, with Benjamin settled comfortably on my lap, I spread my hands over his, using my fingertips on top of his to hit the keys. As we played some pretty two-note harmonies, I heard little humming sounds emanating from Benjamin. He was matching various pitches, and his singing was perfectly in tune. Thrilled at this new development, I kept on playing so that Benjamin would keep on humming. I recognized that music was his special muse, speaking to his soul and awakening him.

Since Benjamin's use of sign language was developing well, I decided to add another means of communication, using pictures. When Benjamin had identified the picture book teddy-bear as playing "Row your boat," and when he had tried going down Rhea's toy doll-slide, he had demonstrated his grasp of the connection between a *symbolic representation* of something and the corresponding *real-life object*. For many children with autism, this understanding might come only after much drilling, and I was thankful that Benjamin hadn't had trouble with the concept.

Using index cards, I now drew an apple, a banana, a cluster of grapes, and a cucumber. I posted the four cards on the refrigerator and asked, "Benjamin, what do you want?" Placing my hand over his, I helped him to point at the apple and to then take the card and hand it to me. I gave him a piece of apple, exchanging it for the picture.

Later, I tried again. "Benjamin, what do you want?" He immediately took the banana picture and handed it to me. "Honey, you're brilliant," I praised, giving him a slice of banana.

Inspired, my mom pulled out her gardening catalogues. Cutting out pictures of various fruits, vegetables, and flowers, she made a comprehensive set of cards for expanding Benjamin's vocabulary. Lining up several pictures, I repeatedly named each thing while pointing at it. "Now Benjamin points," I said. "Point at sunflower." I helped Benjamin to correctly identify the card. "Point at broccoli." After several days of playing this game, Benjamin began pointing on his own, and whenever he didn't remember what something was called, I would collect the picture into a "review" pile, to be worked on until Benjamin could consistently identify it.

Around mid-April, I got a call from someone at the Developmental Disabilities Center. "We are sponsoring children with special needs to participate in an ongoing movement class for typical toddlers and preschoolers. Would you like to join?" Delighted by this unexpected opportunity, I brought Benjamin to the designated dance studio the following week, and we joined a group of moms with their little ones. We started off sitting cross-legged in a circle on the floor, our children on our laps, echoing and copying 'Dance Nancy' as she sang a series of songs accompanied by vigorous movements and broad acting.

"Stand up and follow me, everyone," Nancy called out and then sang, "*Head, shoulders, knees and toes, knees and toes,*" while motioning for the children to follow her movements. Benjamin stood still, not understanding what to do. "This class is going to be the perfect challenge," I thought, taking Benjamin's hands and helping him to touch the various body parts named by the song.

Nancy now directed, "Children on your backs, moms grab your kiddos' ankles." She started singing again. "*I had a little bicycle and rode it through the town...*" The cheerful tune was new to me, and Benjamin's legs first wobbled and then kicked as I manipulated them to bicycle in the air.

"Everyone on this side of the room, line up, and let's go for a swim," Nancy called out. Invigorating music pulsed, and a line of children moved across the floor with Benjamin and me joining them as a tandem unit. Nancy kept calling out directions: "Now walk backwards. Now side-slide. And gallop." Surrounded by the effervescence and chaos of the other children, we tried to follow.

"Everybody run..." That we could do. I chased Benjamin in the right direction, tickling him so that he would run and grabbing hold of his hand when he veered sideways, trying to leave the group. Class time flew by, and then the kids lined up in front of Nancy, each receiving a cute little animal sticker. She knelt down, smiling at Benjamin, and I was struck by her vivacious, high spirits. "Hi Benjamin."

I prompted him to wave at Nancy.

"Do you want a sticker?"

I helped him point to one of the darling little whales.

"Ooh, that's a good one," Nancy said affixing it to the back of Benjamin's hand. Using his pointer finger, Benjamin began pressing the sticker as if it were an on/off button, touching it again and again with immense excitement, face glowing, hands twirling, leg muscles tensing and making him rise onto tiptoe.

Nancy stood up, regarding Benjamin thoughtfully. "Benjamin's eyes are amazing, there's so much light coming from them. He seems radiant...angelic." I looked at her, at this new person who was providing such a joyful learning environment, and I got a bit teary eyed at her quick discernment of Benjamin's spiritual nature. He was indeed my angel.

It was the end of April, and Benjamin was having another cranio-sacral appointment. After a while, Cheryl told me, "That area near the back of his head is super-tight again." As she worked on releasing the spot, Benjamin began swinging his arms up, gesturing, "*Whee*—happy."

"That feels good to him," I exclaimed, laughing.

For several hours after we left Cheryl's office, I watched Benjamin repeatedly nodding his head, making large emphatic motions rather than the tentative little head jerks that he had recently managed to produce when indicating "yes." Benjamin's new freedom of motion seemed exhilarating to him; between nods, he babbled intensively, making new sounds that I hadn't heard before. Best of all, that evening, he spontaneously gave me two kisses, lightly puckering his lips as he touched my cheek with them. My heart flip-flopped. Benjamin was intentionally forming a specific shape with his mouth. This was a breakthrough!

At bedtime, I asked Benjamin for another kiss, hoping he would be able to repeat his spontaneous impulse, but he wouldn't do it, and I had to have faith that the earlier kisses hadn't been accidental. "I love you," I said to Benjamin, signing as I spoke.

Then I helped him to make the signs back to me.

Two days later, Benjamin again developed a high fever. "This is the same pattern as last time," I thought, observing no further symptoms of illness. "Benjamin's learning curve has been accelerating, and now he again needs time to rest and assimilate his new level of understanding."

7

The Merry Month of May
May 1997

May had arrived with a profusion of fragrant flowers, and we were sitting outdoors eating breakfast at the picnic table in my parents' back yard. Several vitamin bottles were lined up next to me, and I poured a spoonful of special "autism formula" into a sippy-cup of juice for Benjamin. I had read about a number of nutritional supplements that might help relieve autistic symptoms and had also found literature confirming my earlier suspicions that foods containing gluten and caseine (milk protein) could cause an exacerbation of symptoms. (Butter and ghee were not considered problematic due to their minimal caseine content.)

While Benjamin was making great strides in his learning, he wasn't displaying any of the obvious changes in behavior that I had read about in testimonials touting the autism-specific formula with its high vitamin B-6 content, and I now planned to discontinue its use. My sense was that mega-dosing with something that wasn't making a clear difference might actually be harmful. Nevertheless, I would continue feeding Benjamin fish oil and other food-based supplements in modest doses, knowing that these would provide subtle support without the likelihood of stressing his body.

We were in my parents' living room, working on identifying colors while stringing beads. "Get red. Get blue. Get yellow. Get more blue." I directed Benjamin's attention, helping him to push a thick cord through enormous wooden beads.

Then, for a change of pace, I pulled out some "stitching cards" that our neighbors had lent us. These colorful pasteboard cards came in various shapes—round, square, heart-shaped, etc.—and had holes punched at regular intervals around their edges. I guided Benjamin in threading a long, skinny shoelace through the holes, teaching him the basic whipstitch pattern. Benjamin's eye/hand coordination was remarkably good, and he threaded the cards with surprising ease while my mom sat nearby, knitting a sweater for him. Her weaving loom leaned against the table, and I could see that a rustic woolen pillowcase was in the making.

"When Benjamin becomes a little older, we should teach him to weave," my mom suggested. "We can make a very large, rudimentary lap loom for him." This was an excellent idea. My mom had once been a teacher of handcrafts at a Waldorf school and had taught both me and my brother to weave, embroider, crochet, and knit, all before we had entered Kindergarten. In addition, we had begun learning several musical instruments as children, beginning with the soprano recorder at age four. These childhood experiences were still vivid in my memory. They had shaped me, instilling discipline and requiring a balance between intellectual thinking and creativity. Now I was looking to these skills as possible therapeutic influences for Benjamin.

As Benjamin and I finished with the stitching cards, my mom joined Dad in the kitchen to make lunch. I was grateful that she didn't want me helping her. We had all noticed that if Benjamin was left alone, he would immediately slip back into his pattern of solitary, self-stimulatory obsessions. At this early stage of therapeutic intervention, Benjamin needed to be actively engaged during every minute of his waking hours, and I was beginning to wonder how I would manage household chores once we had moved into our own house.

After the meal, I drilled Benjamin on his picture-card vocabulary. I was now combining several therapeutic modalities for maximum effectiveness. I seated Benjamin in his hammock cocoon and began swinging him, then handed him two cards. "Give me broom. Now give me table." Benjamin had to decide which card was which, and he had to hand the correct one over as he swung near me. "Mommy's turn." I held the card up near my face, asking for eye contact. "Look at me. See table. Benjamin's turn." I handed back the card as Benjamin again swung my way. In this manner, Benjamin's sensory system was being soothed by swinging, and we were simultaneously working on language, eye contact, making choices, and taking turns.

Benjamin loved playing in water and, as breaks from our ongoing skill drills, we were taking regular baths in my parents' large old-fashioned tub. Immersed in warm, lavender-scented water and surrounded by various bath toys and colorful plastic cups, I began pouring streams of water onto Benjamin, making him giggle with delight. After a while, I encouraged Benjamin to play with a large ocean sponge, helping him to squeeze it and to poke his fingers into the intriguing plethora of holes that riddled its round, beige mass. He had initially disliked its squishiness, just as he had hated the feel of Play-Doh, but I kept insisting that we play with it. Now Benjamin was getting to be friends with this ocean creature.

The tub was also a fun place to work on oral motor skills. "Blow," I encouraged, holding a cup of water to Benjamin's mouth. This was becoming easy and Benjamin vigorously blew bubbles, but when I deftly slipped a fat straw into his mouth in place of the cup, his blowing was thwarted. He couldn't keep going with this differently shaped object obstructing his mouth. His lips closed loosely around the straw, but he stopped blowing.

"We're going to need a stroke of luck to get the concept across," I thought once again. Benjamin had been trying to drink through variably sized straws, motivated by the mouthfuls of delicious juice that occasionally rewarded his efforts, but he was having difficulties with pursing his mouth adequately. And blowing? Benjamin wasn't making the connection.

After our baths, I would usually give Benjamin a full-body massage, kneading his muscles and stimulating his skin using massage oil which smelled soothingly of calendula and lavender. I was very picky in selecting body care products. Even those that were "all natural" could contain scents which would give me an itchy nose or even a headache, and I was keeping an eye out for any similar reactions in Benjamin.

Most of the autism-specific materials I had perused during the past three months had included discussions of common hyper-sensitivities (tactile, visual, and auditory), and I knew that Benjamin had issues with all of these. However, I hadn't yet run across any mention of olfactory sensitivity.

"That's an unfortunate omission," I now thought. I remembered a brief encounter that I'd had in San Diego, shortly after Benjamin had been diagnosed. I had met with a young mother whose little boy also had autism, and at the time of our meeting, her son had been an irritable, crying mess. The little boy had been throwing himself around, refusing to walk, allowing his frustrated mother to drag him along as she gave up on conversing with me.

She had explained, "This is typical for my little guy; it is part of his autistic behavior," and I had thought, "Wow, she's got it rough. I hope Benjamin doesn't start doing that kind of thing." After our visit, the smell of the young woman's perfume still lingered in our driveway, and I realized that I was getting a headache from it.

I mentioned this incident to my parents. "Maybe the little boy's behavior was being aggravated by his mom's perfume. When I consider how crummy I feel when exposed to certain smells, I can easily imagine myself throwing a tantrum and acting out, just like that little boy was doing." My mom nodded vigorously in agreement; she too was hyper-sensitive to perfumes and the like.

I went on. "I think that, because so many commercial products have strong synthetic smells, folks become habituated to them and forget about the impact that they might have. Likewise, we are inundated with sounds; it's hard to evade elevator music or traffic noise. Ceaseless sound like that can drive me absolutely nuts. Just imagine how someone with autism must feel when overwhelming sensory input can't be evaded. Wow."

Fortunately, I could spare Benjamin from such overstimulation.

During the first weeks of May, Benjamin's sign-vocabulary expanded exponentially. I had purchased a sign language dictionary and had been gradually teaching nouns and verbs that would be of interest. Benjamin had already learned "go," "stop," "want," "sleep," "swing," "slide," "turn," and "jump," and was trying hard to sign "sun," "rain," "clouds," "sky," and "music." He was finally becoming hungry for language and was soaking up new vocabulary like a sponge.

I hadn't given up on my long-term goal for Benjamin to grow up bilingually, and so I was playing some of our language games in German, teaching the names of objects. One of Benjamin's favorite rewards was a game that we called *Engelein fliege* ("little angel, fly"). Jiggling with anticipation, Benjamin would grab my hand and pull me over to my mom whose hand he would also grab. Then my mom and I would each hold tight to a wrist and an ankle; we would swoop Benjamin off his feet, swinging him back and forth between us. *"Engelein fli-i-i-i-ege,"* I would sing as Benjamin crowed and giggled. I had vivid memories of my parents doing this with me when I was little; the wild, flying sensation was unforgettable, and I could understand why Benjamin loved it so much.

Halfway through May, I had an appointment to learn about a therapy called "chirophonetics." Corinne, the practitioner, was a Kindergarten teacher at the local Waldorf school and had a background in sensory integration therapy as well. When I told her that I was teaching Benjamin some German, she declared, "You need to choose a single language and stick with it until Benjamin is fluent."

Seeing that I was taken aback, Corinne elaborated. "The words of every language have a particular feel to them. Take the English word 'tree' for example. When you say 'tree,' your mouth makes a very narrow, focused space to produce the 'ee' vowel. The sharpness of the 'ee' sound might evoke the image of a fir tree with its slender, elegant shape like a piercing arrow. Such an image resonates within the soul, giving a specific subconscious feeling."

"In contrast, the German word for tree is *'Baum'*. Say it slowly: *'B-a-u-m'*. Do you feel how round and full the sounds feel in your mouth? The vowels are more evocative of a deciduous tree with a full, leafy crown and thus, your soul receives quite a different impression than when you speak the English word, 'tree'."

"What a thought-provoking perspective," I thought, trying out the two words and sensing the subtle shift Corinne was referring to.

She went on. "You'll better understand how this pertains to Benjamin if I first review some salient developmental milestones as seen from a Waldorf teacher's viewpoint. The young child's soul and spirit are distinct but invisible entities which aren't yet fully integrated with the child's physical body.

Integration occurs as the child grows and, over time, the individual personality emerges and is developed through life experiences. We call this individuality the 'ego'." I nodded my understanding as Corinne looked at me questioningly.

"During the first three years of life, this process of incarnation gives the child an increasingly strong sense of willpower and feeling of individuality. This is why children go through 'the terrible twos'; as they become more integrated, they develop a sense of self and begin exploring their emerging will. During these early years, children learn through imitation and emotional interaction, and you are currently striving to develop such a capacity in Benjamin."

I nodded again. My favorite book on early childhood development, *You Are Your Child's First Teacher,* by Rahima Baldwin, had furnished me with detailed analyses of the basic principles that Corinne was now touching on.

Corinne continued. "By age three, the child's memory has developed considerably, and the capacity for imagination begins to emerge; the child becomes increasingly social and interactive. Around this time, the typical child will begin saying 'I' and 'me' when referring to him or herself—the child has become fully aware of its separateness from others. This is a basic shift in consciousness; the child has its first inkling of being a unique individual."

"Before this developmental stage is reached, children are still purely imitative and therefore call themselves by name, just as they hear others referring to them. Right now, you are having Benjamin say "Benjamin's turn" rather than "my turn," correct? This is appropriate for his current age and stage of learning."

The importance of this point struck me. Children with autism require a great deal of help in learning the phrases "my turn" and "your turn." Reading about teaching the "Me/You" program in *Let Me Hear Your Voice* had made the challenge of this abundantly clear, and I had been wondering about when to introduce the concept to Benjamin. Corinne's statements made me realize that I should wait a while yet; Benjamin was just two-and-a-half years old, and prematurely drilling pronouns with him would only cause mutual frustration. Developmentally, he was not at the stage where he should be expected to use the pronoun "I."

Corinne now presented me with an illuminating interpretation of autism. "When a child develops autism, the incarnating soul struggles in its unification with the physical body: the soul becomes blocked by the physical barrier of faulty brain structure. In working with such a child, we must be sensitive and must nurture the soul, strengthening it so that further integration might occur."

"I believe that my approach to working with Benjamin is well aligned to this," I told Corinne.

"My intention is always to awaken enthusiasm and joy, and to thus develop intrinsic motivation. That is what willpower is all about."

Corinne agreed and went on explaining. "The child with autism is comforted by repetition and can learn more easily when we create an inviting soul-atmosphere. This is, in part, achieved by the repeated presentation of carefully chosen impressions. On the other hand, the soul of such a child is easily overwhelmed and weakened by what it perceives as conflicting information. This is why you should stick with a single language; you need to keep things clear and simple. You are already expanding Benjamin's sign language to include nouns, verbs, and adjectives. When you begin adding pronouns and creating sentences, you will find that teaching a single language is plenty difficult."

I interjected, "That makes sense. But, later on, I should be able to add German again, right?"

Corinne agreed, but added the caveat, "Benjamin's soul must become strong and confident; he must first overcome his current issues with speech formation. In my opinion, chirophonetics will support this."

Now Corinne gave me a brief description of the therapy. "I'll be teaching you specific strokes and forms that you'll be tracing on Benjamin's body with your hands. At the same time, you will intone the particular vowel, consonant, or combination of sounds that correlates to each stroke. There is a certain rhythm and dynamic inherent to each stroke which you'll pick up easily, considering that you are a musician and have also had massage training. In addition, specific mental images go along with each stroke and sound. As you've told me, you are well versed in the use of imagery, and have experienced the power of combining physical work with focused intention. Now, working with Benjamin, you also want to connect with the spiritual realm."

"Absolutely," I agreed. "Maintaining awareness of a higher dimension will keep me inspired."

The end of May had arrived, and Rick was coming to Boulder for his first visit since transferring to Whidbey Island. When he finally walked through the door of my parents' house, Benjamin and I were waiting. "Wave 'hello.' There's Daddy," I said. "Daddy. Hello, Daddy," I prompted, reminding Benjamin to make the sign for "father."

I couldn't tell whether Benjamin recognized Rick. Over half a year had passed since Rick had been with us, and so much had changed. "Let's go into the garden," I suggested. "We can get reacquainted there."

Rick followed us to the swing set and there, Walker greeted us with a vigorously wagging tail. My parents had purposely absented themselves, respecting our need to reconnect in private. Now I assisted Benjamin in going down the slide and began showing Rick a few words in sign language. Gradually, I felt the three of us becoming a family again; the detached feeling that had resulted from the many months of separation was evaporating. Rick and I had been emailing of course, but little opportunity had arisen for telephone conversations; between my intense work with Benjamin and Rick's erratic work schedule, there hadn't been much overlap in free time for phoning.

"I can't believe how much Benjamin has grown," Rick observed, watching as Benjamin and I reviewed our most recently learned action signs. Benjamin was turning around in place, keeping his balance as he slowly twirled.

"Good turning," I said, signing, and Benjamin easily signed back "good." Then he tried to sign "turning," needing a little help from me. Then he turned himself around again and glanced up at both of us, looking satisfied. Applause was in order.

The three of us were spending time in a rustic log cabin in the mountains. My parents had bought the little hut as a retreat from daily life, and now Rick, Benjamin, and I were enjoying some family time there, hiking along a nearby trail. A gentle breeze played through delicate aspen leaves; a small creek burbled, meandering through wildflowers and tall grasses. As we sat down on the planks of a little footbridge, I heard Benjamin humming.

A single pitch. Then silence. Then the same pitch again. With surprise, I realized that Benjamin was matching the musical tone discernible in the bubbling of the stream.

"He is hearing music in everything," I told Rick. "When my dad mows the lawn, Benjamin will hum along with the engine. Or he'll match his voice to various clinking utensils or dishes—they all have different pitches, you know. When crickets start chirping, Benjamin will sing along as well. And he is humming actual melodies, picking them up from me and from Nancy at dance class. It's quite marvelous."

Back at the cabin, Benjamin worked to finish a puzzle, his eyes meeting mine as I held the last, missing piece up by my face. "Good looking," I exclaimed, rewarding him with the puzzle piece. "All done," Benjamin now signed. Grinning, I grasped him under the armpits and propelled him upwards like a rocket. "*Whee!* Good job." I looked proudly at Rick. "Lots of progress, do you see? Now, can you help me with something?"

I explained. "Benjamin has been fearful of any sensory exercise that requires him to lie on his tummy. He needs to get over that issue. Let's try swinging him in a blanket so that he feels enclosed and safe. We'll start him out on his back."

I laid out a sturdy blanket and directed Rick to hold onto the two corners nearest him. "Come lie down," I said to Benjamin, helping him get comfortably settled. I grasped the blanket corners opposite to Rick and together we swung Benjamin back and forth, gently at first, then in ever greater arcs. Benjamin looked blissful.

Then I told Rick, "I'm going to turn Benjamin over, cushioning his tummy with a pillow." Repositioned, Benjamin remained peaceful and happy as we swung him gently. My idea was working. Eventually, when my strength gave out, I stepped outdoors for a breather and Benjamin followed. He tugged at my hand and then ran back inside, plumping down upon the blanket, snuggling his chest against the pillow. I followed, laughing, tickled by Benjamin's obvious request. "I see you, angel. Say 'more'."

Benjamin signed "more" and looked expectant.

I spoke to Rick, signing my entire next sentence, slowly repeating it so that Benjamin might copy me. "Come, Daddy, more swinging."

The few quiet days of reconnecting were over. Our household goods had arrived from their sojourn to Europe, and now we were moving into our own house. The last half of Rick's short visit felt like a circus: I bounced back and forth between setting up house and running over to my parents' in order to do some language drills with Benjamin. Keeping him engaged was a fulltime job and, while my parents could take Benjamin on walks and look at picture books with him, they couldn't manage the program of therapeutic games.

Instead, my mom did some baking, getting Benjamin involved in making a batch of gluten/casein-free cookies. Once, she showed him how dandelions could be braided to create a crown, and Benjamin seemed happy to wear the handsome new headpiece. My mom even attempted to work on turn-taking, and one afternoon, she engaged Benjamin in decorating a roughly woven fisherman's net that she had suspended between the lowest branches of an old apple tree. "What a beautiful surprise," I exclaimed, admiring the pattern of sunny golden dandelions. The flowers had been tucked into alternating loops of netting, creating a wonderful effect.

8

Home Alone
June 1997

The whirlwind of moving had passed, and now that Benjamin and I were settled into our new place, it was time to establish a daily rhythm of activities. "We'll start off with a morning walk, just like always," I thought, seating Benjamin in his jogger and tying Walker alongside so that Benjamin might reach out and pat him.

We had a choice of several nearby trailheads. Just four blocks from our house in a southward direction, one could enter Boulder's extensive open space and trail system to hike up onto a thickly wooded mesa. In a more westward direction, four blocks of steep uphill walking would bring us to Chautauqua Park which had, over a century ago, been part of the nationwide Chautauqua movement. There, presided over by a large, wooden auditorium, a grouping of cabins and small houses nestled into an arc of steep terrain. Farther on rose a set of magnificent granite cliffs dubbed "the Flatirons."

Today I would be introducing Benjamin to a nature trail which looped around below the Chautauqua auditorium. Here the walking was easy, and on either side of the trail stood tall deciduous trees, forming a canopy of cooling shade. Alongside the path, a little streamlet bubbled. "We'll come here whenever it gets hot," I decided, planning out various therapeutic activities which could take place along the trail.

After a little bit of walking, we reached a small footbridge. I tied Walker to a tree and encouraged Benjamin to sit on the bridge with me so that we could play "patty-cake" and "copy me." Then I pointed to an enormous boulder which rose from the ground directly next to the bridge, its knobby sides inviting passersby to scramble up and sit upon its flat top, fifteen feet up. "You can fly," I exclaimed, lifting Benjamin onto one of the lower ledges that protruded from the boulder. Holding him under the armpits, I encouraged Benjamin to jump, and then I "flew" him through the air and back to the ground where wild grasses swayed, their tasseled heads dancing lightly in the summery breeze. Now I picked one of the long stems for Benjamin to carry like a flag; he tended to collect pebbles compulsively, and I wanted to keep his hands busy with something else as we walked on.

Soon we came to a second bridge which bordered a steep, wooded embankment, and again I tied Walker up. High above the treetops, I could see the roof of the Chautauqua auditorium. By the end of this month, the gentle burbling of the streamlet would be accompanied by the sounds of a symphony orchestra; music would be floating down to this secluded spot. For six wonderful weeks, the auditorium would be home to the orchestra of the Colorado Music Festival, with musicians arriving from all over the world in order to rehearse and perform.

Now I looked down from the bridge at a shallow pool whose sandy bottom glinted with little sparks of gold and silver. "Water-striders" were dimpling the surface, skating upon the water, and I showed Benjamin how little leaf-boats could be set sailing alongside the insects. The earthy smell of decaying leaves scented the shady refuge, and an abundance of emerald-green moss pillows lined the pool. "Feel—soft, like velvet." Benjamin cautiously ran his hands over the moss, becoming increasingly bold with my encouragement.

Walking on, we passed an apple tree with wild roses clambering up it and eventually skirted a profusion of poison ivy before stepping onto a third footbridge. Here, the streamlet chuckled and bubbled busily as it ran over steep steps of mossy boulders. Benjamin happily dropped sticks and pebbles into the water, and we watched them being tumbled and rushed away as the streamlet disappeared from sight in a nearby thicket of thorns. Beyond the bridge and almost drowned by tall grasses, enormous poppies swayed, their fringy purple centers surrounded by glowing orange petals. The drone of honeybees and bumblebees filled the air. A hummingbird darted by, a shrill trill marking its passage.

"Come smell," I encouraged Benjamin, and he obediently put his nose into a poppy's flaming chalice. He loved sniffing at flowers and fresh herbs, and when I held the crushed needles of a pine tree under his nose, he inhaled pleasurably. Then we sat down on the bridge, and I pulled out a picture book and a snack. "This trail is going to become an extension of our home," I thought. "We can get a lot of work done here."

We had returned from our morning walk. "Benjamin, push open the door," I requested after unlocking the front entrance. The main floor of our house consisted essentially of two large rooms. We had just walked into the extra-wide, rectangular living room with its large French windows; they flanked the doorway on either side. Walking across this broad room, we entered a short hallway and went through to another rectangular space, equally as wide as the living room. Our dining table and chairs occupied one end of this second room, while the kitchen was at the other end; a peninsula of counter space delineated the transition from one area to the other.

The back door was centered too, just like the front door, and led out onto a wooden deck; this overlooked a somewhat weedy back yard with a collection of haphazardly situated trees. The house was built into the slope of a hill and, looking at it from the front, our living room appeared to be the first floor. However, from the back, one could see that the house had basement rooms which were at ground level; this was the portion that I would be renting out. Anticipating an eventual housemate, Rick and I had put together our family sleeping area in the finished attic of the house, and we had already discovered the drawback of this charming space: it could get beastly hot.

Now Benjamin and I were in the living room, getting ready to play some games. I had arranged the space to mimic a Waldorf Kindergarten and so, aside from a futon couch and our little spinet piano, the primary furnishings were a toy cabinet and a set of wooden "play-stands" which my brother had recently built for me. Each play-stand consisted of two narrow side-pieces, connected to one another by a shelf that was about 3 ft. wide and 12 inches deep; the shelf was about 2 ft. from the ground. Near the top of each stand, at a height of about 4 ft., a dowel ran parallel to the mid-height shelf, connecting the tall sides to one another.

Currently, I had the stands set up to form a little playhouse. I had placed them parallel to one another, about six feet apart, and had created a delicate archway from one stand to the other using very thin, flexible doweling. I had purchased a soft, translucent fabric (similar to cheesecloth) to drape over the structure; this way, we would have a roof and walls that allowed in plenty of light.

After cutting and hemming the fabric into large rectangles (3 ft. x 4 ft.), I had dyed the cloths using colors reminiscent of pale yellow moonlight, golden sunshine, the rosy, pink glow of sunrise, and the cooler blues and lavenders of evening skies in summer. Now I had a stash of extra cloths which could be used to add "rooms" to the house, or which might represent a lake or meadow on the living room floor.

Enclosed on three sides, the playhouse looked out into the room, and I had placed Benjamin's little work table and chair inside. On the play-stand shelves, I had arranged wicker baskets containing various small wooden toys. Soft dolls and animals sat side by side, many of them handmade by either me or my mom. A wooden bowl containing acorns, chestnuts, and pine cones was paired with a basket of smooth black stones. On the floor below stood sturdy baskets containing the bigger toys and also the cylindrical wooden blocks that I had asked my brother to make by sawing a fallen tree limb into variably sized pieces. Next to the playhouse stood a tall cabinet containing the toys I had either bought or borrowed for specific therapy exercises, their clutter neatly hidden away from sight.

The entire room had an inviting, orderly feel to it and thus would serve Benjamin well.

Benjamin had correctly identified a line-up of pictures taken from a "Memory" game, and as a sensory break, I was guiding him to tumble head-over-heels across the living room. "Count the somersaults," I exclaimed. "One, two, three….eight, nine."

Benjamin could fit in nine somersaults; that's how long the room was. We had been practicing this skill for three months, and by now, Benjamin hardly needed help. He was also getting strong enough to try playing "wheelbarrow": with his hands placed on the floor as if to do a push-up, Benjamin would let me pick up his legs and balance him like a pushcart. "Now march your hands," I would encourage. "Be strong, don't crumple."

Benjamin and I were on the nature trail, working on imitation skills, when a woman carrying a camera accosted me. "I'm a photographer," she told me. "Would you allow me to snap a few shots? I want to capture the deep connection that I'm observing between you and your little boy."

Pleasantly surprised, I assented. This wasn't the first time a stranger had felt moved to comment on the bond they observed between me and Benjamin.

"There is something special about the two of you," the woman tried to explain.

"Well, my little one *is* 'special'—he has autism," I told her. "Playing these games is part of his therapy."

"Ah. But that's not what I mean," she said, looking thoughtful. "It's something about your energy together."

I knew what she meant. She was seeing the effects of my focused intent. And, she had perceived the radiance that could emanate from my beautiful child. My angel.

Around this time, Benjamin jolted me into renewed hope that speech might be just around the corner. I was getting ready for bed, listening to Benjamin tossing and turning in his sleep. Suddenly, I heard a softly muttered, "Mama." My heart gave a big thump—the syllables were unmistakable—but when I looked, Benjamin was still fast asleep. The next morning, he awoke with the sound of "Mama" on his lips, stronger this time, almost like he wanted to call me. I zoomed across the bedroom to Benjamin's bedside. "Yes, sweetheart, Mama is here," I exclaimed eagerly. Benjamin still looked sleep-drunken, and my excitement seemed to puzzle him.

"Mama. Say Mama," I encouraged.

Even with repeated cajoling, Benjamin did not respond, and I had to resign myself to a continued state of hopefulness. The sweet sounds of "Mama" must have been spurred by Benjamin's subconscious mind; he still couldn't produce speech intentionally.

It was mid-June, and Benjamin had slid into a slump. After two weeks of sunshine, the sky had become gray and rainy, and an unwelcoming atmosphere seemed to pervade our house. For several days, I had been unsuccessfully trying to spark Benjamin's interest, trying to get him playing with me, and now I was feeling tearful and somewhat depressed by his lack of engagement. I tickled him with a perky squirrel hand-puppet, trying to elicit a smile, but Benjamin remained languid, sitting limply. Changing tack, I took him to the futon and put him on my lap. "Let's play horsey," I said and began bouncing him on my knees.

Benjamin's face remained uninterested and his eyes looked dull, unresponsive to the movement and the rhyme. Usually, he loved this game. I thought, "It's as if all willpower has left him. He is completely bereft of desire." Benjamin seemed like an empty shell, and I was frightened by the apparent retreat of his soul.

As the blue days stretched on, I became increasingly depressed and worried. "Am I just reacting to this slump, or might I be a partial cause of it?" I questioned myself one evening as I sat at the computer, surrounded by piles of papers, typing up my thoughts about Benjamin. "If the weather were good, would I have enough energy to buoy Benjamin up? Are we both reacting to being home alone without my parents around to liven things up? Or am I sabotaging my focus by embarking on a writing project?" I stood up and walked around the room.

Each evening, after cleaning up the house and journaling about Benjamin, I had been dabbling with the beginning stages of writing a book. Files, papers, and books covered the floor of my basement office space. "My work with Benjamin is more important than anything else," I reminded myself, surveying the overwhelming volume of materials. "He needs me to be completely present and available, both spiritually and physically. And yet, I need some small outlet for my professional aspirations."

For several years, I had been itching to write an accessible handbook for musicians, covering a wide range of topics; I wanted to transform the thesis papers I had written as a doctoral student into something that would benefit others. But life had changed. I was no longer on the course I had charted for myself in earlier years; instead, Benjamin was now my guiding star.

I began boxing up files, having finally reached a compromise with myself: I would abandon the comprehensive book project I had once envisioned and would focus on a single topic. "Realistically, I can only write while Benjamin is sleeping," I concluded. "I know I can't allow this project to extend over the course of years; that would make it an energy drain. It needs to be a rejuvenating goal instead." By the time I went to bed, the floor had been cleared of three quarters of its paper burden; the comparatively small amount that remained would form the basis of my "manageable project."

We were in Julie's office, and I was describing the vacant quality of Benjamin's slump. "This doesn't feel like an 'assimilation' break. I feel like Benjamin is gone, like he has simply flown away." Julie had been watching Benjamin closely. "I see what you mean," she said. "I think we need to stay with the same homeopathic remedy, but I'm going to give him a different dosage. I think it will help him to reconnect." Praying that she was right, I coaxed Benjamin into swallowing the little cupful of liquid that Julie handed me.

Within the week, Benjamin's delight in learning had returned. His agitated hand-flapping had relaxed, and he was enjoying the increasingly acrobatic approach I was taking to our sensory integration exercises. I could bounce and swing him harder and higher than before, and he didn't become afraid. Benjamin's sign-vocabulary was rapidly increasing as well, and when I wrote out a list of words that he was familiar with, I was astounded to realize they numbered close to one-hundred. Best of all, Benjamin had finally figured out how to suck liquids through the variably sized straws of the sippy-cups that we had been messing with for months. Perhaps he would now learn to blow through them as well.

Now I was introducing a new game. "Let's play tea party." Benjamin joined me in the playhouse, and I showed him how to drape his little table with a silk scarf as a tablecloth. I brought out my old china toy tea set and put out four little blue-and-white cups with their saucers. Benjamin sat at his usual place while a teddy bear and a pair of sibling dolls that I had christened Alexander and Katrina occupied the remaining spots. "Just look. Don't eat yet."

I put some raisins in each of the cups and demonstrated to Benjamin how he was to feed his little doll friends. Animating the teddy-bear from behind, I made the cuddly toy wave and jiggle as if it were eagerly awaiting a snack. "Feed Teddy," I prompted.

Benjamin looked nonplussed, and I gently lay my hand under his elbow, guiding his hand to the bear's serving of raisins. Benjamin grabbed a few, and then I guided his hand so he was holding the treat up to Teddy's snout.

"Mm, yummy." I made the teddy bounce delightedly and then I let go of Benjamin's arm; he automatically popped the raisin into his own mouth.

"Good job. Now feed Alexander."

After a few more tries, Benjamin started feeding the dolls without my physical support, his face lighting up with happiness.

"Now feed Mommy."

Benjamin knew what to do. Maggie (my physical therapist friend) had mentioned that even very small children will spontaneously try "feeding" their moms as a reciprocal gesture of nurturing. On hearing this, I had immediately begun familiarizing Benjamin with the concept. He had picked up on it quickly and now, when we picked raspberries in my parents' garden, he would occasionally reach towards me without prompting, striving to put a juicy, jewel-red berry in my mouth.

Shortly before the end of June, Benjamin had another cranio-sacral session with Cheryl. As I watched him interacting with her, my heart felt so light that I wanted to laugh out loud with happiness: Benjamin kept looking directly at Cheryl's face, smiling and remaining connected with her in a manner I had never seen before. He reacted to each of Cheryl's comments with a playful, joking, almost flirtatious manner that was utterly charming. After the session, I practically floated out of Cheryl's office, so uplifted was I by Benjamin's interactions.

However, a shock was in store for me. When Benjamin awakened the next morning, he seemed unhappy and withdrawn. His mood had completely reversed from the previous day's joy, and as the morning progressed, he became increasingly frustrated, expressing his upset with voluble screams.

Dazed by the change, I wondered at its cause. Was it possible that the previous day's openness and feeling of connection had overwhelmed him? Did he now feel overly vulnerable? Or was there something about Benjamin's brain chemistry that could fluctuate so dramatically? Had Cheryl's work released something that was now disturbing his equilibrium? Was Benjamin just having a bad day, or was this the beginning of another slump?

I phoned Julie immediately, thinking that another dose of homeopathic remedy might help us to avert an extension of this scenario, but she requested that I wait for a week. "Let's see whether Benjamin can assimilate Cheryl's work and regain his inner balance without intervention," she counseled. "If not, call me back, and I'll try a different way of administering his current remedy which might give it a more lasting effect."

Not surprisingly, the next few days continued in the same vein, with Benjamin remaining upset and irritable. However, in contrast to his mid-June decline, I now sensed that Benjamin had gained a certain degree of willpower and had strengthened in his desire to assert himself; his frustrated discontent didn't have the quality of limp vacuity that I had seen previously. In fact, he was now trying to put on some of his own clothes and was working hard at buckling his own sandals.

One morning, just at the end of the month, it occurred to me that a novel experience might lift Benjamin out of his tempestuous mood. I settled him into the jogger and pushed him uphill to the Chautauqua auditorium. The Colorado Music Festival orchestra was now in residence, and they were starting their season with a children's show featuring Beethoven. Benjamin sat on my lap with a fruit juice lollipop in his mouth, watching the actors and the orchestra. He remained quiet as a mouse, and by the end of the concert, he was rocking back and forth in time to the music. I breathed a deep sigh of relief. The beauty of Beethoven's music had temporarily tamed Benjamin's beastly feelings and had given me a respite.

9

Onwards and Upwards
July 1997

We were enrolled in a six-week mother-and-baby swim class offered by a local physical therapy/rehab center, and on the first day of July, Benjamin and I attended our first class. The therapy pool was warm and soothing, and the teacher animatedly led our little group. We moms stood in a circle, almost shoulder-deep in water, singing nursery songs in unison and guiding our children to float on their backs, to kick, or to make paddling motions with their arms.

I was glad to be in the company of other women since Benjamin's irritable mood had wiped me out; I had spent the morning determinedly working through a variety of therapeutic activities, in spite of Benjamin's resistance. As children laughed and splashed around us and the playful class progressed, I could feel my tension melting away; Benjamin was clearly comfortable in the warm water, and the songs were a helpful distraction.

Once we came home from the pool however, Benjamin reverted to his withdrawn state and remained prone to screaming at the slightest provocation. "Today was a real low point," I thought later, after we had eaten dinner and I had put Benjamin to bed.

The next morning, Benjamin was still in his funk, and he remained thus as we arrived at our weekly "Dance with Nance" class. As always, Nancy passed around a drum which each child got to play, saying their name and receiving a unison greeting from the group. Playing the drum was a ritual Benjamin had come to enjoy, but today, he seemed unable or unwilling to cooperate.

Once Nancy launched into song, I prompted Benjamin to participate, carefully gauging how far I might push him. Everyone was singing, *"Head, shoulders, knees and toes, knees and toes,"* when Benjamin unexpectedly clicked into focused attention. Intently watching Nancy, he began following her motions without any help from me. I sat back on my heels to watch and suddenly, tears welled up in my eyes. I had been practicing the class songs with Benjamin, targeting those which seemed to cause him the most trouble, hoping that he might learn them well enough to eventually blend in with the other kids.

Benjamin's sudden accomplishment was both unexpected and astonishing. Nancy's face registered surprise as she noticed Benjamin's independent participation, and when she caught my eye, I saw her blinking back tears of her own. We hadn't missed a day of class since beginning in April, and now Benjamin was reaping the rewards of consistent attendance and review.

On hearing of Benjamin's continuing inner turmoil, Julie recommended administering a low potency dose of remedy on an ongoing, daily basis. Within twenty-four hours, I began observing an upswing in Benjamin's mood. During our morning walk, he showed a refreshed interest in the dragonflies, bees, and butterflies that I pointed out to him, and when I transferred a ladybug onto Benjamin's hand, he was happy to watch it crawling up his fingers.

Later on, he began trying out some harsh consonant sounds such as I hadn't previously heard from him. *"K-k-k-k-k-rrrrrrrr!"* Within moments, I understood. Firecrackers! Independence Day had arrived, and Benjamin was mimicking the crackling sounds that were occasionally rending the air. I pulled out our sign-dictionary, looked up "firecrackers," and demonstrated explosive motions to go along with Benjamin's noises. Perhaps we were moving closer to speech?

After two further days of homeopathic support, my "sunshine boy" had resurfaced, and I began teaching Benjamin to play "catch," using a medium-sized feather pillow rather than a ball; this would enhance Benjamin's chances of catching rather than dropping. As we played, a vision of childhood pillow fights flashed across my mind, and I impulsively flung the cushion into Benjamin's torso. After an initial startled reaction, Benjamin giggled, tossed the pillow back to me, and then hopped around with his hands twirling, clearly anticipating the pillow flying at him with another firm *whomp*. After a few more repetitions, it was clear I had stumbled upon a highly motivating activity.

"Let's do our ABC's, just like in dance class," I now suggested, and made the signs for "A" and "B." Benjamin struggled to copy me, and I rewarded him by slinging the soft pillow into his chest. *Whomp*. Benjamin bounced happily, anticipating more of the same. "C, D." *Thump*. "F, G." Benjamin crowed with delight, and we continued forming letters and tossing the pillow back and forth with unflagging energy until we had gotten through the entire alphabet.

Inspired by Benjamin's enjoyment when getting slammed by the pillow, I dragged out our enormous beanbag cushion/chair, set it up in the middle of the room, and called to Benjamin. Picking him up, I gently tossed him onto his back, making him flop into the middle of the beanbag. Benjamin squealed with excitement and bounced up like a jack-in-the-box, signing, "More." With each successive body toss, I became more vigorous until I was whirling Benjamin in a circle around me and then letting him fly into the cushion. He laughed and laughed seemingly insatiable, hungry for the sensory stimulation provided by our new game.

Our first therapy session with Corinne was taking place at our house, and we started off with a review of sensory integration activities. I showed off the cocoon-like hammock swing that hung from a beam in our basement, explaining, "When I spin Benjamin, I always sing the same short song so he has the security of knowing when the spinning will stop. His eye-nystagmus is becoming more normal."

Corrine handed me some sheet music. "Here's my favorite song for swinging." I settled Benjamin in the hammock and began. *"How do you like to go up in a swing, / Up in the air so blue..."* The lovely melody rose and soared with Robert Lewis Stevenson's poetry, but by the third stanza, Benjamin was beginning to look a little pale and so I coaxed him out of the hammock. "He's getting motion sick," Corinne observed. "Hold his hands, and have him focus on your eyes while jumping vigorously; that will settle his queasiness."

"Jump like a frog. *Ribbitt, ribbitt*," I exclaimed, steadying Benjamin, and soon his cheeks returned to their normal rosy glow.

Now Corinne asked for a sturdy blanket to wrap Benjamin in. "Roll him up as tightly as you can manage. The overall sensation of being contained and squeezed is very soothing, just as being tightly swaddled is calming to a baby's nervous system. Now, while Benjamin is wrapped up, apply pressure with your hands."

I mentioned reading about Temple Grandin, a well-known woman with autism who had observed that cattle would become calm when placed into a body squeezing chute. Feeling a close kinship with the animals, Temple had developed a "squeeze machine" to use on herself, finding that its firm pressure helped calm her nervous system and reduce feelings of anxiety.

"You can create a similar effect using a weighted blanket," Corinne suggested. "Take a large pillow case, sew parallel baffles along its entire length, and fill these baffles with rice. Then sew the top closed so the rice kernels can't escape. When Benjamin lies down to rest, lay this heavy blanket on him."

As we talked, Benjamin had remained tightly wrapped, and now Corinne directed me to unroll him and then keep him rolling across the carpet like a log. Benjamin grunted as I propelled him across the room. This new motion was awkward.

Next, we moved to our medium-sized gymno-ball. Corinne had Benjamin sit on it as she held his hips and guided his seat in a big slow circle. She began singing, *"I like to ride a horse and buggy...I like to see those wheels go 'round and 'round..."* Benjamin tipped this way and that, trying to maintain his balance, but when Corinne unexpectedly moved him sideways, there was a moment of delay before he leaned in the opposite direction to keep from falling. "We need to sharpen Benjamin's response time," Corinne commented. "Expose him to these balance challenges on a regular basis."

"Benjamin still has a lot of tactile sensitivities," I now told Corinne. "I'm exposing him to all kinds of textures. We have a sandbox, and we are working with play-dough that I make myself—the chemical smell of the commercial stuff is revolting."

Corinne nodded in agreement. "Add a few drops of pure rosemary oil to your dough; it will enliven and refresh his senses. You might try lavender oil for a more calming effect."

I showed Corinne a baking tray filled with dried kidney beans. "I hide various objects in here, and Benjamin has to dig around to find them. When he's ready for more imaginative play, we'll scoop landscapes into the beans and populate them with little dolls and animals. I have another box containing rice for the same purpose; it feels quite different from the beans."

Corinne looked approving. "Have you tried finger painting yet?" she now asked me.

I nodded, remembering. "Benjamin couldn't stand the slimy, sticky feel on his fingers and I didn't push the issue. I should try again. Summertime is the perfect opportunity for making a mess outdoors."

Corinne now inspired me with further ideas. "Try adding some liquid watercolor paints to dollops of fragrance-free shaving cream. If you get a big piece of plexi-glass, Benjamin can finger paint on it, and you don't have to worry about your furniture getting stained. Another place to try this is in the shower. Have Benjamin 'paint' the wall with both hands. Guide him to make lots of circles, and see if you can get him to paint his own body; that would be a good exercise for self-awareness."

Now Corinne asked Benjamin to lie down on his belly so she could show me some chirophonetics patterns. "We'll start with a descending rhythm to support Benjamin's incarnation process." Corinne laid her palms on Benjamin's back, near his shoulders, and then stroked them in a repeated swirling pattern, gradually making her way down Benjamin's back. The rhythm of *slow, quick-quick* repeated itself with each set of big and small swirls.

"As you trace downward, imagine the power of a waterfall," Corinne instructed. "Then, let the quick, small swirls become lighter, like taking a breather before diving back into cascading water." Dynamically forming the pattern, I felt like my hands were singing a poem on Benjamin's body.

"You've got the right feel," Corinne commented, watching me. "Now I'll show you forms that connect the soul to speech formation. *Rrrrrr*," she intoned, rolling her 'r' and tracing a new pattern down Benjamin's sides and legs. For the remainder of the therapy session, Corinne showed me a variety of strokes correlating to specific sounds, suggesting imagery to accompany each one. She prescribed some to be done in the morning while others were to be carried out in the evening.

Feeling inspired, I observed, "When things get difficult, I sometimes forget about the 'unseen world' and find my imagination running dry. I lose my sensitivity, my spiritual antennae. This daily chirophonetics work will help keep me on track."

"Time to visit Cheryl," I said, gathering our things and shepherding Benjamin out the door. He vehemently shook his head, "no."

"Well, that's interesting," I thought. Benjamin might resist me or withdraw into himself when he didn't want to do something, but this was a clear expression of opinion that I hadn't seen before. As we climbed the stairs to Cheryl's office, Benjamin hung back and again began shaking his head, "no, no, no."

When Cheryl welcomed us, Benjamin looked worried and hung back. He didn't want to get near the massage table, and only after much cajoling did he consent to let Cheryl work on him. "You are safe here," Cheryl gently assured him. "I am here to help you."

I was amazed at Benjamin's continued apprehension and thought, "He seems afraid, like he remembers how open and connected he was during last month's session, and remembers, too, how awful he felt the next day. He is afraid of that happening again."

Back home, we met with the piano technician who had come to tune our instrument. As the man finished up his work, playing octaves and checking whether all the pitches were true to one another, Benjamin sidled over, clearly wanting to play. As the technician packed up his tools, Benjamin began picking out octaves, imitating what he had just heard while I watched in astonishment.

"How is he gauging the distances?" I wondered. Benjamin wasn't making any mistakes. "He must be cluing in to the black-and-white pattern of the keys, even though I haven't taught him what to look for." I thought on, musingly. "Maybe the brain differences of autism can account for enhanced pattern perception."

The concern I had expressed in Cheryl's office proved unnecessary. Indeed, Benjamin's happy mood had only heightened since the appointment, and he was now taking great interest in his surroundings. One morning, as we walked past a neighbor's flower garden, Benjamin stopped and began inspecting the bees that hovered and circled around fragrant blossoms.

"*Bzzz...bzzz*," he announced, clearly imitating the buzzing of an enormous bumblebee that had just entered the fray. Surprised and delighted at Benjamin's new sound, I thought, "His will to express himself is strengthening." Once home, I looked up the sign for "bee" and taught it to Benjamin, accompanying it with the "*bzzz*" sound.

Later that day, Benjamin was snacking on a juicy peach when he made the sign for "rain."

"Rain?" I asked, puzzled. The sky was clear and blue, with nary a cloud to be seen. Benjamin was still eating, juice from the peach running in rivulets over his fingers and splattering on the table. Then the light bulb went on in my head, and I laughed out loud, amazed at Benjamin's communication. The peach was "raining" droplets of juice.

In swim class that week, we moms learned to safely take our children under water for a few moments, and Benjamin did beautifully, showing some surprise but no fear as I momentarily dunked him, following the teacher's directives. The next week however, at our next class, Benjamin became tense and reluctant whenever I turned him onto his tummy. "He is anticipating going under water again, and now he's afraid," I thought.

I was tempted to "accidentally" dunk Benjamin a few times and to hope that he would get over his fear with repeated exposure, but my gut instinct told me not to push the situation; Benjamin might stop trusting me to keep him safe, and then any further progress would be stymied. I certainly didn't want to destroy his enjoyment of being in the water. We needed to keep building positive associations around the act of "going swimming."

During the last week of July, Benjamin had a breakthrough moment which happened as he drank from one of his sippy-cups. This particular cup was transparent and had a hollow handle which extended from its bottom to its top, simultaneously serving as a handle and a drinking straw. Benjamin was tilting the cup, making the juice flow to his mouth through the handle, when he suddenly began blowing bubbles, keeping his lips tightly pursed. He had done this, momentarily and accidentally, on several occasions during the past week, but this time was different.

As Benjamin blew, he clued in and noticed that the funny burbling sounds in the cup were linked to what his mouth was doing. He kept at it, experimenting and becoming increasingly confident about blowing hard. I watched breathlessly, feeling sparkles of joy, excitement, and hope leaping around inside me. As it became clear that this was no longer an accident, I quickly ran to gather up some "blowing" toys.

I slipped a soap-filled bubble pipe into Benjamin's mouth, replacing the sippy-cup's straw, and a satisfying mound of shimmering bubbles began frothing up. Then I held a whistle to Benjamin's lips, and his blowing was rewarded by a pretty trilling sound. Eventually, I even slipped my wooden soprano recorder into his mouth and rejoiced as musical notes filled the room. Four months of intensive work were culminating in this special performance.

Following his "blowing breakthrough," Benjamin quickly learned to direct his airstream across space, managing to blow without the aid of a straw. We started off chasing feathers across the table, using our breath, and soon Benjamin was able to send soap bubbles cascading from a standard bubble wand; he was also learning to blow out a candle flame. He loved seeing the effects of his airstream and was thus motivated to practice.

10

A Miracle
August 1997

Within days of learning to blow, Benjamin's enthusiasm had waned. He seemed exhausted by his latest leap in understanding, and so I took him to see Julie, hoping for a bolstering homeopathic. "We'll keep on with the current remedy; it has clearly been helpful," Julie decided. "I'll administer a single, high potency dose today. You'll need to discontinue the daily support dosages, at least for now."

Expecting good results, I was shocked when, twenty-four hours later, Benjamin had turned into a tortured little beast, screaming at intervals throughout the day, shrieking and screeching as if he were being eaten alive. By the end of a solid week of this behavior, I was absolutely at the end of my rope. Benjamin's screeches felt like needles in my ears, and I was so tense from being around him that my gut was in knots. How could human vocal cords possibly produce such a high pitch and such volume?

Unbelievably, severe welts had begun to bloom in Benjamin's diaper area. "If anyone ever doubted the power of homeopathy, they should just take a look at this," I thought. I notified Julie, and she asked me to hang in there and wait out the storm. "Benjamin is definitely reacting to the remedy. There's a good chance that once he bottoms out, he'll rebound and show some real improvement."

Thank goodness, Julie was right. During the second week post-remedy, the screaming tapered off, and Benjamin gradually began regaining his inner balance. We had an appointment with Cheryl, and she noted that the area of Benjamin's head which so consistently became tight and resistant was now feeling pliable and open. "This is dramatically different," she told me.

Feeling encouraged, I decided to take Benjamin on an outing to the county fair so that he might take in some new impressions. Initially, the sounds of bleating sheep and bellowing bulls tickled Benjamin's fancy, but soon he was humming incessantly, insulating himself from further connection. Nevertheless, I took him through all the exhibits, and when we eventually reached the pony rides, I swung Benjamin up onto a fuzzy, brown Shetland. As the pony walked, Benjamin's body swayed gently back and forth and a bemused smile slowly crept over his face. The sturdy little animal had completely captured his attention.

"More," he signed when the ride was over. I paid for another round. "More,

more." The soothing motion of the pony's body fulfilled Benjamin's craving for sensory stimulation, and I fantasized about taking the cute little equine home and stabling it in our back yard. Impossible of course, but from now on, I would be putting out feelers, searching for further horse opportunities.

A full two weeks had passed since Benjamin's mega-dose of remedy, and the baking heat of mid-August was upon us. Benjamin had regained a reasonable amount of connectedness, seemed relatively content, and was no longer screaming about anything. We were still working on blowing, and I was encouraging Benjamin to make a firmer "O" shape with his lips in order to focus his airstream.

"Copy me," I exclaimed once again. I blew kisses. I made a fish-face with a comically pursed mouth. I tickled Benjamin's lips with a stick of candy. My strategies weren't working very well; Benjamin's lips remained overly loose and open.

We went to sit on the front steps of our house, taking a break, and I watched Benjamin as he stared into space. My mind was drifting, searching for fresh inspiration, when I suddenly saw Benjamin's lips form a small tight "O." My heart skipped a beat.

"Benjamin," I said softly. "Copy me. Oh…oh." I pursed my lips tightly, cooing to him. Benjamin's head swiveled toward me, his eyes coming into focus as he shaped his mouth precisely and deliberately.

"Yes, sweetie, that's it." I kept my burgeoning excitement tightly under wraps, focusing intently on Benjamin. "Say 'Oh'." The hairs on my arms prickled as I kept my eyes fixed on Benjamin's, willing him to respond. There was a palpable flow of energy between us.

"Oh…" A soft sound emanated from Benjamin.

"Oh," I said again, and Benjamin echoed, "Oh…"

Keeping my eyes on his, I now slid Benjamin onto my lap and cradled him so he relaxed in my arms, laying back, gazing up at me.

"Mm." I hummed softly.

"Mm," Benjamin hummed back.

"Ma," I said quietly, stretching out the sound. "Mm-aah."

Benjamin watched my mouth intently, taking in the changing shape of my lips. "Ma-ma," I said slowly.

Hesitantly, Benjamin began to mirror me. "Mm…ah. Mm-aa. Ma-ma. Mama."

The miracle I had been praying for was happening. Benjamin was beginning to speak.

Now the gift of language was within reach, and Benjamin's progress was remarkable. Only days after his breakthrough, he was copying me in intoning all the vowel sounds, his voice still sounding odd as his lips, tongue, and vocal cords struggled for coordination. We were working on consonants too, combining them with the vowels.

"Benjamin, say 'mah, mee, moo'. Mah. Mee. Moo." Benjamin joined me as I slowly and clearly enunciated each set of sounds. He stared intently at my lips in order to copy and follow.

"Now say 'bah, mah, kah.'" Gradually, we made our way through all the sounds of the alphabet, and began combining vowels. "Say 'mee-ah-oh'. Like a kitty-cat: miaow." Every syllable was practiced repeatedly, and I made a game of it, keeping up Benjamin's enthusiasm by playing "pillow fight" or by offering him various edible treats.

After a week of speech practice, Benjamin was already attempting three-word sentences, following along as I slowly enunciated each syllable. Only the consonants "l" and "r" were causing real problems, partly because Benjamin couldn't see what my tongue was doing inside my mouth, and partly because his oral musculature wasn't yet strong enough to form these two sounds.

Benjamin was beginning to come up with single words on his own, and he amazed me as he began answering the riddles contained in a favorite book. "Is your mama a llama?" I read. Several rhyming clues followed, and then I turned the page, announcing, "Your mama must be a…"

As I lapsed into silence, Benjamin looked at the picture and supplied the correct response: "Kah-oo."

I rewarded him with a drawn out "*moo*," and went on. "Is your mama a llama? …oh no, she must be a…"

Benjamin glanced at the picture and then looked to me for help while his lips already began forming an "*f*" sound. I joined him, clearly enunciating, "F-i-sh. Fish." He still needed to watch and copy in order to produce the "*sh*" sound, but was clearly retrieving the word from his memory instead of depending on me to supply it. Language acquisition was truly a miraculous process, albeit taken for granted by most.

One of our regular activities involved putting crayon to paper. Benjamin's initial explorations of color had been thoughtful, but he had gradually moved into a wild, scribbling style filled with tension and excitement. Observing this overstimulated activity, I now thought, "Benjamin is becoming fixated on scrubbing the paper. We need to take this in a different direction." While a toddler might scribble, a typical child of Benjamin's age would be attempting to draw a picture.

I laid my hand over Benjamin's, stopped his scrubbing, and exclaimed, "Let's draw together. Here, we'll make a lazy eight...and a circle...and this is a triangle." Benjamin was still trying to scribble, and when my hand kept blocking him, he began to cry. I rubbed his back, trying to soothe him, yet insisted that we go over the shapes again. "Look, we'll use another color; see how pretty red and blue are together?"

Benjamin's crying now turned into intense sobbing, and I hesitated, unsure of whether to work through this or not. He wasn't screeching, and this was not a tantrum; instead, Benjamin was weeping as if I had wounded his soul. Tears of empathy welled up in my eyes, and I thought, "Benjamin's scribbling expresses his inner chaos—upon which I am imposing form and order. It's painful for him; he is being prevented from following his natural inclinations."

My poor child. At times, combatting autism must truly feel like a form of torture. But I couldn't just stand by and watch Benjamin becoming inextricably stuck in fixation; I needed to show him that he had other options.

I took a deep breath, blinked hard, and pressed on, guiding Benjamin's hand, striving to keep my voice steady and warm as I asked questions. "What shape is this? What color?" Benjamin was still sobbing, but as we worked, he gradually became more present, began trying to respond. I sensed his craving for love and praise, and felt that we were reconnecting, heart to heart. Together, we were overcoming the compulsions of autism.

I was teaching Benjamin to interpret facial expressions, pointing out the clues that help in reading another person's emotions: the look in the eye, the activity of forehead and eyebrows, the shaping of the mouth.

To teach Benjamin basic labels like "happy," "angry," "frustrated," and so on, I had introduced a simple puzzle called *Moody Bear* which had a choice of six different facial expressions. Benjamin liked the puzzle, but when I first showed him the "sad" and "scared" faces, he became spooked and very resistant. I didn't push the issue.

A week passed with Benjamin overreacting to anything connected with "sadness," whether encountered in a story, a picture, or in passing conversation. Even when spoken in a neutral tone, the word "sad" would invariably trigger great upset, and so I tried to steer clear of the distressing emotion. However, just now, Benjamin had plumbed the depths of sadness during our difficult drawing session, and my instincts prompted me to address this.

"Hugs can help sadness to go away," I commented in a carefully neutral tone. My statement drew Benjamin's instant attention, but he didn't get upset. I rejoiced inwardly and pulled out the bear puzzle. "Look, here is Moody Bear. Let's put in his happy face." Benjamin did so.

"Now take it out and put in the sad face." Benjamin drew back in trepidation but remained quiet, so I went ahead and replaced the bear's happy face with the one that showed a down-turned mouth. Benjamin composure remained intact. "Now let's practice making faces," I suggested. "Copy me..." As I turned down the corners of my mouth, I was careful not to project any overt emotions. I just wanted Benjamin to settle with the intellectual concept of sadness; dramatized feelings could wait until later. Benjamin followed my lead, arranging his face appropriately, and then, suddenly, he was on the verge of crying.

"Happy face," I said quickly, hoping to rescue him from his overly tender emotions. I smiled brightly at Benjamin. Looking tremulous, he made an effort, turned up the corners of his mouth, and tentatively smiled back. Laughing, I enveloped him in a hug. Benjamin's display of increased emotional resilience called for celebration.

11

Autumn Gold
September, 1997

The heat of August hadn't yet mellowed when the first day of September arrived. Benjamin and I were out in the front yard playing toss with a small beanbag when the garden hose caught Benjamin's eye and he ran over to it. He tugged at the heavy coil, dragging it towards me while patting his chest with one hand.

"Ah…ah-ee…" He struggled to sign while simultaneously pushing the hose at me, clearly desperate to tell me something using verbal communication. "Ah… Oo-ah-nn-t…" Benjamin was on his tip-toes, looking at me intently, working his lips. "Oo-ah…tah." His hand formed a "W" and he tapped his mouth: the sign for "water."

"*I want water,*" I exclaimed, translating Benjamin's halting sounds and then whooping with joy. He had just spoken his first independently formulated sentence.

Later that day, Benjamin surprised me again, saying the words, "I'm all done." The sentence came tumbling out so unexpectedly that, for a few seconds, I didn't quite register what Benjamin had said. I just stared at him blankly, wondering whether my ears had been playing tricks. No, they hadn't. Benjamin was now tapping the table for emphasis, signing. I echoed his spoken words, smiling and getting a grip on myself.

"All done. Wow, honey-bun, good talking. Yes, you are all done."

The following week, as Benjamin became increasingly adept at pronouncing words, he also became proficient at opening and closing everything that was contained in our bathroom drawers. At first, his fascination with the various tubes, bottles, and boxes was just as one might expect in any young child. However, he quickly became fixated on repeatedly opening and closing the drawers, and he didn't want to stop uncapping and then reclosing various items like chapstick and deodorant.

Now, I was suddenly wishing I could be in two places at once. Whenever I was busy preparing a meal or was otherwise distracted, Benjamin would escape me and run into the bathroom to resume his repetitive actions. He ignored my calling, and I had to keep interrupting my work to retrieve him from his dead-end activity.

I tried setting him up at a nearby table, giving him a puzzle to work on, but

Benjamin's thoughts were stuck on the objects of his fixation, and he would slip away at the first opportunity. I tried to thwart him by installing child locks, but Benjamin simply found other objects that would satisfy his mania for opening and closing. I was stymied by circumstances, and all I could do was to hustle through meal prep and leave everything else for later, to be done after Benjamin was in bed.

I was on the phone, learning about a class called "Kindermusik."

"Parents stay with their children throughout the weekly thirty-minute sessions," the instructor told me. "We sit in a big circle and I lead the songs, most of which have body motions to go along. You'll get a CD to take home—the featured ensembles are of high-quality—and a picture book is included, with illustrations for each song. The elements of music are introduced in a playful and developmentally appropriate way."

I was impressed by this description, and when Benjamin and I arrived for our first class, I was equally taken by the teacher's sparkling and warm personality. "Miss Amy" had a knack for engaging children, and I marveled at her unflagging energy. She would be a perfect fit for Benjamin.

"On. Off. On, off. On...off." Benjamin was repeating the two words, nonstop, while I was tied up in the kitchen, making lunch. "On, off, on, off..." Now he was flipping the light switch, correctly labeling his actions. *"An. Aus. An, aus. An...aus."* What? Were my ears deceiving me? Benjamin was speaking German, correctly saying "on" (*an*) and "off" (*aus*), even though I had stopped talking in German since Corinne's warning about language confusion.

"Papagei," (parrot) Benjamin now proclaimed, giggling and repeating himself. Woah. He had only heard that word once before, near the beginning of summer. We had been visiting Ursula at her house when Benjamin had become enamored of a whimsical toy parrot. *"Magst du den Papagei?"* Ursula had queried, not realizing that my parents and I were speaking only English with Benjamin. Comically animating the toy bird, she had chanted, *"Papagei, Papagei,"* (parrot, parrot), and now Benjamin was recalling the moment with great amusement.

A few days later, Benjamin again astonished me. This time, the word was *"Geige"* (violin). Could he possibly have retained some memory of speaking this word at the age of fifteen months? "The brain is such a mystery," I mused. "Who knows what goes on in there."

Benjamin was beginning to echo words immediately upon hearing them, and I was teaching him about opposites, making up playful drills around concepts like up/down, in/out, hard/soft, smooth/rough, and so on. The downside to Benjamin's progress with pronouncing words was that he no longer depended on looking at me in order to speak or to sign. The bridge of language was replacing the physical connection of eye gaze, and I had to redouble my efforts at gaining visual contact.

During the third week of September, Rick arrived in Boulder for an extended visit, and we immediately dived into a pressing home improvement project. Toxic lead paint had once been used to protect the surfaces of our house, and I knew of the dangers this posed. The paint would chip from typical wear-and-tear, and moveable surfaces such as doors and windows were prone to releasing microscopic particles of lead paint into the air. (Babies and young children are particularly vulnerable to ingesting or inhaling such paint debris and, because of their rapid brain development, are prone to developing abnormalities as a result of lead toxicity.)

I had recently taken Benjamin for a blood draw, and his test results showed a small burden of lead in his system. While it wasn't enough to cause alarm, I wanted to do everything possible to maximize Benjamin's brain functioning and his overall health. So now, Rick and I decided which of our home's doors and windows needed to remain functional; the rest would be caulked shut. The painter I had hired would remove the remaining doors and windows, taking them to his shop to scrape the old lead paint from their edges; he would then protect these crucial moving surfaces with safe latex paint. In addition, each functional door jamb and window opening needed to be scraped and repainted and, while the work was going on, these sites needed to be encased in plastic sheeting so that toxic paint chips and dust would not escape into the house or fall upon the ground.

It was a tricky project and while the work was going on, we kept several high-power air filters running as I repeatedly wiped any possibly contaminated surfaces with a cleaning solution of TSP; this was recommended in the book about lead abatement I had borrowed. Since scraping and repainting our entire house was not a feasible option, I used clear book tape to cover baseboards and entryways that were at a higher risk of chipping.

Benjamin stayed with my parents while Rick and I worked and, when the project was finally done, I felt a pang on observing that Benjamin's eye contact and sense of connection had waned markedly. Clearly, continual one-on-one therapy was the only means for counteracting his autistic tendency to withdraw. Nevertheless, the effort that we had put into our project was worth it: when I had further blood work done on Benjamin the following month, the test results showed a clear decrease in the amount of lead in his body.

During the week that followed the completion of our house project, Benjamin displayed another leap in his speech development. We were in dance class, and it was Benjamin's turn to choose which song the class would sing. "What song would you like?" Nancy asked.

Benjamin looked at her for a moment and then opened his mouth and began to sing. *"A, b, c, d..."* The group joined in after the first few notes, and I sat next to Benjamin, watching him as he sang every single letter and every last word of the alphabet song. I was absolutely astounded. Just a scant ten days ago, Benjamin had struggled with singing a few words, exerting much effort in his attempts, and now he was singing an *entire song* without my having practiced it with him. Remarkable.

The next day, we were on our way to Kindermusik class, and as I drove, Benjamin began a series of proclamations. "Rosehip," he announced from his car seat behind me. "Painting. Band-Aid." Then he was silent for a while before casually saying, "Dried applesauce." I laughed, knowing that Benjamin was referring to the fruit leather my mom made by dehydrating homemade applesauce.

Benjamin's collection of words was eclectic, and I marveled at how his brain had finally become a sponge for language.

I was at the piano, playing a scale for Benjamin, singing the note names, and he immediately copied me, singing perfectly in tune, requiring no explanation or practice. Then Benjamin spontaneously sang the scale again, this time using solfege syllables. *"Doh, re, mi, fa..."* I was speechless. Months had passed since I had sung such a scale, and now Benjamin was repeating what he had heard, with flawless auditory recall. Something dawned on me.

"Sweetie, sing me a G," I requested, and Benjamin immediately did so, plucking the note out of thin air. I played the correlating key on the piano, confirming Benjamin's correct singing of the requested note. "How about B, sing me a B," I now asked, and again Benjamin complied effortlessly.

After a few more trials, I ran to the deck where Rick was taking care of a much needed repair. "Benjamin has perfect pitch," I exclaimed exultantly. "Come inside and listen."

We were in Cheryl's office for our monthly cranio-sacral session. Working on Benjamin's chest, Cheryl commented, "There's a lot of stress here," and within minutes, Benjamin confirmed her impression. He began to cry, melting under Cheryl's hands, sending an intuitive thought flashing across my mind.

"Benjamin's heart is aching—the relationship with his Daddy is so confusing." Outwardly, Benjamin might appear oblivious to Rick's comings and goings, but the soul connection to his father was intact. Autism could not prevent him from feeling loss or abandonment, nor did it preclude a longing for connection, however paradoxical that might seem.

At the end of September, my parents came over to help us celebrate the European harvest festival of Michaelmas. Our dining room table was heaped with the bounty of my parents' garden. Glowing orange pumpkins were stacked to form a pyramid and were flanked on either side with cascades of vibrantly colored fruits and vegetables. Bouquets of fall flowers accented the display, and a Renaissance print of the Archangel Michael fighting a dragon was discreetly tucked in behind two fragrant beeswax candles.

Gazing at the beauty before me, I meditated on how the festival went beyond giving thanks for the earth's abundance. Michaelmas was traditionally a time for gathering fortitude, a time to begin questing for inner light and strength—as was symbolized by the bright angel overcoming the dragon's dark powers. For me, the winter months with their increasingly short days could be depressing, but this could be counteracted by deepening spiritual activity, and so I took to heart the festival's call to consciousness.

Now, my parents, Rick, and I sang traditional European songs, and Benjamin sat on my lap, absorbing the festive mood and plucking the strings of a small lyre (lap harp). Then I recited a German Michaelmas poem which I had learned as a child and which I had begun speaking for Benjamin as we walked the trails each morning.

All of our language development was taking place in English, as per Corinne's recommendation, but I couldn't imagine cutting Benjamin off from the legacy of European culture I had inherited from my parents. I had decided that morning walks would be an ideal time for exposing him to German songs and poetry, neither drilling nor explaining, but nevertheless planting seeds of understanding. As he had already done, Benjamin might continue to surprise us with what he picked up.

Over the past few months, I had begun burning the midnight oil. After Benjamin was in bed, I would complete the household chores and then spend several hours practicing my violin and/or writing. I had signed a job contract after successfully auditioning for our local professional orchestra, the Boulder Philharmonic, and was scheduling rehearsals with a pianist-friend, preparing for a solo performance. These musical activities took place at night, and I was blessed by my parents' full support; they were always willing to come over and babysit while Benjamin slept. And just now, Rick was home to help out as well.

"It takes a village to raise a child," I thought, grateful that I could fit in some soul-feeding activities for myself.

With Rick taking care of Benjamin while I rehearsed, the father-son bond was growing stronger and, by the time of the season's first concert, Rick felt that he could bring Benjamin to the performance. My heart glowed as the two of them met me at the edge of the stage during intermission. "Did you see Mommy playing violin?" I asked Benjamin, whose eyes were round with wonder.

"Benjamin sat and listened quietly," Rick told me, happy and proud that his son hadn't put him through undue stress. "It's obvious that music really speaks to him."

12

Benjamin Turns Three
October 1997

Rick, Benjamin, and I were walking to the bus stop near our house; Rick was on his way back to Whidbey Island. Around us, trees flamed crimson, russet, and gold, and as we passed a neighbor's garden, I pulled a dried Michaelmas daisy off its stalk, picking it apart, tossing seeds and shriveled, purple petals into the air.

"We have really connected as a family during these past few weeks," I observed, sighing with contentment. I counted off the months until Rick's next visit on my fingers; he would return at the end of January. "When we next see you, Mother Nature will be in her winter sleep, and spring will be just around the corner. That's a long time...we'll miss you."

After Rick's departure, I turned my thoughts to Benjamin's upcoming third birthday and recalled the discussion that I'd had with Corinne concerning the natural development of a three-year-old's individuality. Benjamin was naturally beginning to say "I" rather than "Benjamin" when making spontaneous requests. For instance, instead of saying, *"Benjamin* wants water," as a younger child would typically do, he was saying, *"I* want water." This sign of appropriate ego-development was encouraging since Benjamin was still developmentally delayed in most respects.

Now that Benjamin was developing a sense of self, I felt the time was ripe for toilet training. Whenever we were at home, I kept Benjamin dressed in only shirt and socks, with no bottoms on. This way, both he and I could easily pick up the signs indicating a need for some "potty time." Within a few short weeks, Benjamin had developed fairly consistent control over his functions and was wearing "big boy underpants." I had our carpets steam cleaned, and that was the end of that.

At this time, I began working on developing flexibility in Benjamin's language rather than exclusively drilling the same phrases over and over again. I would model various ways of saying the same thing with different words, and then I would encourage Benjamin to echo each similar phrase in turn, hoping that he would make the connection between them. After several weeks of this, my strategy was already bearing fruit. Benjamin was occasionally making unprompted requests that alternately began with words such as, "I would like..." "I want..." or "Can I have...?"

I also began work on the correct use of pronouns ("he" and "she"), and was introducing the idea of "*my/mine*" versus "*your/yours*." I had read about the difficulties that this concept posed to people with autism. The labeling of "mine" or "yours" involves a shifting viewpoint: the correct usage of the words depends on who happens to be speaking them, and this requires a certain degree of mental flexibility which is at odds with how autism affects the brain. Rigidity in thinking, difficulty with abstractions, a tendency towards literal interpretations, and the need for a concrete understanding of the world; all these are hallmarks of autism.

I began my experiments with teaching "*my/yours*" by initiating a turn-taking game. We were sitting in the playhouse, and I had set Benjamin's favorite shape-sorter on his little work table.

"*My* turn," I said, pointing at myself and then putting a triangle into the sorter.

"Say '*my* turn'," I directed, and taking Benjamin's hand, I made him pat his own chest.

"Benjamin's turn," he said. Technically, this was correct, but now I was intent on changing the verbal pattern.

"No, say '*my* turn'," I prompted, and after several more corrections, Benjamin said the words while patting his chest with my help. I rewarded him with a treat and then gave him a turn with the shape sorter.

After numerous repetitions of "*my* turn," I could see Benjamin was getting the idea, and I thought, "Let's try the next step."

I now pointed towards Benjamin and said, "*Your* turn."

He immediately and automatically echoed, "Your turn."

I paused for a moment, thinking. This was not the response I was looking for. "This would probably work a lot better if I had an assistant," I thought. But I didn't have anyone around just now. We would just try to get this figured out on our own.

Withholding the shape-sorter, I said "*your* turn" while tapping Benjamin on the chest and gently laying my other hand over his mouth to silence him; I didn't want him incorrectly echoing "your turn." I really wanted him to say "*my* turn." I took his hand, helped him pat his chest, and prompted him.

We messed around with this for a while, and then I thought, "Benjamin sometimes surprises me with what he picks up. I'll try another step forward."

I now took his hand and shaped it into a fist with the pointer-finger sticking out. "Say, '*your* turn'," I directed, making Benjamin's pointer tap my chest while I held a raisin near my mouth, letting him see that I was about to eat it.

"Your turn," Benjamin said obediently.

Now I quickly muttered "*My* turn" and popped the treat into my mouth. Benjamin squawked in protest.

"Now it's *your* turn," I emphasized, tapping his chest and stuffing a date into Benjamin's mouth to prevent him from incorrectly echoing me. As Benjamin chewed happily, I prompted him to say "*My* turn, *my* treat."

Throughout our session, I had spoken as little as possible, keeping the target phrases free of extraneous sound-clutter, and now I noticed my head aching from the strain of analyzing each moment and gesture. Clearly, this drill would take many daily repetitions to sink in, and I would probably have to back-track, practicing only a single step for several days before adding the next.

I marveled to think that the typical child's brain could learn such complex verbal juggling as if by osmosis and that most parents would never think twice about it. Indeed, I knew that most of the developments that other people took for granted in their young children would not be coming naturally to Benjamin. Therefore, whenever he *did* produce something spontaneous, I was ready to celebrate the moment and to commemorate it in my daily journal.

Benjamin was spontaneously reciting a particular couplet from the Michaelmas poem, repeating it at various times throughout the day."*Sankt Michael gibt mir die rechte Kraft / die Böses besiegt and Gutes schafft...*" (by Wera Bockemühl). My translation: "*St. Michael endows me with such honest strength / as can vanquish evil, and perform good deeds...*"

Although the verse began with easily understood harvest imagery—apples, baskets of vegetables, the gift of sharing one's crops—Benjamin's attention had been captured by the key philosophical message of the poem. I thought, "The strength and intention of these lines must somehow touch his soul, because he certainly doesn't know what they mean on an intellectual level. What extraordinary sensitivity."

Benjamin had a musical ear, but he wasn't picking up on the natural inflections of speech. Even when I exaggerated the natural ups and downs of verbal phrases, Benjamin echoed in monotone. "Maybe our language drills need to be sung," I thought. "Music will engage Benjamin's heart and emotions, and singing will make his voice more flexible."

"Come to breakfast, come to the table," I now sang to Benjamin, clapping in rhythm to my improvised sing-song. "I'm coming, I'm coming," I continued, cuing Benjamin to sing the phrase back to me. Then, going up the scale, I sang, "Would you like some apple?"

I looked encouragingly at Benjamin, singing a descending minor third in imitation of a cuckoo's call. "Yes please, yes please."

Benjamin joined me. "Yes, please."

Although I had initially felt silly and self-conscious about my singing, Benjamin had responded immediately and with enjoyment, and now I resolved to keep transforming our mundane interactions into a musical production.

Since the middle of summer, the little violin I had bought for Benjamin had rested in a safe place on our couch or on top of the piano, always waiting, always available, just like a good friend. On various occasions, I had shown Benjamin how to hold the instrument, just to pique his interest, and for a while in July, he had become quite motivated to try holding the bow. Now that Benjamin was speaking and was nearly three, I deemed him ready to begin with proper violin instruction.

The place to start was with the bow and the violin as separate entities: Benjamin would learn how to manipulate each individually, without the distraction of the other. Then we would bring the two together, and he would begin truly playing his instrument.

To begin setting Benjamin's bow technique (involving the right arm and hand), we played a bow-simulation game which Benjamin absolutely loved. I would rest one end of a yard-long wooden dowel on Benjamin's left shoulder and hold the other end of the dowel in such a manner that, when Benjamin slid his right hand up and down the dowel, he would automatically be performing the correct arm motions involved in stroking an actual bow across a properly held violin.

The fun of this game was that Benjamin could choose interesting words to say, and these words would determine the rhythm pattern for his "bowing action." For example, he might say "*blueberry, blueberry*" which translated to a rhythm of "*long, short-short, long, short-short*." While speaking, Benjamin would slide his right hand back and forth along the dowel, in the proper rhythm. In this way, we were nailing two birds with one stone: Benjamin was working on his pronunciation and diction skills and, at the same time, he was developing his violin-playing skills.

After he had gotten comfortable practicing rhythms like "*run, pony, run, pony*," "*watermelon, apple*," and "*My name is Benjamin*," I added an element of choice.

"What do you like?" I would ask, and Benjamin would decide. One day, he surprised me by saying "*I like toasted coconut*," and this immediately became his favorite rhythm-phrase; he giggled with glee whenever he repeated these words along with his simulated bow strokes.

As a separate activity, Benjamin was learning how to hold the violin up on his left shoulder and to accurately place his fingers on the strings. "Make that finger hop up and down like a froggie," I prompted, applying the bow to the strings so that Benjamin could hear the effects of his finger movements. He delighted in the changing musical pitches and was discovering how to make a scale and how to finger some simple songs.

"Good job. Now *you* get to play with the bow," I told Benjamin each time he had completed practicing his separate right and left hand exercises. I helped him to position his violin and to take hold of the bow. Then I put my right hand over Benjamin's and guided his bow-strokes so that a pleasing sound emerged rather than the scratchy, screeching sounds that so easily result from a beginner's inaccurate bowing.

I'd had the impulse to set up a play-date. Benjamin was getting regular exposure to the company of other children through our weekly Kindermusik and "Dance with Nance" classes; however, now that we were working on phrases like "*my turn, your turn,*" I felt that Benjamin needed to experience a one-on-one play situation.

I contacted a friend whose son was about Benjamin's age. Claire was happy to invite us over, and I felt a thrill of anticipation as Benjamin exchanged a few verbal phrases with both her and Dennis. Soon however, he discovered the wheels on a toy truck and became absorbed in spinning them, alarming me with his quick regression into old behavior. I hastened to find a game that might pique his interest.

"We have a simple card game here," Claire suggested. "Dennis, can you show Benjamin how to deal out the cards so everyone gets the same amount?" As Dennis did so, counting as he went, I gently encouraged Benjamin to watch, lightly touching his cheek and then pointing to direct his eye gaze.

"Good job counting," Claire exclaimed sincerely as Benjamin's voice joined Dennis's. Now we were ready to see how the card game was to be played.

"Just a second," Dennis said, turning away from us. His interest had momentarily shifted to a little toy piano. "Just a second," he repeated and began tinkering with the keys.

As soon as Benjamin heard musical pitches emerging from the toy, he echoed Dennis, saying, "Just a second," and reaching for the little instrument.

"Wait. It's Dennis's turn. *Then* it'll be *your* turn." I was grinning with delight. Benjamin had just picked up a novel phrase through imitating a peer. Our home drills were paying off.

I was showing Corinne the simple weaving loom that my mom had constructed. "I've been encouraging Benjamin to weave without help, building up his willpower through independent activity. He has to focus on maintaining a pattern, and his hands have to work together, threading the soft wool through the strings."

Corinne nodded approvingly. "Around age three, children are generally ready for actions that cross the body's vertical midline. We can emphasize activities requiring bilateral coordination; this means that both sides of the body are working together in a controlled and organized manner, with the two hemispheres of the brain communicating and sharing information with each other. At this point, Benjamin's weaving is a developmentally appropriate activity."

Corinne now suggested some expansions of old exercises. "When playing patty-cake, you've been asking Benjamin to clap his hands against yours, straight across. Now you should add a diagonal pattern, with your right hand meeting Benjamin's right hand, then your left hand clapping his left in an alternating rhythm."

"When you ask Benjamin to 'paint' your shower walls, have him trace a lemniscate—that's a figure 8 lying on its side. Also, help him to make wide arcs, extending as far left and right as he can reach, like tracing an enormous rainbow. Have Benjamin use both hands, together and separately. If you want less mess, then tape butcher paper to the wall and let Benjamin use block crayons for drawing lazy 8's and rainbows."

"Here's an exercise to help Benjamin with differentiating between large movements and very fine ones." Corinne demonstrated large circular motions that involved the entire arm; then she made circles with just the forearms (from the elbows, as if manipulating a jump-rope); next, she made circles with her hands using her wrist joints (like a hula dancer's gestures); and finally, she tapped her closed fists together, then tapped the heels of her hands together, and ended by touching the fingertips of both hands together in various combinations.

"This movement sequence will heighten Benjamin's body awareness and will foster coordination," she told me. "You can make up a little song to guide him and to keep the motions in descending order, from large to fine."

Now, our discussion turned to Benjamin's preschool readiness. I had already chosen a small home-based Waldorf program, knowing that the focus would be on fostering social development and imagination—the very things that Benjamin needed most. Talia, the teacher, was a good match to Benjamin's personality, and she also had experience working with special-needs children and was willing to let me join her class as Benjamin's assistant.

"Benjamin's soul-strength is growing," Corinne observed. "He should be able to connect with other children." I felt hesitant, acutely aware of how very tenuous and elementary Benjamin's play skills were as of yet, but Corinne's assessment was encouraging, and so I decided we would start with preschool in January, after the holidays.

A few days before Benjamin's end-of-October birthday, a surprise snow storm arrived and within hours, the brilliant fall colors that had suffused our neighborhood were hidden beneath a thick layer of white. There was an air of coziness in our house, and Benjamin was absorbed in holding his violin and following my directions for left-hand finger exercises when he made a sudden request. "I want the bow," he exclaimed, his choppy, stilted pronunciation sounding more marked than usual.

"Here it is," I said, proffering the bow. I held it level as Benjamin excitedly arranged his right hand into a correct bow hold. Then he pulled the bow out of my grasp, rested it on the strings of his violin, and began playing his favorite rhythm, "*I like toasted coconut*." As he tried the rhythm on each individual string, his sound rang out clear and clean, and his right arm moved with impeccable form. Awestruck, I watched Benjamin as he played without any assistance, his face glowing and his smile incredulous as he glanced back and forth between his bow and me, still playing all the while. "Who is doing this?" his eyes seemed to ask. "Is it really *me*?"

My organized program of exercises had prepared Benjamin to successfully assert his willpower.

The next morning, I was up early preparing breakfast when I heard Benjamin's light footsteps pattering around upstairs, and soon thereafter, the repetitive clicking of a light switch in the hall reached my ears. Abandoning my work, I ran upstairs to interrupt Benjamin's fixation. Wanting to redirect him with a minimum of conflict, I whisked him off of his feet with a tickle and a song, and was hit by a pang of disappointment when, instead of giggling, Benjamin protested with a screech.

We headed downstairs and, after we had eaten breakfast together, I hurriedly washed up the dishes. Benjamin was momentarily left to his own devices. When I returned to the living room, I found him magnetized by the sight of an upside-down toy car, its wheels madly spinning as Benjamin propelled them into motion. I teased the toy away from him and began leading Benjamin towards our coat rack. "Let's put on warm things and go play in the snow," I exclaimed.

But Benjamin had other ideas. He had caught sight of the air-filtering device that stood in a corner and was now straining towards it, eager to push its various operating buttons. "This looks like the beginnings of another backslide," I thought, groaning inwardly. How could this be? The positive changes I had seen in Benjamin during most of October had seemed so lasting and solid. Why would the happy momentum of the past several weeks suddenly reverse itself?

We had spent a few hours out of doors, safely away from tempting switches, lights, buttons, and spinning objects, and Benjamin's frantic energy had mellowed. Diving into birthday preparations, I showed Benjamin how to hollow out a pumpkin, urging him to plunge his hands into the gooey, fibrous insides in order to pull out the seeds. "Good job using your hands," I praised as Benjamin reluctantly cooperated. He had made enormous progress in overcoming his tactile hyper-sensitivities. Now I carved a happy face into the orange flesh of the pumpkin, and Benjamin smiled back at the grinning birthday jack-o-lantern.

"Mm, that smells good," I said, inhaling the delicious scent of roasting pumpkin seeds. Once they were out of the oven and had cooled, I filled a bowl with them. "Let's play puppet show, just like yesterday. Come watch." I settled Benjamin on the couch and handed him the crunchy snack.

I set up Benjamin's little work table, added various props, brought out three differently-sized teddy-bears, pulled on a hand-puppet—a charming girl with long braids—and began telling the story of *Goldilocks and the Three Bears*. Benjamin already knew the story from the illustrated book I had been reading to him, and now he was learning to watch the animated characters.

"Hands down," I reminded Benjamin as his attention drifted and he began flicking his fingers alongside his face, stimulating his peripheral vision. "Watch Baby Bear," I directed, gently touching Benjamin's face and then pointing, drawing his gaze to the appropriate figure. While I had already spent several days preparing Benjamin to enjoy the show during his party, I was reserving one element as a surprise: the old-fashioned puppet theater that my parents had built. It stood four feet high and had a little stage, backdrop, and curtains that could be closed for scene changes. Whimsically flowered wallpaper decorated the theater, and strings of bells and chimes hung from the backstage area. Tomorrow, Benjamin would watch the three bears and Goldilocks coming to life without me being in plain sight. "Good watching, Benjamin. Now we clap to show appreciation. 'The end.' The story is over." We practiced applauding, and I made the bears and Goldilocks take a bow.

"Now let's play birthday party, just like we've been doing." I lined up stuffed animals and dolls along the couch. "Say, 'This is for you'," I prompted, reminding Benjamin to repeat the phrase each time that he handed a little toy trumpet to one of his "guests." We would be giving away the little noisemakers as party favors the next day, and Benjamin would perform this little ritual of sharing with each child.

After dinner, I prepared to give Benjamin his first haircut, combing out his fine, golden locks; they reached to several inches below his shoulders. This haircut on the eve of Benjamin's third birthday would be a rite of passage, marking the end of toddlerhood and indicating the beginnings of his becoming a "big boy." As I prepared to cut, tears started running down my cheeks and my hands shook so hard I could barely manage the scissors. Mental snapshots from the past many months flashed before my inner eye, reminding me of the enormous changes in our lives and of the amazing breakthroughs we had achieved together.

Benjamin would never again be a baby or a toddler, and I would never return to the blissful ignorance that had been mine prior to Benjamin's being diagnosed with autism. Somehow this realization struck me with incredible poignancy. The urgency of my therapeutic work had lent a special depth to my experience of being a parent. Not one moment of my son's gradual unfolding had escaped me, and I was conscious of the fulfillment I was experiencing through being a part of his process. If autism was a dark cloud, then the passionate intensity of working to overcome it might well be the silver lining...

13

Things Get Harder
November 1997

I had purchased a set of three boy-dolls who would reside in the dollhouse my parents had crafted for me when I was a child. A pair of sister dolls, a Mama-doll, a Papa, and even a baby already occupied the house, and now the miniature family welcomed the trio of ethnically diverse dolls: "China-Boy," "Brown-Boy," and the blond, Caucasian "Benjamin-Doll." The boys had wooden heads, hands, and feet, and their cloth-covered wire limbs could be bent into action poses. I showed Benjamin how they could easily sit on a toy horse, straddle his "Brio" train for a ride, or stand alone.

Fantasy and make-believe would not be coming naturally to Benjamin, but we would practice mimicking a typical three-year-old's symbolic play. I began by showing Benjamin how the dolls might "talk" together. As the conversation bounced back and forth, I gave each doll a unique voice, making it hop around while speaking.

"Hi, Benjamin-Doll."

"Hi, Brown-Boy."

"How are you?"

"I'm fine, thanks."

Then I asked Benjamin to take over his portion of the familiar script. As expected, we had to drill the sequence, and Benjamin needed help moving his doll around, not yet understanding that his voice was representing the doll's thoughts. I also began teaching Benjamin how to animate our collection of toy animals and showed him how to act out being a creature.

"Watch, I'm being a cat..." I crawled around Benjamin on all fours, making him laugh as I meowed and burrowed my head into him, then rolled over, purring. "Now copy me." I had to break down the sequence and direct Benjamin to practice each little portion before he could follow along with me. Even though Benjamin appeared to be watching my demonstrations, he couldn't perceive the essential parts of the modeled actions.

Years later, I read about a comparison study in which researchers had tracked the eye movements of both typical and autistic persons as they viewed short movie-clips. (Some of these film segments depicted an individual actor experiencing obvious emotions; others featured a dialogue between two people.) As one might expect, the typical person would focus on the actor's facial expressions and eyes. In the case of a dialogue, the viewer would look back and forth between the faces of the speaking actors, intermittently glancing downward in order to pick up on the actor's body language. In contrast, the autistic subjects in the study spent most of their time *avoiding* the actor's faces, instead looking at the background *around* the featured actor(s), their eye gaze often resting on inanimate objects, and their visual attention generally bypassing the relevant aspects of the scene. So it seemed to be with Benjamin when faced with a demonstration: unless I specifically guided his gaze by gesturing at the relevant area and by directing him verbally and through touch, he would miss out on pertinent information.

Sorting was another skill that required much practice. Benjamin needed to learn that, depending on the defined category, the same object might be classified/sorted in different ways. I had gathered a little bag full of buttons, differently-sized beads, tiny wooden crafts items, and so on. When I first introduced sorting, I kept things simple, starting with a collection of beads that differed only by color. "Put all reds here and all blues there." Once mastered, I added larger beads to make four groups. "Let's sort: small reds, big reds, small blues, big blues."

Next, I added the distraction of mixing the red and blue beads with other objects that didn't fit into the blue/red category and needed to be put into a container of their own. Eventually, Benjamin would be ready for greater challenges such as sorting increasingly varied objects by texture, shape, size, color, or material. By experiencing that the criteria for categories are changeable, Benjamin was gaining some flexibility in his thinking.

I had recently read a book by Temple Grandin, a well-known author with autism, and was struck by her description of how, as a child, she had been unable to categorize things. For example, only after seeing countless different boats (both as pictures and in real life) did she grasp that they all had something in common which put them into the single category of "boat." The differences between the many boats had initially overwhelmed her and had prevented her from recognizing key similarities.

Now I began testing Benjamin, wondering whether he might have these same difficulties. He was already able to match physical objects with pictures of similar objects, and now I challenged him to sort the cards of a "Nature Memory" game into basic categories. "Put flowers here, put animals there." In some of the pictures, a large animal would be sitting amongst some small flowers; or, a large blossom might have a tiny insect crawling on it. Benjamin had to recognize which aspect of the picture was most important in order to correctly sort it. Happily, he had little trouble with the exercise, and I was reminded that each person with autism would have their own set of strengths and weaknesses.

Both Benjamin and I were recovering from the flu, and Benjamin's mood was volatile. He whined and screeched, fanatically flipping switches, pushing buttons, and manipulating all the locks throughout the house. "I'll use masking tape to cover up all but the most necessary switches," I thought, getting to work on the project. "But I must also find a way to work *with* Benjamin's fixations, rather than just stopping him." With this in mind, I began requesting that Benjamin flip the light switch for me whenever we entered our dark bathroom. "Now it's *my* turn with the light," I would then announce as we got ready to exit. At first, Benjamin screamed uncontrollably, struggling against my restraining arms while reaching for the switch, but after a few distressing days, he began accepting that he couldn't take sole ownership of the light switch but had to share it.

In contrast to the joyful cooperation that Benjamin had displayed during October, he was now contrary and inclined to say "no" to everything. He refused help, even when terribly frustrated by something, and I began to think that he was catching up on his "terrible two's," exerting his emerging will and testing boundaries. Hoping that this difficult developmental phase might be eased with the help of homeopathics, I took Benjamin to see Julie, and she prescribed the same high-power remedy that had supported Benjamin's speech breakthrough during the summer.

"At first, things might become even more difficult, just as happened in August," she cautioned. "Hang in there, and if things don't improve by the end of the month, we'll go back to mild daily dosing."

Benjamin's screeches were searing my ears, and I was dredging deep to come up with hope and energy for our therapeutic work. Benjamin's vocal onslaughts were a replay of the piercing sounds he had produced in August and now, as then, I felt myself at the breaking point. Fortunately, there were a few isolated days where, without rhyme or reason, Benjamin's mood lightened, affording us both some recovery time.

One particular morning, mid-month, Benjamin awoke, smiling, displaying the mellow sweetness which had been prevalent prior to his third birthday. All day long, he maintained an air of cozy connectedness and contentment and so, that evening, I made popcorn and hot spiced cider, lit a candle, and retold the seasonal story of St. Martin using various dolls and props to make the tale come alive.

Using the blond Benjamin-Doll to represent St. Martin, I settled the flexible little figure upon a wooden horse, tied a red silk handkerchief around his neck as a cape, and used a small tinfoil-covered stick to represent the saint's sword. I arranged pieces of logs to form a bridge for the horse to walk over, and at the opposite end of this passage, placed a doll wrapped in sacking to represent a poor beggar.

Then I began telling the story, showing Benjamin how St. Martin had sliced his cloak in half so that he might share its enveloping warmth with the poor man. Although Martin possessed very little himself, he had nevertheless been willing to give, to help someone in need, to share the light and love residing in his heart. "A worthy example," I thought, bringing the centuries-old tale to a close.

14

Jingle Bells, Jingle Bells
December 1997

"Come, sweetheart, help me carry." I was gathering up fragrant boughs of evergreen, wanting to decorate our house for the holiday season. "Put these branches in the big vase. Good job. Now look, Mommy is making a wreath." Benjamin was finally on the upswing; his screeching had diminished since starting a daily regimen of low-potency homeopathics the previous week, and his mood was stabilizing, making my work with him easier and more productive.

We had progressed into the wonderful world of "W" questions. "*Who* is that?" *Where* is he? *What* is he doing?" We pored over family photo albums and looked through a plethora of picture books. Benjamin was learning to ask for information, and we practiced simple "*Why? Because...*" scripts over and over again. I also drilled Benjamin in answering "*what?*" whenever I called his name.

Benjamin's rapidly expanding vocabulary now allowed me some insight into his thoughts. As he verbalized, Benjamin would jump chaotically from one unrelated observation to the next, clearly displaying his autism-driven attention deficit. Sometimes he would talk nonstop, repeating certain phrases, making it impossible for me to engage him. "The act of talking has become a self-stimulatory fixation," I would think on these occasions.

Now, while talking, Benjamin was either clenching his teeth, or he was keeping his tongue curled into the roof of his mouth, thereby squashing his sounds. When I demonstrated exaggerated articulation, Benjamin seemed unable to copy me, and so I began manually pushing his chin down, making his mouth open wide as he talked. Eventually, this fixed the problem, and I returned to improving Benjamin's robot-like monotone. I spoke vivaciously, making my voice rise and fall with tremendous expression, encouraging Benjamin to mimic me. I also began setting many of our drilled dialogues to melody. While the words wouldn't change until Benjamin had mastered the phrases, I could at least keep the materials fresh by varying the music.

Benjamin was fast asleep when I sneaked to his bedside with a whimsically decorated St. Nicholas stocking. My head was filled with memories of childhood: finding my own magical stocking in the dusk of dawn, discovering almond cookies with silver sprinkles tucked into the stocking's toe, imagining that angel's wings had shed the shimmering decorations onto the delicious sweets. Now, I longed to pass on the enchantment. If I could spark Benjamin's imagination, he would one day have special memories of his own.

When Benjamin awoke the next morning, I was waiting. Bringing his attention to the extraordinary stocking, I showed him how to remove the decorative fir branches that peeked out the top. "You must search inside. Find the surprises." Benjamin dug around and came up with several mandarin oranges which he promptly peeled and ate.

With a bit more encouragement, he also discovered a wrapped package containing a set of shiny, silver bells firmly attached to a pair of red, wooden handles, just like the ones we used during Kindermusik. Benjamin began rhythmically shaking the bells, singing, "*Bell-horses, bell-horses, what's the time of day? / One o'clock, two o'clock, time to go away.*" That was one of his favorite songs from Miss Amy's class.

Watching his sweet delight in the new little instruments, I eagerly anticipated the following week when Benjamin would bring his violin to class and, using open strings, accompany the Kindermusik group in singing *Muffin Man*. His first public "performance" was imminent, and I was confident that Benjamin would shine.

In mid-December, we again had a session with Corinne. "When Benjamin gets fixated on mechanical things, it's like he's getting sucked into them as if being drawn by a powerful magnet," I explained. "I can imagine what it feels like because a similar thing happens to me when I'm around a running television. I tend to get pulled into the programming and become somewhat oblivious to what's around me. If the show is interesting, then it can take some real effort to tear myself away."

"Let me give you an esoteric explanation for that," Corinne suggested. "Just as the soul can be thought of as a distinct entity, we can visualize our emotions as being contained in a cohesive energy body; people often use the term 'astral body' for this. When Benjamin is pulled into a fixation, his astral body is extended and becomes entangled with the object; he experiences real pain in having to withdraw his energy and feelings from the physical object. Be sensitive when interrupting a fixation, and provide a few moments of transition time. It's good that you're not exposing Benjamin to TV, videos, or other such technologies; they are over-stimulating and would only block his capacity for interpersonal connection."

Corinne thought a moment. "Here's an idea. We can call forth the feeling of being out of kilter, as Benjamin is during a fixation, and have him practice returning to awareness. Put Benjamin on the spin-board or in his hammock swing, and have him look at his feet while you spin him around. Twelve rotations should be sufficient to make him dizzy. Then stop the spinning and vigorously squeeze Benjamin's hands and arms in order to override his feeling of dizziness. This is effective because proprioceptive feedback takes precedence over vestibular feedback in the brain. As you squeeze, ask for eye contact and engage Benjamin in a dialogue to get him thinking and connecting with you. As you talk together, help him to remain present by massaging his hands." I nodded appreciatively, liking the new strategy.

Then Corinne asked Benjamin to lay face down on her massage table and taught me a sequence of chirophonetic strokes that would have a calming, harmonizing influence. She placed a small lyre on Benjamin's back and gently plucked its strings, improvising a melody. As the musical vibrations of the wooden instrument transmitted directly into Benjamin's body, he looked blissfully at peace. "He *is* the music," I thought, appreciative of how the new experience was speaking to Benjamin's soul. From now on, each morning would begin with this fulfilling sequence.

Talia's preschool group was gathered for a holiday celebration. There was a ceremonial aspect to the event and, while I expected the large group of three-year-olds to have trouble being quiet, only Benjamin caused a disturbance as he talked to me, his loud voice cutting into the silence. "There's something to be learned from every uncomfortable situation," I told myself, realizing that I hadn't yet taught Benjamin how to whisper. Like most things, this new skill would need practice at home.

Christmas was only a few days away and, as if mirroring the general build-up of holiday excitement, Benjamin's feet were in constant motion. At our appointment with Julie, I half joked, "It's as if he's dancing a *tarantella*—you know, like he's been stung by a tarantula spider."

Julie regarded me seriously. "You know, there *is* a homeopathic remedy that helps antidote such behavior, but I don't want to try it on Benjamin right now. He is learning well and is expressing much physical affection. I don't want to risk derailing this upswing of energy."

We both looked at Benjamin as he began hopping on his tiptoes, jerking his elbows forward and back while flapping his hands. Simultaneously, his torso was repeatedly jackknifing towards his thighs and then snapping upright again, producing a bizarre-looking movement pattern.

"I've tried copying Benjamin's motions to understand what he might be feeling when he does that," I told Julie. "It's pretty stressful, physically, but I think it helps him discharge a build-up of emotional excitement and makes him more aware of his physical boundaries. However, it's odd how Benjamin's self-stimulatory behaviors come and go; sometimes, he'll have a period of several days or even weeks where he hardly hops or flaps. When I added sensory integration to our program, I thought that Benjamin's need for self-stimulatory movements would decrease, but that doesn't seem to be the case."

I went on. "So, I've been experimenting with verbal cues, stroking Benjamin's arms while saying 'quiet arms' or resting my hands heavily on his shoulders to ground him while saying 'stand still.' For a while, my cue phrases were "*stop* flapping' or '*stop* jumping,' but then I realized that I should prompt specific, desirable actions instead. *Stopping* something just leaves an empty space that craves to be filled." Julie nodded, affirming that she liked my reasoning.

"I'm trying cues like 'hands down, stand tall, heels down,' and I hope that someday Benjamin will gain some degree of conscious control over his movements."

Christmas Eve was at hand, and my parents and brother had joined Benjamin and me for a family celebration. Rick, on military deployment in the Middle East, would be present only in spirit. As we sang carols around the beautiful, candle-lit tree which had appeared as if by magic, Benjamin gazed at each of us in turn, obviously delighted at being surrounded by the sounds of a choir. The innocence and joy radiating from him touched me deeply, and I felt privileged to be a parent. The world, as seen through the eyes of a young child, was a gift like no other.

Later that night, as I tucked Benjamin into bed, I was caught up in reverie with childhood Christmas memories floating into mind. The sound of Benjamin's voice brought me out of the clouds. "I want prayers," Benjamin requested and then switched to German, prompting me with the first line of the prayerful meditation I had created for him. *"Mein Engelein, die Mama betet für dich..."*

I began. The meditation focused on five things that I felt were key to Benjamin's growth and healing: heartfelt joy; centered calm; connecting to others through the eyes—as windows to the soul; the desire to be with others; the hope that the music blooming in Benjamin's heart would act as a bridge between him and others. Every night, I imagined these qualities becoming manifest in Benjamin's daily life. Too, I visualized energy, love, and wisdom coming from a higher source, surrounding both Benjamin and me. There was a limit to what I could do alone.

1998

15

New Year, New Beginning
January 1998

The New Year had arrived and Benjamin, now three-years-and-two-months old, was in high spirits. I was joyful in my work with him and had, since Christmas, introduced an element of "playing pretend" when distracting him from his fixations. Benjamin had become newly obsessed with turning the bathtub faucets on and off, and I tried diverting him by *pretending* to take a bath: I mimed turning on an invisible faucet and made rushing, gurgling water sounds, then turned off my pretend faucet. Benjamin giggled at my sounds and was willing to join me in the game, letting me guide him in the miming of actions.

Later, when he gravitated towards a favorite light switch, I called, "Only pretend, Benjamin. Like this." I ostentatiously flipped an invisible switch, and Benjamin stared at me in surprise, completely taken aback. He left the light alone. "I might be on to something here," I thought.

A week later, the strategy of getting Benjamin to "play pretend" had retained its effectiveness. Benjamin was mostly keeping his hands off appliances and wall mounted fixtures, and was even restraining himself around the thermostat which had lately captured his fascination. "If I had tried my 'pretend' strategy any earlier, it probably wouldn't have worked," I thought. "Benjamin wouldn't have had enough imaginative capacity to respond."

But now, he *was* showing evidence of a slowly awakening imagination. Benjamin was pretending to play a piano waltz on the tabletop at breakfast and would sometimes say, "I'm playing dance music," drumming his fingers on his knees or on the wall. Occasionally, without prompting, Benjamin would try some of the animal sounds or actions that we had been practicing. In addition, he was experimenting with the pronunciation of words, giggling wildly at silly things like "pillow bear" (polar bear), "crimp cheese" (cream cheese), or "hump pump" (the hump on a camel's back).

Because Benjamin's eye contact was still lacking in spite of his current liveliness and interest in the world, I redoubled my efforts to gain his gaze *on request*. Once he began attending preschool the following week, I would be asking Talia to use the cue, *"Look at me."* Hoping to increase the likelihood that Benjamin would respond, I brainstormed a new idea. "Let's do some counting," I suggested. "Remember swim class and how I counted while you did the back float? As you got better at floating, Mommy was able to count up to higher numbers. Now we'll count while you look at my eyes."

Benjamin had positive associations with the floating activity and was ready to play my new game. I challenged him to hold my gaze for increasingly longer amounts of time as I counted off the seconds: "Look-at-me, *one*, look-at-me, *two*, look-at-me, *three*..." Familiar with the timing routine and eager for a reward, Benjamin's eyes stayed trained on my face, maintaining a steady gaze. My little flash of inspiration had proved effective.

Lately, Benjamin was becoming overwhelmed by certain feelings. When he took an enormous liking to something, a tremulous smile would suffuse his countenance and then, suddenly, his hands would fly up to hide his eyes or else he would quickly turn his head away, seemingly overcome. At times, the hidden eyes would be followed by the words, "I want to stop," and I would see bodily tension mounting until Benjamin was trembling all over. In the end, he would dissolve, sobbing as if his heart were about to break. This scenario had already played out several times during Kindermusik where it seemed that certain songs touched Benjamin's heart too deeply. "Strange," I thought, "how the autism can either block his emotions altogether, or leave him bare and unprotected—emotionally hyper-sensitive."

At the playground, Benjamin was showing interest in other children and was willing to take turns going down the slide. This was a marked contrast to one month earlier when he had broken into inconsolable sobs whenever someone "trespassed," wanting to try out "his" slide. "This shift in outlook has come just in time for the start of preschool," I thought thankfully, anticipating our first day with Talia's class.

Over the weekend, Benjamin made great progress in his understanding of a new game called *Mystery Garden*. The game board depicted a colorful, whimsical garden with a variety of interesting objects hidden amongst the trees and flowers. A set of little game cards duplicated these hidden objects, and Benjamin had finally managed to match up each of his little cards to its corresponding object on the board. Eventually, the game pieces would come in handy for teaching how to use clues (to identify an object), and then we would work on playing the game "properly" since it was really a type of *I Spy* or *Ten Questions* game. "I'm excited too," I now praised Benjamin, who was reveling in his success with the game.

My eye fell upon the cuddly pair of handmade cloth dolls named Alexander and Katrina. Taking up the boy-doll and making him dance through the air towards Benjamin, I exclaimed, "Look who's coming." Benjamin glanced up from the game pieces and said delightedly, "It's Alexander." His response was so spontaneous and natural, so like a typical child's, that I later celebrated the moment in my journal.

Another such moment happened the next day when I asked Benjamin to bring me Alexander. He went over to the doll cradle and found only Katrina there; he picked her up and gazed at her for a long time, then gave her a gentle kiss. My heart melted at Benjamin's spontaneous tenderness with the doll. Even though I was developing Benjamin's play skills through artificial means, scripting scenarios and practicing certain actions repeatedly, he was beginning to respond with genuine feelings.

Benjamin was settling into Talia's preschool. We had joined the class that met twice weekly in the mornings and were becoming familiar with the schedule of activities that filled each four-hour session. Talia had agreed to me acting as Benjamin's shadow, kneeling behind and slightly to the side of him, whispering directives in his ear and guiding his eye gaze through pointing. However, my goal was to remain unobtrusive as I facilitated interactions; I wanted Benjamin's attention to remain on learning from his peers and teacher.

As I monitored Benjamin, I kept an eye on the other children's play, gathering ideas. If I could script play scenarios to practice with Benjamin at home using materials that were clearly of interest to the other children, I would improve his chances at joining in during playtime.

Story time was a new experience and, as Benjamin kept trying to talk, not following the example of his quietly attentive classmates, I realized I would need to teach a new cue: "*Stop talking. Listen.*" Benjamin was already improving in his whispering skills, and now it was time to learn about maintaining silence in settings other than the concert hall.

"Wet-on-wet" watercolor painting was another new activity for Benjamin. The children gathered around Talia, watching as she swirled her paintbrush in a jar of water. She blotted the brush on a rag and then dipped it into a little jar of watercolor paint. Talia began singing as she touched brush to paper, and a lovely swathe of blue swam across the wet surface, making a lively track with feathery edges. The children watched silently, fascinated. Benjamin too watched carefully and then followed Talia's lead with minimal assistance from me. His paper bloomed with rich ultramarine blue, and Benjamin swirled his brush back and forth, reveling in the color and not wanting to stop. Meanwhile,

I sat on a little child's chair behind him with a song in my heart, thankful that our persistent work on imitation skills was bearing fruit.

Rick was home for his long anticipated visit and, after a few days of happy interactions, Benjamin was experiencing one of his inexplicable shifts. Sweet openness had given way to stormy screeches and tantrum behaviors. Benjamin's eye contact had deteriorated, and he struggled for words, frustrated by the knowledge that his vocabulary was there, inside his brain but hiding, just barely out of reach. Now Benjamin engaged in "echolalia," repeating whatever he heard me say with no apparent grasp of meaning. He had turned into a human tape recorder. Transitions were more problematic than usual too, and during Kindermusik class, Benjamin screeched and growled fiercely between songs, protesting each change in music. The autistic regression was intense.

16

Quick Changes
February 1998

Benjamin had emerged from his internal storm with an expanded vocabulary and with a great enthusiasm for looking at books with Daddy. Now Benjamin was giggling as he pretended to read, reciting the memorized rhymes of a comical counting book. While turning the pages, Benjamin checked the colorfully drawn numbers, correctly identifying each one. Then he picked up a book of Mother Goose rhymes.

"Mother Goose, Guther Moose," Benjamin exclaimed, laughing hysterically as he switched the beginning consonants of the words, thus creating a "spoonerism." (Years down the road, Benjamin would retain his easy capacity for consonant reversals. Eventually, this would become a distinct talent, allowing Benjamin to entertain people with the hilariously twisted new meanings that could result when familiar rhymes and stories were consistently spoonerized.)

These days, Benjamin was also amusing himself by manipulating vowel sounds, making whole words reflect only a single vowel, perhaps a throwback to the speech exercises we had drilled when Benjamin first began talking. The word that gave him most pleasure was in German: "*Mundharmonica*." (Benjamin was referring to the harmonica that he loved blowing on.) He couldn't stop giggling as he pattered through a succession of transformations. "Mendhermenece, mondhormonoco, mandharmanaca…"

I laughed too and couldn't help being impressed by Benjamin's capacity for word-play. "He *is* intelligent," I thought. "Although 'ordinary' things require endless drilling, Benjamin has his own set of talents."

Rick, Benjamin, and I were attending a small dinner party at a friend's house, and after everyone had finished eating, Benjamin expressed his willingness to perform a few songs on the piano. He had recently figured out how to play a melody with his right hand while simultaneously playing a chordal accompaniment with his left hand, and I had been amazed by this progress; we had been spending very little time at the keyboard together.

Benjamin clambered up on the piano bench and proceeded to play with great accuracy and confidence. When we all burst into applause after his first little song, Benjamin looked surprised at the clapping noise—it came as a sudden deluge—but then, when he had come nearly to the end of his second song, he began looking over his shoulder at us, smiling with anticipation, obviously delighted at the prospect of another ovation. The frequent praise and applause that he received from me during our work sessions was finding transference, and now Benjamin appeared as a born performer, craving accolades from an audience.

Benjamin and I were sitting across from one another in the playhouse, reviewing our latest language drills. "Is this a spoon?" I asked. "No, it's a fork," Benjamin corrected me. Smiling and nodding my approval, I glanced at Rick who was relaxing nearby. "Did you hear that? When you got here two weeks ago, the concept of negating—of saying 'no' about something—was still an enormous struggle. Now, Benjamin is becoming confident with it."

Turning back to Benjamin, I held up a wooden giraffe. "Say, *I know what that is. It's a _____.*" Benjamin repeated the phrase, supplying the correct label. "Good job. Now look here. *What is this?*" I held up a kitchen implement. Benjamin remained silent, and I prompted him. "Say, *'I don't know. What is it?'*" Benjamin echoed me, and we kept repeating the verbal exchange until he could remember the entire phrase. Then I finally answered the question. "It's a whisk, for stirring and mixing."

In this way, we were steadily working our way through the outline of language programs found in *Let Me Hear Your Voice*. When starting in on new concepts and phrases, I found that the cozy setting of the playhouse helped Benjamin to focus, its close walls and low roof creating a feeling of protection, like a nest. But soon, Benjamin would have to fly, to start using his newest words in the realistic situations that I would set up for him.

The day before Rick was due to depart back to Whidbey Island, I made a proposal. "I think we should get a cat for Benjamin." Rick reacted cautiously, fearing I might get carried away by my characteristic enthusiasm for animal companions. "Don't you have enough work on your hands without another animal to take care of?"

I elaborated on the reasons for my idea. "Walker is a sweet dog, and Benjamin likes him, but I don't sense a real connection between them. An affectionate cat would sit on Benjamin's lap. He needs that kind of cuddling—sharing space with a warm, furry being."

During a spur-of-the-moment visit to our local humane society, a mellow orange tabby with light-green eyes caught my attention. Something about this feline gave me an inexplicably good feeling and, after a few minutes of interaction, my mind was made up. I filled out the animal adoption papers, and we headed home, brainstorming names for our new family member. "Mandarin, that's perfect...more elegant than Pumpkin."

Once home, we introduced Mandarin to his new living space, and then I called Benjamin over to sit on the couch. He allowed me to place the cat on his tummy, and when I encouraged Benjamin to pet the silky soft fur, Mandarin began to purr, utterly relaxed, enjoying Benjamin's attentions. After a while, Benjamin scrunched down, attempting to look directly into the cat's contentedly slitted eyes. "Meow, Mandarin," Benjamin said then, talking to his new friend and putting out a careful finger to explore the cat's wiry whiskers. "Meow. Meow, Mandarin."

Watching, I felt deep satisfaction at Benjamin's spontaneous communication; a bond was forming before my very eyes. We had found the perfect therapy pet.

At school, Talia had asked if I could help out, baking with the children while she worked with two girls in the playroom, finishing their Valentine's projects. Now I was showing the little group how to roll out cookie dough. "No more bites of raw dough," I reminded the girls. "Benjamin, you too, that was the last bite."

Benjamin began screeching a little in protest. After a week of calm, he was once again in an autistic downturn, hopping and flapping excessively, and having difficulty staying connected. "Hold your ears," one of the girls suddenly called out, a mischievous glint in her eye. The others followed her example, giggling excitedly, hands to ears, eyes fixed on Benjamin. He stood, facing them, looking shocked.

Perceiving that the entire group was laughing at him, Benjamin crumpled and broke down sobbing, hiding his face in his hands. I too felt shattered at the moment of cruelty and, abandoning the baking project, cradled Benjamin as he cried inconsolably. "What a mistake," I thought. "I should have spoken up, told Talia that I didn't feel comfortable leading the group. My gut feeling was that Benjamin needed extra support today, and I should have honored that."

That night, Benjamin fell asleep quickly, overcome by weariness, but after a few hours, he awakened, screaming and crying piteously. My heart was heavy as I held him, rocking him back to sleep. Benjamin had never had a nightmare before, and I felt sure that the morning's events at school had come back to haunt him.

In typical Colorado fashion, the weather was fluctuating crazily between days of balmy warmth and days where low-hanging clouds sent snowflakes drifting into a cutting chill. The fluctuating barometric pressure was taking Benjamin and me for a ride, causing excessive moodiness in both of us.

As Benjamin seemed mired by fatigue and disinterest in our therapy work, I compensated by jumping from one exercise to the next in a playful manner, not dwelling for long on any one activity. "Careful, keep it light," I admonished myself. "Don't insist on working until you get results; just touch on things."

I pulled out the set of wooden "castle blocks" I had recently purchased, encouraging Benjamin to simply watch as I constructed an elaborate fortress with towers and crenelated turrets. Then, using the set's collection of wooden horses and knights, I acted out the basic storyline of *St. George and the Dragon*. Benjamin was already familiar with the tale; I had recently found a beautifully illustrated version and had been reading it to him.

I didn't pressure Benjamin to participate, thinking, "I just want to give him the big picture of what can be done with these blocks. If Benjamin can see what the overall goal is, then practicing the individual steps of construction or storytelling will make more sense." I had previously made the mistake of pushing Benjamin to help me with castle building without first demonstrating the possibilities, and Benjamin had had a complete meltdown. Now I offered him some treats to snack on while watching me, mindful of keeping up his energy and building a positive association with the activity.

As the week went by and Benjamin generally resisted engagement, I kept a tight leash on myself as anger flared repeatedly. "We need to get out and away for a little," I thought finally, worn out by the continual head-butting. I phoned my parents. "Let's all go to the reservoir north of town for a walk and a picnic."

When we arrived, I breathed in deeply. The fresh, tangy smell of lake water mixed with the scent of rotting vegetation, and the rich aroma of adjacent cow and horse pastures floated in on a bracing breeze. A gull's piercing shriek rent the air, and a small flock of Canada geese honked nearby; I could barely see them amongst the reeds of a protective inlet. The unique smells and sounds of this water ecosystem were transporting me, making me feel like I was on a mini-vacation.

As we walked, with Benjamin running on ahead through a stand of cattails, I cleared myself of tension and after a while, fresh thoughts came to me. "Maybe I need to change my approach," I told my parents. "Benjamin has become more decisive when he says 'no' and 'I don't want to,' and he is getting more specific about voicing his desires. Perhaps I need to give him some space to unfold rather than constantly feeding in skills and information. He might also be in need of some assimilation time; we've been working hard on certain concepts, and he's finally gotten the hang of them." I mulled this over and then concluded, "Benjamin's fixations will need monitoring, but I'll try backing off our 'program' and see what happens."

Three days of rollercoaster moods went by, with ear piercing screeches marking the lowest points, but I stuck with my new resolution to give Benjamin room. On the fourth day, something shifted and, right after returning from our morning walk, Benjamin astounded me by *initiating* a play session. "I want to play *One and Many*," he announced, pulling out the appropriate box of picture cards. After appropriately matching up numerous sets of cards on his own, he decided, "I want the insect dominoes." My heart leapt as Benjamin began laying out dominoes, matching ladybugs to one another, adding a grasshopper in the right place, and hunting for another dragonfly to match up with the end of the sequence that he had been building. "This is a 'first'," I thought, marveling at Benjamin's unprecedented display of intrinsic motivation.

Partway through the morning, one of the little girls from preschool arrived to play with Benjamin. I had identified Lily as being the most accepting and easygoing child in the preschool group and had invited her over. Lily became immediately engrossed in our inviting collection of toys, acting out scenes with the figures in the dollhouse, playing dress-up, constructing a store, and occasionally narrating her actions. Throughout, Benjamin sat in close proximity, dumping and refilling various baskets of toys. While neither of them interacted much with the other, I could see that Lily's presence was making quite an impression on Benjamin; he seemed bemused by how comfortably she took up playing with his toys and belongings.

Once Lily had gone and we had eaten lunch, Benjamin resumed the initiative he had shown earlier in the morning. He continued pursuing one exercise or game after another, and I remained largely passive as before. I didn't direct him, didn't try to keep him on task, didn't shape his actions—I merely responded to Benjamin's occasional requests. I could hardly believe how well things were going. I had apparently made the right decision in changing my approach and now, together, Benjamin and I were reaping some rewards.

I sent up a silent "thank you," feeling that, as was so often the case, inspiration to do something different had come to me as a gift. Day after day, I was being called upon to rely on myself, to observe, analyze, and problem-solve, to teach and to love. And, when I remembered to remain open and receptive to guidance "from above," then I also "heard" what was being whispered in my direction.

The next day brought more wonderful surprises. The first thing Benjamin said after awakening was, "I want to play with play-dough." Sure enough, he went for the bucket and dug his hands into the rosemary-scented stuff I had kneaded into proper consistency months earlier. After breakfast, Benjamin pulled out the *Mystery Garden* board game and started playing solo, saying both his and my parts of our usual, scripted dialogue. Barely able to contain my delight, I nevertheless held back from joining Benjamin, reminding myself, "Wait for an invitation."

Of his own volition, Benjamin kept moving through a variety of games while I remained on the periphery, only stepping forward to intercept Benjamin's occasional forays to the humidifier buttons or light switches. Eventually, Benjamin knelt down in front of the dollhouse. He picked up the daddy-doll and began manipulating the figure, saying, "He wants to sit. He wants to sleep. He is eating salad." Then Benjamin inspected the daddy-doll's clothes, wondering whether they could be removed.

A shiver of happy excitement went through me as I watched Benjamin narrating his actions. He seemed to be imitating Lily's style of doll-play from the previous day, and I was thrilled that the daddy-doll had caught Benjamin's particular interest; this was proof to me that his bond with Rick was getting stronger with each successive visit.

That afternoon, Benjamin became inexplicably interested in a pair of wide curtains that hid an attic closet niche from view. He disappeared behind one of the curtains, and I could see the cloth moving around as Benjamin made his way along the length of it. Then he reappeared at the other end, eyes shining with discovery. I exclaimed, "Peekaboo."

Benjamin gave a delighted little hop and disappeared back behind the curtain. When he emerged from the other end, he looked at me and, with his usual choppy and precise diction directed, "I want you to say 'Peek-a-boo'." He emphasized the long, drawn out "*ee*."

So now I had a job to do. Back and forth Benjamin went, joyful in his game, reveling in the sound of my enthusiastic "peek-a-boos." Then suddenly, he stopped stock still and announced, "I want to drive through the tunnel," before diving back behind the nearest curtain.

My jaw dropped, and then I did a little celebratory dance in place, my heart chiming with the wonder of it. "A little fantasy, a real moment of imaginative transformation—and created entirely by Benjamin with no help from me. Yahoo!"

Near the end of February, I invited my parents and a few family friends over for a Mardi Gras party, wanting to introduce Benjamin to the high-jinks atmosphere that traditionally accompanies this celebration. Benjamin was costumed as a clown, and I had painted his face before taking him to look in a mirror. At first, Benjamin seemed uncertain, thrown by the unfamiliar image in the glass, but then he pulled a silly smile and looked flirtatiously at himself, turning his face this way and that, experimenting with various expressions. I stood by, charmed by Benjamin's playful interaction with the twin clown in the mirror.

Once our guests arrived, Benjamin surprised everyone with his animated sociability; he was thriving on the party atmosphere, and there were no overt signs of his autism. The highpoint of the evening came when my mom bent towards Benjamin, smiling at him while slowly hiding her face behind a strange and sinister mask. Benjamin became silently wide-eyed with astonishment. Unable to fathom the transformation, he carefully tiptoed around behind my mom to ascertain whether she was still present or whether some dangerous foreigner had somehow taken over. He continued looking baffled, and when the masked face turned to glance back at him, his misgivings grew. Only when the disguise eventually slipped, revealing my mom's familiar face, did Benjamin's unease finally resolve itself. As my sides ached with laughing, I counted my blessings. "What a gift to witness the magic that can occur in a child's mind."

During our month's end visit with Cheryl, she commented on the remarkably "open" feel within Benjamin's head, contrasting it with the tension that was typical for him. Now, as we left her office building, Benjamin began spitting repeatedly, and I had to laugh. "I know, you are copying Mommy," I said, acknowledging the source of this behavior. Weeks earlier, I had hawked and spit during a trail walk, trying to rid myself of the unpleasant postnasal congestion brought on by a cold. "No more spitting now, we're getting into the car," I requested.

On arriving home, Benjamin was drawn to observing Walker who was drinking noisily, his pink tongue lapping up water from a stainless steel dog dish. After Walker had slaked his thirst, Benjamin got down on all fours and began copying the dog, licking at the water's surface and then spitting into the bowl.

"Honey," I exclaimed, delighted with Benjamin's desire to imitate. "Let me give you a dog bowl of your own." Benjamin giggled and gleefully spent the next forty-five minutes "drinking," spitting, and asking for refills. The scene was very funny, and I was happy to indulge Benjamin's inclination—he was playing imaginatively and was simultaneously working on the coordination and strength of his oral faculties. Then, once Benjamin had tired of his spitting game, I suggested that we read together.

"I want *Is Your Mama a Wama*," Benjamin requested.

"*Llama*, not 'Wama'," I corrected. "Watch me: *l-l-l-l-l*." Obediently, Benjamin looked. For months, I had been demonstrating how to correctly shape the "*l*" sound. "Keep your tongue flat—like this. *Aaaah*. Now touch just the tip behind your front teeth." Benjamin carefully followed my lead, and suddenly I heard it: "*L-l-l-l-l*." No more nasal sound, no more squashed and incorrectly placed tongue.

"That's it, that's it, good job, yahoo," I praised, whooping joyfully, and Benjamin repeated the vocalization, correctly intoning the consonant. "*L-l-l-llama*," he said carefully and giggled as I caught him up in an enthusiastic bear-hug. Another longstanding mini-challenge had been overcome.

17

Back To Work
March 1998

Benjamin's happy and expansive mood had now extended for a period of three weeks, providing me with an unprecedented sense of normalcy as we flowed through our daily activities. As sunny skies and balmy breezes prevailed, I planned various outings and incidentally discovered new avenues for addressing Benjamin's sensory issues.

Benjamin and I joined with my parents in exploring new hiking trails, and on these occasions, Benjamin insisted on carrying the heavy family backpack, filled with water bottles and snacks. "He clearly craves the feeling of weight and compression on his shoulders and back," I observed to my parents. "It must make him feel grounded." Benjamin had such a tendency to flit and flutter that weighing him down with the backpack was having a soothing counter effect. Benjamin hiked along, happy and relaxed, pointing out moss, bits of white quartz, flying crows, and deer droppings.

We also made several visits to a local goat dairy and, while Benjamin was initially fearful around the bouncy baby goats, I kept guiding him to pet them and snuggle with them. Soon, their antics had Benjamin giggling, and he began mimicking their bleating, sidling up to them in hopes that they would rear up and give him a "hug"—which they obligingly did. Eventually, Benjamin even began cutting capers of his own, clearly inspired by his new animal friends.

Benjamin and I were in Corinne's therapy room, discussing ways of expanding Benjamin's capacity for back-and-forth conversation. "Let's try playing 'conversation ball'," Corinne suggested. "Sit on the ground and stretch your legs out to form a 'V'." I situated myself, and Corinne guided Benjamin to do the same, but sitting down opposite to me. "We are going to have a simple dialogue, and whoever is speaking will roll the ball to the other person," Corinne instructed.

"Benjamin," I exclaimed, rolling the ball to him.

Corinne helped him to roll it back as she modeled the desired response. "What?"

We repeated this until Benjamin understood that he was to answer while sending the ball back to me.

Now Corinne explained further. "You can work on any ordinary conversational exchange in this manner. Make sure Benjamin is energetic in rolling the ball so that his words 'ride' upon the physical impetus of the action. Later, when Benjamin is ready, you can *toss* the ball—or you might want to use a beanbag—and you can move farther apart from one another so that more energy is required in tossing. The game provides a literal illustration of how communication operates, of how we exchange ideas and take turns listening and talking. Also, the integration of speech with directed movement will give Benjamin the experience of focused intention."

I nodded my understanding as Corinne went on. "Another variation of the game is to use familiar Mother Goose rhymes and to work on smooth, continuous exchanges: you would say the first line, then Benjamin would continue with the next line, you would take the third line, and so on."

"I love it," I exclaimed, envisioning the expansive possibilities of the game. "What a great way to engage willpower and foster connection."

Close to mid-month, I got the feeling that we needed to get back to "work." Benjamin was running out of play impulses, and the novelty of acting as leader seemed to be wearing thin. As I began reintroducing daily violin practices, I hit upon a new idea. Pulling out Benjamin's favorite booklet of Mother Goose rhymes, I opened the page to *Jack be nimble, Jack be quick, / Jack jump over the candlestick,* and placed it on our music stand. Benjamin looked at the comical picture and observed, "That's Jack."

"Yes, you're right. How about if we play this rhyme as a song," I suggested and made up a simple melodic pattern. After singing my invented tune for Benjamin, I demonstrated by playing it on his little violin and then handed him the instrument. "Now it's your turn," I declared, and Benjamin reached out his hands, ready to try.

"You're doing a wonderful job," I praised as we worked out the playing of the new song. Then I turned the page.

"That's Lucy Locket," Benjamin exclaimed.

"Right. Just a moment." I hummed and experimented, then decided to make this rhyme into an easy finger exercise. I chanted the verse while Benjamin played, getting a thorough technique workout without any sense of tedium. Next came *"The Queen of Hearts, / She baked some tarts..."* and Benjamin happily plied his bow, stroking along in rhythm to my chanting.

"How exciting," I thought. "I can make up all kinds of basic exercises, and they'll never get dull—not with these wonderful pictures and verses being associated with them."

Talia and I had recently discussed Benjamin's inherent gentleness and the likelihood of his getting pushed around by peers if he didn't learn to use some verbal phrases in self-defense. So now, at preschool, I was prompting Benjamin to say, *"I want this... I don't like that... I'm sorry... Please move... Can I have a turn?"* At home, I began using dolls to show Benjamin how certain interactions might require assertiveness. In addition, when we worked on playing with toys, I was purposely *not* always helpful to Benjamin. For example, when I handed him a toy, I wouldn't relinquish it until he looked at me saying, *"Can I have a turn?"* Sometimes I pushed him around a bit and cued him to say things like *"stop that"* and *"don't push."* At other times, I would grab at a toy in his hands so that he could practice phrases such as *"please give it back"* or *"it's my turn."*

I was once again striving to infuse Benjamin's speech with emotion and inflection, experimenting with something called "eurythmy." This expressive movement art is commonly practiced in Waldorf schools and involves specific gestures that correlate to the sounds of speech. I was familiar with the five arm motions that correlated to the five pure vowel sounds—*ah, eh, ee, oh, oo*—and I was teaching Benjamin one of my favorite morning poems, accompanying the words with clear eurythmy gestures as we stood in a patch of golden sunshine.

> *Sonne, Sonne, komm hervor*
> *Aus des Himmels goldnem Tor.*
> *Strahle mich so lange an,*
> *Bis ich mit dir strahlen kann.*
> *(Hedwig Distel)*

> *Sun, sun, come on forth,*
> *From the heavens' golden gates.*
> *Send your gleaming rays to me*
> *Until I too am shining bright.*
> *(my translation)*

I stood across from Benjamin and began. *"Sonne, Sonne..."* I intoned, making an "O" shape with my arms above my head, aware that the gesture was one of capturing and then containing energy. As the poem continued with *"komm hervor,"* I gracefully moved the "O" shape to heart level, holding the energy there with intention and awareness. There were many O sounds in that one line of verse.

Next came, *"Aus des Himmels goldnem Tor."* The *"ee"* sound of Himmel was expressed with one arm pointing upward and the other downward. I quickly stroked Benjamin's opposing arms, helping him to feel the energy flowing outward from his center and through each arm. I thought of the *"ee"* sound as the sense of *"me,* myself," centered between opposing forces, simultaneously striving upwards and reaching for inspiration while also remaining grounded, anchored to the earth. Then came "O" again, for the words *"goldnem Tor."* *"Strahle..."* *"Ah"* was the next sound, one of wonder and openness, the arms radiating out at an angle that reflected the shape of the capital letter "A." Moving on, I chose only the most prominent vowel sounds, placing their correlating gestures either low down, at heart level, or high up, depending on how they might best flow from one to the next. With the final two words came clear *"ah"* sounds which imparted a feeling of awe, and I felt that both in gesture and sound, we were representing the light that comes from within.

Benjamin had entered a new phase where he frequently flopped to the floor and was reluctant to engage in anything, needing me to generate interest and excitement. Now I was racking my brain for inspiration. My ideas flowed more easily if there was something coming from Benjamin and, at the moment, he wasn't giving me much to work with.

"Let's play 'going to the store,' like the children do at school," I suggested. This would be a stretch for Benjamin, but I felt it was time to try acting out simple scenarios as an extension of the work we had been doing with the dollhouse figurines. "Get into your car," I directed, showing Benjamin how to hold a pretend steering wheel and drive around. I showed him how to mime exchanging money for an object and helped him to pretend wrapping it up as a gift. Then I helped Benjamin back into his invisible car.

After a few rounds of playing store, Benjamin picked up one of the brightly colored writing implements I had collected for our "shop." He held it up, inspecting its point and requesting, "I want paper; I want to write." I handed over a notepad, happy that Benjamin's energy had been sparked by our work session. He sat down, and I helped him wrap his fingers around the pencil. Then, with intense concentration, Benjamin began tracing assorted small crosses and other shapes. "This is my shopping list," he announced and began making squiggly lines that snaked horizontally across the paper in imitation of cursive script. I watched, astonished. This was Benjamin's first try at writing, and he was already making neat, precise marks that looked like actual letters.

As March came to a close, I began dragging under the cumulative strain of having to generate enough energy to carry both Benjamin and me through each day of therapy work. Benjamin's moods kept mirroring the crazy weather typical of a Colorado spring, and I was exhausted from juggling the many proverbial balls that were part of my daily circus.

Keeping up with household chores was an ongoing struggle, and I now felt mired in my nightly efforts to rework the initial rough draft of my book manuscript. I was rehearsing and performing with the Boulder Philharmonic Orchestra on a regular basis and, while I was thankful for the opportunity to get out of the house to make music with colleagues, I was overextended by the attendant responsibility of practicing on my own time. It was all simply too much.

How I longed to shed my ever-present concerns about Benjamin's autism and to be like other parents. Surely they could shrug off their children's low days rather than feeling persecuted by fear every time that a bump in the road came up. Living with this thing called "autism" was like living with an insidious monster that shadowed me day and night without respite. My sense of perspective was becoming habitually skewed, and I was finding it increasingly difficult to salvage my inner equilibrium. "I'm losing my resilience," I thought, feeling threadbare and vulnerable, recognizing that my personal monster of depression was gradually insinuating itself into my depths. How was I going to manage?

18

"April Showers Bring..."
April 1998

Corinne was loaning me a book that was fresh off the press. *"Biological Treatments of Autism and PDD,* by William Shaw," I read before thumbing through the pages and examining the table of contents. That evening, I perused the chapter on removing gluten and casein (dairy protein) from the autistic person's diet. Apparently these substances could act as *opiates* and thereby slow down brain functioning. "Ah-ha," I thought. "That's what I observed in Benjamin when I tried giving him goat milk yogurt last month as an experiment; he got all slow and floppy, and started spinning things again. Now I know why." My instinctive decisions to keep Benjamin's diet free of dairy and gluten had been sound.

Once I had read through the book, I decided to proceed with the various recommended blood and urine tests, hoping to gain further insight into Benjamin's physiological functioning and encouraged by the possibility of reducing his autistic symptoms. Within a few days, we were in the doctor's office for a blood draw. I expected things to go smoothly since Benjamin had already experienced the procedure during our lead abatement project, but this time, the attending nurse (who was new to us) seemed insensitive to the needs of a child. When her poking and prodding resulted in a collapsed vein, I began asking questions. Couldn't we see a pediatric nurse?

Rescheduled for the next day, Benjamin was understandably panicky when we arrived at the medical center. His fear was contagious, and I began pulling in deep breaths, trying to keep calm for him. Benjamin cried and struggled against the kind nurse's soothing ministrations, and it soon became clear that, if we expected to get this blood draw done, some adroit teamwork would be called for.

As I got Benjamin to lie back on the padded exam table, I leaned on him gently yet firmly, using my body weight to immobilize him so that he couldn't squirm away from the needle. He was shaking with fear, and my tears of empathy overflowed as I repeatedly sang Benjamin's favorite lullaby, my face just inches from his, trying to draw his attention to the song while simultaneously blocking his view of the nurse's activity with the needle. An assistant had been called in to further stabilize Benjamin's arm, and now the primary nurse successfully slipped the slender "butterfly needle" into Benjamin's vein. After an intense few minutes that made me think of an emergency room, we had managed to get the necessary blood samples.

I released Benjamin from the pressure of my body and quickly scooped him into my arms, rocking him and humming a song as he trembled from his harrowing ordeal. "This will surely have repercussions," I thought then, and indeed, over the next few months, Benjamin would become terrified around any building that resembled the medical center. For a time, he would also express fear at his cranio-sacral therapy sessions since Cheryl's padded massage table reminded him of the exam table in the doctor's office. A single bad experience could do a mountain of damage.

I had forced myself out of bed and into the kitchen to make breakfast, feeling like a wrung out washrag. My upper back and arms were sore, my mind felt dull, and I was acutely aware of the cumulative effect that successive nights of orchestra rehearsals and performances had wrought in combination with insufficient sleep. "Hopefully, Benjamin will be easy on me," I thought, stumbling around, getting ready for the day. No such luck. Benjamin awoke before I was ready for him, and I was struck by his immediate and intense need to fixate on switches, buttons, and handles. The autism monster was taking over once again.

"We'll get out of the house as soon as possible," I thought, and the moment we had finished eating, I suggested, "Benjamin, let's go to the park." As we headed out the door, Benjamin tripped over his own feet and fell hard. Then, scrambling up from the floor, he banged his head against the edge of the door and then again on the door knob. He began to cry. "Oh, honey, my honey-bear-boy," I soothed trying to comfort him.

We got down the stairs without mishap, but once we were at the park, Benjamin tripped again and fell. A bit later, he crawled under some of the playground equipment, then tried to stand up before he had quite made it out from under, bonking his head hard for a second time. "Ouch," I thought, cringing, hearing the dull, metallic ringing of the equipment as Benjamin's skull made contact. What was going on? Benjamin was usually quite coordinated.

For the remainder of that entire day, Benjamin repeatedly ran into walls and furniture, bumping his head or falling down, seemingly disoriented, as if he had lost connection with his own body and was experiencing the world in a warped manner. "Like entering one of those crazy, distorting mirror rooms at a carnival or circus—he doesn't know which way is up," I thought. I had never seen Benjamin behave this way before.

The next day we were back at the park and, while yesterday's physical mishaps now seemed forgotten, Benjamin began displaying a new, bizarre behavior: he became extremely agitated whenever children came to play nearby, squeaking "No!" in a choked and fearful voice, and then running away so fast that he practically skimmed the ground. Having put a generous distance between himself and the oblivious children, he would turn to look back, assuring himself that no one was in pursuit. I gaped slack-jawed with disbelief, observing the scene as it repeated itself several times. My suspicion rested on the new homeopathic remedy that Benjamin had received three days earlier, and after we returned home, I called Julie.

She listened to my description of Benjamin's spacial disorientation and paranoia, then offered me an explanation. "As with standard medications, people sometimes have adverse reactions to particular homeopathics. I agree, this single-dose remedy seems to be having an irritating effect, although by every indication, it should have been a good fit. Even so, the possibility remains that once Benjamin recovers his equilibrium, he will actually be in a better state. Remember, this has already happened several times over the past year. Let's wait things out." This all made sense but offered scant comfort; I dreaded the possibility of the next two weeks being unimaginably awful.

Benjamin was now like a ping-pong ball, bouncing between extremes of behavior. One afternoon, I dropped him off to do some handcrafts with my mom while I ran necessary errands, and when I came back after an hour, Benjamin was sitting with the weaving loom on his lap. He looked directly at me, radiating pride and joy, his smile lighting up his entire being as my mom declared, "Look, Benjamin has woven two inches worth of cloth, and he has been doing it all alone." I stepped closer to see.

"How wonderful," I enthused. "Show me, big boy." Benjamin complied, leaning over his weaving in concentration. I watched as he flawlessly manipulated the shuttle through the "harp strings" of the weaving loom, saying, "Sssstop," as he pulled his colorful yarn through horizontally, stopping before it became too tight. Then he intoned, "Make a mountain." Benjamin shaped the line of yarn into a generous curve and then used his fingers to push it downward, making a line of little mountain peaks. Finally, he carefully flattened these peaks, just as Oma had taught him. I was entranced, watching Benjamin's contented absorption and focus.

As his fingers manipulated the new stretch of yarn, integrating it with the already woven fabric, Benjamin glanced back up at me. His eyes stopped short of meeting mine, and the blissful look disappeared from his face. I had the sensation of a happy enchantment being shattered as Benjamin's gaze became rigid. His eyes were fastened on my waist, on the decorative buckle of the western-style belt I was wearing.

As if drawn by an irresistible force, Benjamin popped up, upsetting his loom and reaching for my belt, grabbing at the buckle and trying to manipulate it. Everything around him receded to unimportance, and the shiny, metallic form became the irresistible center of his universe. Wanting to avoid an abrupt and potentially traumatic transition, I allowed Benjamin to play with the buckle a bit before trying to divert him in a playful way. However, he was not about to cooperate and, when I finally insisted on loosening his fingers from their stranglehold, he began screeching like a banshee. Misery washed over me, and I wanted to cry. Autism was sidelining my sweet boy so often these days, and it was breaking my heart, over and over again.

A late-Friday therapy session with Cheryl had released much tension in Benjamin, and over the Easter weekend, he remained relaxed and contented. On Sunday morning, my parents hid brightly colored Easter eggs throughout their sprouting garden, and I began teaching Benjamin how to hunt for the pretty, oval things. After a bit, he caught on and began actively scanning the ground, bushes, and flower patches, while my parents and I gave him hints on where to search.

"Look at these red tulips," I called, standing by a group of stately flowers. Benjamin came over, and I encouraged him to bend over and sniff, hoping that he would spot the green plastic egg nestled amongst elegantly pointed leaves. Finally, he perceived the egg and pounced on it, pulling its two halves apart to reveal a piece of dried, organic fruit.

As Benjamin became increasingly confident and enthusiastic in his search for eggs, my mom nudged me, whispering. "Remember how it was last year? What a difference." I smiled at her, thinking back to our February arrival in Boulder and the neighborhood egg hunt that had occurred six weeks later. Even the youngest toddlers had excitedly gathered the shiny, foil-wrapped eggs which were strewn about in full view. Meanwhile, Benjamin had stood by, looking vacant, neither attracted by the colorful eggs, nor capable of understanding what was going on. It had been a sad moment of exclusion. But now, having reached age three-and-a-half, Benjamin was able to actively participate in our family egg hunt, albeit with much assistance.

The weekend had provided a brief respite from the past month's-worth of struggles. But Monday morning brought the return of intense fixations and the renewal of extreme, self-stimulatory behaviors. I was now seeing a resurgence of the vigorous rocking that Benjamin had so frequently indulged in when he had been much younger and small enough to be strapped into a sturdy high chair. Now Benjamin had an adult chair to sit in during mealtimes, and his violent rocking was loosening the seat's wooden joints, making it creak in protest.

Kicking was the latest addition to Benjamin's repertoire of "self-stims" and so now, in addition to rocking, he was also thumping his feet against chair and table in a continuous, irritating rhythm. At bedtime, he would lie back and bang his feet on the walls surrounding the bed and already, the plaster was beginning to crack. I wanted to pull out my hair with frustration. How could I keep Benjamin from destroying our house and furniture?

I remembered the child-sized plastic picnic table with attached benches that I had once fished from someone's discard pile, thinking it would be ideal for messy arts and crafts. I dragged the ugly thing into our dining room. "Here, Benjamin, this will be your new place for mealtimes," I announced, feeling vindicated when I settled Benjamin on one of the immovable benches and saw that he was somewhat stymied in his kicking and rocking. Then, I moved Benjamin's bed into the middle of the attic bedroom, away from its cozy nook. Now Benjamin could bang his feet on the mattress, and the walls would be saved from further damage.

That evening, after I had put Benjamin to bed, I came back into the living room and sat down heavily on the couch. There were still a few things to be done before I headed to bed myself: dishes to be washed, the dog to be walked, the cat-litter box to be taken care of, toys to be cleared away, and a brief journal entry to be written. But I just sat there, feeling numb.

"Come on," I urged myself. "Get up, it isn't that much, you'll be in bed within the hour if you get going." My body refused to obey, and my mind felt like it was drowning in a thick fog; I simply could not make myself care or move. My bones had turned to jelly, and I felt disembodied. So I just kept sitting there, knowing that I needed to get some sleep, wishing that someone big and strong would appear to pick me up, undress me, and tuck me into bed like a baby.

I continued to sit, bereft of willpower, sagging into myself as the mantel clock ticked off the minutes. Eventually, there was a little "*mrreow.*" Barely capable of tuning in to the sound, I heard it as if through layers of cotton batting. Mandarin hopped up onto the futon and, seeming to sense my acute state of depression, began kneading my thigh with his paws and purring sympathetically. I dug my hand into Mandarin's soft fur, feeling the comforting warmth of his body and wishing that I could cry and melt into sleep, but no...

My emotions were as in a deep winter freeze, and nothing was stirring in my heart.

The next several days crawled by in a haze of depression, and I managed only the most imperative tasks. Journal entries were out of the question, and the house quickly began looking like a pigpen as I focused on getting some extra sleep, allowing myself an earlier bedtime rather than cleaning things up at the end of each day. After three days of increased sleep, I began feeling somewhat alive again and returned to working with Benjamin.

"Same or different?" I asked as we sat at his little table in the playhouse.

Benjamin looked at the two objects in front of him. "Diff-e-rent," he enunciated carefully.

"Good job. How many pieces?" I laid out three colorful beads.

"One, two, three," Benjamin counted.

"Well done, sweetheart. Tell me about yourself. Are you a girl? Are you a boy? What color is your hair? What color are your pants?" With some prompting, Benjamin came up with the correct answers, remembering the scripted drills we had been practicing off and on during the past few weeks.

"Thank goodness," I thought, relieved that Benjamin was cooperating and that the weather was fine. The sun was shining through the living room windows, and the feeling of inner darkness that had so oppressed me was clearly receding. Musingly, I thought, "I lost all sense-of-self for a while...was so gone, that I was *nothing*. Scary. I'm glad the real me is coming back."

The "real" Benjamin was coming back too. Whilst I had been in my own fog, Benjamin's extreme levels of self-stimulation and fixation had settled down a bit, and he now seemed sunnier and more receptive to interaction. He was making interesting observations as well.

"The floor has an owie," Benjamin announced, looking across the room to where the baseboard heater met the floor. I followed his gaze and saw the melted drips of a bright red crayon staining the hardwood floorboards, making it look like blood was welling up from some small injury. A chuckle bubbled up inside me, and gradually I began giggling, then laughing for real, hugging my precious boy to me. "You're a little poet. Thank you for making Mommy laugh and be happy again."

That evening, I got Benjamin into bed early and began cleaning up the house. On the morrow, Rick would be arriving for a five-day visit, and I dreaded having him see everything so out of control, although it would be worse for him to see me re-flattened by lack of sleep. However, it was one thing to be telling him about the situation on the phone, asking for understanding and sympathy, and it was quite another to have him actually see things coming apart at the seams. Rick was dealing with his own feelings of depression and loneliness, living far away from us in a small and impersonal navy barracks room, working hard to support us from afar while receiving none of the warmth of hugs and interaction that were part of being a family. I desperately wanted Rick to walk into our Boulder home and to feel like he was stepping into an inviting place rather than arriving at a disaster zone.

Rick's parents had joined us for the afternoon—they hadn't seen the three of us since Christmas—and I was filling them in on Benjamin's progress. They seemed nonplussed by my detailed analyses of Benjamin's language development, and they spoke reassuringly. "Benjamin seems just fine, no real problems. He's so affectionate." Well. Just now, Benjamin was "on," and I could understand why he didn't strike them as being much different from other three-year-olds. I knew they couldn't fathom the intensity of what our autism therapy entailed, and I had no desire to give them the gory details. "No one can *really* imagine it," I thought. "Not unless they are going through it themselves."

I fleetingly recalled the terrible state I had been in only a scant week ago. The memory had an eerie strangeness to it, a quality of unreality and drama that was nearly unfathomable. Just now, happily distracted by the atmosphere of conviviality, it hardly seemed possible that I had been laid so low.

Benjamin diverted me from my deliberations. I had served him a glass of juice, and now he was blowing bubbles in it. "I'm pre-ten-ding it's a swimming pool," he said, and as we all cracked up laughing, I commented, "The other day, Benjamin observed paper floating in the toilet bowl and then told me, 'It's swimming in the ocean'."

Benjamin had just begun making such statements, displaying the beginnings of symbolic thinking. Since autism would tend to cause very concrete and literal use of language, Benjamin's small forays into poetic interpretations of the world were an exciting new step.

We had been on spring break while Rick was visiting, and now preschool had resumed. As Benjamin remembered our language drills and spontaneously asked for some toys, the children he was talking to refused to share. "How frustrating," I thought, seeking to intervene. "Adults are predictable while children are not. Benjamin is just getting the hang of asking, expecting to get a positive response, and now he is being confronted by the fact that individuals have minds of their own. At this stage, he needs to be rewarded so that he'll keep trying, keep applying what he's learning. But I'd better start drilling some alternate phrases for situations that require negotiation; difficult for any young child, but infinitely more so for one with autism."

Finally, playtime was over, and it was time for snack. After the steaming oatmeal with raisins had been ladled into each child's bowl, it was time for the usual blessing, and before Talia could choose a child to lead the song, Benjamin spontaneously began singing the simple melody, enunciating beautifully, his clear voice a joy to hear.

I was beaming with pride when Benjamin suddenly broke into tears and screams. The little girl sitting across from him had been making silly faces, and I sensed that Benjamin had interpreted her to be making fun of him and was once again feeling shattered. From my standpoint, the child's silliness had been coincidental, but this became irrelevant as Benjamin shrieked, cried, growled, and roared, remaining inconsolable long after the other children finished eating and went outside to play.

This was no ordinary tantrum. Instead, Benjamin had been struck to the core and was now expressing his devastation. He had been spiritually wounded at a moment when he was most open and vulnerable—while being carried along on the wings of song.

"April showers bring May flowers," I thought as the month came to a close. The loveliness of blue skies, blooming trees, and honeyed breezes was uplifting, and with Benjamin's energy stabilizing, I no longer felt torn between hope and despair. Now we were visiting with Corinne and, amusedly, I told her, "Benjamin has just started overdoing inflections when speaking, putting an upward swoop on every single word. I'm not sure whether he's just being silly, or if he thinks that I want even more inflection since we've been so focused on that."

Benjamin was face down, resting on Corinne's massage table, and she began demonstrating a chirophonetic pattern involving the sounds/strokes of A-O-U-M. "That's an ancient meditative sound sequence, isn't it?" I asked, recognizing the slowly intoned chant from a yoga class I had taken many years ago.

"Indeed," Corinne confirmed. "Sound has been used since ancient times for healing, as well as for meditative purposes. Chirophonetics is a relatively new technique, but it draws on ancient wisdom."

Once I had learned the new sequence, we moved on to review Benjamin's sensory integration program. "Benjamin no longer has any resistance to swinging on his tummy, and he loves playing 'airplane' using our little hammock swing," I reported proudly.

"Good work," Corinne praised. "So now you can play a new game: set out a small basket and challenge Benjamin to toss beanbags into it as he swings back and forth on his tummy."

"The 'conversation ball' exercise has been enormously effective," I now told Corinne. "Just like the 'pillow fight' game that I used to motivate Benjamin when he was first learning to speak, the rolling of the ball back and forth gets him excited and keeps his focus on me." Asking Benjamin to sit a considerable distance away from me, I demonstrated how we practiced our Mother Goose rhymes. "*Jack* (my roll) *be nimble* (Benjamin's roll) *Jack* (my roll) *be quick* (Benjamin's) *Jack* (me) *jump over* (Benjamin) *the candlestick* (me)."

"Well done," Corinne exclaimed approvingly. "Now, as a next step, I would like to see more follow-through in the physical gesture of rolling or tossing the ball. At the moment, there is an abrupt and snatching quality to Benjamin's motions which somewhat matches his stilted manner of speaking and interacting. See if you can encourage more fluidity in both his motions and his vocalizations."

"I totally get that," I assured her. "Passing the ball back and forth needs to be more of a dance; I've been working on that already."

19

Exploring New Avenues
May 1998

My parents were preparing their garden for planting, and Benjamin was discovering squirmy earthworms in the newly turned earth. As I guided him in sowing carrot seeds and planting peas, Benjamin's attention was caught by ladybugs and other interesting insects, but in spite of the idyllic setting, he was gradually descending back into self-absorbed disconnection, becoming fixated on one object after another, emitting ear-splitting screeches whenever I or my parents tried to distract and redirect him.

As Benjamin's bouts of screeching escalated and quickly shredded my nerves, I once again enforced timeouts, but found that the strategy was still ineffectual. Feeling desperate, I decided to try a so-called "aversive consequence." If each screech resulted in an unpleasant consequence, Benjamin might become motivated to reduce his screaming.

I had read about an autistic boy with the same screaming issues as Benjamin: the behavior had occurred whenever the child's autistic obsessions were intruded upon, and also whenever any demands were placed upon him, just as was currently the case with Benjamin. The boy's mother had tried many approaches, had consulted with various professionals, and had asked her son's teachers for help, to no avail. The child's behavior had escalated over a period of several years before someone advised her to use an "aversive" consequence, and this strategy had proved successful.

So now I tried the suggested consequence, consistently reacting to Benjamin's screams by clapping my hands close to his face and forcefully calling out, "No screaming!" The point was to make the consequence sufficiently unpleasant for it to become a deterrent. A few times Benjamin flinched with surprise, but mostly his screams went on regardless, and after a week of intense application, I gave up. The strategy might become appropriate when Benjamin was a bit older and hopefully more capable of self-control, but for the moment, I would trust that the screaming phase would resolve itself, just as had happened in previous instances.

Yet another agonizing day of screeching had come to a close, and I was pondering Benjamin's recurring behavioral nosedives. Could these be correlated to growth spurts? Might the rapid development of Benjamin's body be partially responsible for temporary imbalances in his brain's chemistry or structure? What about the toxins and the bacterial overgrowths that had just been identified through biomedical testing?

I'd had a phone consultation with the doctor who ran the specialized lab to which Benjamin's blood and urine samples had been sent. Apparently, Benjamin had an overgrowth of undesirable bacteria in his large intestine, although he did *not* have the profusion of candida yeast that was being found in many individuals with autism. In addition, there were toxins in Benjamin's body that could be linked to off-gassing; we had installed new carpeting (with foam liner) in our house when moving in the previous year.

The doctor recommended a number of nutritional supplements that would support liver functioning and thereby help Benjamin's body to rid itself of toxins. Since Benjamin was too young to be swallowing capsules, I would have to break them open and hide their contents in strong-tasting foods or juices. The doctor also explained that certain medications might get the intestinal bacteria under control but that the side-effects would probably cancel the benefits. As an alternative, he suggested an herbal formula that he'd had quite good results with and recommended dietary adjustments which would assist with balancing intestinal flora.

I dreaded the extra workload that the protocol would add onto Benjamin's already restricted diet, but the doctor's recommendations made good sense; even if we didn't get miraculous results, at least Benjamin's overall health would be getting extra support.

Benjamin's screaming was putting me over the edge. It seemed like only yesterday that I had been drowning in depression, and now I felt my emotional wounds like fresh scabs, easily rubbed raw and not tough enough to withstand further assault. If I was to regain my equilibrium, then Benjamin needed to be relieved of his inner turmoil.

Praying for a good outcome, I took Benjamin to Cheryl's for a cranio-sacral appointment and then consulted with Julie. "We'll return to the homeopathic remedy that's been so helpful throughout the past year," she decided, and outlined a plan for varying the dosage levels and dosing intervals based on fluctuations in Benjamin's behaviors.

Unbelievably, within a day, my "sunshine boy" was back, and at preschool the following week, Talia spontaneously commented. "Benjamin seems so much more aware of his surroundings than last week. He is making relevant comments and is responding to the children's overtures. He seems happy." These observations were particularly gratifying since Talia was unaware of the two therapy sessions. Not having any expectations of positive change, she wasn't reading anything into the situation. Her observations were impartial and objective, yet matched my own, more subjective viewpoint.

On Mother's Day, in the afternoon, Benjamin and I went to my parents' house for a small gathering. The friendly European couple that joined us for May wine and hors d'oeuvres lived across the alley and had two children, both of whom were several years older than Benjamin.

"Hey, little buddy, high-five," one of the kids exclaimed, and I helped Benjamin to hold up his hand for the playfully slapped greeting. This was something new, and I was excited about its potential. I smiled at the two elementary-school-aged children. "Can we do that again? It's such a fun way to say 'Hi'."

Both the boy and the girl were happy to cooperate, and they gently smacked Benjamin's hand in turns, laughing as they saw his growing pleasure in the interaction. Soon Benjamin was following them around and saying "high-five," holding up his hand without my prompting. Fortunately, the two kids were kindhearted and happy to oblige, not minding Benjamin's repeated requests.

My heart was dancing at this unexpected gift of momentary friendship. "How different this is from interacting with same-age children at preschool and dance class," I thought. "These older kids already understand the niceties of dialogue, of give-and-take, and have learned to be considerate of others. In contrast, children of Benjamin's age are still struggling with learning how to share, how to use their words, how to be caring. They are unpredictable, making it harder for Benjamin to apply the social skills I've been teaching him."

I would have loved for these two well-mannered siblings to become part of my social skills program for Benjamin but knew that this wasn't realistic; they already had busy lives of their own. However, now that we had met, the door was open for future chance encounters. If we were spending time at my parents', we could drop by the neighbors' for a visit.

In the days following this happy Sunday, Benjamin and I enjoyed peaceful interactions and constructive work sessions. When prompted, Benjamin was willing to give me eye contact and, as we reviewed established "pretend" scenarios, Benjamin did particularly well with setting up a little store and taking the dolls shopping within it. He also made progress with the guessing game that I had introduced. For this, I used the familiar picture-cards from our Mystery Garden board game. While shielding a chosen card from Benjamin's view, I asked, "Guess what this is," and then gave a variety of descriptive clues. Benjamin was learning to reciprocate as well: I helped him to formulate clues about cards of *his* choice so that *I* could "guess" what picture he held in *his* hands.

By now, I had fully phased in the various nutritional and herbal supplements recommended to me, and had adjusted Benjamin's diet according to the research doctor's guidelines. I had also re-administered the homeopathic remedy since Benjamin was experiencing a gradual backslide. Thus I was expecting some positive changes, but as the third week of May went slowly by, I observed only a little uplift. True, Benjamin wasn't screaming, but he required my constant vigilance to keep him away from his obsessions. I once again felt worn out as I worked against Benjamin's withdrawn distractibility, trying to review various skill drills with him.

"Maybe I should try backing off like I did in February," I thought now, giving up on the struggle. However, after a few days spent primarily outdoors keeping Benjamin away from 'fixy' objects, I was beginning to feel guilty. We had been to the playground several times in the past two days, but hadn't had any chance encounters with other children or their parents and, not only was I feeling like a slacker, I was also feeling very lonely, with thoughts buzzing around in my head and no one to talk to.

"I would definitely feel better if we accomplished something," I thought, berating myself. "I can't let my own weakness dictate Benjamin's progress." Once we were headed for home, I filled my mind with positive and energizing images, and I made a mental list of activities that might engage Benjamin, formulating a contingency plan in case he resisted. Thus prepared, I shepherded Benjamin back into "work" and, surprisingly, found that he was quite willing. The energy-and-attitude shift within me seemed to have rubbed off on him.

I had tucked Benjamin into bed and was speaking on the phone with Rick. His squadron was going on a three-month deployment, and I knew this would be our last extensive conversation until Rick returned to the States at the end of August.

Just now, Rick was pressing me on details of Benjamin's progress, seemingly impatient with my analysis of how Benjamin was responding to homeopathic support, unwilling to sympathize with my fluctuating energy levels. I was taken aback. Why was Rick being so hard and businesslike?

Rick's voice broke into my flurry of protestations. "Listen, I know things have been difficult for you, but I've been hearing vague answers off and on since before my visit in April, and I am getting concerned." I bristled at the implied criticism.

"What I am trying to say," Rick said, sounding edgy, "is that, from my perspective, it sounds like you need a bit more daily organization in your behavioral program and like you should be outlining some goals. You can't just follow your intuition all the time." Actually, something along those lines had run across my mind recently but I wasn't about to admit that Rick might have a point—not just now. No, I was too caught up in rising anger, feeling that Rick was being unfair and insensitive.

"I don't need you to be an additional slave driver," I snapped. "I already whip myself enough, thank you very much. I've been working myself into the ground trying to help Benjamin, and now you're telling me I need to do better?" My voice cracked with emotion, and I broke into tears. "Who are you to criticize," I lashed out. "You aren't even here, you have no idea." Within moments, I was regretting my angry outburst, knowing that Rick had been trying to say something constructive, even if it had felt tactless to me. But it was too late to rescind my words; their accusatory tone had ignited Rick, and he shot back.

"What, do you think I like being here by myself, working like crazy to support this family? I care as much about Benjamin as you do and yet, all that I know about him is what you tell me, and what I see in person three times per year. So, if you give me the impression that things are stagnating, can you blame me for making an assessment?"

Rick's resentment at being misunderstood was tangled with frustration and, for a while, neither of us could manage to calm down. The cumulative effects of the past year's challenges were rising to the surface, with both of us suffering from loneliness and overwork, both of us longing for "normalcy," both of us grappling with gracious acceptance of our circumstances. Words and feelings were flung back and forth, hurts and truths and desires all mixed together indiscriminately. Only after the storm had spent itself did we begin sifting the debris.

"I've read that one should focus on gratitude…that loving feelings stem from this choice," I offered, addressing the fact that both of us were feeling increasingly disconnected from one another as time went on. "When I truly concentrate on what I appreciate about you, when I intentionally meditate on these things, my heart warms and resentment falls away. Love enters. It is easy to forget that, considering all the daily distractions and worries."

Rick in turn admitted, "Your motto 'see the glass half full instead of half empty' is a good one. I need to work on that too." Through dialogue and discussion, we were now nurturing one another rather than being hurtful; we were reestablishing a heartfelt connection and were reviving the spirit of our marriage.

"I love you," I told Rick finally, really meaning it and *feeling* it, not just saying the words on an intellectual level.

"I love you too," he said, and I could tell he was right there with me.

Our conversation had returned to Benjamin.

"It sounds like you could use some help," Rick observed. "You've been modeling your work on those two books, *Son Rise* and *Let Me Hear Your*

Voice. Why don't you follow their example and put together a team of therapists so that Benjamin gets a predictable amount of therapy each day? He would probably benefit from interacting with different people."

I was hesitant. Yes, some help would be good but, as I had found when working with Rhea the previous year, an experienced behavioral therapist would be costly, and our budget was already maxed out.

I voiced my thoughts. "I'd have to start giving violin lessons again to keep our finances balanced; I would be exchanging work time with Benjamin for time spent with someone else's kid. Yes, that would provide me with some variety, but it wouldn't give me an actual break. Besides, even when we were working with Rhea—and she was one of the best therapists in the area—I was making ongoing suggestions for how she could be more effective with Benjamin. In spite of my own shortcomings and the challenge of keeping up my energy, I still think I'm the best teacher for Benjamin."

Rick cleared his throat and responded cautiously. "I know that you are good at what you do. But you are talking yourself right out of the possibility for getting help. You haven't truly explored the possibility, and yet you're ready to throw the idea out the window."

I was silent for a moment, thinking. Could I find some volunteers or college students and train them to work behaviorally with Benjamin? That was what the family in *Son Rise* had done, and this approach was suggested in *Let Me Hear Your Voice* as well. Certainly it would be more affordable than hiring someone like Rhea. But putting together a team would take time and energy, and there was no guarantee I would find talented people.

Rick broke into my deliberations. "Statistically speaking, behavioral therapy is the most effective approach for helping a child with autism. Forty hours of therapy per week—isn't that what they recommend for greatest gains? Particularly if the child is under age five?"

"Yeah, that's true," I said. "But I can't imagine that every minute of those forty hours should be spent doing 'table work.' I do a lot of our language drills while I'm out walking with Benjamin. And sensory integration is important too. Plus, the social skills practice that he gets during preschool, Kindermusik, and dance class is vital."

Rick spoke soothingly. "I'm sure you're right. But lately, how many hours per day have you worked on specific skills? And has that been every day, or just every once in a while?"

"Okay, okay, I get your point," I said unwillingly. "I need to refocus my program. I'll comb through the therapy outline in *Let Me Hear Your Voice*, and I'll get hold of a new book by the same author; someone told me she recently edited a manual for behavioral intervention. I'll write out some lists of skills and activities, including my own made-up games and play scenarios, and I'll post them instead of keeping everything inside my head."

"There ya go," Rick said supportively. "That'll relieve you of the stress of having to come up with things at the drop of a hat."

I was warming to the theme of evaluating my work and strategizing, no longer feeling that Rick was being critical. I admitted, "Sometimes I work on an individual skill for too long because I want to feel like Benjamin has really 'gotten' it, and also because I'm trying to extend his capacity for ongoing focus and attention. But maybe I'm actually burning Benjamin out, just like I've been burning myself out."

I thought for a bit. "Starting tomorrow, I'll try for more variety in quicker succession. Instead of expecting obvious improvement in one go, I'll keep coming back to certain skills—keep re-approaching them throughout the day. That'll be a challenge for me because I don't by nature jump from one thing to the next in the way Benjamin does. But I know it can be effective, working *with* his ADD tendency instead of just fighting *against* it. I can always change tack if the situation calls for it."

"M-hm." Rick was being a good sounding board, and so I kept on brainstorming.

"You know, maybe I should be using food rewards a little more often. I've really shied away from that because it can be so mechanical, and also because I want Benjamin to be motivated by interaction and hugs rather than by external rewards. But, there is a time and place for everything, and perhaps I've put myself at a disadvantage."

"This all sounds really good; you have some concrete goals to work on," Rick concurred. "But what about our original point of discussion? I still think you should get some help aside from the babysitting that you ask your parents for on occasion."

I sighed, feeling conflicted, but knowing I should give the idea a chance. "I'll call around to see who might be available. I'll also speak to someone at the university's psychology department; there might be some students who already have experience working with autism."

The next week flew by. My long discussion with Rick had renewed my determination to work Benjamin out of his autism, and I had set myself the goal of carrying out intensive therapy for six hours per day, aiming for three hours in the morning and three in the afternoon. If I allowed for Sundays off, that would come to thirty-six hours per week. I had made a long list of games and exercises to work on, organizing them into categories, and was now bouncing back and forth amongst the choices, alternating between skill review and newer tasks. I was giving Benjamin frequent breaks by playing sensory games and was inserting several short violin practices into each day. Surprisingly, the six daily hours of work were melting away like butter under the sun. Both Benjamin and I were enjoying the renewed life force in our program.

In the face of our gathering momentum, Benjamin suddenly reverted to scatter-brained and languidly spacey behavior. He also renewed an old fixation of repeatedly turning on and off the bathroom sink and becoming "lost" in the resulting stream of water. Unfortunately, this change coincided with a May Celebration that was being held at preschool. While Talia held up her hand for attention, and as the assembled children from all her classes stood quietly, waiting to dance around a Maypole decorated with flowers and ribbons, Benjamin was causing me a great deal of stress. He was constantly in motion, and I was trying to remain unobtrusive while keeping him in line. I was courting disaster; Benjamin was on the verge of screeching.

"Come on, let's get started," I thought frantically.

A large audience of parents was standing around watching, and I didn't want Benjamin to ruin the festive atmosphere. Thankfully, Talia began singing, leading the children in their rehearsed little dance, and the music carried Benjamin along. Afterwards though, while the other children played homemade games—Talia had set up stations around the yard in charming imitation of an old-time street faire—Benjamin constantly ran off, away from the scattered clusters of children, and I was unable to capture his attention and interest.

I glanced at the other parents with envy. They stood in little groups, relaxing, conversing, soaking up the sunshine and indulgently watching their children. The tranquil scene, centered on old-fashioned games, was reminiscent of a nineteenth-century painting, and my heart ached for Benjamin and me to be part of it.

Eventually, though, I gave up on the May Faire and took Benjamin home, then phoned my mom and unburdened myself. "When I'm dealing with Benjamin's autistic behaviors, I sometimes catch people looking at me sort of sideways. They don't realize what's going on, and I can see them thinking, 'Why doesn't she leave the kid alone?' It's so embarrassing, it really shrivels my insides. Nevertheless, it's vital for Benjamin to be included in social situations. Hopefully, with sufficient exposure, he'll develop the desire to participate."

My mom tried to calm me. "Maybe you're being hyper-sensitive about other people's opinions? Everyone knows that children can't be expected to act like little adults." There was truth in my mom's words, but I felt she was oversimplifying.

I countered, "Well, yes, kids will be kids. But just when I think that Benjamin is catching up to age-level, I get a fresh reminder of how different he still is. Like today. I was shocked to see how easily Benjamin's peers were keeping quiet, following directions and understanding expectations. There were *so* many kids and yet, incredibly, Benjamin was the *only* one making any disturbance. I'd thought for sure that a few more kids would have trouble with the parameters."

I gave a heavy sigh and then voiced an unpleasant observation. "I don't think most people are particularly tolerant, especially when they don't realize that a disturbing behavior is part of a disability. To others, Benjamin might easily look like a spoiled brat when he starts screeching. And I'm not the type to just shrug off the reactions of bystanders. Instead, I get increasingly tense which only makes things worse. Sometimes I wish I could hang a sign around my neck: *Don't mind us—the problem is autism.*"

Julie had changed Benjamin's homeopathic dosing schedule and within a day, Benjamin was again happy and connected. At preschool, he followed my prompts to hug his classmate Lily when she opened her arms to him, and when we went for our monthly cranio-sacral session, Benjamin eagerly climbed onto Cheryl's massage table. The fear and panic of the past two months were now passé. "Something new, though," I told Cheryl. "Benjamin is developing hypersensitivity to certain sounds that haven't bothered him before; his perception of them is changing. It seems that something in his brain is shifting as he grows."

Benjamin was tucked in for the night, and I was down in the basement office, journaling, when I heard Benjamin's lively voice. "Mama, Mama!"

I popped out of my seat and ran to the stairwell, my heart leaping. Benjamin had never called for me before. "Yes, darling, what do you need?" I remained on the bottom stair, wondering whether Benjamin would keep up a dialogue over such a distance. If so, this would be another first. "Benjamin?"

"Mama, come up, I want to open the gate," he called.

"I love your calling voice, darling. Good job."

"*Mama!*"

I went to tuck Benjamin back in. No sooner had I made my way back downstairs than Benjamin was calling again. "Mama, I want to give you a hug and a kiss." I couldn't believe my ears. For months, I had been striving to overcome Benjamin's autistic reticence, asking him for hugs, showing him how to pucker his mouth and touch my face with it. On winged feet, I now took the stairs two at a time, my heart soaring with joy. Hugging my sweet, blond angel, I felt him squeeze me right back, and then I received a little kiss which landed lightly as a butterfly on my cheek. Heaven was mine.

20

Trial and Error
June 1998

I had talked to several families about their behavioral home-programs and was in the process of hiring a team of tutors plus an experienced "supervisor." "Everyone needs to be on the same page," one mother had told me. "Consistency is vital. For example, you can't arbitrarily change the wording of a directive. The whole team needs to use the same commands and have the same expectations. You'll need regular team meetings and trainings." I felt burdened at this prospect but, wanting to keep my promise to Rick, I lined up a supervisor. Then, as potential therapists came over for mini play sessions with Benjamin, I became increasingly doubtful. I really liked all these college kids and appreciated their desire to help, but there was a wide range in their level of natural talent, and my heart was sinking at the thought of being responsible for their training. Nevertheless, I pressed on, and after countless phone calls, I had a team, a schedule, and an initial training workshop set up.

As I awaited our start date, my sense of trepidation grew and I couldn't stop questioning. "Is my nervousness just due to impending change? Or is my gut-instinct telling me something? Am I doing the right thing?"

Within the week, I had answers. In the course of a single afternoon, my work with Benjamin was repeatedly interrupted by the ringing of our phone. Each of the student therapists was calling to report that something unforeseen and important had come up which would prevent their participation in our program.

At first, I wanted to cry. All that effort, all that time spent phoning and interviewing, fretting and scheduling...all for nothing. "Now what? How will I find replacements?" I wondered miserably. But as the final phone call came in at the end of the day, my upset cleared. "This is a message," I thought. "Something greater than coincidence is going on here." I phoned the supervisor, apologized for the late notice, and explained that I would have to postpone, and perhaps cancel, our workshop.

That evening, after putting Benjamin to bed, I pulled out a videotape that had just been lent to me. It contained footage of one family's training workshop with the supervisor I had chosen and now, popping the tape into our VCR, I observed a highly organized but impersonal style of behavioral therapy that took no loving interest in the personality of the child. My impression was of a cookie-cutter format that was being imposed regardless of the child's individuality, and I felt increasingly claustrophobic, watching. This style of work was definitely not for me—and not for Benjamin. When I finally turned off the tape, I felt queasy.

"Saved in the nick of time," I thought. "I nearly made a big mistake there..." Taking a deep breath of relief, I stretched my arms up over my head. A heavy burden had been lifted from me, and I felt certain that the intervention of heavenly powers had steered me away from error.

Summer vacation was just around the corner, and Benjamin's last days of preschool were notable. He had progressed to sustaining some interactive play (with support) and just now, he and Lily were feeding some doll-babies. Leaning close to Benjamin, I whispered, "Say: *Please give me the bottle.*" Benjamin repeated the phrase, and Lily smiled at him, handing him the bottle. "Here you go, Benjamin."

Lily now talked directly to Benjamin without being distracted by me, and she also responded to Benjamin's words as if I wasn't prompting them. She had become an ideal playfellow, accepting my presence as Benjamin's sometime-shadow, realizing there was no need to keep acknowledging me.

Then, during the final outdoor play period, Talia instigated forming a train of children on the slide. We had been encouraging hugs between Benjamin and his classmates for several weeks, and now he was somewhat comfortable with physical proximity. "Would you like to be the caboose?" Talia asked, and Benjamin was willing to try.

The entire morning had been suffused by a sense of accomplishment and completion, and as we said our final goodbyes, Benjamin gave Talia a long, quiet hug, truly connecting. Talia's eyes glimmered with tears as she smiled. Benjamin had come a long way since joining her class in January.

Talia's school had closed—she was moving to another city—and so now I was speaking with Sophia who also ran a small, home-based school. During this phone interview, Sophia answered my questions with an extraordinary level of insight, and once I met her in person, her creativity and spiritual nature were altogether confirmed for me. I felt certain that both Benjamin and I would be blessed to have her as a teacher.

"I haven't had a child with autism in my school thus far," Sophia admitted. "So I would like to develop a relationship with Benjamin prior to our first day of class. He'll be in my two-day group with considerably younger children; they are all attending preschool for the first time. If Benjamin knows my style and expectations, and if he is familiar with the toys in the schoolroom before class officially begins, he'll be much more comfortable, and so will I." Sophia's self-deprecating laugh was light and lively. I was finding that she could be intensely thoughtful, but also quick to express humor and joy—a wonderful balance of attributes.

We had agreed on meeting for an hour every two weeks throughout the summer, and the very next afternoon, I was waiting on Sophia's doorstep with Benjamin who was hopping around, discombobulated by windy weather, seemingly overstimulated by the proximity of the doorbell. When the door opened, Sophia stood there, smiling and singing a simple welcome song. "Wow, what a beautiful soprano voice," I thought, smiling back and then looking down to see Benjamin's reaction.

Benjamin had stopped hopping and was now studying Sophia's face, clearly drawn in by her singing. Then he willingly entered the house and followed Sophia into the schoolroom while I seated myself in a chair just outside the doorway. Sophia waited to see whether Benjamin would become interested in any of the toys and, when he just stood, looking lost, she invited him to join her in a specific play scenario.

"Benjamin, come to the kitchen, we'll make some tea." Sophia kneeled by the wooden toy stove, mimed tea preparations, and then handed Benjamin a hand-carved wooden cup, sipping from her own toy cup and making gestures that indicated her wish that Benjamin might imitate her. The session went on from there, with Sophia leading Benjamin through a range of household activities, playing at cooking, washing dishes, building a house, dusting, and ironing.

I watched, marveling at the expressiveness of Sophia's gestures: every intention was crystal clear, and she wasted no words. Songs and occasional spoken directives left the play space feeling open and uncluttered, and I sensed that Benjamin was becoming increasingly present-centered. He was responding to the calming energy of Sophia's inner strength.

Her infectious laughter punctuated the session with lightness and humor, but when Benjamin began twiddling his cup, Sophia recognized a budding fixation and immediately redirected him. She used elegant eurythmy gestures to draw Benjamin's attention and to help him become more grounded.

I sat silently watching as if mesmerized, my heart swelling with joy and excitement. "This is better than opening night at a marvelous play," I thought. "Sophia is so attuned to Benjamin that their interactions are like a harmonious dance. Her work will complement mine, and together, we'll balance out the intellectualizing effects of behavioral therapy. Benjamin will have a real chance of developing his imagination and thus growing more whole."

The middle of June was turning into a time of transition. A phone call had come in, notifying me that Benjamin would be required to undergo an intake-assessment by our local school district's team of special education teachers. This meeting was mandated by law and would potentially provide Benjamin with an official IEP (Individualized Education Plan) due to his autism. After hearing an explanation peppered with legal jargon and acronyms, I had scheduled the appointment, feeling intimidated and confused.

Now the morning of the feared IEP appointment had arrived. It was early and I hadn't yet arisen when I heard Benjamin rolling out of bed and heading immediately for the nearest light switch; he began rapidly flipping it as if imitating a strobe light.

I raised my head and looked. Benjamin was hopping madly, alternately digging around in his mouth with one hand and then holding it out stiffly, making bizarre shapes with his fingers; at the same time, he kept the lights flickering.

"Oh my God," I thought, leaping out of bed and running over to Benjamin. I tickled his sides and nuzzled his neck. "*Grrrr*...a tiger is here to eat you all up. You'd better run away." I pointed Benjamin in the right direction and began nudging him towards the stairs. Today was the worst day for him to be in such a state. "Odysseus and the siren song of light switches," I thought, laughing bitterly at the absurd analogy.

I was worried about demonstrating the effectiveness of my behavioral work with Benjamin during our appointment. All that legal mumbo-jumbo on the phone had scared me into thinking that, if I couldn't prove the efficacy of my work with him, my right to determine Benjamin's therapies and educational path might be impinged upon and become dictated by the district.

A few hours later, Benjamin was sitting across from a surprisingly young woman who asked him to try a variety of tasks, some of which he had already mastered at home. The woman was friendly but not enthusiastic, and I was struck by her blandness. Her neutral voice engendered little interest in Benjamin, and he repeatedly failed to complete the tasks, even the ones *I* knew *he* knew.

"Believe me, Benjamin actually knows how to do that one," I said, feeling agonized. "If you use the command *"match—put with same,"* he'll probably do it."

"I'm sorry, I need to follow our standardized protocol; I'm not allowed to prompt him," was the impassive response.

I began to sweat as Benjamin remained unmotivated. Behind my carefully controlled face, I was fuming. "If only she would connect with him like a 'real' person instead of remaining so darn neutral. Her approach is practically a recipe for failure," I thought as I strained to send little telepathic messages into Benjamin's brain, hoping that he might perk up and suddenly find some of the tasks familiar. Nothing happened, and I felt like crying, thinking, "*Anyone might have a brain-freeze in this kind of a situation.*"

Finally, the agonizing stage of testing had run its course, and we moved on to the next step. Here things loosened up a bit as Benjamin was encouraged to try the swing set, to carry out some balancing tasks, to try climbing on a small jungle gym, and so on. Eventually, all phases of testing were done, the parent questionnaire had been filled out, and a team discussion was taking place. To my unending relief, my fears about legal issues were now being allayed.

"Actually, you'll be happy to know that our district currently provides automatic tuition support for children with autism that are attending licensed private preschools."

"Really? The district will support Benjamin's attending a Waldorf preschool?"

I could hardly believe my ears. This was incredibly good news and was most unexpected after the grueling experience I had just endured—that of watching my child's many developmental short-falls being highlighted.

Once we got home, Benjamin's poor frame of mind was still in glaring evidence; he was throwing tantrums whenever I removed him from a fixation. Prior to our appointment, I had been so tense with worry that, whenever Benjamin got stuck, I had nearly exploded. But now, with the IEP process completed and my fears dispelled, I was able to take deep breaths, to center myself, and to approach Benjamin with a fresh clarity of mind.

Rather than becoming emotionally wrapped up in his upsets, I remained calm and loving. I insisted on a work session, pulling out some of our well-known games, and began arranging one of them on the playhouse table. As we progressed through the familiar steps of play, Benjamin's psyche seemed to smooth out—I could practically see the snarls in his brain becoming untangled—and after we had carried on playing for some time, a harmonious feeling was present between us.

"You see," I thought, carrying on an internal conversation with myself. "Sometimes you *can* pull Benjamin out of his autism by sheer force of will, but you need to have utter clarity and calm within yourself if you are to succeed."

With some extra homeopathic support, Benjamin was back to being relaxed, responsive, and happy, and he seemed ready for something new. I had brainstormed the idea of extending our basic doll-play into scenarios which mirrored Benjamin's real-life experiences.

"Come watch, Benjamin," I said now. "I'm going to build a cabin; this will be like Oma and Opa's little place in the mountains." I quickly constructed a small hut and then used a few Lincoln Logs to make a tiny outhouse. "We need some grass and trees," I explained, laying out a moss-green piece of felted wool cloth to represent a meadow.

Handing Benjamin a pinecone, I said, "This will be a tree. Can you plant it in the grass?" I pointed towards the green felt cloth and contributed a pinecone of my own. Then I added a blue silk scarf to the scene, gathering it up to form a long narrow curve. "Here is the river. Do you remember the river that flows near Oma and Opa's cabin?" I placed a toy fish in the "water" and then set a carved wooden squirrel near the "trees." My imagination was on fire with ideas of how this basic scenario could be expanded. "Here's Benjamin-Doll," I said, handing Benjamin the blond little figure that represented him. "Now copy me. We're going to take a walk around the cabin and then go down to the river."

I was narrating my actions while manipulating another figurine. "Brown-Boy is calling you," I now clarified. In a high little voice, I piped, "Come along with me, be my friend." I made Brown-Boy hop up and down encouragingly and, with my voice sliding back into its normal register, I prompted, "Come on, sweetie, make Benjamin-Doll hop along behind Brown-Boy."

Benjamin was following my directions, but I could see that his attention was fading; my requests for ongoing focus had tired him. Playing was such hard work, all the more so when something new was being introduced.

"Good job, you're a great friend, Benjamin-Doll," I praised. "Let's take a nap now. We can play again some other time." I laid Brown-Boy on his back in the meadow and directed Benjamin to do the same with his little doll. Then I stood up. "It's time to move around a bit. Let's go play chase."

A colleague of mine who was also a horseman had invited us to meet a special horse named Captain. "He's an exceptionally kind-natured animal and is highly trained," Adwin had told me. Now Benjamin was riding bareback on the jet-black horse as it walked in a large circle around Adwin.

"Lean back a little and say 'woah'," Adwin directed, and as Benjamin followed directions, Captain promptly stopped. "Now squeeze with your legs and make a clucking sound—like this." Benjamin did so, and the horse promptly responded, stepping into a brisk walk. Intrigued, Benjamin tried the two cues several more times and was consistently rewarded by Captain's obedient reactions. I marveled. "Such an enormous animal, yet so sensitive to a small person's desires."

Now Adwin began asking questions, and Benjamin responded spontaneously, not needing any prompting. "How unusual," I thought. "The horse's rocking motion seems to be integrating Benjamin's brain, making it easier for him to talk." I fervently wished that rides on Captain could become a regular part of

Benjamin's therapeutic program but, regretfully, this was not to be. Captain was shortly being moved to another barn, far away.

I was preparing Benjamin for his first visit to the dentist. I had borrowed a dental mirror for this purpose and had discovered that Benjamin was terribly frightened of the penny-sized mirror with its long metal handle. Perhaps it reminded him of the shiny medical equipment he had seen during his ill-fated blood draw.

I was repeatedly bringing out the mirror, putting it in my mouth to demonstrate that there was nothing to fear. "Look, Benjamin, it's just like putting a spoon in your mouth." After many days of nonthreatening exposure, Benjamin was willing to hold the handle and put the mirror in *my* mouth, but weeks passed before he finally allowed it near *his* mouth. I repeatedly tempted him by putting a dab of honey on the mirror, suggesting, "Pretend it's a lollipop. You can lick the honey right off."

Finally, Benjamin consented to try and, after this mini-breakthrough, I was able to build up the length of time the mirror spent in his mouth, starting with one second. Eventually, Benjamin could handle my counting up to ten while holding the mirror against his tongue or the inside of his cheek. Then it was time to test Benjamin's tolerance: I asked my father to come over and play dentist with us. I had to be certain Benjamin would allow someone other than me to handle the mirror and to look into his mouth.

Though agonizingly slow, this desensitization process was vital. Benjamin's ongoing fears following the bumbled blood draw had taught me how damaging a single negative experience could be, and I had realized the importance of preventative preparation. For this reason, I also briefed the dentist on Benjamin's perceptions and needs just prior to the actual appointment. "My priority is to create a fun experience that feels safe to Benjamin. It doesn't matter whether you can actually look at his teeth."

The dentist took my lead, playing along as I sat in the exam chair, mouth wide open, and then encouraged Benjamin to do the same while perched on my lap. Thus, the groundwork was laid for an eventual "real" exam, with the odds for success stacked in our favor.

I was preparing Benjamin for a family celebration of the midsummer solstice, and as we walked the trails each morning, I taught him German poems filled with evocative images of summer and nature's beauty. Although English remained the language of our daily interactions, I still cherished the hope that Benjamin might become bilingual in the future. Poetry would lead us towards this goal: during the autumn, Benjamin had already surprised me by quoting salient lines of the "September" poem, and by Christmas, he'd been able to get through an entire verse of poetry—so long as I was face to face with him and he could watch my mouth in order to follow the words. Now, Benjamin was actually memorizing the short poems I had chosen.

Midsummer's eve. As the sun's rays slanted low over the foothills, filtering through trees into my parents' garden, I was weaving a crown of flowers for Benjamin to wear. My parents joined us, and we settled around a low table decorated with flowers and a lit candle, ready to begin our little festival program. I strummed my guitar alongside the chirping of crickets, accompanying the songs that had been a midsummer tradition since my childhood, and then Benjamin took the grassy stage, facing my parents as he played his violin and recited two German poems. Finally, ceremonial atmosphere aside, my mom dished up a feast of elder blossom pancakes and fresh fruit, and we crowded around the picnic table to eat.

Suddenly, magic was in the air: haunting sounds of panpipes drifted from the vicinity of the raspberry patch and, from the shadows of an old apple tree, a gnome-like figure cautiously appeared. The creature danced languidly, weaving its way throughout the garden. Animated by strains of increasingly energetic music, the gnome began leaping and twirling, trailing a swirl of golden silk until, with a frenzied crescendo, it disappeared into the dusk.

I bit into a piece of watermelon, watching Benjamin who was silent, his eyes enormous as he repeatedly looked up from his fruit plate to scan the surrounding bushes, hoping to catch another glimpse of the mysterious figure that had danced for him. Clearly, he hadn't noticed my absence during the gnome's dance, and I was thrilled at the enchantment that had overtaken him.

Now it was time for the bonfire, and I sat holding Benjamin on my lap, rocking him gently as my mom and I hummed various European melodies. Eventually, when the flames had settled into small flickering tongues, I said to Benjamin, "Opa and I will help you jump over the fire. You'll soar through the air, just like the firefly in your poem. You're becoming brave and strong."

Benjamin looked somewhat anxious at the thought of leaping over flames, but when my dad and I took his arms (one of us on either side of him) and reminded Benjamin that this was similar to his beloved *Engelein fliege* (little angel, fly) game, he became willing to try. We helped Benjamin with a running start towards the glowing embers and then lifted him high, carrying him in an arcing path over and beyond the hot coals. Benjamin shrieked with excitement, and as soon as he had landed, I could see he was ready for more.

"Wait, Benjamin, Mommy needs a turn." I stood at attention, sent up a silent prayer for Benjamin's continued progress, and then recited a summer poem. As I jumped over the little patch of fire, remembrances of childhood flashed into mind, and I *knew* the exhilaration Benjamin was feeling. Then it was his turn again. Stretching out his arms for us to hold, Benjamin said a line of poetry and then—*run, run, run, leap!*

Again and again, Benjamin sailed over the flames, and I was struck by the symbolism of the act. "Summoning courage...evoking inspiration...and repeated leaps of faith," I thought. "This represents what Benjamin and I do together, every day, in striving to overcome autism."

June was nearing its end. Benjamin and I were escaping the sun's heat, taking a walk along the cool and shady nature trail. "Stand still...and listen." I was teaching Benjamin how to be silent on request. "Funny," I thought. "All year long, I've worked on developing language and encouraging Benjamin to talk, and now his ability to speak has become a means for tuning out the world. What an ironic turn of events."

This new tendency had become prominent during our last few weeks in Talia's preschool when, throughout story time—while the other children remained still and quiet—Benjamin had often been in motion, repetitively chattering to himself as he alternately rocked, flicked his fingers, or otherwise engaged in self-stimulating behaviors.

"Be quiet and listen," I said again, centering myself and breathing deeply, consciously countering Benjamin's current, fluttery agitation. I gently stroked Benjamin's shoulders and arms, and then—imagining an aura of golden peace settling around him—stroked downwards through the air immediately surrounding Benjamin, quickly moving from head to toe with generous sweeps. The tingling sensation in my palms told me I was sensing the subtle energy surrounding Benjamin's body. Then I whispered to Benjamin, "I hear birds singing...the stream burbling...a bee buzzing..."

Benjamin stopped struggling against my hands which had returned to resting on his shoulders. Inner quiet stole into his being, and a budding smile turned up the corners of his mouth. He was finally tuning in to the forest sounds. "This is how we listen at story time," I whispered, gently kissing the top of Benjamin's head.

As we continued along the trail, I stopped Benjamin several more times in order to practice the new skill of listening and was gratified when he became increasingly quick in understanding my expectation. "This is lovely...I can *hear* the silence," I whispered in Benjamin's ear.

Eventually, a fellow hiker came walking along the path.

"Here comes someone, let's say 'Hi'," I instructed, having recently decided that Benjamin was ready to wake up to the wider circle of people that were part of our world and community. I said "Hi" first, and then prompted Benjamin who dutifully echoed me and seemed startled when he got a response.

"Hey there, bud."

Benjamin looked up to locate the source of these words, apparently nonplussed that such a friendly response was coming from a stranger. As we walked on, numerous further opportunities presented themselves, and Benjamin became increasingly delighted at the power of this little syllable.

"Say 'Hi'," I would whisper with each oncoming person.

"Hi," Benjamin would exclaim.

"Hey, how'ya doin'?" That was a different response.

"Hi."

"How's it?" Another way to answer.

"Hi."

"Hello there." So many ways to greet someone.

Wow. This was becoming as fun as pushing the "play" button on our answering machine at home.

On the last Sunday of June, my parents and I took Benjamin on his first long hike—four miles roundtrip—into a wilderness area located near the family cabin. Our destination was a pretty, hidden lake tucked away amongst small mountains, and once there, we spent a good hour dropping variably sized rocks into the water or setting "fairy boats" afloat. I crafted these from leaves or chunks of bark, piercing each "boat" with a twig to form a tiny mast, and sometimes adding a miniature leaf-sail.

The afternoon passed with an amazing feeling of normalcy, and all too soon, we had to pack up our picnic leavings and retrace our footsteps down the trail. Suddenly, Benjamin spotted one of the wild roses that proliferated at this elevation. "It's a rose," he cooed, drawing out the "o" and sitting down next to the diminutive bush with its lovely pink flowers.

"Yes, a rose," I echoed. Benjamin sniffed one of the fragrant blooms and settled himself more comfortably, as if expecting to spend a considerable amount of time there. "Come, we need to get back to the cabin," I said, reaching for Benjamin's hand and pulling him up to standing. We walked along the path for a while before Benjamin spotted another blooming rosebush and rushed to sit down beside it, gazing at it reverently, melting my heart with his expression. As we continued down the trail, however, Benjamin became increasingly reluctant to part with each successive rose bush, shrieking whenever I insisted that we continue walking. Clearly, a new fixation was developing before my very eyes.

Who would have thought that the great outdoors, which had heretofore been the ideal escape from mechanical fixations, would ever present a problem?

21

Focus on Peer Play
July 1998

Benjamin's capacity for interaction was rapidly expanding, and I deemed him ready for consistent one-on-one play sessions with peers. Lily, Benjamin's friend from preschool, was a natural choice for facilitated playtime, and her parents agreed to drop her off once or twice per week for the remainder of the summer. Now I was searching for a second child to come over regularly and, since everyone I had spoken with already had summer plans, I was phoning agencies which served persons with disabilities.

In this way, I got two good leads. A social skills class for preschool-aged children was just starting up. And, an agency volunteer had a son Benjamin's age. "Let's meet and see if our boys get along," Eliza suggested, and the next day, she and Rowan came to visit. Rowan was quiet and reserved, content to explore our toys without Benjamin's participation, and Eliza was enthusiastic about bringing him to play on a weekly basis.

So, my hoped-for social skills program was set: four times per week, Benjamin's afternoon work sessions would be pleasantly interrupted by a period of peer interaction.

As usual, the Colorado Music Festival was starting its six-week season with a children's concert, and we were attending both the dress rehearsal and the performance; the double exposure would help Benjamin get more out of the experience. When Benjamin and I entered the century-old wooden auditorium, the orchestra was already rehearsing, but Benjamin's attention was entirely captured by the little brass number tags that were affixed to the armrest of each individual seat.

He resisted following me and began using his index finger to push on each brass tag as if it were a button, excitedly reading the numbers. "One...four... seven...nine...ten..." The farther up the numbers he got, the more tense and bouncy he became, his free hand twirling wildly as his other hand remained busy with the repeated pressing of tags, the joints of his pointer finger becoming hyper-extended from excess muscle tension. A quality of desperation pervaded Benjamin's fixation, and I thought worriedly, "This is extreme. I'd better increase Benjamin's homeopathic remedy and see if that mellows him."

At the performance the next morning, Benjamin was already in a better state. He was receptive when I lightly touched his cheek and pointed to the orchestra, redirecting his attention away from the number tags, and once the narrated story of *The Little Engine That Could* began and costumed train-actors came chugging down the aisles, Benjamin became engrossed in watching. What a difference from the day before.

Ding dong. Our doorbell was chiming.

"Hi, how are you?" Benjamin greeted Lily, opening the screen door for her, and thrilling me with his natural manner; I had been rehearsing him on typical social scripts, and now our playacting was paying off.

Benjamin followed Lily into our play area, standing by as she explored a wicker basket filled with toy animals. Listening in, I could hear Lily alternating between narrating a storyline and creating dialogue between various figures. "Hey," I thought. "This is just like what I'm doing with Benjamin: enacting scenes from real life, using dolls and talking all the while. It is age-appropriate behavior, and Lily is the perfect role model."

After a while, Lily pulled out a box of "duplo-blocks" (like Legos, but much larger and designed for very young children). Benjamin moved in close, looking worried, and when Lily pulled apart a stack of blocks, he began to scream. Lily looked briefly at Benjamin, glanced over at me, and then, surprisingly, returned to her activity as if nothing was going on. "Atta girl," I thought. As long as Lily remained unfazed by Benjamin's reaction, I could experiment with solving the problem.

"That's what these blocks are for," I explained, repeatedly joining several blocks together before pulling them apart again. I was trying to desensitize Benjamin by "flooding" him with the visual experience. Interestingly, Benjamin would calm down each time the blocks were put together, but as soon as I reversed the process, his screeches would resume. After a while though, his protests were no longer so vehement and, as Lily and I continued building things and pulling them apart, Benjamin became increasingly tolerant. "We'll keep working on this outside of play sessions," I decided, pleased with the improvement.

The following day, an older boy from our neighborhood came over to play. Feeling himself superior to Benjamin, he declined to interact much and instead, amused himself by climbing around on our swing set, acrobatically negotiating the trapeze. Then he spent time balancing on the variously sized tree trunk segments that formed an obstacle course in our back yard. I encouraged Benjamin to watch and imitate, and later, after the boy had gone home, Benjamin spontaneously began climbing around on the stumps, announcing, "Just like Robby." Clearly, the older boy had acted as a motivating role model for Benjamin, and I thought, "Even if very little interaction happens, there is great value in having children over here, playing with Benjamin's toys and 'invading' Benjamin's space. They are providing natural instruction." Like Benjamin, I too was learning something new with every play-date.

Building up the mountain cabin scenario and conducting dialogues between Benjamin-Doll and his friends had become a staple of our work sessions. Now I was expanding this doll's world to reflect additional real-life experiences and locations. I showed Benjamin how to build the road and tunnel which led to the family cabin. I added a nearby riding arena, and also a farm with many animals. Since I had recently taken Benjamin to visit the Denver Zoo, we recaptured the experience by building mini animal pens out of twigs, stones, and wooden blocks, and then populated the pens with tiny zoo animals I had purchased in the gift shop. Roads or railroad tracks connected the different places, and Benjamin-Doll drove a pick-up truck hither and yon, always accompanied by friends.

Benjamin and I were attending music festival concerts several times per week, being the fortunate recipients of complimentary tickets from my orchestra colleagues. The repeated concert experiences allowed me to work on Benjamin's behavior in a real-world situation that displayed a clear-cut expectation: the audience was to sit at quiet attention while the orchestra played.

Normally, we stayed only for the first half of the concert. That was plenty and didn't disturb Benjamin's bedtime by much. Sometimes he sat surprisingly still and listened, allowing me to breathe and absorb the music. More often though, he got wiggly, became distracted by the brass number tags, or started making sounds. Then I would stroke his arms and rub his back, or take him onto my lap whispering, "Be quiet and listen," praying that our regular work with this phrase would enable him to respond appropriately.

When Benjamin got particularly restless, I would be on pins and needles, recognizing that he might let loose with a squawk or shriek. I would be sitting there, feeling this terrible nervous sensation, trying to make sure that my child was behaving properly while also fearing that my apprehensive tension might transmit itself to Benjamin and thereby *cause* precisely the thing I was hoping to avoid. In moments like this, I would begin visualizing: sunshine radiating from my center; a cloak of serenity enveloping both of us; the orchestra's music as waves of golden energy, enchanting Benjamin and drawing him in.

Perhaps my energetic intentions were exerting some influence; we were indeed getting through concerts without disturbing other audience members. Nevertheless, I always made sure we were in an aisle seat near the back of the auditorium, close to an exit, just in case.

Rowan was at our house, engrossed in laying out an extensive system of train tracks while Benjamin sat nearby, stacking blocks and keeping an eye on Rowan's activity. Suddenly, he surprised me by *initiating* an interaction. "I want to give this to Rowan," he announced into the silence, placing a rectangular, red block next to Rowan's knee like a little offering. Rowan glanced up from his train in acknowledgement of Benjamin's overture and took the block, placing it a few inches farther up the track.

"I want to give this to Rowan," Benjamin said again, this time holding out a blue, square block, clearly expecting Rowan to accept his gift. Rowan took the blue block, added it to the red one, and continued playing with the train.

"I want to give this to Rowan," Benjamin intoned once again, this time handing over a short, yellow dowel.

Over and over he did this, either placing a block on the carpet near Rowan, or expectantly holding out his hand until he got a reaction. I was amazed at his persistence and at the overall role reversal. Benjamin was clearly craving interaction, and Rowan was the one who seemed reticent which, oddly enough, was opening up the space for Benjamin to express himself and to share.

The next day, Lily and Benjamin were together, playing, when Benjamin started up with, "I want to give this to Lily." I interceded, feeling that his impulse could now be shaped into something more natural. "Here, can you use this?" I said, cuing Benjamin to repeat after me as he handed over a wooden block. Then, "How about another one?" And, "Here's this..."

Initially, Benjamin echoed the phrases only with prompting but then, propelled by his strong desire to interact, he began saying them without waiting for cues. Lily, in turn, answered in a variety of ways, clearly gratifying Benjamin with her vivacious receptivity.

Benjamin had been building up his sorting skills for many months, identifying which group or classification something might belong to, and he now responded correctly when I asked, *"What belongs? What doesn't belong?"* So, I was expanding our drills, challenging Benjamin to think about "real" things. For example, I might ask him to identify the appropriate placement of furnishings in the dollhouse. Setting up a bed in what was clearly the bathroom, I would ask, "Does the bed belong in this room? No? Show me where it *does* belong. Yes, in the *bedroom*. Now show me what belongs in the bathroom. Here are your two choices..."

One of our newest challenges involved following simple, three-step directions, to be completed *without* an initial visual demonstration. I would say something like, "Simon says: touch your nose, touch your tummy, touch your feet," and Benjamin would have to use auditory recall in order to follow the sequence.

I was also working on visual recall, playing a game called, *"What's Missing?"* I would arrange four or five objects on a plain surface and then ask Benjamin to look and memorize them. "Now turn away, hide your eyes," I would say before removing one of the items. "Now look again. Ooh, what's missing?"

Simple board games were on the program now, and so were speed exercises; I was making a game out of getting Benjamin to move and think more quickly on demand. "See the red bucket over here? And the blue one over there? Drop this ball in the red bucket. Then come back for another ball; it will go into the blue bucket. Ready, set, go! Go, go, go!" I would cheer and applaud, coaching Benjamin to run and fulfill the task, rewarding him at the end with an enormous bear-hug.

Our language drills were becoming increasingly complex as I expanded the scripted format which had been the bread-and-butter of our program thus far. Now I was drilling open-ended questions such as, *"What do you see?"* or requests such as, *"Tell me more…"*

I also worked on Benjamin's linguistic flexibility, teaching him different ways of saying the same thing. For example, Benjamin was learning that when I said, "I have on a red shirt," he was expected to check his own shirt and respond with either *"so do I"* or *"I do too."* At first, he blended the two phrases, saying "so do too," but with consistent corrections from me, he was beginning to understand. Eventually, I would be teaching him the possibility of saying phrases like, *"I don't have a red shirt,"* or *"Mine isn't red,"* and then elaborating: *"My* shirt is *green."*

Benjamin and I were downtown, sauntering along the brickwork of Boulder's charming pedestrian mall, taking in the performances of various buskers and musicians. Now Benjamin stared, fascinated, as a woman played the hammer dulcimer, mallets nimbly bouncing and skipping on myriad metal strings, producing a sprightly, purling sound. After a while, Benjamin's look of blissful absorption gave way, and with a little shriek, he dissolved into heart rending sobs. "It's broken, broken," he wailed. "Mommy, please sing me a song…"

What was going on?

Within moments, it came to me. Benjamin loved the dulcimer music, and the enormity of the feeling was overwhelming—he actually felt shattered by his experience of beauty. I began crooning into Benjamin's ear, rocking him, hoping that a favorite lullaby might bind up the pieces of his soul. "It's not so strange, really," I mused. "I too have been moved to tears by music. I too have felt utterly permeable, as if my protective inner barriers have dissolved, laying me bare to the depths of experience...a mixture of bliss and pain."

A brief wind storm had damaged our deck umbrella, snapping its stem in half, and I had salvaged the umbrella canopy, using it to shade Benjamin's sandbox. The enormous mushroom top leaned at an angle, resting on the ground, and whenever we came near it, Benjamin was inexorably drawn to look at its struts and stem—and to burst into tears, crying, "It's broken." At first, I tried to comfort him and to change his thinking, pointing out that we were still making good use of the umbrella. Then, as Benjamin became so hypersensitive that a mere glimpse of the umbrella would set him off, I considered putting the thing in the trash in order to avoid the dreaded emotional collapses.

But life with Benjamin was filled with emotional triggers, and running away from them wouldn't solve any problems. It had dawned on me that Benjamin was empathizing with the umbrella, experiencing its broken-ness as if it were occurring within his own body, and most likely, he'd had a similar sensation during his upsets with the duplo-blocks. Flooding Benjamin with purposeful, repeated exposure would be an appropriate strategy, and I augmented this approach with matter-of-fact acknowledgement. "Yes, it's broken. I understand. It hurts to be broken."

The phrase, "It's broken," was becoming a recurring theme, expanding beyond beautiful music and busted umbrellas, and I was ready to explore a new strategy. "I'll make up a 'curative story' to strengthen Benjamin's emotional resilience," I thought. "Storytelling is a powerful tool; this is why Waldorf educators create teaching tales which *indirectly* address specific problems."

I had recently discussed such storytelling with Corinne, and she had given me some guidelines. "Your main character, representing Benjamin, should develop the target trait or behavior as the plot unfolds. He needs to be accepting of outside support, so you'll want to create characters that aid in producing positive change. Keep it short and simple, and tell the story repeatedly to make it sink in."

Now, as I tried to develop a curative tale for Benjamin, I felt terribly inadequate. I wasn't a natural storyteller and thus had to sketch the thing out on paper. I came up with a plot and with wording that would resonate with Benjamin's current understanding and vocabulary, and then tested the story. I told it to Benjamin while walking along the nature trail. Listening to myself speaking the sentences out loud, I squirmed at the artificiality of certain phrases. Time to edit.

It seemed laughable that such a short and simple story should cause me such difficulty, but evidently, my perfectionism was getting in the way. "Simplify, simplify, and speak from the heart," I told myself. "Don't get too intellectual about this." Finally, I had worked the tale out to my satisfaction.

Once upon a time, there was a boy. His hair was blond, just like yours, and he loved to play his violin: this boy had music in his heart. One day, out in the woods, the boy heard the sound of someone crying. He followed the sound and—what do you think he saw? A little elf, sitting next to a broken flower. Its stem was bent, its petals were ragged, and the poor elf was crying bitterly, hiding his face in his hands.

"I want to help," thought the boy. "I will play music for him."

He put up his violin and began to play, and do you know? That little elf looked up, and the longer the boy played, the happier the elf became. The music was lifting his heart. He tucked his flower into a special place and held out his hand. The boy held it, and together they danced out into the forest.

Along the nature trail, there was a singular stand of trees and bushes which formed a welcoming niche, carpeted with soft mulch: a gnome home. For several mornings in a row, I invited Benjamin into the cozy and charming space for his special story. He listened very carefully, watching my face— unusual for him. By the third day, Benjamin joined me in saying, *"This boy had music in his heart."* He also spoke along on *"heard the sound of crying"* and *"broken flower."* The story had caught him up; its key images were clearly finding resonance within Benjamin's soul.

Benjamin and I were again downtown, on the mall, and I was daring to dream big. A colleague of mine was directing a large violin ensemble consisting of variably aged children, all students of his. They were playing a public concert of standard Suzuki Method repertoire, with bluegrass fiddle tunes thrown in for fun. "Wouldn't it be amazing if Benjamin could join this group in performance someday?" I thought, struck by the audacity of the idea. "He already plays well enough; he knows many of the beginner's pieces." I settled on the thought, watching Benjamin's intent interest, listening to the concert. By the time the final rounds of applause were rippling around me, I had made up my mind. "I'll project this as a concrete goal, not as wishful thinking, and we'll see about developing the necessary social skills. Maybe by next summer..."

Benjamin was learning to act out scenarios based on poems and short stories, and just now, he had a gold-painted wooden sword in hand and was mounted on an old, wooden hobbyhorse. I prompted him to chase after me, and we galloped through the house with me providing sound effects, whinnying while clip-clopping coconut shells in imitation of hoof beats. Finally I shouted, "Ho, there's the dragon." As we arrived back in the living room, I thrust my sword into a pile of pillows wrapped in a dusky, woolen blanket.

"Get him with your sword, Benjamin, like this," I exclaimed, and as soon as Benjamin was consistently imitating me, I changed roles. Animating the "dragon," I made the pillow bundle jump around and lunge towards Benjamin while roaring fiercely.

"*Raauargh!* It's okay, Benjamin, keep hitting the dragon with your sword. *Raaauargh!* Keep going, that's it—we have to kill him..." As I kept coaching, Benjamin really got into the spirit of the game, vigorously jabbing with his sword, laughing, giggling, and screeching with excitement—and a little bit of fear too—as the dragon kept plunging towards him.

"*Rrrkkk...ahhh...*" Finally, with great choking sounds and drama, the dragon sank to the floor. It had been boldly slain. "Congratulations, King Arthur," I said to Benjamin.

"Yes, Lancelot, Sir Gawain" Benjamin replied, and I gaped at him, astonished. Those names hadn't surfaced since our knights-and-castles phase of February, and yet Benjamin was appropriately pulling them out of his memory.

"What a mystery the mind is," I thought. "You just never know *what* it is taking in..."

A new self-awareness was growing within Benjamin. All month long, he had been riding a "high" of accomplishment, learning many things more quickly and easily than in the past. However, this positive trend was beginning to reveal a downside: when a particular concept or skill required extra effort, and if Benjamin felt stymied—unable to "get" it—feelings of frustration would well up with little delay. Now that he'd had a taste of quick learning, he was less tolerant of the slogging hard work that had been our norm for so long.

Sometimes, frustration would erupt because Benjamin knew precisely what he wanted to do but couldn't make it happen; like when he sang a familiar song and his tongue got mixed up. The words had come out imperfectly, and Benjamin had become extremely upset, screaming and throwing himself about. The time was ripe for Benjamin to expand his vocabulary of emotion-labels and to identify the increasingly complex emotions bubbling up within him.

"Say, 'I'm feeling frustrated'," I prompted whenever the angry screeches surfaced. Within a few days, Benjamin was using the phrase at appropriate times with apparent relief and less need for noisy vocalizations.

22

New Ideas, Further Progress
August 1998

Benjamin was at my parents' house while I did the weekly shopping. He couldn't yet handle the temptations of a grocery store. Rows upon rows of bins, enticing levers and knobs, shelves loaded with stackable cans, a small army of revolving greeting-card stands; all these would invite Benjamin to a fixation fest. When I returned, my mom beckoned me to the dining room table where I saw a completed crafts project. She had engaged Benjamin in constructing a little mailbox out of flexible tagboard of a light-blue color. The box was complete with a door that opened and a red flag that could be raised, indicating the presence of mail. "Benjamin," I prompted. "What do you want to show me?"

This was one of our newest skill drills—showing and sharing—and I was teaching Benjamin to say phrases like, *"Mommy, look at this,"* or *"Hey, I want to show you something."* Benjamin picked up his little mailbox and held it up for me.

"Say, *'look at this,'*" I reminded, waiting to hear the phrase before I took the mailbox. "Beautiful," I enthused. "Did you do the cutting? And the pasting?" Benjamin nodded and opened the mailbox door. Inside was a postcard from Rick.

"*L-l-l...*" I prompted, and Benjamin remembered. *"L-l-l-look,* Mommy, my card from Daddy." I looked admiringly at the dramatic depiction of Mt. Fuji; Rick's squadron was currently flying out of Japan. Benjamin turned the card over and looked at the neat lines of large block lettering. "I'm reading," Benjamin announced as he followed the memorized sentences with his pointer finger and quoted, *"I'll be home soon. Love, Daddy."* I glanced at my mom who was shaking her head sympathetically. We had a full month to go before Rick would be back for a visit.

"Come, Benjamin, it's time to play with the dollhouse." Benjamin joined me willingly, kneeling down and poking his head all the way inside some of the rooms, looking around. I laughed. "Wouldn't it be funny if you could shrink and become as small as Benjamin-Doll?" I asked, thinking of how Alice-in-Wonderland had done just that. I handed Benjamin some dolls and, after prompting him through a familiar sequence of actions, suggested, "Can Benjamin-Doll and China-Boy play together? How about making them jump on the trampoline?"

I sat back and waited, wondering if Benjamin would make the small leap from the concrete to the abstract. Up until this point, most of our play had revolved around miniature objects that clearly represented their full-sized counterparts, but I was beginning to insert requests that would require imaginative transformation on Benjamin's part. Overcoming autism would require moving beyond a purely concrete conception of the world.

Benjamin looked inside the dollhouse and found a little woven rug. He laid it on the floor, picked up the two boy-figurines, and made them jump up and down on the hand-woven square of material. As I smiled, delighted with his success in transforming the rug into a trampoline, he began singing one of the songs we had learned in Kindermusik class. *"Now we are jumping, jumping, jumping..."* I felt a zing of excitement at Benjamin's spontaneous elaboration of the scenario; this was great progress.

Now I decided to introduce something new. "Come, Benjamin, I want to do a little puppet show for you." For the past few days, I had been racking my brain for ideas, trying to come up with something that might allow Benjamin to move through a play scenario independently. Currently, he was entirely reliant on my lead or that of his peers, and while he might become inspired to create a short burst of action such as the one involving the "trampoline," he didn't seem to understand that one thing should lead to the next, and so on, to form an ongoing storyline. So I had come up with a plan: Benjamin's favorite Mother Goose rhymes would provide the necessary scaffolding for him to independently act out a story sequence.

First, I would have him say the rhyme along with me. We would clap in rhythm or play "patty-cake" while speaking the rhyme.

Second, I would perform the rhyme for him, acting it out using small dolls and other figurines. Because of the brevity of each rhyme, I could repeat it several times in succession, and Benjamin could practice being quiet, watching and listening.

Third, I would play "conversation ball" with Benjamin, encouraging him to speak the rhyme with much vigor as he alternated lines with me, tossing a beanbag or rolling a ball back and forth in accompaniment.

As a fourth step, I would guide Benjamin in manipulating the figurines himself, teaching him to "perform" the puppet show. This would be the new, challenging aspect of the exercise and might take considerable time to achieve.

The concluding activity would be for Benjamin to watch as I performed the show one last time; I reasoned that this would help synthesize and reinforce the four previous exercises in his mind. Ideally, the entire sequence wouldn't take longer than a few minutes. Rhymes that were ideally suited to my plan included *Jack and Jill, Little Miss Muffet, Humpty Dumpty, The Queen of*

Hearts, and *The Pussycat and the Queen.*

"Eventually," I thought, "we might even act out the verses in person, each of us taking on different roles. We could use simple props and costumes to help define the characters and actions." Putting my plan into action, I now found that the five-step sequence took much longer than I had anticipated. The fourth step posed enormously difficulty, and in addition, Benjamin had trouble transitioning quickly from one activity to the next. "Interesting," I thought. "His natural inclination is to flit about like a butterfly, following the attention-deficit dictates of his brain, but with me directing the changes in activity, the transitions are a problem. We'll need to practice this sequence a lot."

Benjamin hadn't been swimming since the previous summer's parent-tot class, and now we were in the warm-water pool, reviewing skills. Benjamin loved splashing about and floating on his back as I cradled him, but as soon as I tried to turn him over onto his stomach, intense fear gripped him. "Oh, no," I thought, groaning inwardly. The phobia that Benjamin had developed after his first facedown submergence in water hadn't lessened with time.

Pushing the envelope of Benjamin's tolerance, I placed a kickboard under his belly and added a few foam "noodles" for extra security, promising, "You will stay on top of the water, I will *not* make you go under." I sang to him and massaged his back, and once he relaxed a bit, asked him to blow a few bubbles. That was it for the day. Benjamin's ongoing reluctance told me that this would be a long haul, and I resigned myself to building up trust and whittling away at fear over the course of many months.

I was taking Benjamin to spend a day at the county fair, and I had a plan. Benjamin had been oblivious to the sights the previous year, overwhelmed by the many new impressions. This time, we would make repeated passes through the exhibits, thus creating layers of experience.

On arrival at the fair, Benjamin immediately fell into fixation, clambering up and down every four-rail fence panel in sight. He ignored the animals, wholly obsessed with exploring the boxy, geometric shape of the panels. Suppressing my growing impatience with Benjamin's stuck behavior, I cajoled him to look at the sheep and to sniff the pungent, dung-tinged air.

"Let's pet the sheep, it's so soft," I coaxed, somewhat forcibly curtailing Benjamin's manic climbing. He screeched in protest but I didn't back off; the sheep wouldn't mind hearing some noise, and there weren't any onlookers to glare at me. Benjamin struggled while I determinedly ignored his screams and pushed his hand into the curly wool of the nearest sheep. After long moments, Benjamin seemed to break through the mental barrier formed by his climbing fixation; his eyes came into focus and, taking in the sheep, he stopped fighting me. He relaxed, digging his hand into the soft, greasy wool, petting and stroking with increasing enjoyment. I let out my breath in a *woosh* of relief.

Once Benjamin had become conscious of the appealing animals, things improved; although he still wanted to climb the fencing, I was able to negotiate with him. "*First* look at the pigs with me, *then* you may climb up and down one time. Good job. Now come to see the cows, *then* you may climb up once again Woops, *stop*—only once, not two times. No screeching. The calves don't like that; it hurts their ears."

As we kept cycling through the same exhibits, Benjamin settled down, looking ever more closely at the animals with each visit. My plan was working.

Benjamin's sessions with other children were stimulating his imagination. Lily in particular brought new ideas for play. Currently, she was interested in playing "fire—the house is burning down" and "hospital/doctor" with the dollhouse figurines, and Benjamin was keen to join in. I addressed the gaps in his understanding during private work sessions, and then noted increased participation when Lily returned to similar scenarios.

Spontaneous moments of imaginative play were happening with growing frequency as well. For example, when I laid out a big, blue blanket on the floor and suggested it could be a swimming pool, Benjamin jumped into its middle and then lay down on his tummy, pretending to blow bubbles without any prompting from me.

On a different day, Benjamin surprised me with an imaginative creation all his own: he picked up a wooden footstool and, turning it upside-down, set it upon the sturdy seat of his rocking horse. He stood, thoughtfully rocking the horse, looking down into the container formed by the footstool. Then he commented on the horse's imaginary load. "It's carrying a box...there are rubies in it...and almonds...and vitamin capsules."

"Vitamin capsules," I echoed, chuckling at Benjamin's perception of the world. Every day, he would watch me emptying various vitamin capsules of their contents during mealtimes, mixing the powders into strong-tasting juice for him. The discarded gel caps would form a glistening heap, a pretend treasure trove. Whenever we ate meals somewhere other than at home—picnicking in the park or going to the family cabin—I would be toting a small cooler containing Benjamin's vitamins, nutritional oils, and ice-packs; this cooler was reminiscent of the "box" the rocking horse was currently carrying.

Now I began adding a fantasy component to our familiar "family cabin scenario," thus exercising Benjamin's imaginative capacity on a regular basis. Benjamin-Doll and his friends would go on a walk, heading towards a wooden block sitting in the "meadow." My doll would gesture to the block and ask, "Hey, look there, what do you see?" My goal was for Benjamin to fabricate an answer, but as of yet, he was unable to do so and thus I would give him three choices. For example, I might say, "Is it a rabbit, a bird, or a tree?" Benjamin consistently picked the last thing on my list, and so I was encouraging him to choose different options. We were taking baby steps towards playing make-believe.

Benjamin's awareness of the world around him was expanding. We were sitting on the deck eating lunch when Benjamin said, "I hear Mr. Joe." That was our next door neighbor, clattering dishes in his kitchen. Minutes later, Benjamin commented, "I hear Miss Dana and Robby talking." Dana lived four houses away, and only after Benjamin drew my attention to the voices could I make out the faint conversational sounds. Benjamin, on the other hand, could clearly distinguish the voices with ease. His hyper-acute hearing was astounding.

An afternoon rain shower had drenched us, and now a bright, full rainbow stretched across the purple-clouded sky. When I pointed it out to Benjamin, he gazed with awe and then announced, "I want to draw the rainbow." Benjamin followed through on his impulse and created his first independent drawing—a significant step forward from the scribbling he preferred.

As the last week of August neared, the momentum of the summer's productivity seemed to stagnate. Throughout the past few months, I had been judiciously administering Benjamin's homeopathic remedy as needed, using varying dosages to prevent him from entering a behavioral nosedive, but now its effectiveness was clearly waning. Benjamin was retreating into old behaviors—contrariness, screeching, and fixation—and my nerves were quickly fraying.

One of the worst days occurred while we were taking a day off of "work." My parents had joined us in hanging out at the cabin and in hiking around nearby. Inexplicably, all day long, Benjamin had found reasons to erupt into screams, spoiling a perfectly beautiful day. Even as we ate dinner together, Benjamin was unable to settle down, and the meal was unpleasantly punctuated by his screeches. Eventually, my parents and I packed up the food coolers, gathered the toys and books I had brought, and headed back down the canyon in separate vehicles.

As I drove with Benjamin silently sitting in his booster chair behind me, I thought, "At last, some peace and quiet." The respite didn't last long, however.

Soon, Benjamin began chanting, "We're going through the tunnel, we're going through the tunnel." He repeated the phrase over and over, articulating the words in his usual choppy way, his voice a flat monotone that drilled deep into my brain.

Benjamin went on, nonstop, a broken record player, and soon I felt I was losing my mind. Forcibly concentrating on the road, I yelled for Benjamin to stop chanting but was ignored. A solid half-hour of torture later, we finally reached the anticipated tunnel, and Benjamin quieted. My ears were ringing, my head aching. "I need to start packing earplugs," I thought, wondering why I hadn't come up with this simple strategy ages ago.

In spite of the deterioration in Benjamin's behavior, I insisted that we keep working because his new skills were so tenuous. Whenever I neglected to review a skill for more than a few days, the slippage in Benjamin's retention was significant. However, I did begin questioning myself, wondering whether I had been pushing him too hard, for too long.

In regards to our violin practices, I thought, "Maybe his resistance stems from a perception that we are going to keep repeating things without end." To remedy this, I put together a simple visual aid that would show him the number of times we were going to practice something. I filled a small bowl with pennies and set it next to a large dinner plate, then told Benjamin, "Look here, sweetheart. I am laying seven pennies in a row on the plate. Each time that you play this little exercise on the violin, I will move one penny away from the row and put it right here."

I gestured to an empty area on the plate. "This will make a little pile of pennies—a little heap of treasure. When all the pennies are in the treasure-place, we can change to a different exercise." As I guided Benjamin through repetitions of various music exercises, he began catching on to the concept. He enjoyed monitoring the dwindling rows of pennies and, after he had completed a few rounds of repetitions, I let him play with the coins as a reward.

As far as play scenarios went, I finally had an epiphany of realization: I could build frequent snacks into the scenarios as a natural part of the action. In this way, I would harness the motivating power of food, while eliminating the sense that Benjamin was being trained in the manner of a dog. "What a simple and obvious solution. Why didn't I think of it before?" I berated myself and immediately tried it out.

We were working through a variant of the cabin scenario: Benjamin-Doll was going swimming in a lake as well as catching toads, just as Benjamin and I had recently done at the local reservoir. I jiggled my doll around, giving it a voice. "Hey, Benjamin-Doll, let's have a snack, I'm hungry." I sat down my doll and handed Benjamin a slice of apple, prompting him to "feed" his doll before popping the snack into his own mouth. Then, we carried on. Several more times, I inserted doll-picnics, making sure that these breaks occurred *before* Benjamin expressed resistance. I wanted to create a natural, playful association between the snacks and the dolls, rather than overcoming poor behavior with bribery. Benjamin rewarded me by sticking with the ongoing action for longer than was usual, and I thought, "This is a 'keeper' of a strategy."

Rick's flight squadron had finally returned to Whidbey Island, and now we were on the phone. "Benjamin got a new homeopathic remedy last week," I explained. "He's feeling much better now. You're gonna be blown away with his language progress. Hang on a second." I laid down the receiver and retrieved Benjamin. "Say 'hi' to Daddy," I whispered to him, positioning the handset against his ear.

"Hi, Daddy," Benjamin said dutifully. His eyes brightened with recognition as he heard the voice on the other end. He was silent for a while and then said, "I ate bean soup for lunch." More silence as Rick apparently asked him something else. Then, "Lily is coming to play today." Another silence. "Walker stinks."

Trying to suppress a laugh, I leaned over, wanting to catch Rick's reaction to this cryptic statement. Misunderstanding my intention, Benjamin handed me the receiver, saying "Bye, Daddy."

"That was incredible; we just had a real dialogue," Rick exclaimed as I got back on the phone. "Before I left for deployment, you were modeling practically every sentence for Benjamin, and now he is talking and answering on his own. I am absolutely amazed. But, what happened to the dog?"

"Oh, he got skunked about six weeks ago, and he still reeks," I explained, confirming Benjamin's earlier declaration.

23

A Push for Independence
September 1998

An air of anticipation pervaded our house as Benjamin kept repeating himself. "Daddy's coming to play with me. Daddy's coming." At long last, the metallic sound of a key came from the front door, and then Rick was standing in the living room with his suitcase. "That's Daddy," Benjamin observed and began hopping around, unable to contain his delight. Rick looked bemused and happy. He had never yet been greeted by his son with such joy.

Rick and Benjamin were sitting together, looking at a book, and I settled down next to them. "I consulted with a speech therapist last month," I told Rick. "He had some suggestions for getting more spontaneity out of Benjamin. Now, when I read out loud, I add some wait-time before starting on each new page. The hope is that Benjamin will come up with some comments or questions. If he doesn't, I make little inquiring sounds while pointing at the pictures, looking at him as if to say, 'What do you think about that?' I also encourage him to conjecture, asking things like, 'What would happen if this character did x or y?'"

Benjamin turned the page, looked at the picture of a smiling girl, and observed, "He's happy."

"*She*," I corrected. "*She's* happy." Benjamin echoed my statement and then looked up, beaming. "He's happy," he exclaimed and this time, I felt sure he was referring to himself.

"Yes, *you* are happy. Now say, '*I'm* happy'," I directed, smiling. "*I* am happy too, and so is Daddy." As Benjamin looked back at the illustration, I explained to Rick. "Using correct pronouns is another one of those linguistic issues. We've been working on them all year, but they still seem to be guesswork for Benjamin. That is common for kids with... *You* know." I assiduously avoided using the "A" word around Benjamin, not wanting the term "autism" to enter his consciousness, feeling that his mind ought to remain unfettered by the label until sometime far in the future.

Sophia had arrived at our house for a brief visit, and Benjamin was gazing at her with an enchanted expression in his eyes, as if seeing a vision from a fairytale—a magical Godmother, perhaps. Sophia smiled warmly, ceremoniously handing over a small cloth bag. "Here is something special, just for you."

Beaming, Benjamin tugged at the drawstring and withdrew a large, five-pointed star that had been cut from matte gold cardboard. He pursed his lips, sucking in his breath with wonder, gently tracing the pointy star tips with his forefinger. Then he looked up at Teacher, speechless, eyes glowing.

"Your mama will hang this star by your bed. The star will watch over you at home, just as Teacher will watch over you at school," Sophia explained. Benjamin nodded, and then regained his speech. He was suddenly eager to play and banter. "Teacher has purple hair," he teased, dissolving in giggles. Benjamin's sense of humor had lately become quite pronounced.

Sophia played along, her expressive face reflecting astonished amazement. "And *your* hair is *pink*! Oh *what* shall I *think*?" she rhymed, and Benjamin burst into fresh gales of laughter. After a few more comical exchanges, Benjamin played a song on his violin, and then the visit was at an end. "Good-bye, Benjamin. I will see you at school tomorrow morning."

Thursday morning dawned, fresh and sunny, and I drove Benjamin to Sophia's, parking a few blocks away so we could begin the school day with a short invigorating walk; this was to become a regular feature of our school mornings. When we reached the house and I quietly opened the door, Sophia came to greet us, knowing we had intentionally arrived a little bit late. I had wanted to avoid the chaos of multiple children and their parents milling around in the entryway.

"Heel-to-heel and toe-to-toe, / Where my shoes go, they know," Sophia sang, gesturing for Benjamin to place his sandals neatly on the "shoe train" in the foyer. She had taught him this little ritual during our summer play sessions. Benjamin arranged his sandals properly and then padded through the adjoining living room and into the spacious school room. There, he stood still, taking in the scene and sensing the calm atmosphere that prevailed; then he looked up at me with a radiant smile, delight and joy beaming from his eyes.

His new classmates were already engrossed in play: a pair of twin girls so young that they were still in diapers, another girl who was close to three years old, and a boy of Benjamin's age. The disparate age-range of the class was actually ideal, I thought. Being at different developmental stages, the younger children would tend towards parallel play, while the somewhat older ones would be more interactive and imaginative, and Benjamin would benefit from ongoing exposure to both ways of playing; he still had a lot of catching up to do.

Benjamin went to the rocking chair and sat down, accepting a cuddly, handmade doll-baby to hold while looking around. Time and again, he glanced at me or Sophia, saying blissfully, "He's happy…" For my part, I sat quietly on the floor beside the rocking chair, my hands folded and my "antennae" attuned to Benjamin. I would be his unobtrusive shadow throughout each school morning.

"Let us form a ring," Sophia sang after playtime, guiding the children to form a circle in the center of the classroom. Then she spoke: *"The sun is shining, the sky is blue, / Let's go to the orchard, you come along too..."* (from *Acorn Hill Anthology,* edited by Nancy Foster). Sophia was leading a so-called "circle play," a collection of seasonal rhymes and songs that formed somewhat of a narrative. Simple gestures went along with each line, helping to tell the story. As the circle unfolded—a pony pulling an apple cart, then being fed some hay, and finally needing to be shod by a farrier—the children picked up on imitating Sophia, while Benjamin simply hopped and flapped with excitement. "We'll need to practice the play at home," I thought, knowing that further songs and poems would be added as the weeks went by. Benjamin was already familiar with acting out songs and poems but not in an extended sequence; thus, the charming circle play was the perfect "next step."

After a short nap, the children were sitting around a low round table, eating a hearty snack. "Bees are in the bushes," Sophia commented, thus quelling the annoying hum that emanated from one girl's stuffed mouth. Sophia's observation that "horses are in the stable" effectively quashed the *thunk thunk* of someone's feet bumping on a chair. And eventually, Sophia commented, "Benjamin look, there are sheep in your meadow." Little bits of rice had escaped his bowl, landing on his grass-green napkin, and I drew Benjamin's gaze to the rice, whispering, "Those are your sheep." His face gradually reflected understanding, and Sophia's rippling laughter brought an answering smile to Benjamin's face—and mine. I marveled at the playful elegance with which Sophia taught table manners, indirectly addressing transgressions with colorful imagery.

At home, we were practicing familiar doll scenarios when Benjamin spontaneously embarked on playing hospital as he had done with Lily the previous month. Pretending that his gaily painted truck was an ambulance, he laid Benjamin-Doll into the truck bed, cushioning the little blond figure with a miniature towel from the dollhouse bathroom. Then he surveyed the scene. As I sat quietly, wondering what Benjamin might initiate next, a thoughtful expression crossed his face and, speaking under his breath, he said, "Maureen..."

My heart lurched with recognition. Maureen was the kindly pediatric nurse who had helped us after the botched blood draw, during the spring. The fact that Benjamin remembered the incident didn't surprise me, but I *was* astounded at his recall of Maureen's name. In spite of the trauma he had undergone, Benjamin must have recognized Maureen as a caring individual, and now he was focusing on his memory of her. After a minute, Benjamin turned away, clearly done with the scenario. Having witnessed these moments of recall, I came up with a new idea: our dolls might help Benjamin with processing other negative experiences.

Within days, an opportunity arose for me to try out the new strategy. Benjamin was referring to a scary experience: he had climbed into my parents' heavy, metal wheelbarrow, wanting a ride, and had tipped over in a painful crash. I quickly crafted a tinfoil barrow and placed Benjamin-Doll inside. Seeing this, Benjamin dissolved into tears, the fearful situation flooding back in its entirety. "He's scared…the wheelbarrow is shaky," he whimpered.

I brought out the Mama-doll. "Look, now Mama is holding the handles so Benjamin-Doll can climb in safely. Next time you want a ride, call me to help. I'll make sure the wheelbarrow stays upright." I was reinforcing my words with visual aids, increasing the likelihood that Benjamin would remember my advice. In response, Benjamin quickly got over his tears; the modeled scenario was presenting a solution to his woes.

Benjamin's interest in playing piano had recently returned after a hiatus of several months, and now he was picking out songs in exotic tonalities. He had even made up a game which involved the folk tune of *Pop Goes the Weasel*. Benjamin would stack an arsenal of pillows on the piano bench before playing the song with its several verses; whenever he got to the "*pop*," he would toss a pillow up into the air before finishing the melody. I was thrilled to see him coming up with play ideas of his own.

Benjamin was experiencing another of his characteristic nosedives, and by the last day of Rick's two-week visit, beastly autistic screaming was peppering our activities, accompanied by much arm-flapping and body-tensing. I observed this with dismay, realizing that these self-stimulatory motions had virtually disappeared during the summer months and that, over time, I had begun taking for granted this more "normal" state of affairs.

Although Benjamin was responding well during some of our work sessions, his mood wavered disconcertingly, and I wondered at the cause of this latest regression. Following an earlier line of thought, I mused, "With the rate of growth happening in these early years, there's bound to be disproportional development in various areas of body and brain, interrupting the smooth functioning that might already have been established. After all, typical children have unpleasant phases too. It's just that everything is so extreme and unpredictable in Benjamin. Besides, his development is being artificially fostered, so who knows? It's all a matter of guesswork."

We were at preschool, and Benjamin was in a withdrawn, fixated state, when one of the twins threw a full-out tantrum. Watching her without becoming upset himself, Benjamin commented, "She's dramatic...she's tired." My ears pricked up in surprise. Benjamin was drawing a parallel between the toddler's squalling and his own tendency to screech. He was remembering that *I* sometimes said things like, "Stop being dramatic," or "I think you must be tired," and now he was recognizing the similarities between what *I* sometimes observed in *him*, and that which *he* was seeing in his classmate's behavior. This was a definite step forward out of Benjamin's characteristically autistic perception into greater awareness and understanding of another, and I mentally applauded his "un-autistic" observation.

Sophia was gently establishing some boundaries for Benjamin. One morning, as snack was being served, Benjamin started playing with his green cloth napkin, unfolding it and spreading it over his placemat. He quickly became fixated on the action of smoothing it down, continuing to adjust and stroke the napkin even though it was lying perfectly flat. "Benjamin, I can't serve you until the napkin is folded again," Sophia said matter-of-factly, while also giving Benjamin an encouraging smile.

I waited to see how Benjamin would handle the minor consequence. For the moment, he wasn't ready to back down and so we all held hands, saying the blessing, and then the others commenced eating while Benjamin kept smoothing down his napkin. I knew he must be hungry, and eventually I whispered in his ear. "Mm, this tastes so-o-o good. Fold the napkin now. Then you can eat."

With a few squeaks of protest, Benjamin allowed himself to be persuaded and was promptly rewarded with a steaming bowl of buttered rice and peas. Relieved that the issue hadn't escalated, I watched Benjamin out of the corner of my eye. He ate only a little, gazing thoughtfully at Sophia, seemingly bemused at her power to influence his world.

I caught Sophia's eye and gave a small nod, telegraphing my satisfaction. In this context of communal activity, Benjamin would have many opportunities to learn about consequences, both by experiencing them himself and by watching his peers as Sophia shaped their behaviors.

As the third week of September arrived, beautiful autumn weather beckoned us to my parents' garden, and we began helping with the harvest. All around, fruits and vegetables lay piled in myriad bins and buckets. "They're plum pillows," Benjamin observed, gently laying a succulent, purple-blue fruit amongst its fellows. I had taken a break from picking plums and was sipping some tea, swishing it around my mouth to clear residual bits of fruit from my teeth. Benjamin watched me curiously and then commented, "Gotta eat the tea bag..."

Tea sprayed from my mouth as I burst with hilarity, nearly choking as I tried to swallow. "You are too funny," I coughed, catching Benjamin up in a bear-hug. He struggled to get out of my arms. "Oi woint to goi on the sloide," Benjamin giggled, clearly wanting to fuel my laughter further. Then he mangled his words in a different manner. "Oo-ah oo-want to-ah gwah..."

"So it *is* on purpose!" I thought. Benjamin had recently developed a rounded "foreign accent" which was getting increasingly pronounced, but I hadn't been sure whether he was creating it intentionally. Now I knew. "Time to straighten that out then, before it becomes an ingrained habit."

We were visiting with Julie, and I had briefed her on the return of Benjamin's most challenging autistic behaviors. Having decided on a homeopathic remedy, she put a few drops into a little cup of water for Benjamin, who gulped it down with a smile. He had been charming and responsive throughout the appointment, seemingly interested in all that was going on around him and remaining undisturbed by my commentary.

"I feel badly, giving negative reports about Benjamin's behaviors when he is being so sweet," I exclaimed. "It's like I'm pooh-poohing his progress. But he embodies such extremes. He has a golden heart and a beautiful mind, and yet he can be totally subverted by his—you know, the "A-word"—and become unbearable to deal with. I can't just shrug off his bad days; they have too much impact on our progress."

Julie nodded sympathetically. "Your fears are justified, but don't let them take over; that would be self-destructive."

Interpreting the world in a concrete manner might be a hallmark of autism, but Benjamin was nevertheless coming up with colorful, imaginative observations that extended beyond literal understanding. At school, Benjamin had given Sophia's mailbox a smart whack, giggling at the hollow, vibrating sound. *"The mailbox sneezed,"* he had announced, precipitating laughter from Sophia and I. Now, when our old refrigerator made a strange whooping sound, Benjamin remarked, *"It's yawning."* Recently, on watching Walker's excited capering in anticipation of a walk, Benjamin had commented, *"He's doing a doggie dance."* And a few weeks ago, when Benjamin had noticed me feeling upset about something, he'd made an astute remark: *"There's a mistake inside Mommy."* His symbolic use of language was striking, and this prompted me to consider how generalizations about autistic thinking might be overrated.

Throughout the past few weeks, I had begun pushing Benjamin for independence in his daily living skills, wanting to build strength of will and self-confidence. Now I was stationed outside our bathroom, playing the sentinel while Benjamin dragged out each step of his toileting procedure to impossible lengths. Nevertheless, I refused to step in and take over, knowing that Benjamin was perfectly capable of completing the bathroom routine on his own.

"Finish up, we have games to play," I reminded, using a cajoling tone even though I felt like screaming. This forced patience was putting me over the edge. "I'm between a rock and a hard place," I thought. "If I give in to Benjamin's slowness and start helping him again, the underlying message is that he doesn't *really* need to do this on his own. On the other hand, there aren't enough hours in the day to provide all the necessary 'wait-time' and to *also* get through our learning programs. If we don't review constantly, we backslide. What a conundrum, searching for a balance between these extremes."

That evening, with Benjamin in bed, I began writing in my journal. Soon, I found myself giving in to tears punctuated by occasional howls of frustration; despair was overtaking me, and everything seemed suddenly futile. "What's the point?" I thought, feeling hollow. "All this effort, the insane amounts of work, and it seems like it's going nowhere. For an entire year, I've been giving the same old prompts for dressing, bathrooming, and eating. Where's the progress in that?" My fingers were flying over the computer keyboard. "Benjamin is capable but unmotivated. I *must* find a new solution—*I need inspiration...*"

Throwing myself onto the floor with a pillow hugged to my chest, I began taking inventory of my bodily sensations. I was way short on sleep, my head was aching, my lower back griped with pain, and I felt like an emotional powder keg, ready to explode. It dawned on me that Benjamin's behavior wasn't the sole reason for my bleak outlook. "It's that time of month again," I thought. "No wonder my resilience is down to zero. But that won't last forever. Now I've got to come up with something positive."

I began massaging my scalp, racking my brain for ideas. "Benjamin needs to feel like a 'big boy' who can *do* things. He needs to feel empowered and *able*," I thought. "I'll start visualizing him as such—as a 'big boy.' That's the least I can do until something else comes to me. I must send energy in the right direction instead of chasing my tail in circular thinking; I *must* have faith in inspiration. I'll go to bed and let the 'committee of sleep' work on this."

The next day, my parents, Benjamin, and I were exploring a new trail together. "It's nearly Michaelmas," my mom reminded me, trying to bolster my spirits as I wrangled with last night's issues. "Why don't we have our festival a little early? We could put together a harvest table and celebrate this afternoon."

"Let's do it," I said, glad to train my thoughts on something positive. The focus of Michaelmas was on gathering courage and inner resources, and this spiritual task was being required of me just now in regards to Benjamin. Needing to clear my mind, I began jogging up the trail, leaving my little group to follow, and soon an idea came to me. Benjamin was too young to understand the flow of time and therefore had no sense of urgency about completing his daily routines. However, I might produce an awareness of time through the use of music: I would create a song to keep him flowing through his bathroom procedures.

Humming the tune of *Twinkle, Twinkle Little Star*, I began putting words to melody, imagining Benjamin going through a sequence of actions. I figured, "One phrase per action, sung slowly, and with a small pause at the end of each phrase; that should allow enough time for each step to be completed." Soon, I had a final version:

> _Bathroom Song_
> _Now I'm pulling up my pants,_
> _Pulling up, and pulling up._
> _Now I'm dressed and ready to wash,_
> _Wash my hands and rub, rub, rub;_
> _Now it's time to dry, dry, dry,_
> _Dry my hands-oy, what a big boy!"_

That was it. And surely it would work.

It did. Once back from our outing, I used the first available opportunity to test the new song on Benjamin. He seemed tickled by its novelty and moved through the dictated sequence quite willingly. When we got to "*what a big boy*" with Benjamin emerging from the bathroom, I gave him a bear-hug and made a big deal out of his successful completion of the routine.

"You are so big, and I am *so* proud of you—*big* kiss from Mommy." Then I thought, "What a relief; payback for last night's emotional pain. I just hope it lasts."

Benjamin was darting around the house, toe-dancing and hip-hopping, his mouth spouting the chaos that was in his head. "What does the camel say? What does the elephant say?" he asked repeatedly, not stopping for an answer. Clearly, Benjamin's thoughts were looping 'round and 'round, and I pushed him for some real exchanges, tossing a conversation ball to emphasize turn-taking. I insisted on moments of silence too, interrupting and calming

Benjamin's jumble of disorganized thoughts. "Be quiet...and listen," I whispered, reviewing the cue that we had so intensively practiced during the early months of summer. With these interventions leading him out of chaos, Benjamin settled down.

We were at table, eating, and I was insisting that Benjamin feed himself every bite. Benjamin's regression in independent eating habits had been evolving since May when I had begun popping spoonfuls of unpleasant vitamin mixtures into his mouth. Benjamin had adapted by becoming less motivated to feed himself, remaining content with me plying the spoon. Now he needed to be weaned from this insidious habit.

However, this meant that meals were going very slowly, and I practically had to sit on my hands to prevent from picking up a spoon and feeding Benjamin. "Come on, big boy, I know you are hungry, put in another bite." I couldn't leave him unattended—Benjamin would either stare into space or hop out of his seat—and I cast about for something to occupy me. My solution? Instead of sitting, wasting time and feeling frustrated, I would bring song/ poetry collections to table and busy my mind with memorizing new materials.

I had laid out Benjamin's clothes, lining them up along the couch, and now I was cuing him to get dressed, starting with the first article. My goal was that Benjamin would someday organize the clothes himself rather than requiring the daily, ritualized set-up, and that he would recognize tags, buttons, pockets, etc. as indicators of the proper way to wear something. Currently, these clues needed pointing out, but I was nevertheless insisting that Benjamin put his clothes on with minimal help. "We need a 'dressing song' to move things along," I thought now, and began making up a lively chant.

> *First come the underpants, tralala, la.*
> *Then comes the undershirt, ladeeda, dee.*
> *Turtleneck, tag in back—going through the tunnel..."*

Benjamin's customary resistance dissolved, and he began moving more quickly, propelled by the song. My push for overall independence was gradually generating some momentum, energizing both Benjamin and me.

The dollhouse was getting a rest. I had shifted Benjamin to playing out familiar scenarios using Alexander and Katrina, the medium-sized twin dolls, as props. My idea was that Benjamin should play "Daddy," thus taking on a role that represented independence and responsibility. Furthermore, carrying the cuddly dolls around and caring for them could be a genuine and heartfelt experience. Feeding, burping, rocking—such nurturing actions would be a healthy role-reversal from Benjamin's day-to-day experience of being cared for by me.

As the "Daddy," Benjamin would also have a sound reason for acting out household activities. I had borrowed a picture book called, *I Can Help*, and Benjamin had taken a strong interest in the illustrations of a child sweeping, washing dishes, cleaning windows, and so on. However, when I attempted to teach Benjamin some skills, he became fixated on the various tools, spinning and tossing them about. I decided that *real* helping could wait until later and that, for now, we would only pretend. However, in keeping with my new "big boy" focus, I did insist that Benjamin carry his own dishes to the sink after meals, and that he give Walker and Mandarin their replenished food bowls each evening. Little chores would add up to a big step forward.

24

Benjamin Turns Four
October 1998

Benjamin was cocooned in Corinne's hammock, content to be swung while we talked. "Here's something to try when Benjamin starts flapping and tiptoeing," Corinne suggested. "Instead of making him stop, have him purposely act out being a 'busy bee' while you sing a little melody; encourage him to move in as fast and hyper a manner as possible, but only for the duration of the song. Then he should intentionally let go and relax. By giving Benjamin a designated time in which to flap and hop, you might find that he gets it out of his system for a little while; eventually though, he'll need another 'bee break.' No guarantees that this strategy will work, but it is worth a try." I nodded.

"I would also introduce finger-knitting and other simple crafts," Corinne said. "As Benjamin grows in independence, you'll want him to experience the satisfaction of creating tangible objects with his hands—pretty little things that can be looked at and enjoyed, or that can be given away as gifts."

Corinne now recommended emphasizing puzzles and games where individual parts would come together to form a whole—a complete picture or form. "Putting together a puzzle is essentially an act of integration. It symbolizes what we are ultimately striving for with Benjamin—the harmonious integration of his many aspects: his physical body, his emotions, his personality and thought processes, his soul and spirit, and so on." As Corinne spoke, a mental image of Benjamin consisting of many harmoniously interwoven bodies floated through my mind.

"I can imagine such integration and wholeness for Benjamin," I told Corinne. "But, I must admit that my worries around fully recovering Benjamin from autism are growing. The brain is most malleable and responsive to therapy from birth to age five, and Benjamin is nearly four years old now; we're getting close to the end of that optimum time period. Although Benjamin has made incredible progress, he isn't as far along as the children described in the 'recovery stories' I have read."

A tangled web of thoughts and emotions welled up inside me. "Thinking back to last year, I'm amazed at the calm acceptance I maintained towards Benjamin's autism. Even though my goal was recovery, and even though I was striving hard, my work with Benjamin had a sense of discovery and adventure to it. But these days, I so often feel like I'm fighting: I go head-to-head with the autism monster. There's an aggression embedded in that attitude which makes it more emotionally painful when things don't go well. My sense of fear is counterproductive, but I can't seem to let go of it."

Corinne nodded her understanding. "Let me suggest a sequence of visualizations. Start off by projecting an image of Benjamin in the *future*, integrated and whole, divested of his autism, and send up your prayers for him. Then settle into thinking about Benjamin as he is *right now*, with all of his challenges, and consciously let go of the negative feelings that this image might trigger; imagine your fears flying away like a flock of birds. Finally, settle into a feeling of calm acceptance. Reiterate your intention to keep working for growth and change, and imagine doing so while maintaining your inner peace."

"Thank you, Corinne. I will do that," I said quietly, feeling taken aback by the shrinking sensation that had overtaken my gut at her words, *"Benjamin, as he is right now..."* Clearly, there was a lot of fear there—a destabilizing flock of painfully pecking birds that needed to be ousted.

"As you work with Benjamin, maintain a feeling of 'breathing' and allowing space," Corinne now counseled. "Feelings of fear and panic in *you* will only block Benjamin, will harden his etheric forces and make it even more difficult for his astral body to integrate with his physical body. Be careful when you are tempted to force things along. You may have to push for progress, but don't do it *just on principle*. Remain sensitive to when Benjamin needs you to back off; maintain some level of trust in his process. Your instincts are sound."

Benjamin had developed a head-cold, and at preschool, he contentedly watched his friends as they played. The mild illness had apparently subdued Benjamin's excessive jumpiness, allowing him to be fully present and aware. Soon, Sophia called Benjamin over for a turn at watercolor painting. The paper gleamed dully from soaking in a water bath, and Benjamin chose to begin with yellow. The glowing color swam, each stroke becoming increasingly diffuse and fuzzy as the paint soaked into the thick paper. Next, Benjamin added strokes of red, evoking an autumnal mood as he played with the two colors, melding them into various shadings of orange. His attitude was contemplative and he laid down his paintbrush, leaning back, tipping his chair onto its hind legs.

Boom. Benjamin had tumbled to the floor, his small chair lying overturned next to him, and Sophia was reaching out a hand to help him up. Fighting back tears, Benjamin cuddled into her. She had cautioned him about tipping over in his chair, and now she held him comfortingly and talked quietly. Watching, I was deeply touched by Benjamin's utter trust in Sophia, and I was overcome too by the poignancy of Teacher being his source of comfort even though I was available and sitting only a few feet away. I longed to wrap my arms around Benjamin but instead breathed deeply, consciously releasing my proprietary feelings, wanting to support Benjamin in his developing independence. It was good that he could look to someone other than me for help.

Benjamin eventually left Sophia's embrace and moved over to where some cuddly dolls, similar to our Alexander and Katrina, lay in a basket. Benjamin picked one up and cradled it in his arms. "Hi, Baby," he said to the dolly. "Hi Benjamin," he said to himself, creating a dialogue by giving the baby a voice. "I love you..."

Benjamin paused, then said musingly, "Baby is walking to the forest..." He sat down and, taking hold of the doll's arms, began reciting our German *Morning* poem (the one I had used to teach basic eurythmy gestures during the spring). We hadn't reviewed this poem for many months, but now, Benjamin began making the vowel shapes with the doll-baby's arms, speaking the poem all the while. I watched, warm of heart as Benjamin handled the doll with exquisite tenderness, love in his face, his soul alive with the movements and the poetry.

Now fatigue overcame Benjamin, and I made a little house for him to retreat into. Setting two play-stands opposite one another, I used thick woolen strings to fashion clotheslines that reached from one stand over to the other. Then I draped lengths of softly colored cloth over the structure, securing the side-cloths with large, wooden clips. The house now had a roof and four sides, and Benjamin crawled inside, still holding the soft baby-doll.

He had nearly fallen asleep when I crept into the cozy space, humming a gentle melody. "It's time to awaken. Children are cleaning up," I murmured. Benjamin eyes fluttered open, and he reached out to gently brush a strand of hair off my face. Moments like this were gifts to be cherished, and I was put in mind of the few other times that Benjamin had touched my hair or brushed a crumb off my cheek. His endearing gestures revealed the gentle, loving soul that was his essence and that so generously showed itself when the clouds of autism were lifted.

We were having an exceptionally productive week abounding with special moments. For example, with the dollhouse figurines, Benjamin spontaneously acted out a round of *Duck, Duck, Goose*, apparently recalling the game from Talia's preschool. For the first time, Benjamin began actively playing with Mandarin, dragging strings along the ground for the cat to chase, and he also got up the courage to hold Mandarin in his arms, cradled against his chest. And, several times, Benjamin went through his bathroom routine with *zero* prompting, causing me to dance little jigs of joy.

At preschool, as the children played at horseback riding, Benjamin joined in, announcing, "This is Captain." I smiled. My work—teaching Benjamin to mimic real-life occurrences during play—was coming through. As the free play period ended, I went to the foyer for a sweater and was surprised to hear Benjamin say, "Mommy's going home."

I stopped in my tracks, wondering. "Should I interpret this to mean that Benjamin is ready to continue his school day without me?" Still standing outside Benjamin's field of view, I sought to catch Sophia's eye. She looked at me, smiling and nodding, discreetly pointing me towards her living room couch, and I saw we were both thinking the same thing. I would remain present and available, but would stay out of sight while Benjamin went through the remainder of the morning's activities with only Sophia to guide him. If successful, this would be a significant step towards Benjamin's becoming a "big boy."

As I eavesdropped and occasionally snuck a peek into the playroom, I could see that Benjamin was not at all perturbed by my sudden absence. During circle time, he kept his eyes on Sophia although he imitated only a few of her motions, and at snack he was very quiet, seemingly deep in thought, forgetful of eating until Sophia prompted him. He didn't even look for me at story time and, once the children were outdoors playing, I spied on him, observing that he was actively engaged with his classmates.

"Look, Teacher, I see a grasshopper," he exclaimed, spontaneously using the "look/see" phrase that we had drilled so diligently in the previous months. I was thrilled. Only a few weeks earlier, Benjamin had been getting hyper-fixated on insects, quivering with tension as he watched a butterfly or a ladybug, blocking out everything else. But now, he was displaying flexibility and a desire to share his experience.

For three weeks, Benjamin had been meeting the challenges of my intensive "independence program." Now however, halfway through October, I was seeing signs of regression. Benjamin again needed my intervention in the bathroom as he became fixated on sink handles and on the stream of water coming from the tap. "The novelty of singing through his routine has worn off," I thought. "Benjamin's motivation is waning." Hm. Perhaps I could entice him with some new reward that would come at the end of the song since my hugs and praises were no longer providing a sufficient incentive.

Brainstorming, I came up with the idea of tempting Benjamin with little music boxes; I had quite a collection of these from my own childhood. The next time he headed for the bathroom, I pulled out a surprise. "Look here, Benjamin. If you do your entire bathroom song without any help, then you may play with this."

I demonstrated turning the hand-crank on a little decorative box, watching Benjamin's face as the tinkly sounds of Tchaikovsky's *Swan Lake* began sounding. Benjamin's eyes widened and he became suddenly animated, zipping through his routine with nary a pause. He hopped out of the bathroom for a hug and then reached for the music box. "Well," I thought. "Looks like that's going to work. I sure hope it lasts a while."

Benjamin may have been backsliding in his independence routines, but at school he was still moving forward. Just now, Benjamin was using his practiced dialogue skills during playtime, and he was coming up with spontaneous comments. Joining his classmates in "cooking," he sounded completely natural. "My turn. Here, the spoon is for you. Can I stir too?"

When the immediate activity waned and Benjamin began looking a bit lost, I set out a flat wooden disc that had been sliced from a log. Placing it onto the play table, I topped the slice with a wooden spool that had once held sewing thread. "Here's a cake and candle," I suggested, wondering whether a game of "birthday" might be sparked.

Benjamin gazed at the pair of wooden objects and began singing, *"Little candle, golden flame, share with us your bright light..."* There was reverence in his voice as he imitated Sophia's story time ritual, and I was touched by his undiluted expression of awe.

We were having a second consultation with the speech therapist. Knowing that I had made up some curative stories for Benjamin, he suggested I also create a few mini-stories based on my own childhood memories. "See if you can develop a repertoire of three or four little vignettes, and encourage Benjamin to say, *'Mommy, tell me about the time that you...'* You might also add a memory exercise to your bedtime ritual. Review the day's main happenings, and do this in backwards order. Benjamin can probably tell you what he did just before bed, but you might have to help him with what happened earlier than that, and especially with remembering what he did during the morning." This was an excellent suggestion, and it reminded me of a meditation exercise which I had come across in some readings on spiritual development.

I had reviewed my lists of behavioral therapy programs and had marked the language exercises which Benjamin now seemed ready to tackle. We were working on phrases such as, *"What's your name?"* or *"I have a _____,"* followed by a description of an object. We discussed the rooms in our house: *"What's in there? What do we do there?"* I drilled "when" and "where" dialogues: *"When do we eat breakfast? Where are we going?"*

I now began working on Benjamin's awareness of things around him that might be a bit distant from his current location. Particularly at school, I had noticed his difficulties in finding toys that weren't immediately in his vicinity. For example, if I pointed at a doll for him to retrieve from across the room, he couldn't seem to follow the trajectory of my finger in order to find the doll. So now I made up "searching" games, giving Benjamin many opportunities to hunt for something as I pointed at the object.

I also put a fresh emphasis on finding an object based on clues, challenging Benjamin to imagine what I might be hinting at. Benjamin had already learned about identifying something based on a verbal description; we had been practicing this using our *Mystery Garden* board game, and Benjamin had become quite adept at the guessing game in that context, since there were a limited number of objects that he could essentially memorize. Now I was expanding on the exercise, asking Benjamin to locate specific objects *in our vicinity* as I gave him broad clues such as, "I spy something round, red, and shiny."

In addition, we were playing "hot or cold." We would agree on an object to be hidden, and then Benjamin would search for it as I gave him feedback. Using the metaphor of temperature, I would indicate how close he was to finding the object. I would say things like, "Remember, you're looking for the blue ball. Now you are getting warmer; that means you're closer...now colder...*brrr*, ice cold; that means you are very far away...ooh, now you are hot, you're so close you're practically burning your nose."

Benjamin's current state of happiness reminded me of how, during October the previous year, the time before his birthday had been golden and filled with a sense of buoyant anticipation. This year's lead-up seemed to be following a similar pattern. Benjamin's special day was only a week away, and thus I began reviving the puppet show I had performed the previous year, rehearsing it for Benjamin so he would fully enjoy it at his party. Using dollhouse figurines, I also enacted the ritual birthday celebration that Sophia would be conducting at school. Such a mock-up would show Benjamin what to expect and thus help him with the transitions, as well as bolstering his comprehension of this meaningful event.

We were in Denver, consulting with a well-known autism expert, and I was describing Benjamin's waning motivation in regards to his "big boy" routines. "Try making picture schedules," the woman suggested. "Many people with autism respond well to concrete visual cues. Use simple illustrations and lay out the sequence of actions that you want Benjamin to follow. Then post the schedule in the area where the routine takes place. For example, you could make a pictorial version of the bathroom song that Benjamin just demonstrated to me."

I nodded in assent. I would try this out although my gut feeling was that a set of pictures in the bathroom would not keep Benjamin moving. Nevertheless, it was a proven strategy, and I felt sure I could find an effective application for the concept. As we wrapped up our session, I mentioned my hope that Benjamin might one day leave his autism behind.

"I have yet to meet a child that has completely recovered," the expert told me. "In my experience, residual autistic traits remain, regardless of progress." I looked at her in shocked disbelief. Then, feeling a bit desperate, I asked, "Isn't there a fair bit of ambiguity surrounding the definition of recovery? It's not a clear-cut thing... And it seems that full recovery *is* possible if one considers the doctors' reports cited in *Let Me Hear Your Voice*." The expert shrugged noncommittally and didn't argue her point. We were out of time.

The proverbial rug had been yanked out from under my feet, and I moved as if dazed, shepherding Benjamin out to the car. Driving back towards Boulder, painful thoughts regarding my beautiful boy's future kept dogging me. Now how was I going to maintain my optimism? What would keep me going if I couldn't be hopeful?

Soon the car topped the final rise leading into Boulder, revealing a stunning view of the continental divide. The highest peaks already sported some snow, and the closer mountaintops reflected sunlight in earthy tones. Blue-green foothills were layered in front, and the city of Boulder nestled right up to the foot of these lesser summits, its many deciduous trees flaming with autumn foliage. I drew in a deep breath and, taking in the beauty before me, finally admitted something to myself. "I've been in a form of protective denial that has kept me strong. By imagining an end in sight—an end to the demands of Benjamin's autism—I've been able to push myself beyond limits, time and time again."

Now Pandora's box was open and self-doubt began bleeding into me, released from a hidden, seeping place. I wondered, "If I truly accept that Benjamin may not recover, how will I find the strength to go on—to keep working at the level of intensity that is needed? I'm afraid I'll somehow give up. Can I maintain faith and truly believe that, whatever happens, the future will turn out alright?"

Back at preschool, Benjamin's interest was drawn to his same-aged peer, Colin, who was building a house, draping cloths over two play-stands. Benjamin meandered over to the "building site," seemingly intent on helping.

"No, Benjamin, those are *my* walls," Colin said possessively.

Benjamin looked stunned and then, after a moment's silence, he fell to pieces, crying and screeching. The phrase "It's broken" emerged repeatedly through his sobs, and his heartbreak was palpable. I felt for him. "This is rough," I thought. "Sophia and I keep encouraging Benjamin to interact and play, and now—just as he finally reaches out—he gets the door slammed in his face. How painful."

And yet, how real. This was how life could be. Clearly, I needed to think of ways to prepare Benjamin for these things; perhaps by modeling such scenarios with our dolls and by demonstrating some options for dealing with them. While this thought crossed my mind, Sophia's clear voice came from the table where she was painting with the twins.

"Colin, when you are ready, you can share with Benjamin." Colin made a resistant moo. "I will help you," Sophia assured him, letting Colin know that, while he would be allowed to finish his project, it wouldn't be acceptable for him to cut his classmate out indefinitely.

Now Sophia turned to Benjamin. "Colin will soon be ready to play with you. Can you find another friend for the moment?"

With this series of deft interventions, Benjamin's upset cleared up surprisingly quickly and Colin realized that he would like to share after all. I was impressed by the definitive clarity with which Sophia handled the situation; I would follow her example when making up those teaching scenarios.

The next day at preschool, during free play time, Benjamin reached a "high" of achievement: he remained engaged with his peers throughout a sequence of four "imaginations." First, Benjamin joined several children sitting on a play-stand, pretending to ride a boat, fishing for an invisible catch. Eventually, he disembarked and began "baking muffins" with the little girls. Then there was a "horseback ride" with Colin, and finally, Benjamin joined the others as they became bunnies with corncobs as ears. Then fatigue hit him. The scenarios had been quite elaborate, and Benjamin could no longer keep up as his peers developed further storylines.

Rather than allowing him to flop onto the floor, Sophia handed Benjamin a washboard and some cloth. "Can you wash our aprons?" she asked, demonstrating. Benjamin nodded and, glad to be in a corner by himself, slowly rubbed the fabric across the riffled surface of the antique tin washing tool, his mind clearly elsewhere.

"He needs assimilation time," I thought. "Imaginative play takes a lot of effort, and the simple, repetitive 'work' with his hands is an integrating sensory break." Sophia's clever strategy was calling forth physical engagement from Benjamin without requiring an exhausting expenditure of energy. Sophia had already introduced the children to playing at "work," and I was impressed by the interesting range of activities and materials provided. There were skeins of yarn to be wound into balls in preparation for knitting and crocheting. Sandpaper was available for smoothing down assorted blocks of wood, and the children had already done some hammering using a big, wooden mallet. Dried corncobs sans kernels could be rubbed across a handheld grater, and nuts could be cracked using an old-fashioned nutcracker. A *metate* for grinding corn stood near the hearth, and several children had already tested their strength by moving the smooth, oval river stone back and forth in the stone trough. Sophia owned a hand-operated grain mill for grinding flour which the children operated on bread baking days, and butter could be churned by filling a jar with whipping cream and then shaking it until the butterfat solidified into a clump. Inspired by these myriad activities, I had already added similar "work materials" to our home play area.

Our repeated practice with following the trajectory of a pointing finger (in search of an object) was having an unexpected but desirable outcome. This pleasant surprise revealed itself at preschool. During snack time, I was watching from afar when Benjamin looked over at me. At table, a conversation was in progress, and Colin was just saying, "Hey Benjamin, guess what?" Using hand signals, I cued Benjamin to keep eating, and then I pointed, indicating for him to pay attention to Colin. To my delight, Benjamin responded immediately to my prompting, even though it was coming from across the room. Clearly, his awareness was now bridging distances in a way that hadn't been possible before.

Benjamin's emotions had taken an unexpectedly volatile turn. Periods of frustrated screaming and tearful irritability alternated with chunks of time where he seemed quite happy. A few times, Benjamin experienced extreme screeching episodes which, after some hours' duration, stopped as suddenly as they had started. What could possibly cause such intense shifts in energy?

Hoping for clues, I spent several evenings combing through my journal notes of the past twenty-one months, color-coding and organizing materials, extracting developmental trends, recording treatments and interventions, and finally making a comprehensive chart.

While this process highlighted the enormous gains we had made and reminded me that cranio-sacral therapy and Julie's homeopathic treatments were helping on a large scale, I was still none the wiser in regards to the precipitating causes of Benjamin's difficult periods. His recurring attacks of hyper-autistic behaviors remained a mystery.

As Benjamin's fourth birthday dawned, low-hanging rainclouds made for a subdued mood. Festive smells of candle smoke and homemade chocolate cake pervaded our house, but Benjamin didn't perk up until he had unwrapped a tiny gift-box from my parents. On a ground of dark-blue velvet lay two lovely moths that my mom had found dead in her garden. One was an enormous hawk moth, its outstretched wings a pearly salmon color, patterned with grays and browns. The other was an ordinary miller moth with silvery wings, and Benjamin touched it gently.

"Fairy dust..." I murmured, pointing out the pearly, grey substance that shimmered on his fingertip. Now Benjamin began hopping and flapping, becoming fixated, and my heart sank. Throughout the past month, Benjamin's burgeoning obsession with insects had led to highly distressing scenes, with him screaming interminably when he captured various critters and they either escaped him or needed to be let go.

"Please, don't let this day be ruined by these moths," I pleaded silently, shoving my hands deep into my pockets to keep from snatching up the box. Then, admonishingly, I thought, "Let go of your fear and don't assume the worst. Give Benjamin a chance to take it in."

After an eternity, Benjamin's gaze finally wandered to the other small packages lying on the dining table, and I sighed with relief as he opened them. There was a shiny red wagon too, prominently placed directly next to Benjamin's chair and inviting him to climb in, but he was oblivious to its presence, and I didn't point it out. I was curious to see how long it would take for Benjamin to perceive it. "Sometimes, Benjamin's autism sends him to a different planet," I mused. "He often gets lost in details, funneling down into a micro cosmos, but at other times, he's somewhere else altogether."

Thankfully, by the time his afternoon birthday party began, Benjamin was awake to the world and was happily greeting his guests. After a harmonious play period, Benjamin even took in my puppet show with great attentiveness. Then it was time to light candles and sing. *"Happy birthday to you... How old are you?"*

"I'm four years old, I'm four years old..." Benjamin's pure, clear singing voice filled the room, resonating with perfect intonation, and I had to swallow hard as the beauty of the moment overtook me. The entire afternoon had been a resounding success.

I had come up with a fresh idea which extended the "picture schedule" concept. One of my goals was for Benjamin to act out scenarios independently rather than requiring my continuous presence and input. My long-term hope was that, as Benjamin memorized a repertoire of scenarios, he would become spontaneous in his play and that this would lead him to fabricating stories and action sequences, just as typical children do. Perhaps I could support these goals by making a set of cue cards. To test my idea, I chose our familiar "going to the store" scenario. On a strip of tagboard, I sketched five simple pictures representing a sequence of actions: a car (for driving), some fruit (to buy), money (to pay), the car (to drive home), and a house (bringing groceries into the home). Then, referring to the pictures, I told Benjamin the "story" of going to the store and explained what each picture meant.

Next, I asked Benjamin to verbalize the sequence of events, having him use the pictures as memory cues. The final step was for him to act out the story, referencing the picture schedule in order to remember the actions of the scenario. After several days of practice, Benjamin caught on to the concept, and I could see that he liked looking at the picture sequence and "telling the story." Thus, I made an entire collection of tagboard picture sequences, all based on the various doll scenarios we had practiced over the past many months.

In addition, I experimented with a variation of my initial idea. I didn't want Benjamin to think that there was only one "right" way to go through his play scenarios, and so I built some variety and flexibility into the game. I made a duplicate copy of some of the picture sequences and then, I cut these copies into individual, square playing-cards, each of which displayed a single picture. Using these card collections, Benjamin could arrange the pictures in whatever order he liked in order to narrate or act out a story.

25

Power Struggles
November 1998

November arrived with variable weather that shifted around as unpredictably as Benjamin's state of mind was doing. Sunny, bright hours were being wrested away by threatening storm clouds and, analogously, Benjamin's happiness was being chased hither and thither by miserable moods. Now we were back in Julie's office and, as I talked with her, Benjamin monotonously opened and closed a set of sliding closet doors, as withdrawn and fixated as could be.

"We *do* have good moments," I told Julie. "But these days, Benjamin will 'blank out' on me, acting like all he's learned has gone out the window. True, he *does* forget things, but lately, some of these blank-outs seem purposeful—an evasion tactic. Also, there's a new element of defiance that I haven't seen before. For example, Benjamin will tug on the dog's ears, and when I tell him to stop, he gets this rebellious look on his face and purposely ignores me."

Julie gave me a wry grin. "Benjamin may be four years old, but what you're describing sounds like what two-year-olds go through," she observed. "At that age, most children become defiant, testing boundaries, exerting their will power, and though this can be hard on the parents, it's a healthy part of growing up. Also, children often experience a regression before taking a big step forward developmentally. You've worked hard on independence during the past month, and perhaps Benjamin is on the brink of more fully 'owning' that." I nodded thoughtfully, glad for the positive perspective on my troubles.

We had been drawing and painting regularly, and Benjamin was now comfortable with collaborating on a picture, practicing his imitation skills. "Today, let's draw an autumn tree. Next time, we'll make a field with haystacks," I suggested, pulling on seasonal inspirations. "Watch while I draw."

Using the flat side of a brown block-crayon, I drew a broad, dark line, forming one side of a gnarly tree trunk and then swooping left to form a low-hanging branch. "Now your turn; trace Mommy's line." Benjamin did so, and then I asked him to draw a line of his own that would mirror mine, thus forming the other side of the tree's trunk, with a branch swooping to the right. Over and over, we took turns making broad crayon strokes that followed the pathways of rising sap within a tree until the many layers formed a solid trunk and an impressive crown. Then we took turns adding dynamic curves of russet, gold, and flaming red, evoking the glory of the maple and oak trees scattered about our neighborhood.

Having done well, but tired from his effort, Benjamin escaped to the bathroom while I glanced at the clock—time to hustle. I had an orchestra rehearsal to attend and still needed to make dinner. Heading towards the kitchen, I heard the *plop plop* of the plunger and the *click click* of the flusher being manipulated in rhythm like a drum kit. Changing course, I went to disengage Benjamin from his fixation. "Sit down if you need to 'go'."

I got him settled on the toilet and then hurried into the kitchen. Soon I heard Benjamin twiddling the toilet paper roll, spinning it on its axis. I returned to the bathroom. "Wipe," I commanded, confiscating the roll and handing him some paper.

Hearing our meal sizzling, I ran back to the kitchen to stir the pot and turn down the heat. By now, the bathroom sink faucet was being rapidly turned on and off, on and off, and so I raced back to the bathroom. My head was spinning. "You are finished." I had to bodily pull Benjamin away from the sink as he couldn't disentangle himself from its temptation.

Passing the dual light switch on our way out the bathroom door, I switched the top lever to its *"off"* position, and Benjamin began howling with outrage; he had wanted to flip the light switch. Hoping to appease him, I suggested, "You may flip the bottom one." Benjamin began shaking his head wildly with frustration, screeching, and I thought quickly, my nerves frazzled. "Look. Let's do this in harmony, like when we play the piano together." I turned the upper light switch back on. "We'll flip the switches at the same time; you do the bottom one, I'll do the top."

Benjamin quieted down, mollified that his opportunity for flipping a switch hadn't been entirely taken away. He also seemed intrigued by my analogy of playing the piano. "Ready, set, go." The lights went off. "Ta-dah—teamwork." A power struggle, averted.

A heavy snowfall was underway, and we were making our way slowly through accumulated drifts of white. I enjoyed tramping along with Benjamin in my wake, but when we got four blocks away from home, he became fixated on a wrought iron fence, repeatedly banging its rails.

No amount of cajoling would convince Benjamin to budge from his spot, and eventually, when we had spent a full twenty minutes in place, I decided to pull him bodily away. Benjamin began having a tantrum, upset that I had interrupted his clanking "music," and I—ignoring the tantrum—began pushing and pulling him, step by step, in the direction of home. He actively resisted me and then allowed himself to sag, heavy as a sack of potatoes, while I propelled him forwards. Hot pains shot through my back and shoulders, and tears started down my face as I thought, "Benjamin is getting so big and heavy; my body's not up to this anymore." Gritting my teeth against the pain, I felt enraged as Benjamin started giggling and leaning into each push, apparently enjoying the sensation of being shoveled onwards.

"Terrible twos indeed," I thought, flushed with frustration, resentful of feeling so weak and inadequate. I wasn't prepared to stand around, freezing, waiting for Benjamin to cooperate, and walking away wasn't an option. At the moment, Benjamin had all the power.

Later that day, Benjamin's defiance pushed me over the edge of reason. We were practicing the violin, and he was resisting me every step of the way, acting like he couldn't play a single note without my help. Stuffing down my feelings of frustration, I determinedly remained calm and insisted that Benjamin play through one song properly before quitting for the day. As I prompted him, he defiantly pinched and twisted his fingers against the violin strings and then pulled his sack-of-potatoes trick, letting himself go limp, dangling the violin and dropping the bow.

In that moment, my self-control snapped and I began screaming with rage, pounding the pillows of the couch, wanting to strike out at Benjamin, my bottled-up feelings of helplessness pouring out in an insane flood of fury. "Even if you don't want to play music, *I do,*" I raged into his face and, snatching up my own instrument, I began improvising a storm, hacking out furious chords and hideous dissonances. After a prolonged musical tempest, I gradually calmed into a haunting melody by Rachmaninoff, searching for inner peace.

Benjamin was sitting silently on the couch, looking at a book. I paused, and Benjamin's lips quivered. "Mommy, please play more music." I resumed playing, and when the melody came to an end, Benjamin began to cry in earnest. Laying away my violin, I sat down, cradled Benjamin against me, and rocked him soothingly, heavy hearted as I repented my earlier lack of wisdom. Instead of locking into a battle of wills, I should have let off the pressure and returned to the contentious issue at a later time.

I thought, "Perhaps some watercolor painting will bring us back into a harmonious relationship." I prepared the materials and then, sitting kitty-corner from one another, Benjamin and I silently applied paint to paper, playing with watery forms, letting the colors speak through their luminous beauty. Serenity pervaded the room. Once finished, I cleaned up the project and then went to find Benjamin in the living room.

A shy smile crept onto his face. "I want to play violin," Benjamin requested.

"Are you sure?" He nodded, picked up his violin, and began playing— beautifully.

That evening, after Benjamin was fast asleep, I devoted myself to journaling. A crisis point had been reached during the afternoon, and I needed to fully process what I had learned. "Power, control, and communication—these are the key variables," I thought, and after generating pages of free-flow writing, I was ready to summarize and to draw a few conclusions.

Benjamin's autism has required me to control and direct everything, and this has become a habit. The time is ripe for a clear shift in consciousness: I must focus on giving choices. I'll also explain to Benjamin that sometimes I get to choose, and sometimes he gets to choose.

As a parent, I'm responsible for providing consistent boundaries and consequences. However, I must also be ready to change course in midstream, to side-step resistance, to be flexible...

I've been sounding like a broken record lately: irritation, anger, and the word "no" are coloring my daily interactions with Benjamin. "No" is important to say, but if it becomes an outlet for my anger, if I'm a brick wall to Benjamin, then I shouldn't be surprised if he runs up against me with a defiance that equals my anger. "No" can be firm and neutral, and not an automatic reaction—I can establish authority and still be kind.

The next day, I began making good on my conclusions and resolutions of the previous evening. I explained to Benjamin that, "Mommy sees what a big boy you are now," and that he would be helping me with making choices. In addition, I started providing explanations for certain actions, teaching Benjamin about the why's and wherefores. "We do this because...but we don't do that because..."

When I sensed a tantrum coming on, I would give a clear cue. "Use your big-boy words. If you want something, you can tell me with words—then I can listen." Oftentimes, I had to guess at what Benjamin might want to say and to give him the proper words and phrases, but as the days went by, he caught on and realized that I was "on his side."

Whenever possible, I rewarded Benjamin's "big-boy words" by following through on his requests. Eventually, this lenience in favor of Benjamin's choices could be tempered, but first he needed to be convinced that communication was powerful. Simultaneously, he needed to realize that tantrums would not get him anywhere.

We were in the park adjoining the old Chautauqua auditorium, flying a kite, watching it climb higher and higher into the sunny, clear sky. As it steadied, tugging at the end of its tether, Benjamin giggled with happiness, holding tightly to the handle that secured the twine. "I'm doing it all by myself," he announced repeatedly, clearly reveling in a new awareness of independence. Making choices was waking him up.

We were working on language drills, and I was keeping up Benjamin's motivation and energy by repeatedly flinging a soft feather pillow at him. However, since having a "pillow fight" was becoming hyper-stimulating for Benjamin, I eventually changed course and invited him into a calm dialogue, giving him a new cue that I had brainstormed. "Palm-to-palm," I said, kneeling down and holding my hands up in front of my chest, palms facing outward. Benjamin eagerly placed his hands flat against mine, giving me his rapt attention.

This idea of holding "palm-to-palm" while talking had come to me after a recent cranio-sacral session. On that day, Cheryl's quiet way of speaking hadn't filtered through to Benjamin's attention, and I had wondered, "How might I teach him to listen and focus when someone speaks calmly?" So often, I captured Benjamin's interest by acting super-animated, by singing, or by doing something unexpected. However, other people wouldn't do that, and my job was to connect Benjamin to the "real world."

After conversing for a bit, I ended the exchange. Slowly, gently, I drew my hands away from Benjamin's, asking him to do likewise rather than snatching his hands away. "We want to keep our connection, even if we aren't talking," I explained. Benjamin's eyes glowed as he sensed the warmth that remained even though our hands were no longer touching. "It tickles," he told me, and I nodded. "That's energy."

I had been preparing Benjamin for Martinmas, retelling the traditional tale of compassion and generosity, and—like the previous year—had enacted the story using dolls. This year, I was adding a further activity: my parents and I, with Benjamin, were acting out the story using a script plus simple costumes and props. We would go through the short play several times so that Benjamin might get a feel for the two key roles: first, he would be St. Martin and act out the giving of the cloak, and then, he would be the beggar and thus experience receiving compassion within the context of the story.

I waited for dusk to fall before taking Benjamin over to my parents' house; as we walked in the door, the delicious scent of apples baking in the oven instantly brought back my own childhood memories of this festival. A feast of baked apples and a lantern walk in the dark accompanied by the singing of traditional songs had always followed our playacting, and now my mom was reviving the family tradition.

As we embarked on the opening of our play, Benjamin's attention was diverted by a glimpse of my dad's wristwatch, and his immediate fixation threatened to ruin the evening. Aided by deep, calming breaths and a resolve to avoid head-butting, I finessed Benjamin's attention back towards being St. Martin and gestured for my parents to continue with their lines. The play unfolded, gaining momentum, and Benjamin became increasingly engaged in the action, forgetting the now hidden wristwatch. The second time through, he even joined in speaking some of the lines, clearly benefitting from the repeated run-throughs and from the previous week's "doll performances." The layering of strategies was having a satisfactory effect.

I was feeling light of heart about Benjamin's growing comprehension. As I kept talking with him, giving him explanations and reasons for things, a new level of maturity was glimmering through—a positive response to my expanded style of communication.

I was keeping things simple, careful not to over-intellectualize, and was vigilant in monitoring my words. Soon, I noticed the phrase, "We don't do that," coming up with some frequency. "A dead-end comment," I thought critically. "Be proactive instead. Present an alternative choice before squelching an action."

I thought back to how Sophia handled undesirable occurrences in school. When a child threw a toy, Sophia—singing rather than speaking—would direct, "The doll may fly, it may *not* toss," and she would demonstrate, carrying the doll high through the air, "flying" it to a gentle landing in its cradle. Now I began using this example to shape my own admonishments.

Benjamin had developed a vocal tic overnight. Every few seconds, he was saying, "yes, yes, yes…m-hm…yes, m-hm." Even when eating, the sounds kept going, and after several hours of Benjamin's uninterrupted vocalizations, my nerves were shot. "Earplugs," I thought finally. "I've got to wear earplugs, or I'm gonna go nuts." The tics were clearly involuntary—all my efforts to interrupt them were ineffectual—and I observed that they intensified in the afternoons when Benjamin became tired. Strangely, after three days, the tics disappeared, and I was left scratching my head, wondering.

Sophia was crafting Martinmas lanterns, teaching the children to handle scissors, and Benjamin was showing himself quite adept. Now he was cutting a piece of yellow tissue paper into little snippets, gradually accumulating a fluffy pile. As he bordered on fixation, I made a suggestion for transforming his repetitive cutting activity into a game. "Take a handful of snippets, stand on your chair, and blow the pieces into the air. That will make a confetti storm."

Benjamin took my cue, and a whirl of gold filled the space around him. "I'm being an autumn tree," he exclaimed, surprising me with his beautifully poetic interpretation. "I want to be an autumn tree too," several children now requested, and I assisted Benjamin in sweeping up the paper bits for his friends, thrilled to see them crowding 'round and making Benjamin the happy center of attention.

Benjamin had made an unprecedented leap forward: during violin practices, he was independently playing through several songs in succession, freeing me to accompany him at the piano. This was an enormous change since I often had to sit directly opposite Benjamin, lightly touching his bow arm to keep it moving, or even propping up his left arm so that he wouldn't give up on holding the violin. My touch helped to focus Benjamin's mind and, although the hands-on approach seemed ridiculously overdone, I kept on with it because, whenever I could rouse sufficient motivation in Benjamin for him to play without my help, he showed considerable skill.

At the piano too, something had "clicked." Benjamin was no longer struggling with the independence of his hands and was now playing simple melodies with his right hand while his left hand accompanied with arpeggios or a "rocking horse" pattern of broken chords. Now that the need for hands-on help was lessening, I tried teaching through demonstration but found that, as was the case in every context, Benjamin had great difficulty taking in the salient information. Other children might learn easily through imitation, but Benjamin's brain simply didn't work that way.

My mom had come up with a new idea. Handing Benjamin a comb with a piece of wax paper folded over it, she explained that he should rest his lips against the paper and try singing. Curious, Benjamin followed her directions, giggling as the crinkly paper buzzed hilariously like a kazoo. He proceeded to sing various melodies, recalling them from times past, thereby demonstrating what an enormous repertoire of songs (minus lyrics) was embedded in his mind. I was astounded at his musical memory and wondered whether this might be a so-called "splinter skill." I had read about this phenomenon: in spite of the learning difficulties associated with autistic brain functioning, someone with the diagnosis might also develop certain highly specific, isolated skills, and might show real brilliance in those areas.

Benjamin's vocal tic had returned, but now it had changed from *"yes, m-hm,"* to *"we're gonna go,"* and that phrase went on nonstop for an entire day. By the next day, the words had disappeared and instead, Benjamin was repeatedly saying *"hck."* For me, this was the worst tic yet because my own body involuntarily empathized with the momentarily stopped breath that accompanied the pressurized little sound. Within a few hours, I was so wound up with accumulated tension that I had a hard time drawing a deep breath.

I tried to interrupt the tic by asking Benjamin to sing with me, figuring, "If he is singing, he's got to breathe deeply and then let things flow," but the moment our music stopped, the tic was back in full force. Then I tried the simpler strategy of having Benjamin say a drawn-out *"ah"* every so often, just to "un-stopper" him. Although this helped Benjamin to breathe more normally himself, it didn't end the tic.

"Please don't let this become a regular part of our days," I prayed fervently. Thus far, the various disturbing behaviors that had already cropped up as a part of Benjamin's autism had all become an integral part of our lives. They waxed and waned, and occasionally seemed to disappear, but not for long. While I had been hoping that they might shrink in proportion to Benjamin's positive growth and progress, this simply wasn't happening—at least, not yet.

26

Close of the Year
December 1998

I had stepped outdoors to fill our bird feeder and, on returning, was hit by the sight of Benjamin perched on a small tower—a stepstool placed atop a dining room chair—madly flipping the hallway light switch. His quick planning in response to my brief absence was stunning. How had Benjamin even found the stepstool, tucked away in the basement? The drive to satisfy his fixation struck me as analogous to someone with a chemical addiction, and I suddenly dissolved into hopeless tears. What if Benjamin never fully escaped the grip of his compulsions?

I retreated, howling with sadness, hands covering my face, temporarily incapable of maintaining a balanced perspective. Benjamin, meanwhile, continued rapidly flicking the light switch, seemingly impervious to my anguish. Just now, he was acting completely autistic even though I knew he was capable of giving and receiving love. *Click, click. Click, click. Click, click.*

Eventually silence fell. Getting myself together, I went to investigate and found Benjamin looking at his flower fairies book, calmly turning the pages. Was the obsession out of his system for now? Might we have a good day after all? "What do you think, can we practice violin?" I asked, and Benjamin willingly put aside his book. To my utter astonishment, he played through all of his songs with virtually no help from me. "From the depths of despair to the heights of heaven," I thought as my feelings soared, propelled by the restorative power of Benjamin's music making.

I had made a list of playground games that children commonly engage in and was now teaching these to Benjamin, with my parents joining in to create some semblance of group dynamics. I had already tried out games like "red light, green light," hide-and-seek, and tag during play sessions with Rowan and his mom, Eliza, but realized that we needed more bodies to make the logistics of these games clear to Benjamin. I also recognized that with group games, Benjamin would have an easier time understanding the actions if adults were sedately playing along instead of a group of squirrely children. So now, my parents and I played "Red Rover" and "follow-the-leader" with Benjamin, and then formed a "snake," holding hands and having the front person lead the way through various twists and turns. In the absence of chaos, Benjamin became able to settle and learn.

Benjamin was once again having screaming fits, throwing himself to the ground and shrieking for no discernible reason. His frustrated contrariness tainted each day, and after a visit to Julie for a new homeopathic remedy, I decided to take a break from our learning programs. Engaging in daily combat seemed pointless, and I suggested that my parents take Benjamin on long walks while I edited my book manuscript; I was desperate for some daytime hours in which to work.

Soon, guilt was nipping at me. Benjamin's mood had mellowed within the week, and as I reviewed various games with him, I noticed an obvious decline in his skill level, a direct result of the reduced number of hours spent working with him. "He's ready for me to take up the reins again," I thought, feeling torn. I didn't want to slow the momentum of my writing just now, not when I was so close to being done. "A few more days should do it," I thought, and made my decision: I would plow on and pick up the pieces afterwards.

Finally. Midnight. Mid-December. My manuscript lay printed, a neat stack of paper, ready for its final polish. I regarded it lying so harmlessly on the chair next to me. Those pages represented years of work; not just the time it had taken for me to write it, but all those years as a music student, researching and exploring practice techniques that might help musicians to overcome or prevent music-related injuries. I picked up the manuscript and rifled through the pages. "It's real. I've really done it—I can hardly believe it."

I shook my head with wonder and scrunched up my shoulders, then dropped them again, wishing that I could feel light and easy, relieved of this long-standing burden. Now would come the fun part: my pen-and-ink drawings to illustrate key points, and my art for the book's cover. When Rick came home for a visit in late January, we would create the final layout on the computer, and the book would be at the printer's by Valentine's Day. But my happiness at this prospect was weighed down by worry about Benjamin's slackening progress. A fresh infusion of energy and inspiration was called for.

We'd had a lengthy respite from worn routines, and I was determined not to slide into an old rut. Reintroducing Benjamin to playing with dolls and animal figurines, I avoided drilling scripted scenarios, instead focusing on the genuine joy of play; it wouldn't do to go through the motions with an empty heart. I watched Benjamin carefully, trying to intuit which activity might spark genuine interest. I played out myriad scenes and stories, inviting him into my world of fantasy but not demanding specific participation; if Benjamin became engaged, I would expand from that point of connection.

As the days passed, the appropriateness of this approach was validated by

Benjamin's increasing moments of imaginative play and also by some beautiful mornings at school. One particularly special moment occurred after all the children had been sitting together, busily sanding pieces of wood, altogether enveloped in a bubble of concentration and mutual camaraderie. Eventually, Benjamin's stamina had run out, and he had moved away from the circle to rest in Sophia's rocking chair.

Seeing this, Sophia placed a lyre on Benjamin's lap, and he began absently strumming its strings, plucking gently, his eyes softly gazing into space, his face tranquil. As if enchanted, the other children stopped their activity and spontaneously joined in gathering 'round Benjamin, silently listening, intent on taking in the delicate sounds. The somnolent spell of the music prompted the twins to lie down, and Sophia silently bedded down the others as Benjamin played on. Then he too lay down, and a heavenly silence pervaded the room, the delicate sounds of the lyre reverberating only in memory.

Such moments of beauty were sprinkled amongst more challenging times where I had to hold myself firmly together, keeping patience and a positive outlook in the forefront of my thoughts. However, when Benjamin began screeching or was taken over by vocal tics, I quickly felt pushed to my limits. These rough patches might have been tolerable if I felt energetic and healthy, but at this juncture, I was suffering from a bone-deep weariness that came from two years of pushing myself beyond reasonable measure. Every day, I was pulling myself up by the bootstraps, trying to generate the necessary output of energy, trying to produce a mind-set that would allow for creativity.

An observation I made during this time was that when frustration, anger, or even just impatience began welling up inside me—even if I acted calm on the outside—Benjamin would sense my negative energy and would begin acting up, screeching, resisting whatever was going on. Clearly, my internal state was actually *causing* some of our clashes; I was inadvertently sabotaging my intentions. "A powerful lesson," I thought, recognizing the dynamic. "I must find *genuine* patience within myself; just acting the part won't do the trick."

Rick's squadron was still deployed overseas, and connecting on the phone was difficult, but just before Christmas, we managed, using a special military phone line. Now I was sharing my recent decision to cut back on Benjamin's therapy appointments. "I get so much out of watching Benjamin at school and seeing how Sophia handles him that I feel alright about transitioning away from the occasional consultations," I now explained to Rick. "Clearly, there's no magic recipe for getting Benjamin out of his autism by age five. I need to settle in for the long haul."

Such a perspective would have been depressing to me just a few months ago, but I had recently spoken with an autism researcher in California, and this person had given me a renewed sense of hope for Benjamin's long-term improvement. He had described the case of a young woman with autism, now in her late teens, with whom he had worked with since her childhood. By continuing with various therapies over the course of her life, the young woman's autistic traits had receded to the point that her autism was virtually undetectable.

The researcher had stressed that a great deal of brain development and maturation would be occurring well beyond the so-called "window of opportunity." As Benjamin got older, he would become more self-aware and would be able to learn self-advocacy skills and other personal management strategies.

Now Rick imparted some new information. "I recently read about the MMR vaccine possibly causing autism in some kids." "Hm," I said, thinking back to the time around Benjamin's first birthday. "Benjamin's loss of eye contact and speech *did* happen within a few months of his MMR, but I was already noticing odd things when he was tiny—only six months old. I'll follow up on the new info though, just in case."

Our allotted phone time was running out, and I quickly shared a bit of holiday spirit. "We've been sledding," I told Rick. "And Ursula had a festive party where Benjamin got to perform, singing while I accompanied him on the guitar. You should have seen his face; he was positively beaming, looking around at all the folks while he sang, acting like a real 'ham'."

I hung up, melancholy about spending another Christmas apart. Hopefully, this would be the last time.

My parents and brother had joined us for an evening family celebration, and now I was telling the Christmas story, narrating the familiar tale as simply as possible while manipulating a set of "standing puppets" through a manger scene. In the dim candlelight, Benjamin eyes glowed, and he soaked up the story, no longer antsy and distractible as he'd been when watching me rehearse it throughout the previous week.

Then, Benjamin and I "performed" our prepared festival program: the *Winter Circle* that Sophia had been teaching in preschool and the German Christmas poems which Benjamin had learned, accompanying each line of song and rhyme with expressive movements. The Christmas story had set the mood, and now Benjamin's heart was in every gesture and lyric, imbuing everything with genuine feeling. We all felt it—the beautiful energy coming from Benjamin's being.

Then it was time for gifts, and I led Benjamin to something large hidden beneath a woolen blanket. "Are you ready?" I asked and dramatically unveiled the thing. Benjamin looked and then started hopping and flapping wildly at the sight of an enormous rocking horse with a sturdy metal stand and heavy-duty springs that suspended the horse from each of its four legs. I lifted Benjamin onto his steed, and he began rocking, carefully at first, and then with increasing abandon, laughing and crowing with joy. We were looking at the face of pure ecstasy.

As a gift from my parents, I had received a copy of *The Man Who Listens to Horses*, by Monty Roberts, and being a lifelong horse lover, I was devouring the biographical story of the "horse whisperer." In his youth, Roberts had spent countless hours watching the wild mustangs of Nevada, and over time, he had figured out the subtle but complex system of communication that exists amongst equines. I was inspired by Roberts' example of patient watchfulness and by his manner of tuning in with great sensitivity, and I thought that Benjamin might be observed in a similar way. "On occasion, I should try settling into Benjamin's time frame and see if I can figure out what's going on in his head. Now that he's developing opinions and more personality, this might be quite instructive."

One morning, when I was feeling particularly tolerant and mellow, I got Benjamin started on his dressing routine and then stepped back, letting him know that he was to complete the task himself. Although he had shown himself capable of this during October, he had regressed to being so slow and sluggish with the routine that I often intervened, unable to ignore the ticking of the clock.

Now I sat, mending torn clothes, sewing on missing buttons, not hurrying Benjamin along. The entire experiment lasted about forty-five minutes, and in the end, Benjamin did manage to get himself dressed. "Interesting," I mused. "A two-minute task took him nearly an hour. But, his mind did seem to be busy with something; he seemed contemplative rather than being fixated. I wonder what he was thinking about."

Perhaps he was meditating on mathematical concepts. Just recently, Benjamin had—on his own—developed a basic understanding of addition, and these days, when he played with dominoes and dice, he correctly added together the dots on various faces of the game pieces. I was delighted to observe Benjamin's emerging intelligence, but at the same time, was determined that he progress in as balanced and well-rounded a manner as possible. It would be all too easy for him to develop splinter skills and to become fixated on these to the exclusion of the many other thought processes that needed fostering.

The last day of the year was at hand, and we were spending a cozy evening in the company of my parents, playing simple board games and such. As we had done for the past several evenings, we lit the Christmas tree candles, drank spiced cider, and enjoyed the leisurely feeling that surrounds family game playing. Benjamin no longer considered the games a chore, in contrast to four months earlier when he had struggled with them, and he was requesting certain favorites.

One of these was a card-matching game called *Black Peter*, and Benjamin became blissfully happy when he drew the final *losing* game card. A chimney sweep wearing a top hat was depicted on the card, and—according to family tradition—this called for the use of a scorched, sooty cork to sketch a moustache over the loser's upper lip, and to mark a black dot in the middle of his forehead. "Black Peter, Black Peter," Benjamin chanted, looking at his black-smudged face in the mirror. "Let's play it again."

This time, my dad ended up with the penalty card, and I helped Benjamin to draw the curling moustache and the dot onto his grandfather's face. "Ooh…" Benjamin marveled at the dramatic transformation that he was effecting.

Now, the candles on the tree were guttering, and we all gathered 'round to make a "big wish" as the final candle sent its smoke heavenward. "Transformation— more transformation for Benjamin," I prayed. "Please let him keep growing out of his cocoon and into his wings…"

1999

27

Learning About Consequences
January 1999

We were in Julie's office, and Benjamin was strutting about impatiently, bumping and tugging at handles and knobs in a manner that was quite unlike his usual self. "He's really become fierce these days," I told Julie. "He's in a state of extremes, having nightmares and vocal tics, and he's so contrary that, even in his sleep, he's saying 'I don't *want* to, I don't *have* to.' I've gone into survival mode, feeling bombarded by his screaming. It's awful."

Julie nodded. "You've been working on independence and building up will power, but this upheaval is excessive. I have a new remedy in mind; we'll see if it takes the edge off."

Winter break was over, and preschool was about to resume. In anticipation of this, Sophia and I were speaking on the phone. "Benjamin's rebellious attitude is lessening a little," I told her. "I think he's ready for us to put a strong emphasis on boundaries and consequences." We discussed possibilities, and we agreed that—whatever Sophia came up with at school—I would follow through in a similar manner at home, thereby giving Benjamin a consistent message about the expectations for his behavior.

The next morning, Benjamin eagerly entered Sophia's playroom and went directly to sanding a block of wood, picking up where he had left off before Christmas. This sense of continuity was a new, positive sign; Benjamin was remembering what had occurred several weeks earlier, and he still knew which supplies were needed and also where to find them. Then, after a while, Benjamin wandered into the kitchen where he stared fixedly at the clock on the stove. Sophia addressed Benjamin. "Your eyes may look, Benjamin, but you must stay in our playroom. The kitchen is Teacher's kingdom."

Reluctantly, Benjamin backed into the playroom but continued staring at the clock. Suddenly, he let out a yell of protest. *"Naaaaah!"* Startled, I jerked slightly. Then, I twitched again as Sophia reposted unexpectedly. *"Naaaaah—is not a kindergarten word."* Sophia had perfectly imitated Benjamin's yell before continuing to speak in a normal manner, and now Benjamin looked positively shocked.

"What a clever strategy," I thought. "To be used sparingly though, otherwise the shock value will wear off." Benjamin moved away from the kitchen, and I heard him muttering, "Teacher screamed at me." Clearly, he was trying to process what had just happened, and I hoped that he would think twice before letting loose another yell at school. The time was ripe for him to begin exercising some self-control.

During circle time, Benjamin was causing a disturbance; in response, Sophia placed him in timeout, setting a chair for him nearby. Benjamin sat, momentarily watching, and then popped out of his seat, appropriately imitating Sophia's expressive movements. "Timeout will end when this song is done," Sophia said, returning Benjamin to the chair.

I was puzzled. For months, we had been working on getting Benjamin to participate more during circle. Now Sophia was keeping him in timeout even though he was imitating voluntarily. Why? The song ended, and Sophia's voice was encouraging. "Now you may join us, Benjamin."

"Ah," I thought, the light bulb going on in my brain. "He'll learn that participation is not just arbitrary and that he cannot bargain his way out of timeout."

A different lesson was introduced later, during snack, when one of the girls started talking about poopy diapers. "Bathroom talk may happen in the bathroom. At table, we have table talk," Sophia said, clearly setting the boundaries for all the children.

"Wise," I thought. "Rather than forbidding something outright, Sophia is designating a place where the child *can* do it and get it out of their system. She is teaching that there is a time and place for almost everything."

The next day, at school, Benjamin again experienced timeout, as did one of the girls. The two of them were misbehaving during snack time, and so, Sophia had them sit together at a separate table with only bowls of plain rice to eat. Delicious nectarines were then distributed to the well-behaved children. Benjamin was sorely missing his opportunity for some fruit, and I hoped that this would motivate him to remember the lesson.

I had decided to start Benjamin on some needlework, expanding our handcrafting beyond weaving and finger knitting. Guiding Benjamin in his first attempts at "cross stitchery," I was astonished to observe his fine-motor control as he carefully pushed a fat darning needle through little holes in the roughly woven, mesh-style cloth. He was clearly ready for the activity, and it would be an excellent exercise for focus and coordination.

At preschool the following week, the children were laying on the floor for rest time. As I watched from the adjoining room, Benjamin began talking and banging the floor with his feet. "I'm silly. I'm messing with Teacher." Sophia directed him to the timeout chair, and after a while, allowed him to return. Three times this scenario repeated itself, and Benjamin was again sitting in the chair when circle time began. From there, he imitated Sophia's motions beautifully. *"Early in the morning, beneath a blanket of snow, / Dwarves awaken in their caverns below..."* (from *Acorn Hill Anthology,* edited by Nancy Foster).

"Now you may join us, Benjamin" Sophia said after the first verse. As the circle continued, Benjamin started flopping around, purposely *not* participating. "Benjamin, when children can listen, they may stay at school," Sophia announced, and my ears pricked up. Did this mean she was sending him home? Benjamin kept acting like a rag doll, and Sophia's eyes beckoned to me. "We will see you next week; I am sure you will remember how to listen then. Good-bye, Benjamin."

The circle continued on, and I ushered my disbelieving child out the door. Sophia had aimed the lesson like an arrow; the clear consequence had cut short the power struggle with a minimum of fuss. "Situations like this remind me of why I stay at school even when I'm not in the actual classroom," I thought. "I'll keep reminding Benjamin to be a 'big boy' who can listen, and I'll drive the point home by withdrawing 'privileges'—that is, if being allowed to open or shut the car door, to fasten the seatbelt buckle, or to be given the PLU stickers from our groceries might be considered privileges."

The vocal tics that had plagued Benjamin for the past two months were finally gone, and now Benjamin was trying out different voice qualities. Using a very low pitch, he rasped, "Hi, Benjamin." Then, looking up at me, he explained. "Like Opa." Excited, I reached into the dollhouse. "Try that deep voice for Daddy-Doll." We had been working on "voices" for quite some time without success, but now that Benjamin had settled with the idea, our roleplaying could take on a fresh dimension.

Benjamin's fixation on numbers had become a constant source of discord. Page numbers, digital clocks, telephones, the car's dashboard dials, speed limit signs. Everywhere I looked there were numbers, and Benjamin was counting ceaselessly. "If you can't beat 'em, join 'em," I thought, feeling at the end of my rope, and proceeded to show Benjamin a little bit of math. He already had the concept of addition figured out, so now I introduced the idea of subtraction. A few days later, Benjamin startled me by spontaneously doing some basic multiplication. "4 and 4 and 4 again...makes 12," he told me. My jaw dropped.

"He may be screaming a lot," I thought. "But he is also developing some real brain power."

At preschool, Sophia was regularly providing Benjamin with a tub of warm soapy water, along with cups and ladles for pouring. Benjamin, who so easily fixated on water, now had to share with the others. Furthermore, Sophia was using the water as a teaching tool, giving Benjamin many opportunities to listen and follow directions. "The bubbles may not fly around. Here is a sponge for wiping up the floor. Now it's time to dump the water in the kitchen sink; can you keep the clock's numbers from catching you?" These little boundaries, tasks, and consequences in the midst of playful activity were sinking in, and Benjamin was becoming quite tractable during his water play.

Rick had arrived home for a week-long visit, and now he was upstairs, unpacking his suitcase. Benjamin was getting warmed up on his violin, and I asked, "Shall we play a concert for Daddy?" When he nodded enthusiastically, I directed, "Go find him. Go find Daddy. He's upstairs." I had recently begun exercising Benjamin's capacity for carrying out tasks that involved him going to a specific location, finding an object, and then coming back to me. I had made "retrieving" into a game, but sensed that this was too artificial. Benjamin needed a "real" reason to focus and follow through.

Here, for once, was a natural opportunity. "Go upstairs," I prompted as Benjamin seemed to lose his direction. I waited and then went to the stairwell. "Did you tell Daddy what we're going to do?" I prompted, projecting my voice to the top floor of our house. Benjamin piped up. "I want to play for you, Daddy." A few minutes later, we were performing a series of violin duets while Rick sat listening, clearly astonished by the musical progress his son had made during the past few months.

I was mining the riches of my German and English poetry collections, choosing verses that would "speak" to Benjamin and inspire action. Often, I would work a single poem in a variety of ways. For example, one of our favorites featured a horse traveling over varied terrain, and Benjamin was learning to trot and canter in time to the rhythmic meter of the poetry. In addition, I would have Benjamin recite the poem while rocking on his big "Christmas horse" with the sturdy steed moving according to the poetry: slow, gentle motions for the walk, bouncy, up-and-down movements for trot, and wildly exuberant rocking for canter. As a final exercise, I would hand Benjamin a toy horse and have him recite the verse while acting out its storyline.

Benjamin was doing well with poetry, but these days, whenever I asked questions, he would tune me out, looking through me as if I were invisible, or else turning his head away, refusing to give eye contact. I wondered, "Is Benjamin bored? Or is the effort of thinking and answering overwhelming? I've stayed away from drilling, not wanting to burn him out, but maybe he's now getting rusty from lack of sufficient practice." I experimented with various motivators: treats, toys, tickles. Nothing worked. Was I wrong about Benjamin's capacity for answering? Perhaps his memory really did blank out on him?

One afternoon, as Benjamin was clambering into his car seat, I had a momentary inspiration. When Benjamin sought to "click" shut his seatbelt, I blocked him, presenting a choice and a mini-consequence. "You may close the seatbelt *if* you answer Mommy's question. Otherwise, *I* will close it. Tell me, what did we just eat for snack?"

Motivated by his attraction to the seatbelt, Benjamin's answer came immediately, a marked contrast to his earlier resistance. "There ya go," I thought. "He *can* answer but would rather not. I'll need to be clever with giving weighted choices—and identifying motivating consequences."

Sophia was introducing a new activity: beeswax modeling. The children would be sculpting small figures using a specially prepared wax intended for this purpose. Handing each child a chunk of the colorful material, she directed, "Make a nest with your hands and keep your baby chick warm." Sophia demonstrated, and soon everyone's wax pieces were soft enough to mold and shape. Little fingers busy, the children discovered an inviting, fragrant medium that easily stretched, squashed, and twisted. "A perfect sensory activity," I thought, watching.

"Look, a little bird." Sophia held up her piece of wax, displaying a well-formed bird, its thin waxen wings outstretched in flight, its tail fanned out for balance. "I have an elephant here," one of the boys ventured, holding up a lump with a protrusion that might be a trunk.

After a while, Sophia began gathering up the children's beeswax figures, and when she came to Benjamin, he resisted. "It'll be going home with you," she said, holding out a wooden tray and encouraging him to place his figure on it. With great effort, Benjamin relinquished his orange blob, but then he broke down, hiding his eyes and sobbing, small screams punctuating his crying. "I promise it will be safe, and you'll have it at the end of school," Sophia soothed.

Hearing this, Benjamin escalated into greater screams, and Sophia abruptly changed tack. "Benjamin, I am sorry. You may *not* have it; you are screaming, and it is story time."

Now Benjamin choked back a sob, and I could see him fighting to contain himself. "Wow," I marveled. "He totally 'got' that consequence." Benjamin continued with his internal struggle, trying hard to keep quiet as a beeswax candle was lit and as Sophia began telling a story. Even so, little squeaks and sobs occasionally escaped, and then Benjamin would slap his thighs, trying desperately to quell himself. I watched, impressed. This was Benjamin's first real try at self-control. Sophia's teaching and my supporting efforts were bearing fruit.

The school morning was over, and Sophia and I were comparing notes while Benjamin busied himself with a Powerbar snack. As he twisted and manipulated the stiff-but-flexible candy bar, it came apart in two large chunks, and Benjamin began screaming at the top of his lungs. Hastily bundling him into the car, I blocked the noise with a pair of earplugs and began the fifteen-minute drive home, ignoring Benjamin's meltdown with utter calm. "I wonder what will happen if I simply don't react," I thought, feeling the placid detachment of an objective observer. Today, my calm mindset and the protective earplugs would allow me to keep my cool.

Benjamin kept up his screaming unabated all the way home, caught up in an obsessive rage. Clearly, he required some intervention. "I need to stop his emotional momentum, to provide a shock that will bring him to his senses without harming him," I thought. I left Benjamin screaming on the deck, filled a small bucket with water, and then shouted into his face. "You must stop screaming! If you don't stop, I'll wake you up with cold water."

Benjamin was entirely oblivious to me, lost in screams as it were, and after a few more tries to get through to him, I resorted to the wet and chilly consequence. As the water doused him, Benjamin gave a shocked screech and trampled his feet; then I wrapped him in a warm towel, rubbing vigorously, drying him. Amazingly, Benjamin's screaming fit had stopped, and now he was spluttering in surprised shock, shaking his head and looking dazed, as if he had unexpectedly returned from a chaotic trip to unknown realms.

Benjamin calmed down surprisingly quickly, and once I had changed him into dry clothing, he was ready for some normal interaction. Unexpectedly, the remaining afternoon was productive, and Benjamin seemed relatively happy. "Well, now I've got an emergency strategy for use in dire situations," I thought, relieved that my seemingly draconian idea had worked.

Snow had fallen in the high country, and we were at the family cabin. Benjamin was in a mellow mood as he explored the hills of snow that half buried the little log hut. Eventually, he found an inviting trough between two snowy swells and sank down into the powdery cold. There he lay, staring into the sky through a lattice of bare-branched aspen trees.

I was craving exercise and could easily have become impatient with Benjamin, but instead, I reined myself in and settled into Benjamin's time frame, remembering my own childhood and how the simplest things might give the greatest pleasure. I plunked into a neighboring snow mound, lying back as Benjamin was doing. My hood kept the snow from sliding down the back of my neck, and I too contemplated the sky, feeling cradled as I sank deeper into my drift of snow.

"Every step of raising a child seems to require letting go of selfishness," I thought. "But I must remember that, even as I am giving something up—freedom, or career, or whatever—I am receiving something in its place. It's all about seeing the glass half full..."

I stretched out my arms and legs, sliding them back and forth in the snow. "I'm making a snow angel," I exclaimed to Benjamin. "Copy me, then you can stand up to look." Our angel imprints lay side-by-side, a big mommy-angel and a small child-angel, both sparkling as the sun peeked out through the slight veils of cloud. "See?"

28

Moving Beyond and Going Up
February 1999

Benjamin was sounding like a broken record. "Fifteen-neh-neh-neh, sixteen-neh-neh-neh, seventeen-neh-neh-neh..." The mechanical sound of counting went on and on. As my nerves frayed, I lost my cool and let out a shriek to rival one of Benjamin's. "Just stop it, would you?!" My back was on fire, my head was aching, and I was behind on sleep; I was in the painstaking process of creating my final book layout and had been burning the midnight oil once again.

The next day, having gotten a decent night's sleep, I felt more capable of handling Benjamin's number obsessions. For the past six weeks or so, he had taken to displaying the number "four" with each of his hands, tensely tucking in his thumbs and rigidly spiking out his fingers, becoming hyper-stimulated by the sight. "This is four, these are my 'four' hands," he would say, unable to focus on anything else. Recently, these "four hands" had become a consistent distraction at school. Benjamin now had an issue with transitioning *into* circle time as he insisted on his tense hand shapes, and then, caught on his fixation, he would be incapable of participating until several verses had gone by.

Today, I was determined to tackle the issue during our home-practice of the *Winter* circle. As I started the introductory verse, I encouraged Benjamin to follow my motions properly, but he began shrieking and screaming, not wanting to release his "fours." "This has become a real mental block," I thought, feeling quite certain that Benjamin's new habit would not fade on its own, and that I would have to take a strong stance in curtailing it.

I began repeating the problematic verse, insisting that Benjamin open his tensed thumbs, physically wrangling with him and using a forceful voice to gain his attention, but consciously keeping anger out of the picture. In spite of the realizations that I had come to during the autumn—about letting go and letting things breathe—I still felt that pushing Benjamin's envelope of tolerance was a valid strategy, if used judiciously. Such an approach had its place and could be effective, so long as I remained capable of flexing if a stalemate was in sight.

The scene was pretty ugly that morning and was certainly devoid of all enjoyment, but the following day, when I again introduced circle time into our activities, Benjamin offered almost no resistance. I corrected his hand shapes, and he happily followed me through the subsequent circle rehearsal. His mental block had been removed—at least for now.

Benjamin had received a "booster" remedy from Julie, and the very next morning, he woke up sunny and calm, happily inspecting the Beatrix Potter figures on his nightie. Beatrix Potter was the Victorian-era author of the "Peter Rabbit" tales. She had written and illustrated a whole collection of animal stories besides, and the charming storybook figures covered Benjamin's nightgown. While looking at the pictures, he slipped into making his "four hands" and became distracted by the sight of his rigidly extended fingers.

On this morning, I decided on a playful approach to overcoming the fixation. "There's Jemima Puddle-Duck, on the sleeve of your nightie, see? Remember, she laid *nine* eggs, not eight," I pointed out, hoping to expand Benjamin's "four hands." "Can you put out one thumb so that we have *nine* eggs?"

I was attempting to transform the obsession rather than squelching it entirely, and after some hesitation, Benjamin complied. "Good job. And now, the eggs will hatch. Can you soften and wiggle your fingers to make the little ducklings?" I wiggled my own fingers and then surprised Benjamin with a quick playful grab. "Here comes the fox! Quick, hide those ducklings and keep them safe." The "four" hands disappeared and Benjamin giggled. Whew.

At preschool, I was sitting on Sophia's living room couch, watching Benjamin while recording observations and thoughts on my laptop computer. Now there were shrieks and words of protest coming from Benjamin. "I don't have to!"

Benjamin's screeching gradually escalated, and Sophia waved me over. "I think he needs to go home. He feels entirely inaccessible to me and doesn't have the energy to be here. Perhaps he's wiped out from his remedy yesterday, do you think?"

I nodded reluctantly. This might well be. But, for the first time, I was realizing that Sophia too had her limits and that perhaps she just didn't have the energy to deal with Benjamin this day. He certainly required every ounce of *my* energy and concentration, so why should it be any different for her? To me, Sophia was such a paragon of masterful teaching that the thought had never even crossed my mind during these many months of collaboration.

I had hit upon a fresh inspiration. We were once again rehearsing the familiar scenario of Benjamin-Doll going fishing in the stream near the family cabin. I had placed a toy frog and some carved, wooden fishes onto the length of blue cloth that formed the stream, and now my mind was tickled by the sight.

"Benjamin, look, there's Jeremy-Fisher, the frog," I said, referring to one of Beatrix Potter's animal stories. "He's sitting on a lily pad, and the stickleback fish is nibbling his toes."

I manipulated the little animal figures, and Benjamin giggled with recognition. For months, I had been reading to Benjamin from our complete collection of Beatrix Potter's stories and, although these tales had initially been much too long for him to follow, over time and with repeated readings, he had gotten to know them well enough to recognize key scenes.

Now I encouraged Benjamin to copy me in acting out the frog-and-fish interaction, and then I laid a green silk handkerchief next to the stream-cloth, suggesting, "Here's Mr. MacGregor's garden. Look, I've got Peter Rabbit here, nibbling on the cabbages." I got a woolen bunny out of our basket of toy animals and, picking up the daddy-doll from our dollhouse, I made the figure chase the rabbit out of the field. "Wow, that was close. Mr. MacGregor nearly caught Peter under his sieve," I exclaimed.

Benjamin commented, "His buttons got caught."

Excited by Benjamin's correct reference to the story, I elaborated. "That's right; and Peter wriggled out of his little blue coat to get away." Now my imagination was stoked, and one scene after the other came tumbling out, each taken from a key moment in one of Beatrix Potter's charming stories.

Peter Rabbit joined his cousin, Benjamin Bunny, in stealing onions in the field before popping under a basket to hide. Then, a cat jumped atop the basket, trapping the two culprits. Next, I used a girl-doll to represent Lucy, the little girl who visits Mrs. Tiggy-winkle (the hedgehog) and ends up helping with the washing of all the neighboring animals' clothes. I had Benjamin join me in rubbing doll clothes up and down our antique washboard's ribbed surface, singing Sophia's "washing song." Then, I strung up a line between the play-stands, and we hung up the "clean clothes"; Benjamin's coordination with the clothes clips improved with each try. Now, according to the story, it was time for tea, and so I set up our china toy tea set. As Benjamin helped feed the various dolls and animal characters, he too was allowed some treats, and afterwards, we delivered the "washed" laundry to all the animals scattered around our "hillside."

After negotiating our way through this web of storytelling, it was time for a sensory break. As I bounced Benjamin up and down on his big, red gymno-ball, I glowed with happiness. For months, I had felt my imagination running dry with the constant repetition of the real-life doll scenarios we had been practicing since the previous summer. Now, finally, I had hit upon a fresh animating spark, and Benjamin was showing himself ready for it: after half a year of working with concrete scenarios and short poems, his capacity for imaginative play had progressed sufficiently for us to enter the world of story and fairytale.

I was pondering the connections between snippets of story, sharing my newest realizations with my mom. "Our daily doll scenarios—and also the Beatrix Potter stories—all hang together in the manner of a 'mind map'," I observed, and then explained. "A mind map is a diagram which is used to visually outline information. On paper, it looks a bit like a spider web: it is created around a single idea, placed in the center, to which associated ideas, words, and concepts are added. Then you can have sub-concepts that extend out from the bigger ideas. Furthermore, you can organize your materials in such a way that related strands of material are near one another, with relevant links drawn between them to bring attention to their interconnectedness."

I continued. "By working with scenarios or stories that are linked to one another, I've been building up Benjamin's thinking as if constructing a mind map. I'm creating a web of flexible connections, in spite of the linear, step-by-step approach that is often necessary in building up Benjamin's individual skills." I let out my breath in a gratified sigh. "My understanding of how to work with Benjamin is evolving all the time."

During the next few weeks, I watched Benjamin's joy in life grow stronger and more present as the homeopathic remedy took effect and bolstered his mood. While bouts of screeching still occurred regularly, there was an overriding sense of contentment, and Benjamin warmed my heart with his frequent displays of sweetness. Smiles abounded as we played with dolls and games, read stories, and practiced violin. Benjamin continued astounding me with his facility at embroidery, and he was eager to learn the waltz and polka steps that I was introducing in preparation for Mardi Gras. We would be having a dance-and-costume party with a few family friends, just as we had done the previous year.

"Do you remember the *Black Peter* game we played with Oma and Opa over Christmas time?" I asked, brainstorming a costume for Benjamin. I pulled out the game card depicting Black Peter as an old-fashioned, soot-smeared chimney-sweep, dressed all in black, and wearing a black top hat. Benjamin looked delighted when I told him, "For our party, you can be dressed up just like this, and I will draw a curly moustache and big black eyebrows on your face."

Benjamin was talking to himself. "When Benjamin screams, children laugh…" Hearing this phrase being repeated over the course of days, I noted the following: *Benjamin has begun thinking about his actions in terms of cause and effect. The children at Sophia's preschool have never laughed at him, and I think he is recalling that terrible Valentine's baking incident at Talia's school—it happened exactly a year ago. I'm amazed at how deeply such an occurrence can touch a child, and how lasting and hurtful it can be.*

Benjamin's use of language had taken a leap forward, and I wrote: *An exquisite day at school: Benjamin is full of delight, truly talking **with** Teacher rather than talking **at** her. He is determinedly combining words into more complex sentences, trying to express himself with a new level of depth and feeling. He is stretching beyond his usual parameters—very exciting.* Now, Benjamin was able to take on a greater variety of "voices" when animating different dolls and animal puppets. In addition, his recitation of German poems had become noticeably easier. And, for the first time, Benjamin spontaneously said "I love you" to his father on the telephone.

Interestingly, even with all these positive developments, Benjamin still remained quite fierce in his fixations and occasionally displayed behavior that would be typical of a two-year-old: he would flip-flop back and forth between extremes of wanting and not-wanting something. For example, if I gave him my wristwatch to look at as a reward for good work, he would become fixated on holding it, wanting to stare at the numbers on the watch face. But if I set a limit to the time spent with the wristwatch, he would suddenly turn the tables, shouting, "Fly the watch up to the high shelf. I don't want it—I don't want my turn!"

Of course, he *did* desperately want his turn, but the fact that he could not be in total control of the situation called forth this emotional contrariness.

My uncle from Germany was visiting, and I was giving him an overview of autism and of my therapeutic work with Benjamin. "I'm rewiring his brain, sparking new pathways and connections, and simultaneously strengthening those neural pathways which might compensate for problem areas. Apparently, autism can cause *too much* brain matter to develop, and this slows down the transmission of information—things kind of get lost in there. It's like negotiating a maze with a lot of dead ends."

I went off on a tangent. "I recently had an illuminating dream experience. It happened during the last stages of laying out and proofing my book manuscript. I was wrestling with the computer, dealing with faulty manuals and flawed programs, trying to figure out which commands were relevant to my situation; it was nerve wracking, and all of it was happening at night, just before bedtime."

"When I finally went to sleep, I'd spin into these nightmares where I'd feel myself being squeezed into a dark tunnel, desperately searching for a missing dot or letter. I would feel the tunnel going into a curve, whirling me into ever more constricting circles, sickening and dizzying me, and eventually, I would slam into a box, my entire being mashed into a rectangular shape as I followed ever more angular convolutions that kept turning sharply inward, becoming smaller and tighter until I thought I would *become* the very dot I was so desperately chasing after. I felt as if trapped inside the maze of a computer chip—except that it was *my own brain* that had me trapped."

"On waking, I was utterly convinced I had become autistic overnight. The dreams felt so mechanical, so devoid of all human feeling; I was acutely conscious of my inability to escape and unfold into expansive thinking or creativity. I longed to scream and shriek, to kick, roll, and thrash about, and to thereby shatter the bonds that ensnared me..."

I paused, my throat constricted with remembrance. "My nightmares mirrored what I've observed in Benjamin; I glimpsed the horror of having autism."

29

Staying "Up" For a While
March 1999

Mild, almost summery days were luring us outdoors, and we were spending much of our work-time on the back deck. There, I had hung up Benjamin's hammock swing and also a newly purchased swinging/twirling toy which Benjamin was learning to use.

"Come, reach up over your head and hold onto the padded metal bar. Now try swinging back and forth." At its midpoint, the bar connected—like an upside-down "T"—to the rope used for hanging it up. The rope was fused into a special ball-bearing joint which would allow the metal bar to twirl smoothly around its center without the rope ever twisting or kinking.

"Watch out, Benjamin, don't let go of the bar. Now bend your knees a little so your weight is completely supported by the Twizzler. That's good... and now use your feet to propel yourself around and around." With a little help, Benjamin began spinning around his axis, giggling with the joy of the sensation. This was much easier than using the spin-board which required Benjamin to passively sit while I propelled him.

Board games were fun to play out on the deck as well. I would bring Benjamin's little work table and chair outside, along with a collection of games and a few stuffed animals or dolls for company. Until recently, I had used many of the individual components of these games as teaching tools, devising little exercises to work on skills like sorting, matching, expanding memory, learning to use clues, and various aspects of language development.

But now, Benjamin was ready to learn how to properly play the games, according to the rules they had been designed with. I could easily reduce the complexity of the games by removing half of the matching cards, for example, or by reducing the number of available game pieces, and Benjamin was enjoying the new ways of playing with the already familiar game components.

On some days, I even brought Benjamin's violin out onto the deck, delighted at his being able to practice in the fresh air and sunshine. Benjamin was now playing a dance piece called *Minuet*, by J.S. Bach, and was learning an advanced technique called "vibrato." As with his embroidery, I was stunned at his dexterity and relative ease in learning this complex left-hand motion. He was learning to shift up and down the fingerboard as well and was playing two-octave scales in higher positions. I thrilled in watching his progress as I had only once before had such an advanced young student. Most of my violin pupils of the past hadn't been ready for such exercises until they were more than double Benjamin's age.

In between segments of violin practice, I guided Benjamin in learning physical skills such as simple dance steps, taking advantage of the open space our deck provided. As always, Benjamin had difficulty in learning through demonstration and imitation. I knew that, from his autistic perspective, there was an excess of visual information to be attended to. Even with me directing his eyes and asking him to watch for something specific, he had a hard time picking up on the salient information that would allow him to copy me.

So, as I did with all his other skills, I found ways to break down each motion so that Benjamin could practice its components before performing the complete movement sequence. In working on waltz and polka steps, and also with skipping, I often had Benjamin stand on my feet as I executed the steps, helping him get the feel of the overall motion. In addition, I used verbal cues such as, "*step, together, pause...step, together, pause...step, turn, turn / step, turn, turn...*" Singing such cues, using a distinct pattern of pitches for the various movements, helped Benjamin both to focus and to retain the sequence more easily.

"Donkey kicking" was another new skill that Benjamin seemed ready for. Placing his hands on the seat of a low stool, Benjamin would grip the seat's edge for stability, and then I would help him to kick up one leg behind him, immediately followed by the other, as if beginning a handstand. Constant encouragement was needed. "That'll take a while to learn, but see how fun it is?"

Kicking pinecones, both on our deck and out on the trail, was another coordination exercise, and Benjamin was much gratified when his toes managed to propel the light cones across some considerable distance. Climbing too was something that Benjamin had finally grown into with help, and now he showed little fear when making his way up a rough boulder, while monkeying around on his rocking horse, or when climbing onto our kitchen countertops in search of the honey jar.

When Benjamin became tired from our various activities out on the deck, I would suggest, "Why don't we rest for a little? You can listen to your *Teddy Bear's Picnic* tape while you look at the accompanying picture book." Benjamin would settle into the beanbag chair I had brought outside, and I would hand him a cuddly teddy bear. "Here is your own teddy; he wants to sit on your lap and look at the pictures too. Then we can have a picnic lunch of our own, right out here on the deck."

So our days went, the weeks flying by in a flurry of reviewed and expanded skills. When I refreshed Benjamin's sign language skills, he was delighted by the review and gave me unusually good eye contact. When I pulled out the *I Can Help* book that had been lying dormant, he was eager to try various chores around the house, a clear step forward from the last time I had focused on this book. Polishing a pair of shoes became the highlight of one afternoon, and on another day, Benjamin helped me to make pancakes, an activity which we subsequently played out with our dollhouse figurines. Benjamin was now working on a new weaving project, and we regularly spent time at my parents' house, preparing the garden for spring planting. Digging, raking, picking up stones and tossing them into a bucket—all of these were excellent sensory activities.

During our drawing sessions, I focused on springtime themes, depicting flower bulbs sprouting and bursting into bloom. Through drawing, I showed Benjamin how, if we could magically see through the solid earth, we would perceive the bulb's tenacious roots reaching deep down into the brown soil, and we would find little green shoots industriously pushing their way upward in search of sunlight.

We also took several trips to local goat and sheep farms, and I was delighted to see Benjamin's growing courage in embracing the squirmy newborn kids and lambs. This comfort with animals was supported by the newest addition to our family: a sweet, three-month-old Welsh Corgi puppy which we now adopted from the local humane society. Although Benjamin was initially wary of Acorn's frantic puppy energy, I kept encouraging him to snuggle with her, just as he did with Mandarin, and soon the two of them were forming a real bond. Benjamin was becoming increasingly comfortable with sharing his personal space with her, and she was taking on the role of being a therapy pet.

Refinements in Benjamin's language skills were another big focus of this time. Benjamin had initially learned how to ask questions through parroting various phrases and by being drilled on them over and over again. These phrases had become ritualized patterns, and I was trying to break the old habits and encourage true information-seeking.

"What is this? It's a beanbag," Benjamin might say, using the habitual question-and-answer pattern, and I would correct him: "Say: *Mommy, guess what I have?*"

Or, when Benjamin spotted something he liked, he might say, "What is this? It's a cookie," and I would have to remind him, "Say: *Mommy, I know what this is*." Along with trying to erase Benjamin's habitual *"what is this"* phrase, I was attempting to plant the idea that people usually ask questions about things that they *don't* already know the answer to.

Sophia too was encouraging Benjamin to use varied phrases and to connect with the other children at school through more flexible dialogue. "Hello, Sasha. Good morning, Dasha," she prompted him as he first stepped into the playroom each school day. "Hey there, Colin. How are you, Renee?" Benjamin was completing the round of diverse greetings with increasing ease. At the end of the day, he would also be asked to say "good-bye" as each of his friends was picked up by their parents.

"I want the *Volpas*," Benjamin announced one morning at preschool, referring to a pair of comical ladies who had featured in one of Sophia's stories. "Friends, who would like to play *Volpas* with me?" Sophia prompted, expanding on Benjamin's desire and helping him to include his peers.
"Who would like to play *Volpas* with me?" Benjamin echoed, following Sophia's hand-cue to look to his friends rather than at her. "Me, me, I want to play." Colin came over, and the two boys reenacted snippets of the remembered story. Benjamin began to hop, excited by the peer interaction.
"Froggies jump when they are excited; *people* can use their words. Say: 'I'm feeling *excited*.'" Sophia modeled the phrase with great expression, laying her hands on Benjamin's shoulders to ground him, and I—watching from the living room—appreciatively took note.
Sophia continually struck a balance between giving concrete, unambiguous directions (which were essential for Benjamin's comprehension), and using colorful phrases which contained poetic images and metaphors (these would encourage flexibility in Benjamin's understanding of language). It was an ideal melding of two diverse approaches to communication and was the same style which I used at home.

Benjamin was beginning to tune out others' conversational overtures, fixating instead on various verbal phrases, repeating them out loud or under his breath. The buoyant feeling of the past six weeks was slowly waning, and there was an isolated day of screeching that wrenchingly hearkened back to the hardest days of January. Concerned, I administered a homeopathic booster remedy, and Benjamin was back in high spirits just in time for Rick's brief springtime visit home.
Rick was already on the back deck when we returned from our Friday

morning preschool session, and Benjamin began exclaiming. "Daddy is here. Hi, Daddy. Look, Daddy." Hustling up the stairs, Benjamin held up his Easter basket from school, wanting his father's approval.

"That's beautiful, did you make it?"

"Yes, Daddy."

Benjamin hugged Rick around the legs, leaning against him affectionately while I elaborated. "Sophia engages the children in many beautiful crafts projects. For this, they did watercolor painting first, and then they cut and folded the painted paper into baskets." Benjamin poked his fingers into the basket and pulled out several "eggs" that he had molded out of beeswax. "These look almost like jelly-beans," Rick laughed, putting his arms around me. Our two-and-a-half-year period of separation was almost over, and this visit would be the last one. The next time that we saw Rick—in June—he would be arriving with all of his bags, to stay.

30

Emotional Turbulence
April 1999

It was Easter Sunday, and our dining room table featured a bouquet of daffodils and a grassy nest of sprouted wheat in which hid a pair of toy bunnies and a few chocolate eggs. When Benjamin woke up, he saw the decorations and immediately knew what to do. He began scampering around the house, hunting for plastic eggs filled with dried fruits and nuts.

I watched his determined searching with delight. Last year, Benjamin had only *just* gotten the hang of hunting for eggs, and that had been outdoors where a colorful egg amongst dull, dry grass and leaves wouldn't be hard to spot. This year, he was able to perceive the eggs indoors amongst other colorful objects, and he was motivated to keep looking. Our many months of "searching practice" were paying off.

I had a new concern. Benjamin's mood was destabilizing again, and now, when frustrated, Benjamin was digging his fingernails into his forehead, making red welts appear. Saying "no" to this self-injurious behavior seemed to invite a power struggle—Benjamin would only scratch himself harder in defiance—and so I directed him in transferring the impulse to a pillow, encouraging him to squeeze and dig his nails into a cushion instead of his face.

I also tried deflecting the scratching action by morphing it into something else. In sign language, "tiger" is indicated by making claws with the hands, then miming stripes in the air near one's forehead using these clawed hands, but without actually scratching. I practiced this sign with Benjamin during emotionally neutral times and explained that it would be a good sign to make when he felt angry or frustrated. Thus, Benjamin had a permissible way of communicating his negative feeling using a variant of the physical impulse that was naturally overcoming him at these times.

At preschool, the big, rectangular water pan was a continued item of interest, not just for Benjamin but for the other children as well. Sophia encouraged them to bring smooth stones and small log pieces from the baskets near the hearth. These items could be used to form a water habitat, and acorn "fishes" could swim in these surroundings. She also provided two tin cups: one for pouring, and one to float as a "boat."

On this morning, all the children were crowded around the tub, and

Benjamin was happily engaged, pouring streams of water; a collective bubble of calm seemed to be holding the group together. Eventually, the others tired of the game and moved back into the playroom, leaving Benjamin alone with his pouring. Immediately, his play took on a frantic quality, and he hopped and flapped, no longer grounded by the calm influence of the group's energy.

"What a remarkable contrast," I thought, watching the shift. "At times, Benjamin is tuned like an antenna, sensitive to the currents of energy around him. A moment ago, when the group was still present, their energy kept him centered. Now, Benjamin is by himself, and he is 'flying away.' He needs a grounding influence."

Just as I thought this, Sophia stepped over to Benjamin and, laying soothing hands on his shoulders, she asked Benjamin to help her empty the pan of its contents. Carrying the heavy water pan required a steady gait, and Benjamin settled down, completing the job. Thus, through meaningful activity, and through the joint-compressing effect of having to bear weight, he was brought back to his 'center.'

I had found fresh inspiration in a collection of children's nature poetry and was teaching Benjamin new verses, helping him to act them out. Benjamin was amenable to dancing about our back yard as a butterfly or a bee, with silken scarves fluttering from his arms and shoulders where I had attached them, providing the airy feeling of having wings. I would model each line of poetry and would have Benjamin echo it back as I silently mouthed the words. Then I would guide him in mirroring my actions as I narrated, and eventually Benjamin was able to both act and speak simultaneously, flowing through the verses in tandem with me.

Benjamin was finally becoming aware of how *his* actions were making *me* feel. Our work with facial expressions and body language was taking hold, and now Benjamin was making observations: "Mommy feels happy (sad, angry, etc.)." Sometimes this phrase came out as a firm statement, and other times, Benjamin's voice would indicate a question, as if wondering whether he had gotten the label right.

Benjamin's personal energy had again taken on a hyper quality, and he was constantly flapping his arms and rocking jerkily back and forth. I had to struggle for eye contact, and there was no emotional connection between us. My frustration mounted as my leverage for shaping Benjamin's behavior evaporated; the rewards that generally worked as motivators were currently devoid of power, and the application of small consequences seemed ineffectual.

At preschool, Benjamin was now touchy and tender, defending his water tub with screeches and telling children, "Please, no...go away." Sophia was artfully smoothing over his protests, assuring Benjamin that his friends just wanted to play, that no one would take anything from him. Watching this scene for the second day in a row, I thought, "Time for another dose of remedy."

Waiting for the homeopathic to take effect, Benjamin and I had an up-and-down week that seemed to mirror the tempestuous and changeable April weather. On some days, sunny warmth was marred by blustery winds. Other days were characterized by alternating waves of warmth and chill. And a few times, our moods were colored by the pressure of an impending storm. "It's impossible *not* to be affected by the weather," I thought, trying to reassure myself that things would improve shortly. "Even our pets are a little snappish; they're responding to the changes in barometric pressure too."

On one of these turbulent days, Benjamin started the morning with considerable irritability and with a fixation on gathering and holding any number of small objects. "You are like a magpie," I teased, glancing out the window to where a black-and-white bird sat swaying in a nearby tree. Benjamin's hoarding behavior was fairly new and was becoming very distracting, particularly when I didn't have sufficient energy to deal with conflict and therefore allowed Benjamin to keep his pile of collected objects nearby.

Needing an escape, I took Benjamin out on the windy trail and eventually found a protected spot for us to hunker down in. Sitting amongst tall, dried grasses, I opened up my backpack. "Come, Benjamin, here's a new book: *Der Zauber Apfel* (The Magical Apple)."

I opened the picture book which was intended for very young children, and we looked at the first pages. There, a storage container, in the shape of an enormous red apple, opened up to reveal a wealth of tiny toy people, houses, trees, cars, and animals. As we slowly turned the pages, and as I encouraged Benjamin to make comments about the pictures, the wind unexpectedly died down and the sun began warming us. Benjamin snuggled into me, his previously prickly mood becoming relaxed and happy, right along with the change in weather.

In subsequent pages, the tiny toys were arranged into a charming little town with a market square and a church; then they were arranged into various other scenes that formed the town's outskirts. On the last page, the toys were all neatly packed back into their apple-shaped container, to be played with some other day.

"I have a surprise," I told Benjamin. "We actually own a collection of tiny 'town blocks' that includes little cars and people. I have them in a special box at home, and we can build a toy town, just like in this book." I was excited about the new play scenarios which this book supported and was already considering ways in which I might connect the toy town with the Beatrix Potter stories. Together, these two books would provide the impetus for some engaging play and would help to strengthen and expand Benjamin's "mind map" of storybook scenarios.

"I'll build in little motivating snacks to keep Benjamin going," I thought, planning ahead so that I wouldn't overlook this important detail. Sometimes I forgot about snacks, and Benjamin could get quite cranky from lack of sustenance. "We'll build a farmer's market as part of the town, and that will be the playful source of food."

Guarding against my own residual crankiness—the morning's unpredictable weather had been unsettling—I mentally prepared to respond with equanimity if Benjamin hoarded the tiny objects of my "town blocks" collection. "We can transform any hoarding behavior into a 'building up of the king's treasury'," I brainstormed. "And we might do some trading; objects can be exchanged for food treats."

My two overriding goals would be to infuse joy into the new game and to shed the irritability that had been plaguing us. And that was just how things turned out: my mental preparations kept me from losing my cool when things got challenging, and Benjamin was able to benefit from the work session with enjoyment.

As the last week of April arrived, Benjamin's emotional turbulence subsided, and I began noting positive changes: *Benjamin has returned to being happy and cooperative. There is a remarkable new ease and naturalness in his language: quick responses to my questions, more variety, less repetition, real expression.* With Benjamin in such a good space, play dates could again be scheduled, and I contacted Lily's family.

Now that Lily and Benjamin were a bit older, I was expanding my role as play facilitator. In addition to shadowing Benjamin, I began teaching Lily some specific cues, letting her know that she could be a real "helper" to Benjamin and showing her how to accommodate his difficulties. "Tap Benjamin on the shoulder to get his attention," I would suggest. "Ask him again," I would say if Benjamin seemed to be ignoring Lily's overtures. Lily liked telling Benjamin what to do, and she eagerly employed cue phrases, saying, *"Watch me," "Do this,"* and *"Look here."*

31

A Focus on Friendship
May 1999

Benjamin's renewed buoyancy and joy carried us well into May. Of course, not every day was filled with roses and sunshine, but overall, the difficult moments remained within manageable bounds.

By now, Benjamin had learned to skip, and he frequently bounced into this dance-like step during our daily walks. I had also introduced him to riding a tricycle, and we regularly made the rounds of the neighborhood with Mandarin following along, occasionally meowing to Benjamin from nearby lawns and bushes. "My friend," Benjamin observed on these occasions. The cat usually slept with Benjamin during the night, curling around Benjamin's head like a halo, and my heart warmed at the animal's affectionate companionship.

"Let's read *The Rainbow Fish* again," I suggested after one such neighborhood foray. My newest focus was on using storybooks to teach about friendship, communication, and sharing. Benjamin clambered onto my lap and we began. Benjamin had memorized many of the lines, and now he tried to imitate my deep rumbling voice as I intoned the octopus' advice to the vain, stand-offish rainbow fish. "You must share your beautiful scales..."

When the snobby fish finally realized he would remain lonely and friendless unless he began to share, Benjamin pretended to pick the shimmery scales off the page, saying, "One for the blue fish, one for the purple fish, everybody gets one." On this day, Benjamin was particularly taken by the idea that the arrogant rainbow fish had changed his outlook and had become friendly. Benjamin commented, "He is happy now; he has friends."

"That's right," I agreed. "Friends are *very* important."

We were out in the alley one morning when our neighbor's granddaughter came running over, apparently eager to make our acquaintance. Taking advantage of the situation, I whispered to Benjamin that he ought to share a mint from the tin he carried in his pocket.

Benjamin wasn't really interested in the candy itself. Instead, he was fascinated by the boxy shape of the tin, and by the fact that it contained a hoard of small, round objects which incidentally happened to be sweets. Because he was fixated on the box, Benjamin now became quite anxious and resistant when I suggested sharing.

I kept prompting. "Remember the rainbow fish? You have lots of candies, just like he had lots of scales." After much judicious prodding from me, Benjamin reluctantly held out the tin, and his companion politely took a candy. Then, having overcome his inner barrier to sharing, Benjamin suddenly became willing to engage in an impromptu play session with the girl.

They played two chasing games, "Mother, may I?" and "What time is dinner, Mr. Fox," both of which Benjamin had learned from Lily and which I had been practicing with him on a regular basis. When Benjamin and his new friend stopped to take a breather, Benjamin spontaneously reached out, holding open his candy tin. "Krissy, do you want another candy?" I wanted to applaud. Having overcome the initial bind of his fixation, Benjamin's generous nature was now able to take precedence.

At preschool, Benjamin was responding well as Sophia pushed his capacity for conversation with the other children. We'd had a phone conference about raising expectations, and Sophia had been surprised to hear about the extensive interactions I was facilitating during play-dates. I had suggested that she occasionally try a fairly directive, concrete approach and was grateful to see how facile she was in integrating my suggestions into her teaching style.

Now she was more insistent that Benjamin listen and respond to the other children and was even more active in encouraging him to initiate actions. When necessary, she would give him the words he needed. Benjamin rose to the occasion, and his interactions with school friends increased noticeably.

One morning, after a considerable effort at playing, Benjamin looked worn out and Sophia backed off, providing the water tub as a "down-time" activity. Benjamin retreated into pouring and splashing. However, when the twins came over to join him, he suddenly burst into sobs and screeches and began throwing himself about. "I want to pull on something...I want to hurt myself," he cried, his blatantly self-injurious impulse shocking me, just as it had the previous month.

Sophia, quick-thinking as ever, responded. "Come Benjamin, hold my hands, put your toes right up against mine, and lean back—we will pull on each other. That's it...see how we can balance together?" Her tone was light, and soon Benjamin had pulled himself together and was capable of sharing the water tub.

I admired Sophia's inspired reaction which had provided strong and grounding sensory input (to joints and muscles), and had simultaneously created an energy connection through the holding of hands and the balancing of one body against the other. I thought, "What an astonishing transformation of a potentially scary scenario."

In mid-May, we had an appointment with Julie. As she and I talked, Benjamin played, building a tower with wooden blocks and then making a house out of plastic "bristle-blocks." He asked us who might live in the house and then began driving a truck around between the table legs and chairs. My eyes were round with astonishment because, up until today, Benjamin had never given the toys in Julie's office much notice. He had generally occupied himself with fixated activity. "That is looking close to age level," Julie observed, and I felt a joyful tickle run around in my chest. "Benjamin *has* made a lot of progress this spring," I exclaimed, giving her a summary. Then Julie wanted to hear about the most recent changes.

"There have been some self-injurious impulses, and Benjamin's emotional hyper-sensitivity has just reappeared. As usual, it is primarily triggered by beautiful music that he feels a deep connection to. Also, if I express difficult emotions, he gets upset. For example, if I give a story character a sad voice, Benjamin reacts as if the character's feelings are his own but have been overwhelmingly magnified," I told her. "His reactions are often so forceful that I feel like his spirit, soul, and body are flying apart." Julie nodded her understanding and, on her computer, began scrolling through a list of remedies that might address such a reaction.

"On the other hand," I went on, "Benjamin has just started quoting lines from the curative tale I made up last summer. It was designed to help him overcome his emotional sensitivity, so maybe he is trying to self-manage his feelings by returning to the story. That would be a big step forward."

I glanced over at Benjamin who was still absorbed in playing with Julie's toys. "Benjamin's general awareness of emotions is growing. As I've done in the past, I am labeling emotions as they come up, and we've had little talks about what is causing a particular upset or frustration. Lately, I've tried giving Benjamin a concrete strategy for releasing 'icky' feelings. I say, 'Let it go... *woosh*...away it flies,' and at the same time, I help Benjamin to make arm motions that signify the sweeping out-and-away of the upset energy. That seems to help, as long as he isn't in a hyper-sensitive state." After considering all the different things I had told her, Julie made a decision about which new remedy to try with Benjamin, and then we were out the door.

The next few weeks were turbulent. Benjamin's hyper-sensitivity receded and so did his impulse to self-punish, but instead, screeches of discontent and defiance marred many of our mornings. Fortunately, Benjamin's foul mood would generally resolve itself as the morning progressed, but there were a few days where my fortitude crumbled and I fell into despair, feeling as abused and powerless as I had back after the New Year, during Benjamin's "fierce" phase.

Nonetheless, I would eventually pull myself together and would forge ahead once again.

During this time, I was still focusing on teaching about friendship, and I brought the idea of playful interaction and exchange into our painting sessions. Inspired by a book that we had been reading called *Little Blue and Little Yellow*, I began singing a "friendship narrative" while manipulating watercolors.

"Little Yellow went out to play..." I demonstrated, painting a round, radiant sunshine, and then guided Benjamin in copying.

"Yellow got lonely and called, 'Friend Blue, come play too.'" Vigorous brush strokes accompanied the calling for a friend—golden desire was reaching out from Yellow's center. Then I rinsed my brush and slowly began painting in blue, letting a slender color-trail sneak in from the opposite corner of the paper as I narrated.

"Blue answered, 'I hear a friend calling...'" Little Blue's trail arrived next to Little Yellow, and I let my blue bloom into a satisfying sphere.

Now it was Benjamin's turn to paint, to copy. As I repeated the few lines of my impromptu song, he faltered in his strokes, losing focus. I gestured, trying to redirect his attention, and when he didn't respond, gently laid my hand over his to help guide the brush. Little Blue and Little Yellow had some friendly words, and then they played together, their interchange resulting in lovely shades of flowing green. Finally, Benjamin leaned back, satisfaction suffusing his face as he studied his finished painting.

"That was well done, sweetheart."

At the end of May, our artist-friend Ursula hosted an afternoon garden party, celebrating the approach of summer. All of us breathed a sigh of relief as the grey, wet weather cleared, sunshine chasing away the rain just in time for the party.

In tandem with the elements, Benjamin had begun the day with several hours of horrendous screeching and screaming, but now, with the sunshine, all was forgotten, and Benjamin was in tip-top form, charming and happy, basking in the light energy of the party.

"How do you like to go up in a swing, / Up in the sky so blue..." I sang, helping Benjamin to build up momentum on Ursula's backyard swing. Nearly two years ago, Corinne had given me a copy of this Robert Lewis Stevenson poem, set to music, and in spite of the countless times I had sung it for Benjamin, it was still a favorite. Benjamin sailed back and forth under the enormously tall acacia tree that supported the swing, nearly crashing into a huge, spreading quince bush, loaded with deep-pink flowers.

"I want to help," he eventually declared, seeing Ursula nearby. She was pouring wine into sparkling glasses. I stopped the swing, and we went to assist our hostess. "Say, *'Would you like some wine?'*" I whispered into Benjamin's ear and then sent him over to the nearest guest. Benjamin trotted back and forth, remembering to say his line as he served each person in turn, enjoying the appreciation that came smiling at him with each asking of the question.

Having finished with serving, Benjamin became engrossed in looking for insects in Ursula's garden. Searching near the base of his favorite stone statue—an abstract work that Ursula had hewn out of alabaster and had dubbed "The Angel"—Benjamin spotted a black, many-legged "roly-poly" bug.

He picked it up, and it predictably curled into an armored little ball on his palm. Smiling, Benjamin tenderly poked at the bug before squatting down to search for another. I had just poured a glass of wine for myself, when suddenly, Benjamin unleashed a volley of screams and howls, fit to raise the dead. He had dropped the roly-poly and couldn't find it again.

I rushed over to him, looking desperately for a replacement and finding only a slimy slug. "Be *patient*, wait a little, we will find another roly-poly," I soothed. Benjamin continued screaming.

"Only *patience* will bring him back. If you can't settle down, we will have to leave the angel and go home." I felt hot and embarrassed, not wanting ruin the party by staying, and yet reluctant to leave. I had been looking forward to relaxing and socializing a little; I was *so* in need of a break.

My mom came over, and so did Ursula, laughing understandingly. "Not to worry, everyone knows that kids will scream." She squeezed my shoulders, lightening my mood, and the three of us worked at getting Benjamin over his upset, each of us digging around in the dirt with great hope. Benjamin had set us to acting like overgrown children and, although I had initially been on the verge of tears, I now burst into hysterical laughter; the scene was absolutely ludicrous.

"A ladybug," my mom finally proclaimed, setting the little polka-dotted thing on Benjamin's wrist. He quieted, inspecting the pretty insect.

I had barely turned my back when Benjamin's screams resumed; the ladybug had flown off. *"Patience,"* I admonished yet again, and this time he settled more quickly.

Four times more, the scenario was repeated, with Benjamin's screams becoming progressively less with each lost insect. "Maybe he is learning what the word 'patience' means," I remarked hopefully. Thankfully, Benjamin had relaxed, and I was allowed to enjoy the remainder of the party after all.

32

Looking for Balance
June 1999

As we moved into June, Benjamin's ups and downs continued. Times of exquisite connection were broken up by periods of fixation, bouncy and hyper behavior, screaming, or a glazed, "in-outer-space" quality. Nevertheless, I was expanding Benjamin's exposure to new storybooks, trying to strengthen his capacity for following a longer storyline. Knowing that he didn't comprehend much of what I was reading to him, simple though it was, I would stop every few sentences and either explain, summarize, or reword the story in more basic terms. Over time, and with sufficient repetition of the same story, I hoped to fade out my constant interjections and to simply read through the text.

I also worked on connecting the book materials to Benjamin's life, discussing the illustrations and encouraging him to make comparisons, even if these had nothing to do with the written story.

"I have a shirt like that, but mine is red."

"This bear brushes his teeth in the morning, but I do mine at night."

"I like riding my tricycle, just like the girl in the picture."

Benjamin was getting better at voluntarily sharing information, and such comparisons made the books more alive and relevant to him.

Benjamin's relationship with his dolls and toy animals was also expanding. By now, he was getting quite comfortable with talking to the dolls as if they could hear and understand him, and if I picked up Katrina-doll and initiated a conversation, Benjamin knew to pick up Alexander-doll in turn and to animate him, making Alexander "talk" with Katrina. Occasionally, I tried getting Benjamin interested in both a book and a doll, simultaneously.

"I want *By the Seashore*," Benjamin requested one afternoon, referring to one of the little books we had been reading. "Get it off the shelf and tell the story to Alexander," I suggested, and was gratified when Benjamin easily followed my directions. He sat down with the doll on his lap and began to talk about the book's pictures, explaining them to his little "listener."

Shortly after June started, Rick returned home with the few possessions he had kept with him in Whidbey Island. "I can't believe it, you are finally home," I murmured, swaying in a long embrace with Rick as we stood on the deck, surrounded by several suitcases. Benjamin was in the kitchen, probably getting stuck on something, but I put him out of my mind for a few moments. Pointing out the elegant irises, peonies, and roses blooming in our yard, I reminded Rick of our upcoming anniversary. "I'll pick a big bouquet." This year would be cause for extra celebration: Rick was finally done with his active duty Navy career and would be transitioning to the Navy reserve.

When we finally did go inside, Benjamin put out his arms for Daddy to see. While Rick and I had been out talking on the deck, Benjamin had retrieved the PLU stickers off of every single piece of fruit I had purchased earlier that morning and had pasted them all over his arms and hands.

"I'm the sticker-boy...the sticker-man...the sticker-keeper," he declared, more interested in looking at the myriad numbers than in greeting his father. Nearby, Benjamin also had a collection of plastic tags which had come from the flower pots that our neighbors had recently bought. Benjamin was hoarding these tags, obsessed with the barcode numbers displayed on each one, and I was hard pressed to keep him from screeching and running outdoors in search of more whenever I hid his collection, tired of having it around as a source of distraction.

That evening, after Benjamin was in bed, Rick and I discussed how the upcoming summer would look for us. Rick would do some major house improvement projects in between job hunting activities, while Benjamin and I would continue our usual daily work-rhythm. And on occasional weekends, we would get out into the high country as a family for some hiking.

Rick's short visits during the past several years had given him snapshots of my daily work with Benjamin, but now we would have to find ways to become a more integrated family unit. Nevertheless, our "division of labor" would remain as it had always been: I would continue being the homemaker and Benjamin's therapist, while Rick would remain the breadwinner, responsible for providing the family with financial stability. That was simply the most efficient and effective way for us to keep things on an even keel.

"Just think, if we had to pay other people to do all the things I do, we would go bankrupt," I said to Rick, only half joking. Sometimes, my positive mindset would wilt; I would dream of having the freedom to pursue my professional aspirations, and I would wish that there was an income to show for all the work that I did. At such moments, I had to give myself an attitude adjustment, resolving to appreciate how destiny had led me to a path I was perfectly suited for. Working with Benjamin and dealing with the challenges of his autism had clearly become my primary calling, and I had to be content with leaving my hard-earned identity as a musician/writer in second place; there was no way to juggle all these balls with equal dedication.

Benjamin's last two weeks of the school year were flat. He seemed devoid of energy and was irritable and prone to screaming. Sophia's calm assertion of boundaries kept him somewhat in check, but on the last day of class, Benjamin displayed an uncharacteristic streak of meanness, willfully defying his teacher and screeching, then laughing about the scene he had made. I couldn't believe what I was seeing, and Sophia made the snap decision to send Benjamin home after several unsuccessful tries at taming this strange monster.

When we had an appointment with Julie the following week, I had to admit that last month's remedy had done nothing to steady Benjamin's mood. If anything, it might even have caused some added irritability. As I talked, I glanced over at Benjamin who was altogether fixated on flipping Julie's light-switches; this was a stark contrast to the amazing playfulness and interest in toys we had observed during our last visit.

"There's been one age-appropriate development though," I told Julie. "Benjamin is expressing interest in knowing where babies come from, and he's asking questions about the differences between boys and girls." Smiling, Julie added this to the list of behaviors she had been notating, then called Benjamin over for a new remedy.

"We'll see if this one helps bring him back into balance," she said to me. "I know you are hoping for the sweetness and joy that we have seen at various times. However, the expression of conflict is a normal part of a child's development and of life in general. Realistically, I am hoping to reduce the extremes of Benjamin's negative behaviors. If we *also* get greater happiness, then that is a plus." I nodded, knowing she was right but hoping nevertheless that I would be seeing more of what I considered to be the "real" Benjamin.

That evening, at bedtime, this "real" aspect of Benjamin suddenly rayed forth as he exclaimed, "Mommy, please hug me. I *love* you." I was speechless and deeply moved as Benjamin threw his arms around me, clinging tightly, holding on with all his might as I wrapped my arms around him. I rocked him back and forth, feeling the heart-to-heart connection that was present in that moment, wondering at Benjamin's spontaneous impulse.

Of course he had learned the phrase, "*I love you,*" long ago, and we had practiced saying it often. But Benjamin had never before *initiated* saying "I love you." He had simply parroted the phrase, needing me to say it first in order to echo it back. This evening though, the depth of feeling that propelled his words was overwhelming; Benjamin's heart and soul were manifest in his verbal expression of love, and his vigorous hug was a natural extension of his feelings. In that special moment, I could truly forget about the barriers that Benjamin's autism so often presented.

A few days later, the summer sun had reached its apex, hot and golden, and the longest day of the year was at hand: the Midsummer solstice. Benjamin and

I were atop the mesa overlooking our neighborhood, resting in the shade of a pollen-laden pine tree and reviewing the German poems that would be part of our evening festival performance.

I picked a golden dandelion blossom and prompted Benjamin into speaking his prepared verse about the *Löwenzahn* (dandelion). At the line describing how a breeze might carry dandelion seeds up into the sky and out of sight, I handed Benjamin another dandelion stalk, this one topped by a delicate globe of fuzzy seeds. Benjamin blew vigorously, and the silvery little seed-parachutes went swirling into the air, perfectly illustrating the words of the poem: "*Pusteblume, fliege aus, / Flieg in all Winde...*" (by Marianne Garff)

Then we rehearsed the poem about a firefly flitting through the garden with its little glowing light. During our festival, Benjamin would carry an antique barn lantern with a lit candle inside, and he would "become" the firefly, dancing around the garden with his glimmering light. Benjamin was eagerly anticipating this transformation, remembering it from last year's celebration. "And will the gnome come? And will we jump over the fire?" he asked me now, clearly recalling the magical occurrences that had happened the previous year after the sun slid behind the mountains and after my parents' garden had fallen into dusky shadows.

"I'm sure it'll be like last time," I confirmed, happy at Benjamin's recall of our family's midsummer-night's-dream magic. "Someday," I thought, "when Benjamin is much older, I will teach him snippets of Shakespeare's play, and we will act those out during our solstice festival."

33

A Chock-Full Program
July 1999

Now that preschool was out for the summer, I was again focused on expanding Benjamin's world: for the first time, Benjamin was accompanying me to our local library.

"Books are like treasures, you will see." I had to make my selections quickly as I couldn't keep Benjamin busy just by handing him a colorful book and hoping he would become absorbed in looking at it. Benjamin was much more interested in walking back and forth along the rows upon rows of books resting in their shelves. He became virtually hypnotized as the countless vertical edges flew past his eyes, and at other times, he would be caught up in the endless procession of catalogue numbers that decorated the books' spines.

I hastily browsed the shelves, choosing only the most beautifully illustrated books, excited about exposing Benjamin to new stories, cultures, landscapes, and animals. Once we arrived home, I stowed our treasures in a backpack along with various dolls, stuffed animals, cloths, and finger-knitted strings, added containers of food and water, and then we were ready for our daily "learning walk" on the nature trail.

As usual, we stopped at each of the three footbridges along the path. At the first bridge, I would spread out a blanket to sit on. I would read to Benjamin, would ask comprehension questions, and would encourage observations about the pictures. As this was challenging brainwork, I inserted lots of mini-breaks to refresh his mind and to keep his blood moving. "Let's practice some dance steps. *Slide, together, slide, step.* That's it, let's do that a few times. Now let's try *step-hop, step-hop, clap-clap-clap.*" Outdoor folk-dances were being held in downtown Boulder, and these included occasional instructional sessions geared towards children. I had started attending these with Benjamin and was picking up simple steps we could practice in between the weekly dances.

Once Benjamin and I had worked our way through a book and several dance steps, we would get back on the trail and head towards the next bridge. There, we might work on learning a German poem, or on memorizing and acting out the *Summer* circle play I had chosen for this time period. (Sophia had given me an anthology of circle plays that corresponded to the four seasons of the year, and I was working my way through the collection.) Then, after another walking break, Benjamin and I would sit on the third bridge to again look at books, to memorize poetry, or perhaps learn a song.

At other opportune places along the trail, I might stop, spread out our blanket, and get out a few of the toys I had packed. Then I would engage Benjamin in play. "Look, here is a perfect place to build a swing for Katrina-doll." Low-growing branches of a wild apple tree overhung a cozy nook of flowers and grasses, and this was a lovely spot to rig a dolly's swing set.

"And here is some moss; your frogs would love to jump around here." I had a collection of homemade frogs and gnomes in the backpack. "Let's act out the *Pinke Pank* gnome-poem amongst the pinecones here," I might suggest before reciting that little German verse, demonstrating its story line with a little peak-capped figure.

Sweet as all these scenarios were, they represented work to Benjamin, and I had to expend much energy in focusing his attention and soliciting his cooperation.

On some days, I focused primarily on brisk hiking, wanting to show Benjamin the larger network of trails that branched off from our daily loop.

Sometimes, we would have a wildlife encounter that could make for a little adventure story: a bull snake stretched across the trail, a bear cub glimpsed through trees, even a nest of baby skunks hidden away behind a thicket; these all became the perfect material for storytelling practice.

"Daddy will love hearing this story. Let's talk about it, and you can figure out what to say." I would prompt Benjamin to come up with a small narrative by asking leading questions about "what, where, and when," helping him to string the information together into a mini-report. For several days in a row, we would review the same story until Benjamin could discuss it with only a little prompting. His conversation skills were gradually expanding, and these little happenings provided the perfect springboard for sustained dialogue.

In the afternoons, we generally stayed at home practicing violin and working on the various other skills and games that were part of our repertoire. Sometimes we would have a play session with some of the new children that were appearing around the neighborhood. Or we might head over to a nearby playground for practice in negotiating the jungle-gym and monkey bars. Benjamin had long displayed fear around such equipment, but now he was gaining strength and confidence and was starting to enjoy being a monkey.

Occasionally, we also went to the warm-water pool for swim sessions. Recently, Benjamin had made a breakthrough: he had finally overcome his long-standing fear of going underwater. After a year's worth of slow, patient desensitization, he had finally built up enough trust and confidence to try "going under," and now he was quickly growing self-assured and joyous in the water, hopping in from the pool's edge, making "nose bubbles," and dog-paddling towards me as I stood several feet away, waiting to scoop him up.

Several evenings per week, Benjamin and I attended the summer concerts at the Chautauqua auditorium, reveling in the glorious music presented by the Colorado Music Festival orchestra. Like the previous year, we sat near the back of the auditorium so we could easily exit if Benjamin acted up, but unlike last summer, I no longer spent most of each concert tortured by anxiety about his behavior. The crucial difference this year was that Benjamin had matured enough for me to "bargain" with him and to thereby encourage self-control. Now that he understood the concept of consequences, I could offer him a choice. "*If* you sit and listen, *then* we can stay. *Otherwise*, we are leaving."

Fortunately, Benjamin really did want to be at the concert, and he also knew I would follow through with leaving the auditorium if he didn't behave. Of course, I helped his motivation along with little rewards; if I could figure out what thing Benjamin particularly desired at any given moment, he was usually willing to be persuaded that good behavior would benefit him. "*If* you are quiet, *then*...you may hold this toy. (Or...you may have a candy at the end of this song. Or...you may see Mommy's wristwatch at intermission. Etc.). *Otherwise*, I will have to take it away." *If, then, otherwise*—this sequence of words was becoming extremely familiar. The work with consequences that Sophia and I had been doing since January was paying dividends.

However, as far as numbers were concerned, any attempt at reasoning became futile. Currently, whenever a number came up, even in casual conversation that didn't directly involve Benjamin, there was a chance that he would fall apart, screaming and crying. He often seemed to feel he had a monopoly on the world's numbers and that anyone else's use of them was a terrible breach of ownership. However, this extreme response was entirely unpredictable, and so, sometimes he was fine when hearing someone mention a number, and sometimes he was not.

For over six months, Benjamin's number fixation had been the cause of much heartache. At times, however, his obsession produced funny results. One day, as we were walking on the trail, Benjamin was driving me absolutely nuts with his incessant counting, and I tried to get him to sing a song, hoping that music would help divert him from his numbers. Benjamin found a clever compromise. He complied by making up a little melody, but at the same time, he added the following lyrics, "*I love numbers, I love numbers, one, two, three, four, five...*" I had to laugh, irritated though I was.

Naturally, I kept trying to find ways of getting Benjamin out of his loops of obsessive counting because, whenever he got into such a state, he would be entirely caught up in it, incapable of paying attention to anything else. However, in spite of his counting fixations, Benjamin was making useful mathematical connections that were much advanced for his tender age of four. He had woken up one morning, and the first words out of his mouth had been: "3+3+4+4 is 6+8…is 14. 7+7 is 14 too." Astonished, I had run for paper and pencil to record what he had just said, realizing that the sums must have run through his dreams.

In addition to his apparent aptitude for manipulating numbers, Benjamin was displaying a knack for spelling. "H-A-R-M-O-N-I-C-A," he spelled out one afternoon, looking vaguely into space and speaking each letter very deliberately. I wondered. Was he sounding the word out mentally? Or could he visualize the letters? Or both? He didn't falter or lose his place, and his spelling was absolutely accurate. Benjamin's reading too was becoming fluent without any effort on my part; he was simply picking it up on his own. In fact, Benjamin was becoming "hyperlexic" as he could easily and correctly read things that he clearly couldn't understand.

With the adjournment of preschool in mid-June, Sophia and I had discussed Benjamin's need for a break, and thus I hadn't enrolled him in her summer school program. However, we both felt there was a need for continuity, and so Sophia had offered to conduct weekly, hour-long play sessions, working one-on-one with Benjamin as she had done the previous summer.

Sophia had introduced a new greeting song into these special sessions with Benjamin. "*The sun calls me to the meadow green, / Where I love to dance and play*," she would sing, gesturing for Benjamin to follow her into the play room. There, she would segue right into the *Summer* circle she had chosen (this was a different one than I was working on), and then she would move into playing with Benjamin, always beginning with building a house. "Cloth, strings, and clips," she would remind Benjamin. "Gather up your materials and bring them here."

Sophia had explained the importance of house building to me. "For young children, building a playhouse is particularly grounding and satisfying. During the preschool years, the child is gaining awareness of its own body as the housing for its soul and spirit. Also, the child is finding its place within the family unit which, in turn, is housed in a physical building. And if one looks at the pictures that children make at this age, one finds that they are often drawing themselves and their home. So, at various levels, finding containment and security within a structure—i.e. a house—is an important theme. As an aside: we adults are responsible for providing a sense of security and containment. That is what we're doing when setting boundaries and instating consequences; we are 'housing' the child."

During each play session with Benjamin, Sophia would encourage some domestic activities within the confines of the little house they had built together. Only then would she allow playtime to veer in another direction. And, as the concluding activity of the hour, she would paint with Benjamin, always focusing on the theme of painting the ground, the sky, and a figure representing Benjamin standing firmly on the earth. Through art, she was trying to bring him to an awareness of being fully present and grounded.

After one of these sessions with Sophia, Benjamin and I had a wonderful nature story to tell her. I began. "Remember the bouquet of peonies you gave us at the end of school, before summer break? Benjamin noticed a tiny caterpillar crawling on the flowers when we put them in a vase on our dining room table. Then we forgot all about the caterpillar until Benjamin noticed it again, weeks later. It had become long and fat, just like..."

Benjamin took the cue. "Just like in my *Hungry Caterpillar* book. We saw her make a big diarrhea poop."

Sophia laughed, and I continued the story. "We put her in a jar with some sticks and leaves, and the next day, she had shed her skin. Then, right before our very eyes, she began wiggling back and forth like crazy, exuding a milky substance that hardened to become a cocoon. Do you know how many times I tried raising caterpillars as a child and they always died before anything special happened? Well, we just happened to be watching at the precise moment of transformation—it happened in a matter of about twenty minutes or so—a perfect stroke of luck for us." I shook my head in wonderment, and Sophia looked pleased.

"Then we had this cocoon hanging from a stick inside our jar, and last week, it hatched and became a beautiful, dark-brown swallowtail butterfly decorated with yellow and orange, and with blue spots edging its wings. We were lucky again: we saw the butterfly emerge from its cocoon, and we got to watch the crumpled wings slowly expanding over the course of several hours. However, for some reason, one of the wings remained somewhat curled and kept the butterfly from fluttering away properly." I didn't say out loud that I had thought of the parallels to Benjamin's struggles with autism as I watched the beautiful, ethereal creature, sadly hampered in flight by its malformed wing.

"Mommy took pictures of me; the butterfly sat on my shoulder," Benjamin exclaimed, concluding the story.

Near the end of July, Benjamin reached the lofty goal I had dreamed up during the previous summer while listening to my colleague's violin students performing on the mall. I asked whether we might join in this year's performance since Benjamin's repertoire consisted of nearly every piece in Suzuki Book I, and this friend generously invited Benjamin to a group rehearsal.

When the practice session began, I could tell that Benjamin was tense with nervous excitement because his left-hand fingers kept popping straight up rather than remaining curved, but he soon settled in and relaxed. As the pieces became more complex, my colleague began counting off the beats. "One, two, ready, play." I was sitting directly behind Benjamin, acting as his shadow, gesturing where he should look and whom he should follow, and I felt a jolt going through Benjamin at the count-off.

Oh no. The potential for a melt-down was imminent. Someone else was "doing the numbers." "Candy, I have candy for you," I urgently whispered in his ear. "Keep yourself together, and you will get butterscotch candy." I could see Benjamin struggling for self-control and felt my own vibrating tension as I willed for him to contain himself. Then Benjamin managed to begin playing without crying or screeching, and I let out a shaky sigh of relief.

When we rejoined the group for a mall performance a few days later, I was prepared with candies in my pocket. Throughout the concert, I knelt behind Benjamin, cuing his focus, trying to be as inconspicuous to the audience as possible, but nevertheless immediately available if something should go awry. Fortunately, the excitement of having an audience seemed to bring out the best in Benjamin, and everything went off without a hitch. I was enormously proud of my little performer.

That evening at bedtime, Benjamin was wound up and hyper, and I began soothing him with some calming energy work. Stroking downwards from head to toe, I alternated between gliding my hands lightly down Benjamin's sides and then again moving them downwards through the space immediately surrounding him (without touching him). While doing this, I imagined Benjamin's aura becoming smooth and unruffled. It had been quite some time since I had done this, and Benjamin was being receptive. "Do that some more, Mommy," he said, laying his hands on mine and guiding them to rest on his forehead, causing me a poignant moment of déjà vu.

I was suddenly back in the bedroom of our little Coronado cottage... processing the shocking news about what a diagnosis of autism might mean... trying to reconnect with my lost little boy, lightly massaging him...two-year-old Benjamin tentatively taking my hands and placing them against his forehead—a subtle bonding gesture, a gossamer desire for connection...

34

Negative Energy
August 1999

At the beginning of August, Benjamin came down with a high fever and eventually developed a congested cough. The illness seemed to throw him into a negative space, wiping away the supportive effects of the most recent homeopathic remedy. Actually, the past six weeks had been reasonably enjoyable and very productive, in spite of the many moments of upset that had occurred, but now I saw a return of that little mean streak which had appeared just before school got out in early June.

It began as small expressions of defiance on Benjamin's part—nasty little pinches and experimental slaps—and quickly developed into overt combat. If he was feeling rebellious, Benjamin would forcefully hit me, dig his fingernails into me, or, if I was kneeling or sitting at his level, throw an arm around my neck to squeeze me with a choking grip. That shocked me; it actually hurt. Additional journal notes recorded the following:

An astounding amount of flapping has returned; Benjamin is fluttering like a frantic bird. Also, there is an extreme amount of bouncing and jumping. However, no supportive homeopathics for now; Benjamin must fully recover from his illness first. As the weeks went by, Benjamin began having occasional screaming fits again, some of them reaching near-hysteria as they had in January. At other times, he was terribly clingy, wanting me to squeeze him in a bear-hug, needing to be held and carried.

Along with craving extremes of physical stimulation, Benjamin's obsession with wristwatches took on a new twist. When we were in public, he was drawn to other people's timepieces like an iron filing drawn to a magnet. The person wearing the watch would cease to exist for Benjamin, and if I didn't catch him in time, he would grab at any stranger's watch, intent on staring at its numbers. Then he would screech when I pulled him away. "So sorry," I would mutter, burning with embarrassment as disgusted looks were sent my way.

In spite of the difficulties, I kept up our daily rhythm of work, trying hard not to lose objectivity and self-control. Our play scenarios continued to expand, with fresh possibilities being inspired by the treasure trove of new library books that I checked out each week. Our violin practices too were relatively productive as Benjamin began learning pieces from Book II of the Suzuki Method. I also began taking him on occasional outings to stores so that our pretend shopping scenarios at home would be grounded in reality.

As might be expected, these public situations required me to anticipate problems and to prepare strategies in advance so that the shopping expedition might be successful. For example, when we ran out of painting paper, I took Benjamin along to the art supplies store. Just outside the entrance, I gave him a preparatory talk about expectations.

"You will see people wearing watches. You may not touch them, or we will leave immediately. Also, you'll see many number signs and tags. You may not mess with them, or we will leave. You may not scream. These are the rules if you are to come inside with me: no watches, no tags, no screaming."

Benjamin assented and we went in, with me making a beeline for the pads of painting paper. When we got to the register, Benjamin began sidling around the counter, reaching for the cashier's delicate golden wristwatch. "Remember what Mommy said about watches?" I warned, and Benjamin managed to heed me and to desist as I finished buying the paper.

One positive development of this time was that Benjamin began transferring some of his sporadic clinginess to Rick, often requesting to be carried and squeezed; at bedtime, Benjamin would occasionally send me away, wanting Daddy to come and say prayers instead. I couldn't help feeling a bit rejected, but was thankful that Benjamin and Rick were now bonding more.

Throughout the summer, Rick had of necessity been fairly absent, focusing on his job search and spending much of his time holed away in our home office, studying airplane manuals and preparing resumes. The stress of not yet having secured a job was getting to him, and on days where Benjamin was being difficult, Rick had little patience and would occasionally bark in the manner of a drill sergeant, expecting Benjamin to cooperate.

"That won't get you anywhere," I would tell him, explaining alternative ways of handling his son. While straight-forward and concrete communication could certainly be effective, the tone of voice and the energy behind the words was equally important. Self-awareness and self-control were inescapable requirements for successful parenting.

In response to Benjamin's amplified need for physical stimulation, I increased the time we spent on sensory games and also exposed Benjamin to some new experiences. At the park near the nature trail, I found a tree with a very low fork and sturdy branches that seemed made for climbing. I hoisted Benjamin into the crutch of the tree and encouraged him to act like a squirrel. Benjamin beamed from between the leaves, loving the new perspective, and I could tell that his climbing practice on the local playground equipment had made him more courageous.

On hot days when we had worked hard, I took Benjamin on excursions to the reservoir which was located north of town, surrounded by farmland and rural neighborhoods. The lake had an area designated for swimming, and a playground with enticing equipment located higher up its sandy beach. I encouraged Benjamin to roll in the gritty sand and to splash in the cold water, and was delighted when he eagerly explored the novel climbing apparatus. I also tried building sandcastles with him, but couldn't seem to pique his interest. I gave Benjamin a wooden boat tied to a string so he could tow it through the lake's gentle wavelets, and we practiced tossing balls back and forth, standing in the shallow water near the shore.

During our yearly visit to the county fair, I took Benjamin to try some carnival rides; we had avoided them in previous summers because of their over-stimulating light-and-sound effects. After some initial trepidation, Benjamin found delight in riding on the carousel, in sliding down the long, wavy "super-slide," and in feeling the disconcerting changes in his body momentum as he rode on a twisty little roller-coaster and took a "space-ship ride." All these sensory experiences were intended to fill the craving for stimulation that Benjamin was currently expressing.

As the heat of late August settled over us, Benjamin's recurring rebellious attitude prompted him to run away without answering whenever I called him. This new development was of particular concern because we were now "out in the world." The danger of my losing track of Benjamin—whether on the trail, at the store, or in the library—was very real.

I had already experienced a scare at the library when I had been momentarily distracted in my quest for new books. Benjamin had been sitting next to me, apparently absorbed in looking at the call-numbers on the books in front of him, and I had ducked around the end of the shelf, glancing briefly at the row of books on the other side. When I returned, not half a minute later, Benjamin was gone.

I began quietly calling his name as I combed through the maze of shelves around me, my sense of panic increasing as I failed to find him. The library's main entrance was directly adjacent to the children's section, and I feared that Benjamin might have run out of the building altogether. Heart pounding and mouth dry as sawdust, I rounded a corner near the shelf where we had last been together and—there he was. My knees went weak with relief, and I felt shaky. During my search, I had been having visions of Benjamin being hit by a car on the busy street located just beyond the main doors, of him drowning in the creek which ran directly past the library, and of his being accosted by the myriad homeless people who frequented the benches outside.

"Didn't you hear me calling your name? Why didn't you answer? We just practiced this yesterday," I sputtered, my relieved fear quickly turning into anger. Benjamin ignored me, and I took some deep breaths, struggling to regain my composure. Then, in a neutral tone, I explained, "We need to practice answering, otherwise I cannot take you to special places anymore."

I guided Benjamin outdoors to the grassy park adjoining the library, and after I had given him some more explanations, Benjamin was ready to cooperate. I drilled the previous day's "answering dialogue" repeatedly.

"Where are you?"

"Here I am."

"Please come."

"I'm coming."

"Good job. This is truly important, Benjamin. I don't ever want to lose you."

By the end of the month, Benjamin was still prone to extremes of defiance and to screaming for long periods of time. He was also becoming madly fixated on objects like tea boxes and candy tins, along with the usual buttons, switches, and "number objects." Since his overall negative state hadn't resolved itself, Julie gave him a dose of remedy, and I prayed that Benjamin would be in better shape by the time preschool resumed. With district support, we were expanding his school program slightly: rather than transitioning to the three-day group with same-age peers and facing the difficulties of forming new bonds of friendship, Benjamin would stay with the younger children in the Thursday/Friday class. Additionally, Sophia would work with him on Wednesday afternoons, conducting one-hour play sessions just as she had done throughout the summer.

35

A Growing Sense of Humor
September 1999

The first weeks of September were marked by Benjamin's emotional extremes. Some days were happy and mellow, but on other days, he could move from great joy, to terrible screaming, and then back to happiness, in the course of hours. His defiant impulses continued. Fortunately, the somewhat violent phase had passed quickly, but he still felt the need to push boundaries, and he frequently ignored me or screeched when I called him or requested his cooperation. Also, he had newly discovered that he could put on a silly act which would delay the accomplishment of whatever tasks I had in mind. However, in spite of Benjamin's unpredictable moods and the toll they took on my emotional well-being, he was making progress.

There was clear advancement in Benjamin's use of language as he moved beyond concrete observations to make occasional poetic or imaginative statements. One evening, as he was lying in bed staring up at the white ceiling above him, he suddenly whispered, "There are diamonds in the sky." He might have been quoting the Beatles, except he had never yet heard their music or lyrics.

On a different evening, as we were getting ready to say prayers before bedtime, Benjamin wistfully commented, "I want sunshine in my tummy." Then he observed, "Darkness makes more and more sadness. Gotta fight the dragon." I took this to mean that Benjamin wished to feel lighter and happier, and that the recurrence of his ill-tempered moods was making him sad. His philosophical remarks touched me deeply as I too had been feeling that darkness. Worn out by Benjamin's many weeks of defiance, I was inadvertently slipping into defensive and nasty overreactions rather than staying on an even keel. I really felt like a witch sometimes.

Admonishing myself, I thought, "Girl, it's time to fight your own dragon. Pull yourself up by the bootstraps and shift your attitude. Find the light things to appreciate."

Preschool was the ideal place for me to step back and feel a sense of appreciation. Benjamin's use of language, his social skills, and his capacity for joining in play had grown enormously in the past year, and I was glad to once again have Sophia's modulating influence as part of the picture. Her use of consequences and timeout in the context of the classroom with its group dynamics was so much more effective than my lone, disciplinary attempts at home.

Preschool had begun on a good note, and Benjamin's two-day class was essentially intact from the previous school year. Only the older boy had moved into the three-day group, and now there were two new, younger boys taking his place. During the first days of class, Benjamin had persisted in saying "Hi" to one of these boys, actively trying to get a reaction, insisting that his new peer acknowledge him. Surprised and pleased, I took note; this was the first time I had seen Benjamin taking such initiative towards anyone.

It wasn't long before the new boys warmed to the group, and one of them began letting his sense of humor show, thus adding a new dynamic to the class. This child's love for joking around and laughing about things could get out of hand, but oftentimes, his style drew Benjamin's interest and thus provided an important connecting-point.

Partway through September, there was a funny incident that occurred during baking-time. The boys were helping Sophia with preparing some bread dough, and Sophia handed Benjamin a little cup of honey that he was to pour into the mixing bowl. When the cup slipped out of his fingers and dropped into the yeasty liquid that was already in the bowl, Benjamin began hollering in dismay, upset with his mistake, while one of the other boys started laughing his head off, seeing only the comical aspect of the situation. Then Sophia started laughing, and finally Benjamin couldn't help himself; he joined in the hilarity, giggling with increasing abandon.

I too began chuckling as I watched from the living room couch. "Laughter is something we can all share in, regardless of age or ability," I thought. "It is so wonderfully infectious that one doesn't even need to understand what is going on in order to join." The little incident became like a shared joke that was brought up repeatedly between Benjamin and this one rascally boy, always triggering mutually satisfying giggles.

Another time, Thursday's baking activity again became the focus of humor, and in this instance, Benjamin independently told a "story." As he and his classmates stood watching, Sophia poured a measure of foaming yeast into the spelt flour that was already waiting in the mixing bowl. She had previously made a broad, flat indentation in the center of the flour, and as the poured liquid spread out to fill this space, she made an observation. "You see? It is a crater lake with mountains all around its sides."

The children crowded 'round, watching eagerly. The bowl did indeed contain such a landscape. Then Sophia began stirring. "An avalanche," she exclaimed as she caused some of the flour to tumble from the sides of the bowl, down into the yeasty lake.

"Another avalanche," Benjamin exclaimed, giggling as the next small mountain of flour disintegrated. Then Benjamin had something to share. "We had an avalanche on our car," he announced, and then elaborated when Sophia asked what this was all about.

"In the winter, Mommy stopped the car and the snow slid, *brrrmmmm*, down the window." I laughed from the living room, recognizing Benjamin's reference. The previous winter, there had been an enormous snow storm, and I had neglected to sweep the foot-high layer of snow from the roof of our car before driving it. After a few days, the weather had warmed up, making the snow somewhat slushy, and it had indeed slid voluminously down the windshield when I had braked sharply just outside our driveway.

"I love your story, Benjamin," Sophia praised, and then glanced over at me with a smile. She knew how much effort I was putting into storytelling with Benjamin.

The emergence of Benjamin's sense of humor was a positive development that helped make up for the difficult times that peppered our days. Halfway through September, I notated the following:

I think some of Benjamin's screeching has to do with his difficulty in retrieving words. His desires are becoming more complex, and he is having a hard time keeping up with them linguistically. My sense is that an instant movie of what Benjamin wants to accomplish flashes into his mind, and then he has trouble translating his visualized impulses into words—which of course is frustrating, especially if I seem to be blocking his desires.

After thinking about Benjamin's screeching in this way, I experimented. While on the trail, I explained that he would have permission to carry out his ideas, as long as he made an effort to use words rather than pulling, pushing, grabbing, or running off. We practiced this new "rule" many times as we walked.

There were lots of opportunities as Benjamin continually wanted to climb boulders, throw pinecones, or run out in front of me. At first, his body language helped me to guess his intentions, and I would quickly give him the words to express these. Soon, he got the hang of the "game," and it became easier for him to curb his impulses long enough to state his desires.

Also on the trail, I took advantage of Benjamin's emerging humor to create the lighter moments that we were so in need of. One day, as we walked, I introduced a funny new German poem about a gnome who is harvesting pears into his little sack, when *Pardautz!* An enormous ripe pear falls right onto his head and bounces off his nose. Benjamin began laughing like crazy, asking me to repeat this again and again, and then he was suddenly very motivated to learn the poem. "What a pleasure, being able to tickle his funny bone," I thought.

On a different day, I had Benjamin set up a rural scene with meadows, sheep, and a cow, and then I made Benjamin-Doll fall out of a tree, *splat,* into a cow pie. Benjamin laughed and laughed, taking over the doll's actions; it was a wonderfully light playtime.

As we moved towards the end of September, another facet of working with humor revealed itself. We were chatting with a friend who had a son of Benjamin's age. She shared that her boy was currently enamored of a book called, *How To Eat Fried Worms.* Using a deadpan expression, she joked to Benjamin, "Don't you think that would be yummy? Wouldn't you like to eat a worm?"

Benjamin looked shocked and turned pale, and then he fell into a fit of screaming and crying, not understanding that she was kidding around. "That's his 'literal mind' at work," I explained as my friend apologized profusely for upsetting Benjamin. "With autism, there is an overriding tendency to take things at face value," I told her. "In a way, it's good that this just happened; it tells me that I need to start teaching about jokes, double-meanings, and idiomatic expressions. Since Benjamin is beginning to get a kick out of funny things, this is perfect timing."

After Benjamin had calmed down from his shock, and after we had gotten home, I broached the topic of joking. I explained and demonstrated how people often say silly things with a serious face, and tried to convey the idea that the disparity between the two is part of the humor.

Again and again I demonstrated the process, step-by-step, of being pretend-serious and then breaking into laughter to indicate the joking nature of the words. After Benjamin's initial trepidation wore off, he warmed to the idea and became tremendously animated and giggly. So, I told him a joke about a mean cook who beat his batter and whipped his cream, and after some explanation, Benjamin found it truly funny. A new door was open to us.

Just before the end of the month, we celebrated Michaelmas, setting up the dining room table as usual, decorating it with fruits, vegetables, and flowers from my mom's garden. My parents and Rick were present, and this year—unlike the previous one—I was prepared with a structured "program" for our festival, knowing that Benjamin would get the most out of the celebration in this way.

My mom gently plucked at the strings of the lyre while I asked Benjamin to lay his hand on mine so that he might "help" me with lighting the candles on the harvest table. Then we went through the entire *Autumn Orchard* circle from school, with my parents and Rick all participating, standing in a circle and copying my motions as if we were in preschool together.

Unlike the previous year where Benjamin and I had "performed" for my parents, this year's family participation created an entirely different feeling, and the joy shining from Benjamin's face told me I had made the right choice. There was a sense of his being completely supported, of being an integral part of a unified family circle.

Then we ended our festival with the *September* calendar poem which we had reviewed after Benjamin's philosophical comments about wanting light in his tummy. We had been practicing the poem regularly and now, as he recited, Benjamin shared from a basket of polished apples that hung over his arm, ceremoniously handing the fruits to us during the appropriate line of poetry. Then came the words about slaying the dragon, and Benjamin unsheathed his gilded wooden sword, vigorously speaking and acting out that part of the verse. The final lines about facing the coming darkness with a light-filled heart were accompanied by simple gestures too, and Benjamin looked at me earnestly, meaning every word of what he was saying. It was beautiful.

36

Benjamin Turns Five
October 1999

Benjamin had developed an acute ear infection. Its onset was sudden and its progress so fast that, before remedies or medications could take effect, his eardrum had burst, releasing a quantity of infected fluids and temporarily relieving some of the pain. I knew that the eardrum would likely heal on its own, but worried about the possibility that Benjamin's hearing might be affected, even though the doctor assured me that if this were the case, it would probably only be for the short-term.

The worst was over within a few days, but the next few weeks were difficult as Benjamin alternated between recovery and relapse. As a result, his emotions and his capacity for engaging in our daily games vacillated wildly, and the month of October was well underway by the time that Benjamin completely regained his health and vitality.

Around this time, several things happened that gave me a sense of resolution, a feeling that certain chapters of life were coming to a close and that new ones were beginning. To start with, I began receiving complimentary copies of various professional magazines in our mailbox. My book was receiving highly favorable reviews both nationally and internationally and was being recommended to musicians of all levels, amateurs as well as professionals. This was a sweet reward for all those hours of burning the midnight oil—a recompense for my persistence in writing, in spite of the full days of carrying out autism therapy. Now I was using those late-night hours to fill the inrush of book orders, putting together the requested packages, and writing out receipts after returning from orchestra rehearsals or after cleaning up the house.

Around this time too, Rick received word that he had been hired as a pilot by Northwest Airlines and that he could expect to attend two months of training, beginning in December. Since NWA didn't have a hub in Denver, Rick would be commuting to Michigan or Minnesota for ten-day work periods once he began flying a regular schedule. He would be at home for regular intervals, and we could plan our family life around these. Granted, some of his "down time" would be taken up by Navy Reserve work since, together, Rick and I had decided that his staying with the military (at this reduced capacity) would be a wise choice.

Now that Benjamin's fifth birthday was coming up at the end of the month,

I couldn't help thinking back to that time, nearly three years ago, when Benjamin had been diagnosed with autism, and I had thought that by the age of five, he might be fully recovered and on the path of "normalcy." I had certainly taken full advantage of the "window of opportunity" for making a significant impact on Benjamin's development, and I had worked ceaselessly towards the goal of full recovery, trying to emulate the few stories of success that—even though they were controversial—had provided me with a vision for hope.

And now, here we were, with Benjamin having made enormous strides forward, having broken through so many of the barriers that had first plagued him...and yet, his autistic traits were still going strong, affecting his life and mine every single day.

But I would not relinquish my vision of a happy and fulfilling life for Benjamin. I was going to keep reaching for the stars—who could know what the future might bring? Now that the initial "window" was letting in so much light, and now that the "door" was open to life-long growth and improvement, continued determination and persistence would be needed.

I threw myself into preparations for Benjamin's fifth birthday celebration, choosing a new story to present as a puppet show, developing a set-concept for the show, and making simple props. I memorized the story's text and songs while walking with Benjamin out on the nature trail, letting him hear the script as I recited it out loud. As soon as I was able, I began rehearsing the show with Benjamin as my sole spectator. In two weeks, when his special day arrived, Benjamin would know the story almost as well as I did, and he would be able to get full enjoyment out of watching the puppet show with his party guests.

By this time, halfway through the month, Benjamin had fully recovered from his ear infection, and he began having some exceptionally good days at school. Sophia began teaching the children to play some cooperative games that, for Benjamin in particular, were valuable in demonstrating that each individual's efforts were required in order for the group to succeed.

Sophia invited Benjamin to "be part of a machine" and had him sit in a circle with several friends. Then she showed the group how to hand a beanbag around in a precise manner and rhythm, with everyone keeping up a repetitive motion pattern that made me think of smoothly oiled clockwork. As the beanbag traveled, Sophia added funny sounds: *"hip, hop, clop, mop."*

Benjamin absolutely loved this new game, and he concentrated intently on synchronizing his motions to those of his friends, helping to keep up the tempo of the "machine." Once this teamwork exercise had been mastered, a second beanbag could be added, making the synchronicity exercise even more challenging.

A few days before Benjamin's birthday, he and I had a work session which highlighted the progress that Benjamin was making. He was clearly on a path leading to ever more complex communications.

As it happened, I had pulled out our *Moody Bear* puzzle, thinking we should do some review; many months had passed since we had last played with it. In addition to having six choices for facial expressions, Moody Bear could wear different combinations of clothing, and today, I had encouraged Benjamin to make conjectures about the bear's feelings, not just by looking at his face, but also by considering the clothes he was wearing.

When the bear was wearing his farmer's outfit combined with a scared face, Benjamin speculated that Moody Bear might be frightened of a dangerous bull that was running about in his fields. Then, when the bear had on a fancy suit combined with the smiley face, Benjamin thought the bear was going to a party. This idea led us to an extensive conversation, and I was thrilled at the growth in Benjamin's capacity for verbalizing his thoughts.

The difference between now and the last time we played with this puzzle is nothing short of phenomenal, I wrote later that day, after I had put Benjamin to bed and had sat down with my journaling. *We continued our work with the collection of whimsically decorated nesting boxes. The artwork on the different faces of these boxes shows a variety of animals dressed up as circus performers, and we were able to have much conversation about who was balancing on what or whom, and also to put forth conjectures about where and why. We discussed the outfits in detail and did some size comparisons and sorting by various criteria. Then we did some basic math—a little addition and subtraction—while messing with different box combinations.*

The toys that I was working with during Benjamin's first year of therapy are now lending themselves to enormous expansion. We are using them to playfully practice many aspects of conversation and grammar. Thus, the basic tools are leading to advanced skills. This is analogous to a growing onion: new layers continually form around a central core, building up to a mature crop.

Finally, the long awaited occasion of Benjamin's fifth birthday was at hand. During our family celebration before breakfast, Rick, my parents, and I looked on as Benjamin eagerly unwrapped his birthday gifts. He was beaming and talking nonstop, making little word-plays, pretending this and that, asking all kinds of questions. I watched Benjamin, my heart swelling with joy and pride as I recalled last year's celebration and noted the incredible changes that one year's work had wrought.

Later in the day, Benjamin's classmates from preschool arrived for his birthday party, all dressed up in costumes since Halloween was just days away.

Benjamin greeted them shyly, looking like a little gnome in an earth-toned mantel and a peaked red cap.

He was so proud of the costume that we had made together. Benjamin had helped me to dye the cloth using walnut hulls and black tea, and when I had sat at the sewing machine, he had helped me to guide the cloth as the needle flashed up and down. Even some of the embroidery on the peaked cap had been accomplished by Benjamin's fingers.

As I guided the children through some outdoor games, Benjamin fluttered about excitedly in anticipation; he was going to be giving a little "birthday concert" for his friends, performing an intricate *Gavotte* on his violin while I accompanied him on the piano. Once our little audience of children and parents was seated, and our music making was underway, I saw Benjamin's initial nervous tension resolve itself into confident performance. I thought, "This is like an initiation ritual, requiring bravery; Benjamin is showing his friends what he is actually capable of."

After the performance and some more games, it was time for my puppet show. In the story I had chosen, a boy searches for his friends; they are the flower fairies that have disappeared with the coming of autumn. He goes on a quest to find them and, in keeping with fairytale tradition, overcomes three big challenges. In the end, the boy indeed discovers his friends slumbering deep in the earth and learns that he must plant seeds and bulbs if he expects the flower fairies to awaken; they will reappear when the seeds begin sprout. The boy also learns that he must have patience; winter's slumber will not be hurried.

I had chosen this lovely story because it struck me as an allegory of Benjamin's own experience—and mine. Just like the boy in the story, Benjamin and I were on a quest. We too were searching for friends, i.e. the inner connectedness that would allow Benjamin to communicate, to form emotional ties, and to develop relationships. As in the story, we had already overcome three years-worth of challenges. And, like the fairytale boy, I had learned about planting seeds and tending them with patience: Benjamin had gradually awoken from the frozen winter of his autism, and now the seeds of his understanding were sprouting and even blooming; he was connecting with the friends of his world.

The next day, we celebrated Benjamin's birthday at school, starting right at the beginning of the morning's activities. As she did for every student's birthday, Sophia told the story of a little child who left his spiritual home with the angels and traveled over the rainbow bridge in order to join its chosen parents on earth. The tale was lovely and immensely touching; a lump swelled in my throat as Sophia added a special detail just for Benjamin: *"The beautiful music that the child had listened to in heaven, he now brought with him..."* Then she proceeded to tell some of the memorable events from the child's life—how he had learned to walk and eventually to talk, to play the violin and sing, to make friends and share his heart; and finally, she ended with, *"and his name was Benjamin."* An exquisite look of happiness and realization spread across Benjamin's face as he fully comprehended that the story was about *him* and not just *any* child. His joy was complete.

For the remainder of the morning, Benjamin was in a state of near euphoria, displaying a sense of initiative and awareness that was unprecedented for him. Repeatedly, Sophia and I caught one another's eyes, raising eyebrows and dropping the jaw as if to say, "Wow, did you see *that*? *Incredible*."

During playtime, Benjamin participated in house building with unsurpassable eagerness, and later, when everyone was seated for snack, he observed that napkins were missing. All on his own, he took it upon himself to locate them in Sophia's kitchen, to make a trip around the table handing a cloth to each child and to Teacher as he went, and then to stow the remaining napkins back in their cupboard. "I wouldn't have guessed that Benjamin even knew where the napkins were," I thought, goggling with astonishment.

During outdoor playtime, Benjamin began quoting a part of the *Autumn Haying* circle and then ran over to Sophia, exclaiming, "Teacher, I want to play an outside game." Benjamin began acting out the motions of sharpening an old-fashioned scythe on a whetstone, and then he mimed the action of cutting down wheat and binding it into a sheaf.

"Are we playing an outside game," Benjamin now commented, getting his grammar mixed up as Sophia joined him in reciting the circle and acting it out. Again, my jaw dropped. In all my past year's work of teaching Benjamin various circle plays, he had never once initiated any of them. Indeed, *I* had generally exerted much energy in soliciting *his* participation. And here Benjamin was, eagerly accosting Teacher, wanting her to follow him in reciting poetry. "He is 'high' on birthday energy," I thought, feeling a bit starry eyed. "Let's hope that he rides this wave for a while..."

Part II

Keep Reaching
For the Stars

Age Five to Young Adulthood,
and Beyond

Mapping The River's Flow

Naturally, the euphoric birthday wave crested, and Benjamin's ride on the river of life returned to its typical ups and downs, with the downs being as turbulent and challenging as ever. Not surprisingly, my journaling beyond Benjamin's fifth birthday expanded by leaps and bounds, with thousands of pages documenting his ongoing growth. However, for the purposes of this book, our journey through Benjamin's life story will now accelerate, leading to an overview of the present time, with Benjamin having turned eighteen and still contending with autistic challenges; with me still devoted to Benjamin's continued development and improvement; and finally, with Benjamin and I working together, maximizing his strengths so that his personality and particular talents might shine forth, autism notwithstanding.

My goal in this account remains the same as before: to describe how I have worked with, around, and against Benjamin's autism. I will present you with those vignettes and observations which illustrate various interesting aspects of child development as filtered through the lens of autism, and will share the useful strategies that arose in response to Benjamin's needs.

37

The Final Years of Preschool

Benjamin's Second Year at Sophia's Preschool, Continued

November 1999

Benjamin's improved verbalization of desires was taking on a new twist. Now, when he became upset, Benjamin would exclaim, "May I fall," while throwing himself down upon the ground. Often, screeching or crying would ensue.

Since this was becoming a regular occurrence, both Sophia and I were experimenting with counteracting the behavior. I came up with a roleplaying scenario: I would make one of our cuddly dolls have a mini-tantrum and would help Benjamin to act out the parental role. "Say, *'Stop that and get up. Use your words and be a big boy.'*" Benjamin would say this line to the doll with great gusto, and I hoped that the reversal of roles might give him a helpful perspective on his behavior.

Benjamin was currently fixated on candy boxes, tea tins, and little jewelry cases. We had quite a collection of these pretty things, and Benjamin was hoarding them, repetitively opening and closing them, lining them up "just so" and compulsively tweaking their positioning. I generally hid the collection on a high shelf, but would allow Benjamin to play with the boxes and tins if he would join me in creatively "transforming" them. "Shall they be part of a store? We can play shopping. Or, you can wrap them up as gifts. We could play birthday. What else can we do with the boxes?"

As long as Benjamin flexed sufficiently to use the boxes in a play scenario, I would allow them off their shelf, but as soon as things deteriorated and the boxes became a single-minded fixation, they would have to disappear again. That could get noisy and unpleasant. Sometimes though, the overall situation would be quite funny as I watched the gears turning in Benjamin's mind. He would have an irresistible urge towards his compulsion and would request the boxes; when reminded that he was required to "play" with them, he would look like the cat that ate the canary. "I've been caught," his face would say. "Mommy figured out what I had in mind. Darn it all anyway." Then, as if to cover up, Benjamin would act reasonable.

"I want to be the storekeeper."

"What a good idea. I'll bring Alexander and Katrina over to buy something..."

At preschool, the children were making lanterns for their St. Martin's festival, and Benjamin, eager to help with the supplies, looked up at Sophia with awe and love in his face. Then, while crafting, he became frustrated and let out his feelings by screeching. "You can say it with your nice boy words," was Sophia's consistent response, and soon Benjamin's noises had abated. Watching the interaction, I thought, "If this had happened at home, I might have gotten mad and put Benjamin in timeout. But this was much more effective and shows me another way to react."

By cleanup time though, Benjamin was in timeout for nonparticipation. Now he started acting the rascal, purposely tipping over the chair and sitting on its upside-down frame. Sophia had me come over and take Benjamin on my lap to complete the timeout. Knowing that I was feeling a bit frayed, she explained that "children need to be nixies," that they need to act out wily and mischievous impulses as part of their development. "This tends to happen between age four-and-a-half and five. Like the 'terrible twos,' it is part of the child's need to find boundaries and to thus feel secure in its world," she assured me.

"All the more reason to keep my reactions calm and objective as I enforce consequences," I thought. "If I can accept the inevitability of the behavior, that might keep me from getting so emotionally wrapped up in Benjamin's issues."

Benjamin had difficulty with voluntarily closing his eyes, and I had decided to tackle this issue. Closing one's eyes allows the imagination to flow and is also a first step towards relaxation and inner awareness—important in dealing with autism. Lately, I had been blindfolding Benjamin and giving him various objects to feel and identify. This had become an enjoyable activity and so, one afternoon, I suggested playing the game without the blindfold. "Quick, close your eyes for a moment and guess what this is," I exclaimed, but Benjamin immediately balked, screeching, insisting that he needed the bandana over his eyes. I held firm on my agenda, and suddenly we were engaged in a noisy power struggle which resolved only after I changed tack and tickled Benjamin's interest by making up a "new" game.

"This is the 'open-shut' game," I explained. "Look at me. Do you see my earrings? See their color and shape? Now, shut your eyes but pretend you can see me *through your eyelids.* Can you still see my earrings? Tell me, what color? What shape?" Benjamin's face was tight with the effort of keeping his eyes closed, but he answered accurately, his visual recall clearly intact.

"Now open and look. Did you remember right? Good job. Now look at my hair bauble. Quick, close your eyes. Tell me about the bauble." Benjamin's already tight face squinched up further as he recalled some details, and then his eyes flew open to check his memory. He giggled at his success. Suddenly,

Benjamin was showing his liking for the game, although I could see him struggling to overcome inner resistance each time I cued him to shut his eyes. "Lots of practice needed," I thought, adding the exercise to the list I kept posted in our play area.

During violin practices, I was helping Benjamin to develop his imagination and to engage his emotions. Benjamin was already halfway through the third-level book of the Suzuki Method, playing real repertoire by Bach, Handel, Beethoven, and Dvorak, and these musical compositions lent themselves well to invented storylines. "Now we want to sound like a grand king, loud and confident. And here, this is a shy princess; she is dancing, softly, lightly."

When we practiced together, Benjamin still needed me to orchestrate his every action, and sometimes fifteen minutes would go by with only a few notes being played. Benjamin's slowness and difficulty with focusing would stretch my patience to the utmost, and at times, I would still resort to propping him up physically just to keep things moving. In spite of the challenges, Benjamin was making enormous progress: he was playing three octave scales and arpeggios, had a very nice vibrato, and was working on some advanced bowing techniques that involved bouncing the bow on the violin strings.

Benjamin even participated in a public violin workshop given by a master teacher. Although he was initially shy during his session, he gradually warmed into his playing. However, when the audience burst into applause at the end of Benjamin's performance, he seemed shocked by the sudden noise and began saying, "I need to fall." His excitement and his liking of the music and the new teacher were overwhelming him. Thankfully, Benjamin didn't entirely lose his composure, and the teacher's genuine praise eventually brought a tentative smile back to his face. An important goal had been achieved.

December 1999

For several weeks, Benjamin had been going downhill; his social connection was waning, he was bouncing around a great deal, and he had newly begun episodes of violent rocking accompanied by hyperventilation—worrisome and very strange looking. He was back to being hypersensitive and was starting to lash out again, wanting to hit and scratch. Autism was taking him over once more.

Now, when Benjamin became upset, he would recite a veritable litany—"It's broken, I need to bump, I need to fall,"—before throwing himself down. Sophia was helping him with interpreting those inner impulses. "You didn't know what to do, so you felt like falling. I will help you." Then she would give him some options, suggesting what Benjamin might do or say instead.

Sometimes Sophia would reach out and take both his hands in hers. "You are on the bridge now, Benjamin. You must walk across and get to the other side." Sophia's "bridge" image represented the importance of moving on through the acknowledged feelings. Benjamin was to do so without "falling over the edge," without becoming mired in the upset.

One time, when Benjamin had become calm, Sophia extended an invitation, still holding both of Benjamin's hands. "Can you look into my windows? My eyes are like windows, Benjamin. Can you see me in there? Eyes are windows to the soul." Benjamin gazed at Sophia, looking a little bemused at first and then gradually emanating a deep sense of peace and satisfaction. There was much love to be seen within Sophia's "windows," and caring warmth was flowing from her hands to his...

I was experimenting with tickling as a means for derailing Benjamin's screeches of protest and for getting his attention when he ignored me. He didn't like being tickled vigorously, even though laughter would usually ensue, and soon, the mere threat of being tickled was acting as a deterrent. I was glad of the humor inherent in this new form of "discipline."

Tickling also became an effective tool for counteracting Benjamin's "sack of potatoes" trick. Rather than trying to drag him to his feet, I would give him a quick, hard tickle which would jolt him into action.

One morning at school, Benjamin remained oblivious to his surroundings, entirely caught up in self-stimulatory behaviors. Eventually, his spinning and flapping morphed into giggling and lying on the carpet, and soon Benjamin was banging his feet on the floor in a regular rhythm. "Now he is being a rascal, along with being caught up in a sensory fixation," I thought, and shortly thereafter, Sophia announced that she was sending Benjamin home. She had tried various consequences and these had had zero effect on Benjamin's behaviors. As we were leaving, I showed Benjamin my sadly disappointed face. "Do you understand why Teacher sent you home?" I asked.

"Because I didn't listen to Teacher, and because I bumped my feet. How are you feeling, Mommy? Are you feeling happy?" Thus came Benjamin's immediate answer. Boy, was I ever surprised. Although Benjamin had seemed so far gone all morning, he was entirely clear about what had happened. Also, he was now wishing for me to be happy rather than sad; he cared about how I was feeling. And as the day progressed, Benjamin became very cooperative. "The newest homeopathic remedy is kicking in; the wall is coming down," I thought, and by the next day, it was clear that Benjamin's energy had altogether shifted in a positive direction.

Benjamin, five years old, had made his second-ever independent drawing.

While I was cooking dinner, he had spontaneously gotten out a small, light-blue square of paper and a green coloring pencil, and had sat down to make some wavering marks across the bottom of the paper, narrating as he worked. "I'm making grass...it's like Oma's garden...I need brown for the earth." Thrilled, I brought Benjamin our box of colored pencils, and he finished his picture, adding some delicate orange flowers. Exquisite, and with no help from me.

As we prepared poems and songs for our Christmas celebration, I felt light of heart; throughout the past several weeks, I had been able to apply a "soft" style of discipline. Currently, Benjamin very much wanted to see me smile and was desirous of my praise, and thus, if he began screeching or testing me, I could often turn him around by simply saying, "Let's make Mommy happy." This helped engage him in controlling his own behavior, and he would do so in order to achieve a positive effect in *me*, rather than basing his cooperation on the avoidance of negative consequences.

I had been searching for further horse riding situations and had hooked up with a woman whose retired dressage horse would be a safe mount. Now I was leading the horse around in an enclosed arena, frequently glancing over my shoulder to check on Benjamin who looked very relaxed, clearly enjoying the soothing, rocking motion. Afterwards, as I talked with the horse's owner, I became aware that Benjamin had found some paper and a pencil, and was keeping himself quietly occupied.

When our conversation finished and I came over to look at Benjamin's paper, I saw a beautifully printed line of small, neat words: *Benjamin, box, adventure, children of the forest.* In addition to the words, Benjamin had also drawn a musical staff and had populated it with notes, putting the stems on the correct side of the note heads and creating a little melody on paper. I was astounded. We hadn't ever done any writing practice together, and Benjamin's natural facility with the pencil was clearly outstanding, as was the perfection of his spelling and his recall of correct musical notation.

I was put in mind of a child author from the late 1800's who, at the tender age of six, had begun "making prints" (as she called it), and had turned out to be a poetic prodigy, expressing herself with exquisite beauty as she made keen observations of the natural world.

"It's time to begin reading *The Diary of Opal Whiteley* out loud to Benjamin," I thought now. "He too has a sense of the poetic, and Opal's childhood views of nature will resonate with his soul." This was to become a new aspect of our bedtime ritual in the months to come: the reading of a segment of Opal's personal journal, followed by prayers, and then sleep.

January 2000

I was kissing Benjamin's cheeks when he commented, "I'm a cabbage." After a moment's thought, I got the connection. My nibbly kisses must have reminded Benjamin of a bunny rabbit; thus, the cabbage analogy. "You are being a sweet boy these days," I told him, reflecting on the past three weeks of Benjamin's general responsiveness and my relief at being able to offer gentle guidance. When Benjamin became upset, I could simply hold him, and his negative feelings would diffuse. If Benjamin misbehaved, I could give explanations on more desirable behavior, and he would take in my words. Occasionally, I might need to sharpen my voice or give a quick yell, but this was the extent of my needing to "get strong."

Now, Benjamin stopped being a cabbage and told me a little story: "Once upon a time there was a little fox. He yipped and he yelped, and he went to the meadow and grazed on grass. The end." Short it might be, but Benjamin now understood the general concept of making up a little fantasy tale.

Benjamin and I were holding onto opposite corners of a large silk scarf, dancing together and wafting the silk in an expressive manner while a lovely piano piece by Chopin purled from the stereo set. The length of colorful silk gave definition to the space between us, and Benjamin's body movements were gradually becoming smoother and more poised as I showed him how we could move creatively as a team, making the scarf catch the air currents. I pointed out the waves and ripples that moved through the delicate cloth.

"Listen to the music, Benjamin—take it into your body. Let the music move you, just as we are moving the silk." As the scarf seemed to dance on the sound waves, I reminded Benjamin to notice my movements and to imitate them so that we were mirroring one another. Benjamin still had great difficulty with his imitation skills.

"Now, pretend that we are in a swimming pool full of honey. How would you move?" Benjamin's motions became even smoother and more sustained, and I felt a thrill up my spine. Benjamin was responding to evocative language, was getting a "feel" from an imaginative phrase. A new possibility was opening up to him: rather than depending on me to coax and manipulate his body from the outside, he was making a change that came from within, from an inner understanding.

Now I let go of the silk scarf and placed a beanbag on top of Benjamin's head, asking him to keep it balanced up there. Then I challenged him to walk, still balancing the beanbag. This was a wonderful exercise to keep him grounded; if he got excited and started bouncing, the beanbag would immediately slip and fall, giving Benjamin a different kind of feedback than my oft repeated words, "Settle down."

I wanted Benjamin to be more self-directed during play, but just now, he wasn't coming up with anything and so I began asking leading questions, making him think and answer. "Are any of your dolls hungry? Oh, you say you want to have teatime? What will we need?" Benjamin gradually overcame his inertia as he dredged up answers, chose a cloth to cover his work table, set up doll dishes, and then placed some smooth black stones on each plate.

"What are we eating, honey bun?"

Benjamin looked at me, clearly hoping for a suggestion, but I let my question hang in the air, gesturing to the table and making inquisitive faces to indicate I was all ears, waiting to hear what the black stones might represent. After an incredibly long wait-time, he finally came up with an answer. "Chocolate."

"Yay, yahoo," I cheered joyfully, and Benjamin began bouncing around, beaming with pride and excitement. He'd had to struggle in coming up with this idea, and he now felt a great sense of accomplishment. "Someone is missing some chocolates," I next observed. "And perhaps we should add a little fruit too." Now Benjamin had to figure out who was sitting where and had to decide on what to do about the "treats." He looked around the table, taking in the uneven "servings." He adjusted the number of stones, then added some acorns. I applauded his careful work, pleased that he was now so awake to the play situation. He was starting to think on his own.

Transitions. They could be so difficult, particularly if they couldn't happen on Benjamin's terms. During the holiday weeks, I had accommodated his needs and had managed many a graceful ending or transition, but now we were back to our usual busy schedule. Today, we were nearly late for an appointment, and I couldn't give Benjamin the lengthy amount of time that was so often necessary. Several minutes had passed since my first introducing the idea of leaving.

"We must go *now*," I said urgently, trying to disengage him from the swing set at the playground. The screeching tantrum that followed was absolutely horrendous, and I was glad that no one was around to witness it. My tall five-year-old was once again acting like a spoiled toddler, driven by the rigid thinking that was part and parcel of his autism.

Much later, when the dust had settled, I explained to Benjamin that, as a "big boy," I was expecting him to cooperate and to help me when we needed to be quick about something. Wishful thinking perhaps, but I was attempting to sow the seeds of a new idea, and I would be referring back to today's incident when similar situations came up in the future.

Benjamin's willpower was at low ebb, and I was drained from continually putting forth energy, keeping Benjamin moving, urging him into participation, and curbing myself from taking over and doing everything for him.

"Here we are, back at the 'portal of independence'," I thought, liking the analogy of an imposing entrance that might loom intimidatingly. "Benjamin is retracting from this portal; he is either unwilling or unable to step through and stay on the other side. It's the same scenario that we have cycled through so many times already, and I am once again becoming burned out."

Just now, Benjamin was to be getting dressed, and I had laid out his clothes in order, as usual. Benjamin seemed exceedingly distracted and spacey, and he was trying to put his underpants on over his head. "Look, Benjamin, what do you have there?" I asked and then gulped with disbelief when Benjamin repeatedly answered my question by saying, "It's my undershirt."

How could his attention deficit become so extreme? He certainly wasn't messing with me; it was more like he was blindly depending on rote memory, assuming that he was doing things properly—because he wasn't taking in the very object that was in front of his eyes.

"Benjamin, stop. *Look.* This is not an undershirt. What are these?"

The look in Benjamin's eyes was still vague, and I felt like screaming with frustration. I stared out the window. Snow lay on the ground, and I had a sudden inspiration. I jumped up, grabbed a kitchen bucket, and went outside to fill it with handfuls of clean, white snow. "Now listen here, Benjamin. This will help you to wake up." I rubbed his hands and feet with a bit of snow, and Benjamin squawked with surprise. "Now tell me, what do you have in your hands? Show me how you put it on."

As I held the snow threateningly near to Benjamin, he suddenly came to, focusing his attention. "These are my underpants," he told me, and began pushing his feet through the proper openings.

"Good job. And what is this? Yes, that's right—it's your undershirt. Now tell me where you need to hold it in order to put it on. Yes, good—at the bottom." With the bucket of snow there to help me, I got Benjamin to identify each article of clothing and to verbalize whether he was holding it at the top or the bottom. Then it was time to make his bed, and again I asked him to verbalize the sequence as I guided him through fluffing up his pillow, arranging his blanket, and so on.

Later in the day, I drew out a picture sequence of Benjamin's clothing and bed-making routines, reviewing the morning's "discoveries" with him repeatedly throughout the day. I also asked him to dress and undress several of his dolls.

By the next morning, Benjamin's "brain freeze" had thawed, and he was considerably more responsive to my promptings. I kept on with the "leading questions" rather than directing him with concrete commands, determined to keep him engaged and thinking. "What's next? What's missing? I asked you a question... I am waiting. I need an answer. Benjamin? Hello?"

February 2000

I had brought out our hand-puppets and was showing Benjamin how expressive they could be. "There's more to it than just putting your hand inside," I explained. "Your hand is the magic life of the puppet." I made my Mother-puppet clasp her hands with pleasure, nodding her head, and giving her a voice. "I see my big boy. How is he feeling today?"

I reminded Benjamin to hold up his Boy-puppet, facing the mother and giving the appearance of being in dialogue with her. We had a few conversational exchanges, and then Benjamin lost focus. "What. Yes. Thank you. Please. What?" he rattled irrelevantly, his eyes becoming vague as his mouth automatically ran through a rote list of possible responses to Mother-puppet's question. I persisted in seeking Benjamin's attention, giving him a few tickles and "nipping" at him with my fingers until he resurfaced from his limbo. He came through with a decent response, manipulating his puppet, and I praised him for working so hard to construct a cohesive thought.

"I just gave you a *compliment*, sweetheart," I clarified then, introducing a new vocabulary word. "Giving a compliment is like *words making a rainbow to your heart*. When those lovely words arrive, they make you warm and happy, and so you say, 'Thank you.' That is what we do when someone gives us a compliment—we thank them."

I was still taking Benjamin to the warm-water pool on a regular basis, making sure that he didn't regress in his willingness to go under water. He loved jumping in from the pool's edge, holding his breath and paddling like a puppy to reach me as I stood a few feet away. However, he still showed residual fear and resistance when I used the phrase, "Let's do a dolphin swim." As I pondered this and asked Benjamin some questions, I finally realized we had been stymied by a verbal misunderstanding. Apparently, Benjamin had thought that a "dolphin swim" meant going down deep, near the bottom of the pool, as I often did when I demonstrated.

"Oh, honey, you can do a dolphin swim right near the surface of the water," I exclaimed, finally seeing things from Benjamin's perspective. "All I want is for you to be on your tummy with your face in the water and blowing 'nose bubbles.' That's all you have to do, then you'll be just like a dolphin." And that was the definitive end of Benjamin's underwater fear issue.

I was attempting to take advantage of some "natural consequences" in teaching Benjamin. Currently, the weather was icy and so, when he would resist putting on his outdoor gear, I would simply scoop up boots, coat, hat, and mittens, and dump them on the front steps, locking the door behind us. I hoped that the discomfort of being cold would motivate Benjamin to follow through. "It's time to get ready for our walk," I would say. "Mommy will be getting her exercise running up and down the street in front of our house. You will get dressed like a big boy." And I would take off, monitoring Benjamin's progress with every jogging pass of our house.

Benjamin had become obsessively interested in a "clock book" which was designed to teach a child how to tell time and thus had a set of moveable hands attached to a round clock face. As so often happened, Benjamin's initial interest had been productive, but it had quickly escalated into a raging fixation and so I had hidden the book away. I now had a locked cabinet dedicated to the various objects that Benjamin became stuck on; he had become dangerously adventurous in climbing up to the high shelves that had made up my previous hiding places.

"You are stuck," I explained, forthrightly labeling Benjamin's agitation when he demanded to see the numbers and clock hands. "Being stuck doesn't feel good, and so now the clock book is hiding in the special place where all the 'stuck things' live." Surprisingly, Benjamin looked relieved; I had unburdened him of the strain of dealing with his obsession. Then, his relief gave way to howls of frustration. He couldn't help himself; he still had the burning desire to mess around with the book.

"When you feel more calm and balanced, then the clock book can come for a short visit," I now promised. "I am happy for you to have the book, as long as you don't get stuck on it." Then, to help Benjamin over his inner prickliness, I took him on a vigorous walk. Exercise and other sensory activities were always good for clearing the mind.

Benjamin was climbing around on his rocking horse. Eventually, he settled down in the saddle and, indicating his shoulder and hip joints, he observed, "I'm a nut, with places that crack." I laughed, loving the image and appreciating Benjamin's growing body awareness.

On a different day, Benjamin was wildly flapping his hands, and I asked him what he was up to. Benjamin continued fanning the air as he provided me with a unique perspective: "I am feeling the angels."

Pencils had joined the ranks of hidden objects in my "magical cabinet."

Benjamin had become obsessive about drawing squares and rectangles, so now, when I let the pencils out "for a visit," I would supervise and encourage a transformation of the repetitive squares. "How about turning this one into a horse barn? That one can be the arena, and you could put a wagon there, next to the hay shed..."

After a few weeks of this, Benjamin surprised me with his third independent drawing. Instead of sketching his stereotypical boxes, he began drawing some grass, and then he made four trees, each of which had an intricate pattern of branches. Then Benjamin drew lighting coming out of the sky, and finally, he placed a house in the middle of the paper, giving it a door, windows, and a chimney. Then he added a ladder for climbing, and a knob on the door. After contemplating the picture, he insisted, "The house needs a floor."

I sighed with satisfaction as Benjamin adjusted his drawing so the house was grounded rather than floating haphazardly. I recollected what Sophia had told me about preschool age children and the significance of pretend house-building. She had indicated too, that drawings of houses at this age could be interpreted as representing the child's sense of self. Seen in this light, Benjamin's drawing was an important step forward, coming hard on the heels of a new homeopathic remedy.

Four days after his pivotal house drawing, Benjamin surprised me by pulling out his basket of colorful wooden blocks and constructing a tremendously elaborate building. When it was complete, he announced, "Brown-Boy and China-Boy live there. Look Mommy. Here is the living room...and the dining room...and this is the bedroom." I was astounded. This was another leap forward; Benjamin had never initiated such house-building before. And, on this first autonomous try, he had created a beautiful and extensive living space for his doll companions.

In addition to these achievements—independent drawing and house-building—Benjamin was spontaneously recalling many of our old language games. I would hear him singing the little songs I had made up while teaching various concepts and verbal phrases throughout the past year. Benjamin was newly "awake" after having spent numerous weeks in a state of depressing lassitude.

March 2000

"Springtime is in the box," Benjamin declared one day as I picked him up from my parents' house. He held out a small jewelry case. I opened the lid, and there, nestled in soft, white tissue paper, was a small bouquet of silky, gray pussy willows that Benjamin had picked.

Springtime in a box. How beautiful. And how poetic.

We were practicing violin, and Benjamin began resisting my requests, laughing as I became clearly frustrated by his purposeful antics. I maintained a serious face and gave myself permission to snap at him. It was time to expose Benjamin to the reality of how his behavior might affect other people. "Stop. What you are doing is called 'pushing my buttons.' When you laugh at me like this, it makes me angry, and it even hurts my feelings. If you do that to someone else, it will also push their buttons. Another person might even get so angry that they hit you." I elaborated on this theme, and Benjamin became somewhat thoughtful, taking in my explanations.

Now, I began explaining about eye contact. "If you look away when someone is talking to you, they will think you're not listening. That is called 'ignoring.' People do not like to be ignored. Let's practice looking and listening. Come—make a bridge from your eyes to mine. Look right at me, and you will find there is a bridge for our feelings to go back and forth between us." Sophia's bridge analogy was coming in handy, and Benjamin seemed to understand, although in the next moment, his eyes were floating away again as usual.

"I am not in the window, Benjamin." His gaze floated the other direction. "I am not inside the piano." Benjamin steadied himself and looked right into my eyes. I smiled, letting the warmth of my heart travel directly to him. "I love you, Benjamin."

"I love you too, Mommy."

One morning, feeling in need of some uplifting music, I turned on a recording of *Spring* from Vivaldi's *Four Seasons*. Suddenly, inspiration hit me. Each seasonal concerto was just the right length to accompany Benjamin in getting dressed and making his bed. Each season consisted of three movements, and each of these movements was between two and five minutes long. The music could act as a "timer," and as the last melodious phrases came up, Benjamin would know to hurry so that each of his tasks would be finished by the final resounding chords.

I put my idea into action and it worked out perfectly: outdoors, spring sunshine and singing birds abounded; indoors, there was Vivaldi's invigorating music, with violins imitating birds. Benjamin was noticeably more fluid in moving through his dressing routine, listening intently as I drew his attention to Vivaldi's "sound pictures": a bubbling stream, balmy breezes, a thunderstorm, nymphs and shepherds dancing…

My mind leapt ahead. In a few months, we could start listening to *Summer*, and after that, *Autumn* and *Winter*. If Benjamin lost motivation with any of Vivaldi's seasons, I could choose short violin pieces to serve as timing mechanisms; I had a recording of favorite encores that would be perfect for this purpose.

Benjamin's diction was in need of another overhaul. For the past several weeks, he had begun withholding his energy when speaking, keeping his words all mushed up in the back of his mouth. "Time to sing all our dialogues again," I thought. "That will open up his articulation and make the sounds come forward." Just as in the past, singing helped Benjamin to overcome the new impediment, and his verbalizations regained their clarity.

One morning at preschool, Benjamin was indulging in a fixation, twiddling with one of the porcelain knobs on Sophia's bathroom sink, ignoring me when I came to the doorway and told him to stop. Suddenly, the decorative portion of the sink-handle came unscrewed, fell into the basin, and shattered. I gave a little gasp and stepped back as Benjamin quickly emerged from the bathroom, looking worried and scared. He called out, "Teacher, I need help."

As Sophia led the way back into the bathroom, Benjamin hung back, not wanting to follow, but she gathered him up saying, "We'll be brave. I am proud of you for coming to me." Then she sang, "Accidents happen, we just pick them up." The children often heard this phrase, and Sophia invariably remained calm and objective when things broke.

I greatly admired her self-control and sought to emulate her; there was indeed little point in getting all worked up once something was irreparably damaged. One's initial upset, sorrow, or anger might be natural, but one should let it go quickly and move on to taking care of the situation and to thinking ahead about how a similar thing might be prevented in the future.

Now I returned to my place on Sophia's living room couch and made a journal notation on my laptop computer: *Benjamin's worried concern is an excellent sign; he is beginning to grow a conscience. He knows that he has done something wrong, and he isn't trying to hide it. Just in the past week or so, I have noticed momentary facial expressions telling me of Benjamin's emerging awareness of right and wrong—an important new development.*

Throughout the past three years, whenever Benjamin had become fixated on something, I had tried to distract and redirect him. Now that he was well over five years old, I was adding a new strategy: I was bluntly stating the issue and then requesting that he take charge of it. "You are stuck on that. I want you to put it away, by yourself." Benjamin was gradually rising to this challenge, and I felt hopeful that he would someday learn to self-monitor and control his compulsions.

April 2000

We were observing a worm as it wriggled its way into the earth. "He's taking a squirm bath," Benjamin commented, playing with words and coming close to making a pun.

Now our dog, Walker, meandered over, and Benjamin playfully grabbed him by the tail. Walker looked back at Benjamin, curling his body as he sought to snuffle and then lick the hand that held onto him. Benjamin giggled. "I turned on the sniff," he exclaimed, delighted at the comical effect that his impulsive action had caused.

"It's only for Mommy and Daddy to do." I had been hearing this phrase frequently in the past few weeks. Benjamin had again become very inflexible about sharing or taking turns, and whenever he got upset, he would deal with his feelings by announcing this new "Mommy/Daddy rule," sticking to it rigidly even when I offered him a compromise. Benjamin's "all or nothing" attitude was causing him a fair amount of misery, but apparently, he felt the need to be rigidly in control; thus, the constant rule-making. "Another manifestation of Benjamin's autism," I thought, hoping that the phase would wane soon.

I had been teaching Benjamin to fold origami forms, and he had become fixated on a particular paper construction commonly known as "the fortune teller." "It's my bin-with-a-lever," he would tell me, filling the open spaces in the fortune teller with dried rice or beans and then slowly tipping it over to watch its contents running out.

Benjamin was imitating the rows of levered bins he had seen when I took him shopping in the natural foods market, and now he couldn't get these mechanical forms out of his head. Every time I turned around, I would see a new version of Benjamin's "lever bins." At preschool, the fixation had him turning away from peers as he obsessed on building one type of bin after another, and I was sad to see that Benjamin was shutting out countless opportunities for connection and interaction.

Around this time, Benjamin also began expressing a great interest in death, talking about dead bugs, wondering whether they had died naturally or had been killed, asking whether they might need little coffins, and so on. There seemed to be a parallel between Benjamin's filling and emptying of bins, and his deliberations about a physical body being full of life and then losing its animating spark, thus becoming an empty shell.

Lately, Benjamin had been spending much time in front of our bathroom mirror making the most varied and interesting faces at himself. Sometimes he would ask, "What do I feel?" He was trying to put together a repertoire of labels and facial expressions, wanting to know how one might interpret the look on someone's face.

Benjamin had purposely stepped on a box of puzzle pieces, and I had sent him to timeout. "If we don't treat our things well, they will disappear. What should you say now?" I coached.

"I'm sorry," came Benjamin's immediate answer. "And I won't do it again," I prompted, and Benjamin hesitantly echoed me. Now I hugged him and invited him to come back and finish putting together the puzzle.

After some time of working quietly, Benjamin broke into tears as he touched his chest and said, "There's a cactus in here."

"That feeling is called 'regret'," I explained. "It hurts. Regret helps us to learn and to remember. That way, we won't keep making the same mistakes."

"There's a shattered window," Benjamin now cried, trying to deflect the pain in his heart and to transfer it into an inanimate object. "There are bears coming..." It was hard for him to own his feelings, but today, his upset was not so overwhelming that he couldn't manage it with some help.

"No windows, no bears. It's just that you are feeling sorry and regretful," I murmured, holding Benjamin and rocking him, and soon enough, he had recovered himself.

Since the school year was winding down, one of the district therapists came over to our house to conduct an evaluation. One of Benjamin's weaknesses, identified by this testing session, was something called "visual closure." A simple line drawing would be shown, alongside four incomplete and somewhat varied versions of the model drawing. Benjamin was to choose which of these four choices would match the original model *if the lines were fully drawn to complete the pictures.* He couldn't seem to visualize the completed lines and was unable to recognize what was already there versus what was missing.

"This is the same difficulty we have when putting together puzzles," I commented to the therapist. "I'll start doing more puzzle work with him, and I can make up some interrupted line drawings like these so that Benjamin can practice finishing them."

Also, when Benjamin was asked to do a few very simple mazes, he couldn't understand that he was to trace his way through an open pathway. He would simply draw a direct path from start-point to end-point, not bothering to avoid the "walls" of the maze.

"Really? Typical children just seem to intuit the concept?" I asked, surprised and thinking that Benjamin's trouble with the task was due to my never having practiced it with him.

Now I would expose Benjamin to the task, drawing up little mazes on occasion. I might also lay out a large-sized maze on the floor, using wide colorful strings and challenging Benjamin to walk through the open pathway.

Throughout our time at Sophia's preschool, a district social worker had been coming to class for regular observation sessions, monitoring Benjamin's progress. She was impressed by Sophia's work and was fully supportive of my desire that Benjamin spend an extra year at Sophia's school, working on his social skills. For him, this focus would be more valuable than attending Kindergarten, especially as he already knew how to read and to do some basic math.

"In the upcoming school year, this entire class of children will move up to attending three days per week," I explained. "And next month, Benjamin will begin attending Sophia's summer program as well. This will be a step forward from the past two summers of one-on-one play sessions."

Benjamin's skills were prone to slipping if he wasn't in some sort of maintenance situation, and after some further assessment and a staff meeting, it was agreed that the school district would support Benjamin's continued attendance of Sophia's program. A true blessing.

May 2000

Benjamin had newly begun accosting people, walking right up to them and grabbing a hand or even trying to hug them. Then he would try to look at their wristwatches or would reach into their pockets. "He's not shy, is he?" one friendly couple observed laughing as I pried Benjamin's fingers loose from the mechanized dog leash he was inspecting. I felt both embarrassed and worried. There was no sense of personal boundaries just now, and Benjamin's behaviors in general were becoming a bit extreme. In observing his mental state, the words *fragmented* and *unpredictable* kept coming to mind. Nothing seemed to quite hang together.

We were having a home visit from one of the school district's child psychologists, and I asked her for advice. Benjamin had begun his screeching behaviors again and was expressing protest by tightening up his body to such an extreme that his muscles trembled with the strain.

"Try giving Benjamin a 'thera-band' to pull on; you can get a length of that rubber stuff from any physical therapist's office. Pulling against the resistance of the thera-band will provide Benjamin with a physical outlet for his emotions while you steer him towards using his words," she advised. "To help him with transitions, you might provide a visual timer like a sand clock. If Benjamin literally sees his time 'running out,' he can mentally prepare for the change in activities."

Lately, the monster within had been rearing its head all too often. On the worst Mother's Day ever, Benjamin's ongoing screams, howls, and ugly sounds at lunch had put me over the edge, and now my tears were flowing copiously. I felt completely at a loss, sitting with my face buried in my hands as Benjamin tried to get a response out of me, banging the table, gouging the wooden salad bowl with his fork, tipping over his chair, and finally pinching me and pulling my hair. I left the table, ignoring him, hoping that his destructive impulses wouldn't become too extreme. Sometimes it seemed there was nothing to be done.

In our kitchen, Benjamin stood in front of the blender, making his head whip around in circles as he stared at the "on" button. I snapped, "Quit it, you are not a blender," and Benjamin giggled, finding this funny. I however, had temporarily lost my sense of humor. Benjamin looked bizarre and utterly autistic just now, and I felt myself flushing with a useless anger at autism and at the intrusive way it marked my life just now. I couldn't seem to find my equanimity; the ongoing difficulties of dealing with Benjamin were once again running me down.

I was trying a new strategy for getting Benjamin to control his impulses. Before we sat down for lunch, I handed him three paper "tickets" and explained the rules. "Each time you leave the table during our meal, you will give up one of your tickets. If you lose all your tickets, then you will lose your meal as well. However, if you manage to keep all the tickets, you will earn your dessert." This idea, gleaned from a parenting book by John Rosemond was a great way to visually define the steps towards eventual consequences, both positive and negative. And, on our first try, Benjamin managed to stay seated throughout lunch.

Things were finally looking up. Near the end of May, Benjamin and I were invited to attend a birthday party; a friend's son was turning four years old. Out of the blue, Benjamin insisted, "I want to play violin for everyone." He reiterated this desire several times, even when I probingly asked, "Are you certain?" And so, when we arrived at the party, Benjamin surprised the group of parents and children by performing an entire movement of a violin concerto by F. Seitz while I stood by, thrilled that Benjamin wished to share his music.

Benjamin was unhappy about something and, as he happened to have a collection of popsicle sticks on hand, he was venting his feelings by breaking one stick after another, snapping each one in half. In the process, he accidentally knocked over a small vase of flowers which shattered as it hit the floor. Benjamin was so wrapped up in his stick-snapping that he ignored the broken vase. "This is not okay with me," I thought. "Benjamin needs to react to the situation."

Calmly, I sang the phrase that Sophia so often used with the children at preschool. "Accidents happen, we just pick them up." When Benjamin continued to ignore the vase, I added, "Do you know, that was one of my favorite little vases. I am sad that it broke, even though it was an accident." As Benjamin continued his insular silence, I observed, "You are thinking only of yourself. I have feelings too, and what you are showing me right now is called 'being selfish'."

Finally, my words were getting through to Benjamin. He became a little tearful and said, "I broke the vase."

"Bravo," I thought. "He is labeling the situation accurately and is owning up to his action; this is something new, a step forward."

Then Benjamin began deflecting his feelings and, in his usual way, put the blame on an outside cause. "A window broke…a bear came."

"No, Benjamin, what you said earlier was right. You broke the vase. But I understand it was an accident. I love you, and we will clean it up together. Let's get the dustpan and sweeper."

I had neglected to lock my cabinet of hidden, "fixy" toys, and Benjamin had discovered this oversight; he had extracted a small massager which was painted to look like a ladybug and which vibrated vigorously when switched on. I occasionally used the massager as a sensory tool, running it up and down Benjamin's arms, legs, and back. He had also found a cement truck which had a small windup motor. Now, Benjamin was wildly fixated on the truck's automatically turning wheels, his energy careening out of control, his fixated flapping reaching a feverish pitch, and his cheeks flushed with overstimulation.

"I am casting a magical spell," I told Benjamin. "Look, the ladybug and the cement truck are being transformed." I handed Benjamin a ladybug finger-puppet, cajoling him to trade the massager for the puppet, sweetening the deal with a few raisins. Then I encouraged Benjamin to help me as I built a "cement truck" using his little chair and table to make the body of the truck, and adding our big gymno-ball to represent the cement mixing drum. Next, I formed the cement chute at the back of the "truck" by leaning a board slantwise against the ball. I added wheels, using the large, round slices of tree limbs my brother had sawed up, laid a crocheting hoop on the chair to serve as the steering wheel and, as a final touch, set up several "levers" in the cab of the truck, using clothes clips.

"Ta-dah, now you have a cement truck large enough for you to sit in." I coaxed Benjamin to become the driver of this vehicle, emphasizing the attractions of the levers to distract him from his fixation on the motorized toy truck. "These two will allow you to mix the cement at slow or fast speed, and this third lever will release the cement into the chute." As Benjamin relinquished the toy truck, calmed and satisfied by the substitution we had built, I felt the exhilaration that indulging in child's play could bring. "Even as adults," I thought, "we can recapture our childish imagination, allowing it to tickle our creativity and joy."

June 2000

For the past two weeks, an increasingly strong vocal tic had been emerging, and by now, it had morphed into a repetitive throat clearing that sounded like the grunting of a pig. There would be time periods where the pig sounds occurred every ten seconds or so, and I caught myself empathetically holding my breath or tensing up, becoming increasingly nervous and irritated as I tried to ignore the tic. It was like hearing fingernails being dragged down a chalkboard; I found it impossible to remain unaffected.

"Something must be out of balance," I thought, noting the dark circles under Benjamin's eyes. These had appeared around the same time as the tic, making him look quite unwell, although there were no other signs of impending illness. Furthermore, Benjamin had become terribly prone to getting stuck on every type of lock-and-key assembly, and he had a frequent compulsion to run through the house, turning on every working light switch as he went. I wondered whether a cause would reveal itself, or whether this would be another of Benjamin's mysterious autism phases.

Sophia's summer school had begun in mid-June, and now Benjamin was getting to know some new children. Since we were preparing for our Midsummer festival, I thought that Benjamin might like to play his violin for the preschool group. One morning, I brought his instrument and my guitar (for accompanying), and we set up to play the lovely Scottish lullaby Benjamin had newly learned. As he came to the end of the simple song, he became hesitant, his face reflecting apprehension, and shortly after the last note had rung out, Benjamin fell apart, screaming, kicking, roaring. I was utterly at a loss; normally, Benjamin adored performing. The tantrum took a long time to run its course, and then Benjamin repeatedly began stating, "Teacher, are you sad," mixing up his grammar while trying to distance himself from his feelings. Sophia smiled at him. "No, I am happy. Look, you can see who is sad." Sophia stepped over to the play kitchen, picked up a small metal tray, and held it up in front of Benjamin. Its reflective, silver surface mirrored his tearstained face, and Benjamin drew back in surprise, not expecting to be confronted with his feelings in this way. For the remainder of the morning, whenever Benjamin started in on saying, "Teacher is sad," Sophia would remind him of the reality using the tea tray, eschewing words and simply letting the reflection speak for itself, gently bringing Benjamin to consciousness of his heart's pain.

The entire month of June had been difficult and turbulent, but even so, positive things were happening. At school, I was noticing an increase in Benjamin's imitation of speech subtleties—vocal tone, volume, inflection, character—and would occasionally recognize Sophia's manner of speaking in Benjamin's phrasing. At home, there were periods of extended imaginative play that emanated from Benjamin and that required only minimal input from me. On these occasions, Benjamin built structures, moved dolls around while talking to himself, and fashioned little things out of simple materials like acorns, sticks, and tinfoil.

On our daily trail walks, Benjamin was being moved to use his imagination as well. Cactus plants were currently blooming in luminous, golden groups amongst the ponderosa pine trees, and Benjamin was carefully gathering the dusty, yellow pollen from the cactus flowers. "I'm a bee amongst the ice-cream trees," he explained.

The woods were richly scented with the delicious vanilla smell of the ponderosa pines, and after a while, a gentle breeze began moving through the forest. Benjamin stopped at the base of a tall and slender ponderosa, staring upwards into the sky, observing the swaying treetop. "It's a tree-windchime," Benjamin said softly with awe in his voice.

I too could hear the soft, musical sighing as the wind ruffled the high-up pine needles, and I recognized that Mother Nature was speaking to Benjamin's heart.

July 2000

Benjamin had his own "baby garden": a 4' x 4' plot in the middle of my parents' extensive vegetable garden. He was learning to plant and weed and to identify the sprouting vegetables, and I was introducing the idea of keeping a "nature journal." I helped Benjamin to draw a picture of a baby bean plant next to the dormant bean seed which we had glued to the paper, and then Benjamin wrote out a title for his drawing, spontaneously embellishing his neatly printed letters with curlicues and loops—a budding calligrapher.

Benjamin had already learned the names of all the different types of trees in our neighborhood, identifying them by their leaves, and was now recognizing most of the plants that thrived in Oma and Opa's garden.

The Colorado Music Festival was in full swing, and just as in the past few summers, we were regularly attending concerts. These days, Benjamin was exhibiting perfect concert manners, and so I was able to fully enjoy listening to the music. Afterwards, we would visit with friends that played in the orchestra.

One day, one of these friends went hiking with Benjamin and me. At one point, we were seated on a fallen tree, talking as Benjamin irritably tossed sand and dirt around. I asked him to stop this activity, but he refused, picking up some dirt and resentfully throwing it in our general direction. The handful of debris accidentally hit Laurilyn in the face, and I roughly picked Benjamin up, setting him hard on his bottom on a nearby boulder. "You're in timeout," I barked. "That was not okay—throwing dirt can hurt people. The sand went into Laurilyn's eyes. You must listen to my words when I say to stop."

An amazing array of emotions ran across Benjamin's face as I insisted that he stay on his rock until he was ready to apologize. When the dirt had hit Laurilyn, Benjamin had looked startled and near to tears as he realized what he had done. Now he looked frightened and guilty, and my strong reaction only confirmed that he should indeed feel badly. As he struggled to keep back his tears, I could see Benjamin beginning to worry, hoping he hadn't hurt Laurilyn too badly. Eventually, facial expressions of regret and embarrassment accompanied my urgings that he should say, "I'm sorry." Then, as I kept him in timeout, Benjamin began looking obstinate and rebellious as he half-heartedly struck out at me, obviously feeling too conflicted to follow through with an apology.

"Thanks for being patient," I murmured to Laurilyn. "It's important that we get some sort of resolution on this. To be honest, I am quite pleased to see so many different feelings coming from Benjamin; his emotions have developed much complexity in the past few months." The minutes stretched on, and after nearly half an hour, we were still sitting there. By now, the pressured feeling of expectation had lightened somewhat, and a bit of humor had entered the situation as Laurilyn and I cajoled Benjamin to say something appropriate, teasing him a little but insisting that we would wait all day if necessary.

Finally, Benjamin mumbled, "Wish I hadn't..."

"That's right, that's such a good thing to say," I exclaimed, hugging him. I was struck by the fact that Benjamin hadn't used the stock phrase, "I'm sorry," but had instead expressed his true desire, his wish that the whole thing hadn't happened. Now Laurilyn was holding out her arms to Benjamin, and I encouraged him to relax into her embrace. Both of us were proud of his effort.

Benjamin and I were on the shady second bridge along the nature trail, reviewing the *Summer* circle we had learned the previous year. Then, as a break, we practiced some folk-dance steps; we were again attending the outdoor dance sessions for children. Finally, we sat dangling our legs off the side of the bridge, watching the nimble "water-strider" insects that were "plucking the stream" (as Benjamin would say). I read out loud, choosing one of the fairytales from the Grimm Brothers' collection.

Now that Benjamin was essentially Kindergarten age, I was focusing on these fairytales, knowing that they formed an essential part of the curriculum in Waldorf schools. Benjamin would be attending Sophia's preschool for a third year and then would transition directly into first grade at a public school so that he could be with children of the same age. In order that Benjamin would receive some of the soul-nourishing schooling that would be part and parcel of a Waldorf Kindergarten, I had done some research and had purchased a collection of "teacher suggestions" compiled by a Waldorf teacher: *Path of Discovery* by Eric Fairman. I was delighted at the many new poems, rhyming riddles, and stories contained in this series. This was a valuable resource indeed.

Benjamin was learning how to enter a conversation by using the phrase, "excuse me." I was so often alone in my work with him that an opportunity to enter existing conversation rarely presented itself, but at school, Sophia was helping Benjamin to learn that saying "excuse me" was inevitably followed by a waiting period as other people finished whatever they were saying.

This was the hard part for Benjamin since he wasn't generally interested in the topic of conversation but just wanted someone to hear whatever it was he wanted to say. This single-mindedness of purpose was typical of autism, and both Sophia and I kept urging Benjamin to listen and to take in what others were talking about. "First tell me about what your friend just said. Then you may tell me your own thoughts."

The problem was that this would derail Benjamin, and he would become very frustrated as his own train of thought eluded him. "No wonder Benjamin gets so pushy about saying things," I thought. "He feels that he might forget if he doesn't spit it out right away."

August 2000

Benjamin was back to being excessively bouncy. So much so, that he was complaining of soreness in his legs even though he had a forgiving mini-trampoline to jump on. I stepped up our sensory integration program, trying to provide his nervous system with the stimulation it so obviously needed.

"Let's try drawing with your feet," I suggested to Benjamin, thinking that this might "ground" him. After he was seated on his little chair, I wedged a block crayon between his bare toes and encouraged him to trace lazy eights on the large expanse of butcher paper that I had taped to a board. After a while, I switched the crayon to Benjamin's other foot. He was enjoying the novel integration exercise and was becoming increasingly calm and aware of what both his feet were doing.

Then I did a little stamping exercise to further "ground" Benjamin. As I spoke a poem from E. Fairman's collection, I asked Benjamin to stomp in rhythm and to ball his fists repeatedly, exerting his strength and willpower through these actions.

> *My step is strong, I'll not go wrong;*
> *With all my might, I'll guard what's right.*
> *I'll always know how far to go.*

For the first time, Benjamin was making up a cohesive, ongoing narration. He had drawn line after line of "curly letters" (his imitation of cursive writing) across a sheet of paper, and now he explained that it was a letter to Ursula *Papagei*. Benjamin pretended to read, commenting on his meal, his surroundings, and on various activities. He ended with, "I had bright red firecrackers," referring to the handfuls of crabapples he had tossed high into the sky earlier in the day. "I love your letter," I praised. "And you are getting better at telling stories."

All summer long, Benjamin had been accosting strangers, wanting to touch them or to block their way so he might have an opportunity to inspect a wristwatch or to reach into a pocket. I was continuously admonishing him. "You may not touch people whom you do not know. Your words may reach out to them instead."

Eventually, Benjamin came up with a "solution" that put me in a bind. He would run up to someone and ask, "Can I shake your hand?" Apparently, he had noticed that people sometimes engaged in this ritual, and now he saw hand-shaking as a way of getting what he wanted. This was a clever manipulation which could result in a friendly exchange of greetings and, since people often found Benjamin charming, they would indulge him when he wanted to see their timepieces. Of course, these folks had no idea that Benjamin was following an autistic compulsion, and I didn't always feel the need to explain.

However, just now, Benjamin was going through a thoroughly impudent and defiant phase which involved ignoring me or screaming in protest when I imposed any restrictions on him. Occasionally, he would tip into hysteria, screeching until he was nearly blue in the face. Therefore, if Benjamin got away from me and grabbed a stranger's hand, I had to finesse him when asking that he let go. I lived in fear that he might have a tantrum which would cause an alarming scene. Thus, I built some transition time into my directives.

"Benjamin, it's time to play the 'letting go' game. You will let loose your hands on the count of three. One... Two... Three. Let go." This was somewhat helpful, but if Benjamin was feeling particularly defiant, he would count "one, two, three," and then squash the person's fingers with all his might, letting out a guttural sound of resentment. Thoroughly embarrassed, I would apologize for my son's autistic behavior, hoping that a little understanding would go a long way. Fortunately, most folks were quite friendly and sporting about it all.

It was harvest time in Oma's garden. Benjamin loved picking raspberries and popping them directly into his mouth, and I was taking advantage of this motivating activity. For several days in a row, I had been reading out loud the Grimm's story of *Little Redcap*. Now I called for Benjamin to come out of the berry patch so I could show him the contents of my tote bag. I pulled out a Grandma-doll, a Girl-doll with a red handkerchief which I had fashioned into a cape, and a small stuffed dog which would represent the wolf in the story.

"Let's turn the *Little Redcap* story into a puppet show," I suggested. "If you can help me do that, you may pick more raspberries. Otherwise, we'll have to go home." After Benjamin had complied, he was able to escape for a "raspberry break." Then, after some time, I called him over again. "Now we'll draw a picture of Little Redcap as she meets the wolf," I explained, and Benjamin helped me make a simple drawing.

As he returned to the raspberries, I began planning ahead for the next day. We would physically enact the *Redcap* story using a few props and costumes; Benjamin would probably enjoy being the wolf. Then, I would introduce a new Grimm's fairytale: *The Bremen Town Musicians*. I was already looking forward to the small collection of wooden animals I would use to animate the story, and I could imagine the various drawings we might make. Benjamin was becoming increasingly capable of understanding stories and of engaging in play scenarios, and I knew that our repeated work with fairytales—and the multiplicity of approaches that I was taking in approaching them—was paying off.

Benjamin's Third (and Final) Year of Preschool

Autumn Semester, 2000 Turning Six Years Old

Benjamin's preschool group was now Sophia's "three-day class," meeting Monday through Wednesday mornings. The week after preschool resumed, I sat down to make a set of cue-picture cards. "The time is ripe for Benjamin to become conscious of the specific steps that lead to play and appropriate interaction," I thought.

I made seven simple illustrations, each showing a blond boy with a friend, and as I drew using crayons, I attempted to give a heart-felt quality to each picture before adding a few written cue words using colored pencils. I wanted a feeling of sincerity to come through visually, and thus avoided cartoonish figures. The seven cards showed the following:

1. **Attention getting** (tap a friend's shoulder, and/or say, *"Hey, _____."*)
2. **Sharing** (offer to share something: *"Here, would you like _____?"*)
3. **Interest** (show interest, use eyes, words, body language: *"What are you doing?"*)
4. **Asking** (request to be included: *"May I join?" "Can I try that?"*)
5. **Play ideas** (ask for an idea, make suggestions: *"What shall we do?" "How about if we..."*)
6. **Giving compliments** (encourage, praise: *"Hey, I like that; good job; high five."*)
7. **Patience, persistence** (*"Okay, I'll wait...may I have a turn now?"*)

Sophia naturally facilitated such interactions during preschool, and now I would provide Benjamin with some extra reinforcement using the cards as discussion materials which could be reviewed regularly. I might also use them as visual reminders during home play-dates.

Benjamin had been regressing in his independence skills. He was no longer motivated to keep moving through his tasks, and the use of Vivaldi's *Four Seasons* music was waning in its effectiveness. Sometimes I could get Benjamin going by threatening to turn off the music, but it seemed that I needed to come up with yet another novel strategy to freshen Benjamin's interest and to encourage independent follow-through.

So now, I made a little flip chart for getting dressed and for making the bed. Each page illustrated the next step, and I set up the chart with a cardboard stand that would keep it sitting upright on Benjamin's nightstand. Benjamin became quite enamored of this nifty new tool, and the series of simple pictures kept him moving through each step of his tasks, although I did have to remind him to keep flipping the pages.

I also bought a little sand timer in order to give Benjamin a visual representation of time passing. The timer measured three minutes, and I was trying to make a game out of hustling Benjamin through his bathroom routine before the sand ran out.

A new splinter skill had emerged: Benjamin was now obsessed with asking people for their phone numbers, and he seemed to have a near-instant memory for them. Weeks after a friend had casually answered Benjamin's question, "What's your phone number?" he accurately told me the number and saved me from having to look it up when I wanted to call her. As Benjamin quickly built up a mental repertoire containing dozens of phone listings, I marveled at how his brain might function in order to do this.

Around this time, Benjamin also amazed me by announcing out of the blue, "A-flat minor has seven flats. C-flat major does too." I gaped at him, not knowing how he might have figured out these two theoretical musical key signatures. No composer would use them since they were impractical, but Benjamin was right; if one really wanted to write a song in these keys, every single note would need to be "flat."

"He must be thinking in patterns," I reasoned, although I couldn't figure out how Benjamin would have built up the mental framework for this. He was indeed learning to read musical notes, but I hadn't taught him anything about key signatures or about the complex musical patterns and relationships that underlay such theory. "He must be working it out by mentally 'hearing' the notes and recognizing their relationships," I eventually concluded. I took into consideration that Benjamin had an uncanny ear for chord progressions—this also pointed towards his aural recognition of musical patterns.

Benjamin's speech was once again becoming unclear. He had started mumbling or speaking in a nasal fashion, and I returned to my old strategy of having him sing his conversations with me. I also experimented with "playing back" Benjamin's incorrect enunciation, copying the way he sounded when mumbling or speaking through his nose. I had tried this in previous times, to no effect, but now Benjamin showed great fascination whenever I imitated him, and he was managing to correct himself without much further guidance.

During outdoor play at school, Benjamin had fashioned a mortar and pestle using a flower pot and a stick, and he was mashing up some thyme leaves from Sophia's garden. I had joined Sophia and the children in the back garden, and I now whispered to Benjamin, referring to the cue cards I had made for him. "Invite a friend to share your project," I prompted.

Benjamin ran to one of the boys in the sandbox and invited him over, spontaneously taking his friend's hand and guiding him to where the flower pot rested on a low garden wall. "Look, my grinder," he explained, indicating that his friend might try it out.

I thought, "This shows some real growth. Benjamin is following through with an entire sequence of social interactions without needing direct prompting for each step."

Benjamin's screeches of protest had become somewhat of an ingrained habit and didn't always indicate great upset. Rather, they were often a reflexive reaction and were easily triggered whenever Benjamin was fixated on something and felt disturbed or interrupted. At school, Sophia remained consistent and clear in her consequences, first reminding Benjamin to "use words" and then leading him to a brief timeout, even if his screeching had already subsided.

"I need to emulate this," I thought, recognizing that I had recently fallen into an impatient habit of my own, yelling right back at Benjamin when he screeched and ordering him into timeout, my tone of voice reflecting frustration. "I must stay firm in my role as a pedagogue and teacher," I counseled myself. "I cannot indulge in acting like a worn-out mother. When I listen to myself as if I were a bystander, I do not like what I hear. Benjamin's screeching *is* an ongoing problem, but I shouldn't keep running up against it with ugly behaviors of my own."

One of Benjamin's classmates had chosen a special storybook as a gift for Benjamin's sixth birthday. *The Jewel Heart,* by Barbara Berger, was a beautifully evocative picture book about a pair of magical marionettes; the one was a ballerina, and the other was the boy who loved her and played music for her to dance to. This little violin-playing marionette had a jewel for a heart, but he could not speak. Instead, he expressed himself through his music.

As I began reading out loud to Benjamin, I could see why his classmate had told her mother that the story was just right for Benjamin. The parallels between him and the boy-marionette were unmistakable, and I wondered whether the story would strike a chord within Benjamin. Just like the *Boy and Elf* curative story I had created for him the previous year, *The Jewel Heart* focused on the transformative powers of love and music.

I read on, with Benjamin listening intently and studying the beautiful illustrations. As the result of a mishap, the boy's jewel heart was stolen from him by a greedy wood rat, and thus, the spark of life seemed to have left him. The little ballerina, who loved the boy dearly, worked to repair the damage and to revive him. Not having a replacement jewel, she planted a plain brown seed in his chest. As the boy came back to life and began playing his violin, the seed began to bud, and then it blossomed into a beautiful flower as the boy was once again able to express his love. As the story ended, the enraptured expression on Benjamin's face told me that the tale had resonated deeply. With its dreamlike quality, it had softly stolen into Benjamin's heart and soul.

Playing violin duets together was like having a conversation. As Benjamin and I played the ethnically evocative music of Hungarian composer, Bélà Bartok, I pointed out how we could interact with one another using our violins, just as we did when having a verbal exchange of ideas.

"Open your ears to what I'm playing here," I reminded Benjamin. "Now your melody answers; you play louder while I play softly. Now things switch around, and I get to sound important, while your part is more supportive." As we continued practicing, Benjamin began infusing more verve and energy into his playing, becoming inspired by my sound and energy alongside his.

The language of music was teaching Benjamin about being in a fair relationship. He was tuning in to the balance between giving and taking, between listening and leading.

These days, when something struck Benjamin as funny, he would giggle like crazy and then begin butting his forehead into me, like a little goat. Or, if I was sitting down, he might grab at my head, trying to wrestle me while throwing himself around, apparently in the hopes that I would reciprocate and join in the wild giggling. I could appreciate Benjamin's desire to make me to laugh along with him; this would prolong the hilarity and would allow him to stay on the exciting "high" that can come with sustained laughter.

I thought, "I don't want to squelch Benjamin's fun, but he needs to learn the appropriate parameters for it." Benjamin's exuberance was now causing him to become rough with me. "Ouchie," I exclaimed. "Let me show you how people express this kind of bursting laughter."

I began howling with pretended merriment, clapping my hands, slapping my thighs, bending my knees and hugging myself. As Benjamin watched, his giggles shifted into even higher gear, and I encouraged him to copy my actions. "Very good," I sputtered, laughing for real at Benjamin's antics. "This way, no one gets hurt."

Lately, I had been using the telephone as a means for working on Benjamin's conversational skills. My mom and I would agree beforehand on some topics of discussion, and then, when Benjamin was talking to her, she would occasionally give him a message to pass on to me. "Tell Mama that I have some cake here for you. You'll need to come over for a visit. Also, tell her that we will do some more knitting."

Just now however, Benjamin was having great difficulty with paying attention, and I had to revert to practicing scripted dialogues using a toy phone so that Benjamin would be "rehearsed and ready" before trying another real telephone call with Oma.

The days were growing short as the end of November neared, and now, whenever Benjamin became upset and agitated, he was saying things that were scary for me to hear. "I will cut myself. I'll be in pieces—then there won't be Benjamin anymore..."

"Good God, where has this morbid imagery come from?" I wondered. Just recently, I had read a "Dear Abby" column about teenagers becoming addicted to cutting themselves as a response to deep inner pain. I had been shocked to read of such a thing, and now I was hearing my six-year- old son expressing his feelings in the same way. I shuddered. I would have to keep close tabs on Benjamin to make sure that he didn't actually try cutting himself with a kitchen knife or other implement. Intentional self-injury was certainly a possibility with him.

I was at the end of my rope, once again. There were so many little things that could trigger Benjamin into having an absolute meltdown, and these days, he was again prone to entering a state of hysteria, crying so hard that he seemed in a cramp, either gagging or turning blue with not being able to breathe.

These times were frightening, and I was constantly trying to head off Benjamin's meltdowns. Even though many of his triggers were predictable, it seemed that new ones were cropping up like mushrooms after rain. I reacted in various ways, sometimes being firm in redirecting Benjamin to prevent a full-out crying fit, and other times being gentle and nurturing when he became upset.

Regardless, I seemed to have little influence and was constantly second-guessing myself, wondering whether I should have taken a different approach. I kept thinking, "Would he have cried less if I had done this or that?" In spite of all my experience in dealing with Benjamin, his autism still had the power to put me in a position of complete helplessness.

Just before Christmas, I had a phone consultation with a child psychologist. I described my concern about the increasingly violent and self-destructive imagery that was cropping up during Benjamin's periods of upset. "Benjamin has been grappling with the concept of death for several months," I now explained. "In the spring, the pony I had been leasing for him to ride died of colic. Since we didn't have a chance to say 'good-bye' to the pony, I enacted a little funeral ritual using a toy horse, putting flowers on it and burying it with

Benjamin's help. Benjamin acted pretty matter-of-fact about it all—he didn't seem touched by the incident. His autism seemed to be insulating him from feeling anything."

I went on. "Since then, Benjamin has occasionally commented about dead things like insects, showing his interest in an objective way. But now, it seems like he is getting mixed up, interpreting his overwhelming feelings of upset as having something to do with death and dying."

The psychologist reassured me. "Death can be a very confusing concept to children at this age, and I do have a few simple suggestions to help untangle Benjamin's various feelings. Make sure you give him the necessary vocabulary to label his emotions when he gets upset, and help him to tell or show you how *big* these feelings are. I like your strategy of 'whooshing out' the bad feelings along with taking deep breaths. Perhaps Benjamin might act out 'stomping' on them as well, but I wouldn't have him release his upset feelings by hitting a pillow—hitting is too easily generalized, and Benjamin may end up striking out at others. You could also try having him draw or scribble his feelings."

"In addition, Benjamin needs to have some conversations with you that specifically focus on death. When he gives you an opening, make sure that you elaborate sufficiently; he needs to be given a broad understanding which isn't entangled with immediate feelings of upset. Experiment with different modalities for expressing death: drawing, music, body sensations, emotions; all these can play a part in helping Benjamin to form an overall conception of death."

As we entered into the holiday spirit leading up to Christmas, I decided to put Benjamin's fixations to work. They could be applied in the pursuit of creating something beautiful and useful. "Let's make an advent calendar," I suggested.

This project would provide an outlet for Benjamin's ongoing number fixation and would channel his recent paper-cutting obsession. He would have to do some planning, deciding where to place the twenty-four little windows of the calendar and then carefully exercising his scissor-handling skills. He would need to make small illustrations which would become visible as one window after another was opened, counting up the days until Christmas Eve. And, finally, Benjamin would be allowed to write his beloved numbers—one through twenty-four—on the little paper doors that hid the pictures from sight.

Spring Semester of Preschool, 2001   Six Years Old

I was tucking Benjamin into bed, snuggling a down comforter around him while outside, big, fat snowflakes were rapidly accumulating, covering our neighborhood in soft drifts of white. As sometimes happened just as we were readying for prayers, Benjamin warmed my heart with a few perceptive comments. He started off with, "I can't see thoughts." And I said, "No, only if you write them down or draw them."

Benjamin: "They're yellow."

Me: "Yes, very light."

Then Benjamin, tapping his head: "They're right in here..."

Looking through Fairman's Waldorf teacher's guide, I had found another poem that spoke directly to Benjamin's need for increased strength of will. Now I was asking him to stamp his feet firmly in rhythm to the words and to ball his fists at the end of each rhythmic unit: *quick-quick-slow* (make a fist); *quick-quick-slow* (make another fist).

> *I will work with my will,*
> *With my strength and my skill,*
> *And with courage and grace,*
> *All life's tasks will I face.*

I wanted Benjamin to internalize the sensation of feeling powerful and positive. I asked him to walk forward using the *quick-quick-slow* rhythm and to pretend that he was moving through resistance, carving his way through space. "Remember, like walking in a swimming pool filled with cold honey," I reminded Benjamin. Then I demonstrated. "Lead with your heart, and at the end of each rhythm unit, say "yes." It is like greeting the world; each time you say "yes," send your arms out-and-forward like rays of light coming from your heart."

I showed Benjamin how to step strongly forward on the slow step while keeping the other leg back, the toes of that trailing leg acting as an anchor, representing a bridge between the past and the present. As we practiced this special walk, Benjamin became increasingly coordinated and expressive, and his face glowed as he repeatedly said "yes" with great confidence.

January was nearly over, and these days, Benjamin was overly sensitive, shrieking at the slightest provocation. I too felt hyper-reactive, constantly saying "no" to him, the word flying out of my mouth like a reflex. Realizing that both of us were escalating in our behaviors, I made a great effort to curb myself. Although there were good reasons for my saying "no," the word was becoming ineffectual due to overuse.

I recalled my childhood and my mom's tendency to say "no" to my requests. Eventually, I had stopped asking for permission and had simply begun doing whatever I had in mind even though I might get in trouble, not because I was doing something bad, but simply on the principle of my being disobedient. I wasn't about to repeat this childhood dynamic with my own son. "Life is all about finding *balance*," I thought. "Every day, one must renew that sense of balance. It is not a static state, but a dynamic one."

Just now, I needed to regain a balance between curtailing Benjamin's extreme tendencies and allowing him room for self-expression, even though that inevitably meant that his autistic behaviors would gain the upper hand. In the early stages of fixation though, Benjamin could come up with clever and creative things. For example, his current fascination with our car's odometer had resulted in Benjamin's creating an ingenious paper odometer of his own, with three side-by-side loops of numbered strips that could be manipulated to form hundreds of number combinations.

Benjamin was still prone to the type of uncontrollable hysterics that had begun cropping up three months earlier, and Julie's homeopathic remedies were not helping. He was occasionally kicking and lashing out, and Sophia had sent him home from school when he tried to hit her. I started labeling this kind of behavior as "being like Rumpelstiltskin," realizing that when I used direct language, saying "no hitting, no screaming," it only seemed to rile Benjamin up further. The indirect approach of referring to the devilish fairytale character had a less combative effect, and when Benjamin was in a more reasonable state, he agreed that we didn't want such a character living with us.

Learning to play the violin was not only therapeutic in and of itself, but it also provided Benjamin with a ticket for entering various social situations, for getting to know new people, and for collaboration through the language of music. Our newest project had involved learning a *Trio Sonata*, by A. Corelli, a beautiful piece of chamber music for two violins, harpsichord, and basso continuo.

In mid-February, we gathered with several friends for an evening of music-making. Benjamin played the lead violin part while I was the supportive "second fiddle," and he responded to my body motions, finding the beat when he had gotten off a little, gesturing the *ritardandos* (moments of slowing down) so that the entire group could follow his lead. Everything had been practiced countless times at home, and now Benjamin was having fun, experiencing the beautiful culmination of all that work.

Rick floated in and out of our daily lives as his work schedule with Northwest Airlines kept him on travel for well over half of each month. Recently, Rick had transferred from one of NWA's hubs to a different one, and now Benjamin commented on the change. "They took Detroit down and built it up in Minneapolis," he told me, and I had to chuckle at Benjamin's perception of how things happened.

I had found an affordable horse situation which enabled me to take Benjamin for weekly lead-line rides on an old, safe mare. I would lead the horse around, talking with Benjamin as he rode bareback, reviewing language drills or poems. One day, the horse unexpectedly took a few trot steps, startling Benjamin as he uncomfortably bounced forward onto her withers. I stopped the horse, helped Benjamin to regain his seat, and then we finished up the ride without further incident.

The following week, when we returned to the barn, Benjamin became upset as I prepared to settle him on the horse's back, and I realized he was afraid of being jounced around again. Not wanting to make a scene, I gave in and took him home, hoping his fear would mellow by the next riding opportunity. After all, trotting wasn't something new; Benjamin had become quite comfortable with this gait during the previous spring, riding on the Shetland pony I had leased for a few months until it died of colic.

We came back a few days later, and Benjamin again began to cry and protest once the horse was tacked up (instead of a bareback pad, I had put on a saddle, thinking that Benjamin would feel more secure). "If I give in this time, Benjamin will build up a mental block that could take forever to overcome," I thought. "We'll try to push through this." I swung him up onto the quietly standing horse and tried various calming strategies. Benjamin began to howl. I sang to him, stroked him, and tried to distract him by counting various objects like fence-posts or birds sitting on a rail, and after a long while, Benjamin settled down.

Only then did I begin leading the horse, engaging Benjamin in his current favorite activity of counting by threes, by fours, by fives, and so on. Soon, he was altogether relaxed and happy, and was ready to try a few little balance exercises atop the moving horse. I had him alternately rise and sit in rhythm to his counting. Then, I asked him to lean back and touch the horse behind the saddle. He touched his toes and then reached up into the sky, stretching tall. After an hour-long ride filled with various activities, Benjamin's confidence had been fully restored, and he was looking forward to riding again the following week.

Later in the day, I received a phone call from the barn manager. "I'm sorry, but some folks feel you should have respected your child's aversion to riding. They are requesting that you not come back." I felt the impact of this statement like a punch in the pit of my stomach. They had thought me a cruel mom, torturing her fearful child by forcing him to sit on a horse.

If only they had known about Benjamin's autism and the nature of his mental blocks. If only they could have seen the happy resolution of the situation. But, needing to help Benjamin, I had been unable to give the bystanders what they needed: a mini-education on the challenges of autism.

Benjamin's newest mental block involved the telephone. One day, as we dialed up my parents, Benjamin got the unpleasantly honking "busy" signal, and it freaked him out. Now he had a phobia about phoning, and once again, I decided to push Benjamin through a desensitization process before his fear became a well-established habit. First, I notified my mom of my intentions, and then I phoned her numerous times, insisting that Benjamin put the phone up to his ear for a slightly longer dialogue each time. Benjamin was shaking like a leaf, his hands were icy, and he whimpered with distress, but after many phone calls, these symptoms of fear mostly subsided.

Now we were ready to deal with the busy signal. I asked my mom to leave her phone off the hook for an hour, and then I prepared Benjamin for what he would hear, explaining that we would hold the handset far away from his ear so he could get used to the sound. After many repeated calls, Benjamin's sense of terror had diminished, and I knew that with time and repeated practice, he would be able to manage his residual fear.

We were anticipating a spring snowstorm—the month of March was underway—and Benjamin was developing an earache, so I took him to pick up herbal ear drops at the health food store. Benjamin insisted on using the restroom, and I gave him permission to go into the small, single-toilet room on his own. I remained in the aisle nearby, browsing through various herbal preparations, trusting Benjamin to call out if he didn't immediately see me upon exiting the bathroom. We had been practicing this skill diligently for over a year, and he had become very consistent in calling, "Mommy, where are you?"

After a while, I wondered why he hadn't returned, and when I found the bathroom empty, I began combing the store, calling for Benjamin, a rising sense of panic engulfing me. Benjamin was nowhere to be found and, after begging a store clerk to call the police, I ran out into the crowed corner parking lot where snowflakes were already beginning to fall. This space was bordered by two of Boulder's busiest streets, each having six lanes of traffic.

"Dear God, don't let my baby get killed," I prayed desperately as I ran up and down the rows of parked cars. Then I headed towards the huge traffic intersection where multiple turn lanes went in all directions. Could Benjamin have crossed the expanse of traffic lanes and headed up the hill towards home?

As I waited for the light to turn, the sound of sirens reached my ears, and then I saw the flashing lights of a police car and an ambulance. Howling with fear, I began running alongside the flow of traffic, feeling as in a nightmare. My breath was coming in ragged gasps when I finally reached the emergency vehicles and stumbled into the midst of a group of police officers. There was Benjamin, looking a bit tearful, but otherwise, seemingly unharmed.

"Oh, my God," I rasped, my knees buckling as I rushed to him and threw my arms around him. "Oh, God, my baby, my boy..." My ears rang as I nearly fainted, sobs of relief overcoming me. When I could finally hear again, an officer explained that someone had reported a young child running unaccompanied along the busy street. Might I be a neglectful mother, careless of her child's whereabouts? How did this happen?

After much careful questioning, it turned out that Benjamin believed I had gone home without him. Stunned at first by this revelation, I soon realized how he might have reached such a drastic conclusion. Sometimes, when Benjamin refused to listen and to come when I called him, I would say, "I'm going now, bye-bye," turning and walking away to show that I really meant it. With Benjamin being a tall six-year-old, I no longer wanted to drag him around. I was motivating him to come with me of his own volition and, for the most part, this "bye-bye" strategy had worked.

But why hadn't Benjamin asked someone at the store for help? For some time now, I had been restraining Benjamin from inappropriately accosting people and had once mentioned that not everyone could be trusted. (We had met an unsavory character along the trail, and I had used the opportunity to teach Benjamin a little about "stranger danger.") So Benjamin hadn't approached the strangers in the store. And how had he managed to negotiate the dangerous intersection? Benjamin said something about "seeing red lights." Apparently, he had noticed the traffic signals and had somehow responded correctly. And maybe a guardian angel had helped him along.

Once we were home, I mulled over the incident. Benjamin, like any child his age, needed to be allowed some independent choices and needed to learn from making mistakes; he also derived benefit from being trusted to act like a big boy. However, I needed to continue as his "invisible safety net," allowing him the *perception* that he was being independent while yet watching over him like a hawk. That could be a tricky balancing act since I was bound to let down my guard on occasion—as I had on this day.

The other balancing act involved rule-making. Because of his autism, Benjamin needed "rules to live by," and in order for him to learn these guidelines, they needed to stay consistent. However, real life required that these rules evolve and include increasingly detailed variants. The goal was to move beyond rigid, autistic perceptions and to move towards a capacity for genuine, "in the moment" decision-making.

Thus, I was constantly explaining things to Benjamin, acting as his "interpreter of the world." Everything was worth commenting on, and I continually engaged Benjamin in roleplaying scenarios to support his understanding. I could only hope that in the course of time, my ongoing explanations would facilitate Benjamin's relationship with the complex world around him.

Two weeks had passed since our scary police incident, and Sophia reported that Benjamin seemed to have undergone an "awakening." Although I still spent the initial portion of Benjamin's school time journaling and observing, I was regularly leaving at mid-morning in order to exercise around Sophia's neighborhood, to run errands, or to go for a horseback riding lesson. (My preoccupation with finding horse situations for Benjamin had rekindled my life-long desire to ride, and I was now taking weekly *dressage* lessons.)

"Benjamin has been asking where you are, wanting to know very specifically," Sophia told me. "He also seems much more connected and present in the moment. He is being exceptionally responsive to my prompting."

I nodded. "I have noticed this too. He is often looking for me, calling 'Mommy, where are you?' almost to the point of this phrase becoming a fixation. So I'm being particularly accountable to him, telling him exactly where I'm going. Now he is truly taking in the information rather than letting it go in one ear and out the other. He will actually follow me or actively search for me. It's the unforeseen 'silver lining' of that scary occasion."

The buoyant energy of springtime was finding expression in Benjamin. Just a few months ago, he had occasionally begun saying that he loved one thing or another, and I had taken note of this important development in his emotional life. Now, Benjamin was expressing many loving feelings. "We *love* goats," he would say emphatically, referring to the frolicky baby goats that we had recently visited, just as we did every spring. "They are *angel*-goats— they come in my dreams. Sometimes they fly to me in an airplane while I'm sleeping..."

And Benjamin was hugging all manner of things. His newest love was an old-fashioned sundial that my mom had given him, and he would clutch it to his chest, saying, "I love the sun-clock." He was also expressing his love for our cat, Mandarin, insisting on carrying him around, saying, "I *need* him, my *very best friend...*"

In addition, Benjamin was becoming acutely aware of the internal sensations of his heart beating and his pulse pounding. I had once drawn his attention to these bodily functions, and now Benjamin was spontaneously tuning in to these feelings with great interest and fascination, connecting them with his emotional feelings of warmth and caring. A new understanding of heart-felt love was entering Benjamin's consciousness.

I was anticipating Benjamin's transition to elementary school and had introduced him to the idea. To make the concept more real to him, I took him to visit the Waldorf-inspired public school which he would likely be attending in the autumn.

Benjamin was excited about the idea of going to "big boy school." Taking advantage of this, I worked on heightening his awareness of the behavioral expectations he would be facing. Benjamin's reading had become quite fluent, and so I made a list of essential behaviors that he needed to work on. Using a different colored pencil for each listing, I wrote out a few key words that would remind Benjamin of his responsibilities; then, I drew a representative illustration next to each. Now, whenever Benjamin screeched in reaction to something which displeased him, I could point at the list.

"If you want to go to 'big boy school,' you need to..." Indicating the relevant behavior on the list, I read, "...*get myself together quickly.*" With such feedback, Benjamin's screeches were subsiding more rapidly than usual, and I could congratulate him on acting so grown up.

April was nearly over, and Benjamin was being extraordinarily cuddly and sweet. Nevertheless, his mood could flip on a dime, and he could shift instantly from being happily mellow to howling in fixated protest. At such times, I would be hard-pressed to find something to move him past his obsession. Now, my mom came up with something that worked brilliantly. She had been babysitting each evening as I had orchestra rehearsals, and she reported great success.

"I took a cold, wet washcloth and rubbed it on Benjamin's arms, legs, and face. He didn't like that of course, and now he moves quickly if I ask 'Do you need a cold wash?'" I laughed as my mom's heavy German accent made the threat seem particularly comical. My mom laughed too. "It is turning into an exciting game, and Benjamin begins running and giggling when he sees me coming with that cold cloth. You should have seen how he squeaked and hurried with putting on his nightie."

I was reading about a possible connection between mercury toxicity and autism: researchers were voicing their suspicion that a mercury-derived preservative called thimerosal might be a contributing factor in causing autism.

Apparently, thimerosal was to be found in most childhood vaccinations and, if a child's body was unable to detoxify itself and excrete the thimerosal, it would remain in the body and possibly cause neurological damage. (The many vaccinations that are prescribed during a child's first year of life can result in a considerable accumulation of thimerosal, coming at a time when the body's primary detoxifying organ—the liver—is not yet very functional. Furthermore, many persons with autism have compromised liver functions past childhood; this allows for a higher than average build-up of whatever toxins the individual is exposed to in the course of daily life. Nowadays, thimerosal-free vaccines can be requested.)

Since Benjamin had received all recommended vaccinations as a baby, I decided to test him for mercury toxicity and began looking for doctors with experience in carrying out a detoxifying regimen in case Benjamin had heavy metals in his system. Benjamin's test results came back indicating a *high level* of mercury in his body, along with lower values of other toxins.

There was no way of identifying the source of the mercury, and I didn't assume that it came only from vaccinations. Industrial pollution was known to spread mercury and other heavy metals throughout the environment, making exposure unavoidable. It was even possible that Benjamin had absorbed some toxins in utero. I had grown up with a mouth full of amalgam fillings which had been removed over time; perhaps my body too had retained some of the mercury from these fillings and had transferred the toxin to my growing baby. If Benjamin had been born with a genetic predisposition towards developing autism, his symptoms may well have been triggered by a combination of factors, including his exposure to toxic substances before or after birth.

In any case, chelation therapy was clearly in order. Benjamin would follow a regimen of swallowing capsules containing a chelating agent which would bond with the mercury and other heavy metals. In this bonded form, the toxins could be eliminated by his body.

While some children with autism had apparently experienced obvious reductions in their symptoms after chelation therapy, I restrained my sense of hopefulness. After all, I had already pursued a variety of biomedical interventions, and Benjamin was still on his gluten/caseine-free diet. Although these interventions were probably subtly helpful to Benjamin, he had not experienced anything like the dramatic "turn-around" reported in various testimonials. Nevertheless, mercury was poisonous. My child had a lot of the stuff in his body and, for the sake of his overall health, the toxin needed to be removed.

Using a chelating agent was not to be taken lightly, however. The substance itself could cause serious medical problems and thus, regular testing of certain bodily functions would be necessary. In addition, an intensive program of nutritional supplementation was needed to support the process, and so Benjamin would be taking around fifteen vitamin pills and capsules per day. For five weeks at a time, Benjamin would be taking the chelating agent, and in between these periods, he would have four to six weeks of recovery time. Depending on how Benjamin's body responded, the process of safely removing the mercury could take many months and perhaps even years.

In May, Benjamin's IEP (Individualized Education Plan) status required that he be given a series of aptitude tests. The district therapist who came to our home for testing commented on Benjamin's imaginative perceptions. Her favorite response came when she asked, "What's in the center of an apple?" Benjamin lit up and told her, "It has a core with little brown seeds dancing in there."

"I love you." This wonderful phrase was now crossing Benjamin's lips on a daily basis, and he was giving me frequent hugs to go along with his words. However, the phrase had erroneously generalized itself to everyone around us, and now Benjamin was saying "I love you" to strangers whom we met along the nature trail.

"I *like* you," I would correct him, explaining the distinction between like and love, and once again reviewing the concept that relationships are built over time and that we get to know people gradually, not all at once. "Saying 'I love you' is for extra-special people you have known for a long time like Mommy and Daddy, or Oma and Opa."

In spite of his current loving connection to me, Benjamin's attention deficit was particularly high just now. He became so lost in thought that he only "heard" me if I physically touched him. Getting his attention was like trapping wild birds; it took enormous effort, and Benjamin's focus would shift to the present in increments. However, the moment my hand released him, the faraway look in his eyes would return. I suspected that fixations occupied most of his thoughts, but on occasion, he would begin philosophizing.

Once, Benjamin commented, "My name is Benjamin, but my *real* name is shadows." What an enigmatic statement. Did his soul feel itself in shadow? Did he sense himself as separate from his autism and yet overshadowed by it? Was he like a shade in Hades, longing for full incarnation?

On another day, he brought up a family friend who had died of old age. His train of thoughts progressed with total logic: he observed that one day, Mommy would be old and would die, and that he himself would grow old and die too. There was no emotional upset at the thought; Benjamin was just outlining how things were.

Sophia was recounting the big event of the preschool morning. "Benjamin was enormously brave and strong today. While you were at the barn riding, Benjamin stood up to his fear of 'King Vacuum'."

I knew instantly what she was referring to. During the previous summer, nearly a year ago, we had arrived for a play session with Sophia, and she had been in the midst of cleaning up. The loud whine of the vacuum cleaner had given Benjamin a great shock, and ever since then, he had retained a deep-seated fear of the machine.

Throughout the ensuing school year, Sophia had worked to diffuse Benjamin's terror, occasionally opening the closet where the monster resided, allowing Benjamin to see it from afar, and gradually coaxing him to come touch the vacuum cleaner while it remained unplugged. The gradual desensitization had progressed to the point of Benjamin staying in the play room while Sophia turned on the machine for a few seconds.

"Today, King Vacuum cleaned the carpet while the children sat in a half-circle, watching. And Benjamin became my helper. Would you believe this brave boy? Even though he felt fear, he turned that machine on for me, flipping the switch seven or eight times before letting his friends have a turn." I let my face register obvious pride and astonishment as I exclaimed over Benjamin's courage.

Feeling both pleased and shy at being the hero of the story, Benjamin turned a little bit away from us, smiling, flipping his "number fingers," his head and neck rhythmically reaching forward like a swan about to fly, big proud feelings clearly welling up inside of him...

Benjamin's preschool class had celebrated their "graduation" with a beautiful outdoor ceremony, and now summer break was upon us. To mark the "official" ending of Benjamin's three years in Sophia's preschool, I took him to spend the night at the family cabin. As we sat out on the small deck surrounded by leafy aspen trees, Benjamin brought my attention to a pair of neighborhood canines who were making a considerable racket. The mismatched pair consisted of a large dog with a slow, deep, "woof," and his partner who was a smaller breed with a yowling howl.

"The doggies are doing a duet-bark," Benjamin observed, hearing the music that was buried in the noise. With the help of Benjamin's "duet" image, my mind shifted from irritation to appreciation, and I listened to the rhythmic bass "woof" intersecting the arpeggiated singing of the soprano dog. "I now hear what you hear," I told Benjamin, hugging him. A child's point of view could be so eye-opening.

As the summer progressed, so did the chelation therapy, and Benjamin's moods and behaviors took a downturn. In addition to the chelation pills, the nutritional supplements, and the specifically concocted meals, a regimen of "detox baths" had been recommended, and Benjamin was regularly spending twenty minutes in 105-degree hot baths with Epsom salts and baking soda added to the water. I imagined the various toxins gradually becoming dislodged from their bindings and then moving around his brain and body, causing stress and resulting in behavioral issues.

These days, Benjamin was incessantly chattering under his breath, repeating certain words or spelling them out, frequently "writing" them in the air with his pointer finger. Even when I got right in his face, he didn't "see" me. He was physically agitated, rushing around from one fixated objective to another, and he wasn't calmed by the increased sensory input that I facilitated. He required one-hundred percent of my energy and concentration, and I felt time reversing—we were back to the intensity of previous years, with me shaping every minute of Benjamin's waking time.

Happily, our Midsummer Festival was a day of unexpected calm and clarity for Benjamin. In spite of the difficulties, Benjamin had been looking forward to celebrating, performing, and once again experiencing the magic of the gnome who so mysteriously danced on this special night. I commented to my mom. "In the past months, Benjamin has been happily anticipating our festivals, recalling the special things that happen for each one. And he has been so 'present,' taking in the fullness of every celebration. He has internalized the form and rhythm that our festivals give to the year and its seasons." Benjamin's memories were being built up and nurtured by the predictable and the beautiful.

Once again, I was regularly taking Benjamin to hear the Colorado Music Festival orchestra, and there were many instances where we had to leave the auditorium and listen to the music from outside. Benjamin was exceptionally wiggly these days and was fixated on oral sensations, buzzing his lips, trilling his tongue in a rolling "*rrrrrr*," and squishing his saliva around. Naturally, such behavior couldn't be tolerated in a concert setting, and Benjamin remained generally impervious to my redirection, resisting suggested "deals" or compromises.

"Rhythm, routine, and consistency," was Sophia's mantra for teaching and parenting. Even though it felt like things were going up in smoke just now—Benjamin was having a hard time and so, naturally, I was too— Benjamin required stability and continuity in his life. Thus, he was again attending Sophia's summer program, and although he wasn't connecting much with peers, his imagination was expanding noticeably. "That's the way with Benjamin," I commented to Sophia. "When he's growing in one area, another seems to go dormant. Just now, his impulse to play is surprisingly strong. Yesterday, he built a 'hotel' out of cloth, strings, and clips under a tree in our yard, and then he took a nap in there, looking out through the 'skylight' into the leafy canopy above. And later, he acted as the maestro of an orchestra and 'conducted' along to recordings of Mozart and Brahms. That was lovely."

As August progressed, Benjamin went through another round of chelation therapy, and I again noticed a spike in negative emotions and behaviors. Screeching abounded, there was a rise of pervasive anxiety, and once, Benjamin had an attack of hysterics that had him nearly in a seizure. The chelation process was aggravating him, but since the behaviors weren't new, I decided to keep on with the program; I couldn't imagine quitting and leaving the toxic burden of mercury in Benjamin's body.

Benjamin's philosophical thoughts seemed picked from thin air; they rarely connected to current topics of discussion. Recently, Benjamin had struggled to express his questions about what was in existence before the earth came to be, before people and all living things became manifest. He sensed that there must be an unseen force, a Higher Power. Going off on a tangent, he asked, "When I grow up, will Mommy be there for me? I want to copy Mommy out—that way there will be one Mommy at my house and one Mommy here at home." Then Benjamin mentioned a few children that he really liked. "I want to copy them out too. That way, I can have friends here, even when they go away. But then, we have to copy their spirit too. Can we do that? They need their spirit." Benjamin had an uncanny sense for what lay at the heart of things.

With the impending start of elementary school, I was thinking about leveraging Benjamin's motivation and about how I might convince him to exert more self-control. I decided that I would dangle a very large carrot as an incentive and hope that Benjamin would rise to the challenge.

For the past year, I had maintained an enormous locked cabinet which housed the many toys and objects which were problematic for Benjamin. Now I cleared out the worst offenders and then opened up the cabinet to Benjamin. "You are a big boy now, and you're ready for a big privilege," I explained. "You may play with these toys, but if you begin screaming or can't manage to put them away, then I'll lock the cabinet for the remainder of the day. Each morning, we'll start over. The cabinet will remain unlocked so long as you can show me 'big boy behaviors.' Is it a deal?" Benjamin agreed, and thus began a new phase of strengthening his willpower.

38

The Elementary School Years

First Through Third Grade: Years of Great Change

Benjamin Enters First Grade and Turns Seven Years Old   2001 - 2002

Our public school district had a number of "focus" schools, and I had visited several of these during the spring. The one that seemed most suited to Benjamin was Waldorf-inspired, with the arts being integrated into all aspects of study. In this school, teachers stayed with the same group of children from first through fifth grade and, after observing Benjamin's prospective new teacher, I concluded that she would be an excellent match for him.

Vanessa was interested in developing a relationship before the beginning of school, and now we were at a playground with Benjamin. I described Benjamin's enormous progress and explained how behavioral therapy was an integral aspect of my teaching. "The basis of everything, though, is the energy that comes from love and genuine caring," I told her. "Benjamin feels that and responds to it. You have that vital energy—I sense that. And I think we can act as a real team. I'll support you in every way I can to make your job as Benjamin's teacher easier."

As Vanessa asked me questions on specific strategies for helping Benjamin in the classroom, I brainstormed an idea. "I'll write up a *'Teacher's Guide to Benjamin'* for you. I'll include key concepts and cue phrases that work well. Others on the staff should get copies too: the speech therapist, the school's social worker, and the para-professional who will be Benjamin's one-on-one support in the classroom. That way, everyone will be on the same page."

Now our talk turned to the initial few weeks of school. "Several weeks might pass before we find a para-pro," Vanessa warned me.

"That situation can be turned to our advantage," I suggested. "If you're willing, I can be Benjamin's shadow until things get worked out. I've always been his helper, and I can be unobtrusive. Having me in your classroom would facilitate a smooth transition."

Vanessa was ready to trust me, and we now had a workable plan. At first, Benjamin would attend school only in the mornings. Then, as his stamina increased, I planned to expand his days, maybe adding one afternoon per week, and then building up from there.

On the second day of school, Benjamin became upset and began his high-pitched screeching, thus alerting the class that their new peer was somehow "different." Benjamin had taken a particular interest in a boy named Oliver and, at cleanup time, began following him around asking, "What's your name?" Oliver had already stated his name earlier, and he now ignored Benjamin who became very agitated and began crying, "He won't tell me." A few screeches followed, and Vanessa responded quickly. She encouraged Benjamin to put his palms against hers and to push at her with all his might while looking her straight in the eye. As Benjamin did so, she praised him for cooperating, and then she gave him the words that he needed. "Say, 'I forgot your name. Please tell me again.'" Then Vanessa encouraged Oliver to show some kindness and to answer Benjamin, and the incident came to a close.

I commented, "What you did earlier—having Benjamin push against you—that's something Sophia has also done, to great effect." "That technique is inspired by ancient Greek wrestling," Vanessa explained. "It's very grounding and centering, and I learned about it during my Waldorf training." Images from ancient Greek urns flashed through my mind, and I felt inspired. We would play with this idea at home.

The school was screening potential helpers for Benjamin. After a trial session with one of the school's regular para-pros, I respectfully requested that someone else be assigned to Benjamin. The woman who had helped out was the smothering type; she had monopolized Benjamin's attention by talking constantly and had been heavy-handed in her manner of directing him.

"She means well, but she's the complete opposite of what Benjamin needs," I told Vanessa, and she wholeheartedly agreed with me. After this trial, my thoughts about what to include in my *Teacher's Guide to Benjamin* came into focus, and I quickly put together the document (see next page). "We need to find a better match in order to support Benjamin's ongoing growth," I explained to the school's principal, showing her my guidelines.

Within a few weeks, we had found a wonderful para-pro. I liked Ania immediately; she was calm and athletic, radiating firmness and yet having an easy laugh. Ania had a strong interest in helping all kinds of "special" or disadvantaged children, and I thanked my lucky stars that both she and Vanessa would be working with Benjamin.

Now I would fade out my presence in the classroom and would have all the weekday mornings to myself. Excitement leapt around inside me. Perhaps I could begin taking on a few music students. That would support my dream of becoming an accomplished dressage rider: I could start saving up for a horse of my own. And I might be able to begin practicing my violin more regularly. And maybe I could get some of the housework done during the day so I could write some articles for professional magazines at night. And...and...and...

Teacher's Guide to Benjamin 2001

Overall goals:
- Foster **independence** and the ability to function in the classroom without extra help.
- **Teacher** remains **primary focus** (helpers shouldn't "take over" B's attention unless necessary). Expect that B can and will respond to teacher's directions—allow enough **"lag time"** for him to register information.

Prompting:
Go from least amount of prompting to more:
- Use **gestures** (i.e. pointing) to direct B's attention.
- Use **key words, brief cues** (i.e. "watch"; "quiet"; "put it here"; "go get it," etc.)
- If **physical prompting** it needed, use small gentle touches (be aware of your own energy)
- Use **leading questions** to encourage B to think ("Where is it?" "What should you be doing?")
- Direct B's attention to **imitating** role models ("Copy this." "What are they doing?" "Do what your friends are doing.")
- **Restate** teacher's words (in case B didn't hear or take in the information); if needed, give further explanation, clarification.

General Considerations:
Lack of attention: if B seems spacey and not "present," raise your energy level (extra enthusiasm in your voice, eyes, and touch). Say, **"Look at me."** Try to get true eye contact and attention; do not let B look "through" you.

In case of **emotional upset or outbursts**: remain calm yourself, offer soothing touch, try rubbing B's back. Use reassuring phrases ("you'll be okay"; "we can try again"; "breathe out the icky feelings"; "it's alright to feel frustrated, but screaming is not okay"). Ask if he needs time to sit and calm down (in rocking chair or on gymno-ball).

Do not be shocked by **piercing screams or horrific images** (ie."cut me up," "throw me down" etc.) In this case, try taking a light approach: "That's silly, no one will do that." Label and acknowledge the emotion: "You are feeling _____ (upset, frustrated, angry, sad, etc.), and that's alright."

Negative behaviors: selectively remind B that he'll sit in timeout if he can't act like a "big boy" (only if you are targeting a behavior that you know Teacher will put him in timeout for).

Free-choice time: B may need help in learning how to use/play with toys. You can model possibilities and encourage B to copy. Let peers act as examples.

Relationships:

Facilitate **peer interaction:** key phrases (whisper unobtrusively)
"Ask if you can... (borrow; have a turn; etc.)"
"Ask if he/she needs..." (have him offer toy)
"Ask if he/she can help." (or vice versa)
Remind B to get the other's attention by saying their name/tapping them.
Direct B for appropriate eye contact.

Encourage **helpful behaviors in peers,** and praise them for making an effort: *"I see that you are being a good friend. I like how you _____ (shared; said something nice; etc.)"*

Simple verbal **acknowledgement of feelings/situation** can be helpful: *"Sometimes children need to _____ (cry; have their own space; etc.) We are learning."*

Help peers to **understand** and **be accepting** of B's differences without using "autism" label: *"Each of us is special. We show that in different ways. Differences in our brains can make us do different things."*

Draw attention to how **everyone has things to work on,** rather than emphasizing differences: *"All of us are learning. I learn something new every day. We all need practice with _____ (play skills; communication; being kind, patient, friendly; etc.)"*

After a month at school, the children in Benjamin's class perceived him as being bright and interesting. I had been sending along cool things for show-and-tell time: a jar with a grasshopper, a praying mantis, an enormous horse chestnut, a pair of genuine German "Lederhosen" (leather pants), a colorful theater program.

At home, I was having Benjamin write down some things and illustrate them so he could bring in "stories" to share as well. For example, I took advantage of Benjamin's excessive interest in grasshoppers by having him write a fantasy story involving the green insects. I also suggested that he tell about the friendly donkeys we were regularly riding on, and I had Benjamin show off a small sheaf of wheat and rye that we had picked in the cultivated fields that bordered the donkey pasture.

Benjamin even had a story about a bear encounter on the nature trail: we had been sitting in the shade near the stream, facing each another, singing and reciting poetry in unison, when a young bear had come into view, not twenty feet away. The yearling bear had appeared almost as by magic, startling me into silence while Benjamin continued singing; his back was turned, and the bear wasn't in his line of vision. As my heart pounded crazily, the bear paused, seemingly curious about the pretty sounds coming from Benjamin. Then he

ambled on up the streambed while I gathered up our things and motioned for
Benjamin to remain silent as he followed me. We cleared out of there with
wings on our feet.

With Vanessa's support, I was further cultivating the respect of Benjamin's
class in regards to his talents. One morning, I brought both our violins to
school and together, Benjamin and I performed a *Double Concerto* by Vivaldi.
On another day, I gave a demonstration of recorder playing and taught the
children a little bit about finding the dance rhythms in music. Such educational
contributions were helping to make up for Benjamin's odd behaviors and for the
disruptive screeches that occasionally surfaced. In addition, Vanessa initiated
some storytelling and discussions about "special differences" which helped the
class with their understanding without singling Benjamin out as the focal point.

As in the past, I was still firmly opposed to putting the term *autism* "out
there" as it could become a disparaging insult if a child wanted to make it such,
and because I didn't want Benjamin to be pigeon-holed by a label. My hopes
were still aimed towards eventual recovery from autism, and I didn't want to
sabotage that mind-set or to brand Benjamin's future with the "A word." On
the other hand, I was open to the possibility that the term might have its place
in our vocabulary at some point in the future; I was sure I would recognize the
opportune time when it arrived.

On a crisp, blue-sky October morning at school, the class was lined up
outside the classroom door, waiting to greet Vanessa. As I kept an eye on
Benjamin, I saw him gazing at one of the girls (we had already spent time at
the park with her and had been to her house for a play-date). Now there was a
searching look on Benjamin's face as he slowly inched towards his pretty little
friend. When Benjamin was right next to her, he slowly reached out and gave
her a heartfelt hug, gently holding her, his touch expressing infinite care and
tenderness. My heart swelled with happiness to see Benjamin connecting like
this, of his own accord, his soul bare for all to see. The quality of Benjamin's
hug was mature beyond his age, and a thought struck me: I had just glimpsed
the caring man that Benjamin would someday become.

Shortly before Benjamin's seventh birthday, Ania and I had a brief
conversation. "I have such respect for your son," Ania told me. "And I think
he feels the sincerity of that. I focus on seeing how bright he is, even when
he's having trouble with something. I trust that if my expectations are high,
Benjamin will rise to them." I nodded emphatically. Ania had hit the nail on
the head.

"The other day," Ania went on, "I heard someone 'talking down' to Benjamin, treating him as if he wasn't capable, and I had to shake my head. He may need extra explanations, and yet I get the sense that he understands certain things at a much deeper level than is typical for a child his age." Right again.

This little conversation refreshed me and gave me a needed boost. Lately, Benjamin's autistic issues had taken over again and, as I tried to keep control of Benjamin's fixations, screeching, and tantrums, I found my own "vision" of him slipping. When I went head-to-head with the many negative aspects of his autism, I too could forget who this bright boy was. I needed to remain aware of my communications and to prevent the occasional sarcastic remark or belittling phrase from slipping out. My frustration with autism per se was no excuse for such venting. I expected so much from Benjamin; I should be expecting just as much from myself.

"I need to remember about praising and reinforcing Benjamin, *especially* for the little things that I would *like* to be able to take for granted," I now thought. "I must remind Benjamin of my appreciation for what he *does* do. That will help balance out the fact that I'm often on his case for one thing or another."

In November, around the time of our St. Martin's Festival and lantern walk, I felt that Benjamin was ready for a few lengthened school days, and so he began staying for lunch and for part of the afternoons twice per week. We had already tried extending his days during October and had backtracked on this as Benjamin had become excessively fatigued. Now we were trying again, expanding by only one hour at a time.

It was mid-morning on Thanksgiving Day, and we were getting ready to go on our trail walk. Benjamin was already dressed to go, and he walked out the front door while I finished putting on my coat and hat, gathered up a snack to take along, and then followed him outside. My preparations had taken less than three minutes to complete, but now, as I looked around, Benjamin was nowhere to be seen. I began calling him, and when I met only with silence, I ran to several neighbor's houses, thinking that Benjamin might have gone visiting. No one had seen him, and I began having visions of a possible abduction. Such a thing had happened only a few years earlier in our neighborhood, and the perpetrator hadn't been found.

Frantically, I called the police who arrived with a K-9 search dog and began taking down vital information. Just as I was insisting that Benjamin couldn't possibly be in the house, I glanced out the window and saw a stranger arriving with Benjamin walking alongside him.

"Oh, my God, he's here, Benjamin is here." I ran outside. It turned out that Benjamin had engaged in conversation with the friendly man, accompanying him for the length of several blocks before it had dawned on the stranger that perhaps something wasn't right. Perhaps this child could use some help in getting back home.

Everything had ended well, but I was again faced with the problem of how to keep Benjamin safe without smothering him altogether. "We need more situation-specific teaching, and more vigilance," I thought. "And faith has its place as well; I need to trust in whatever assistance comes from above. I cannot let fear take over. Rather, I need to accept that nothing in life is certain. Even if Benjamin wore a tracking device, his safety would not be guaranteed."

We had followed up the latest round of chelation therapy with some extensive medical tests and had found that the mercury level in Benjamin's blood had *doubled* from the already high level that had been present earlier. The doctor explained that mercury was being released from its protein bindings due to our detox regimen, and he recommended using a more aggressive chelating agent to pull the mercury out of Benjamin's bloodstream.

Now, one month later, we were testing to see whether Benjamin's body could handle the new chelating substance. The results showed that Benjamin's liver enzymes had become elevated and that he needed a break, so we formulated a new plan. Sometime after the New Year began, we would retest Benjamin, and if things had returned to normal, we would adopt a somewhat more conservative approach while still using the stronger chelating agent.

We were celebrating Christmas Eve. At the conclusion of our solemn festivities—singing, reciting poetry, and telling the Christmas story— Benjamin made a beeline for the navy-blue violin case which he had spotted hidden under the candle-lit tree. He went after it with great desire, pushing aside the other colorfully wrapped gifts, his eyes glowing in anticipation. Benjamin opened the case and looked reverently at the new instrument, gently touching its surfaces. With awe in his voice, he softly voiced his feelings. "I love my new violin. I'm so happy I have a new violin..."

Benjamin immediately requested to play, forgetting all about the other gifts, and I could see his thrill as the new, larger instrument put forth a resonance that far surpassed that of his old quarter-sized one. It truly was a terrific violin, a half-sized instrument, made in 1912, and having a balanced, rich, and silky sound. When Benjamin was ready to put it back in its case, he insisted that I help him with the straps which allowed the case to be worn as a backpack. All evening long, the violin remained on his back as if he were carrying a precious baby. Benjamin kept the instrument by his side during dinner and then, when it was time for bed, he insisted on bringing his violin to bed, cuddling up to it as he prepared to sleep, murmuring, "She's lovely... I love her..."

Much of Christmas Day was spent at my parents' house, and Benjamin, overtired from the previous evening's excitement, had several meltdowns as he fixated on one machine after another—the humidifier, the blender, a kitchen timer. The array of buttons to push seemed endless. When evening came and we lit the candles on the Christmas tree, Benjamin seemed untouched by its beauty. He just couldn't get his mind off the machines.

However, there was one special moment when I called Benjamin to make a wish; the last candle on the tree was guttering, nearly extinguished. He came running from his "stuck place" by the humidifier, looked at the small glimmer of flame and, when it disappeared, releasing a gentle curl of smoke, he quietly pronounced, *"I wish that my heart may never break..."* Then he ran off again, returning to whence he had come.

"Woah, where did that deep thought come from?" I wondered, amazed that Benjamin would come up with something so meaningful in the midst of his fixated state. He never ceased to amaze me.

"My daddy's gone, I'm so sad, when will I see my daddy again?" Benjamin was crying bitterly. For years, Benjamin had taken little notice of his father's infrequent comings and goings, seemingly buffered by his autism, but now he had progressed to the point that Rick's extended absence was causing him emotional pain.

Since mid-November, Rick had been away for intensive training at work, learning the intricacies of a new aircraft system, and he had been unable to get any time off, not even for the holidays. And now, after spending only a few days at home, he had embarked on the long drive to Washington, DC. In the aftermath of the 9-11 Twin Towers tragedy, Rick had been recalled by the military to work in the country's capitol for an unspecified number of months. I was stunned by the sudden change in our lives and felt like crying right along with Benjamin. I was on my own again.

Benjamin had received a lovely new book called, *In the Company of Bears*. The story, by Arline Curtiss, was written in rhyme and was accompanied by Barbara Stone's beautiful illustrations featuring polar bears. The deceptively simple poetry contained hidden depths of meaning which spoke directly to Benjamin. Just now, Benjamin was particularly interested in a line that said,

"Things are not always as they seem."

"Like angels," I explained. "We cannot see them, but we might have a feeling that they exist."

Now Benjamin surprised me. "But I do see them," he said. "And colors too."

"Colors?" I looked at him quizzically.

"Colors around you," Benjamin said with certainty. "You are yellow. But not always. And I am mostly bluish-reddish, kind of like purple."

"Ah," I said slowly. "Do you mean to say that you can see auras?"

I explained what was generally meant by the term "aura" (the energy field surrounding a living being), and Benjamin nodded affirmatively. Curious, I began asking Benjamin what colors he "saw" around various friends and family members and was again surprised when he volunteered that our pets, Walker and Mandarin, also had specific colors around them—"but they look kind of muddy and dark"—and that plants had a little bit of a haze around them too.Benjamin's statements struck me as truthful; his innocent commentary paralleled things that I had read over the years, and the quick, definite air with which Benjamin answered my questions was unusual for him. He seemed as confident about describing people's auras as he might be about telling me the color of their hair.

"That's the sound of stars singing," Benjamin told me, listening to a recording of the Vienna Choir boys. A flute part was soaring over the bright, pure voices, and Benjamin clarified, "The boys are singing with the stars."

Benjamin's joy in listening to my extensive collection of tapes and well-preserved vinyl records was gratifying, but I worried that his new interest could easily be taken to an extreme and thereby become a fixation. Indeed, things were already going in that direction. For the moment, however, I was giving him the freedom to pick and choose music.

Benjamin became particularly excited when he found a recording of humpback whale sounds. "The whales are sleeping in the tape player," Benjamin would tell me whenever he listened to this cassette. "They're waking up and singing in there. They're singing a song of seaweed..."

At school during early February, Ania was wondering, "Benjamin has been so absent and unfocused lately. Any idea of what is causing this?"

When Benjamin spent time with my mom, she too was asking, "What is going on? Benjamin can't seem to stay on task with anything. This is worse than usual."

Benjamin had lulled himself into a vacuous and passive state: listening to music recordings had become like a mind-numbing addiction. His thoughts were constantly absorbed by the stereo cabinet and the machineries it contained; he was obsessed with listening to the same few pieces of music; he couldn't refrain from repetitively stacking our large collection of rectangular tape cases. Gone was Benjamin's initial joy and interest in the large variety of sounds and compositions that were at his fingertips. The only way to gain control over Benjamin's latest ultra-fixation was for him to go "cold turkey"; he had to stop listening to recorded music. I bought a new cabinet and put the stereo system along with all our recordings under lock and key.

Benjamin wasn't the only child in his elementary classroom with issues. Oliver, who had been so dismissive of Benjamin during the first days of school, had a tendency to throw tantrums, and his whines and howls sounded like something from a bad cartoon. "*Waaah, waaah...*" If Oliver's sounds hadn't been so nerve-grating, they might have been funny—like a caricature of the "classic spoiled-brat tantrum."

Benjamin had begun copying these sounds with increasing frequency and they had become part of his response to feelings of frustration or displeasure. At times, I might have sworn that Oliver had taken up residence with us, so precise were Benjamin's imitations. "As if it weren't enough for Benjamin to exhibit the symptoms of ADD, OCD, and intermittent tics as part of his autism," I muttered, feeling ready to blow my top as yet another piercing "Oliver sound" emanated from my son. "Now, the behaviors of a child with bipolar disorder are part of the mix." Benjamin might have great difficulty with imitating desirable actions, but no such barrier seemed to exist where aberrant behaviors were concerned.

"Try to see the glass half full," I thought. "Things could be worse." I reminded myself to be thankful for the relatively recent advent of "inclusion" and "mainstreaming" in the world of public education. Even though undesirable behaviors were cropping up just now, the benefits of having Benjamin in a classroom with mostly neurotypical peers far outweighed the drawbacks.

A few weeks after disengaging Benjamin from his stereo system fixation, I was putting him to bed and saying prayers, keeping Benjamin's folded hands tucked inside my own clasped ones. As was usual for me at prayer time, I had entered a contemplative state of thinking-feeling-intuiting, and my mind was on spiritual matters. As I fell silent after the last spoken words of prayer, Benjamin made an observation. "Mommy, you are all sparkly gold around you."

"My aura," I thought. "He can see my spiritual striving. How remarkable." Out loud, I asked, "I thought I have a yellow aura. Does that change?"

Benjamin said, "Yes, the colors move around. Most people look blurry. But some are clear."

Fascinated, I questioned him. "What makes that happen? Do you know?"

Benjamin thought a moment, and then he told me, "When people are sad, their auras get dark and I can't see through them anymore."

I chewed on this thought awhile. I might not be a "seer," but I certainly was practiced at projecting mental imagery. Benjamin statements were inspiring to me, and I thought, "I should be aware of how my thoughts and actions might be manifesting in the colors and energies around me. If I consider the color and quality of my aura at those times when I feel emotionally challenged by Benjamin, the mental projection might help me to diffuse my sadness or anger and thereby move our interaction in a positive direction." I made a resolution. "I will think of settling into my center and will imagine golden sunshine radiating outwards, surrounding me."

For the past year, I had been deliberating whether or not to take Benjamin for psychiatric treatment. Homeopathic treatment had gradually become less and less effective, and finally, we had ended our visits with Julie. Now, I felt I had to give medications a chance. In spite of all I had done with Benjamin for the past five years, his obsessive fixations were as much of a problem as ever, and the prevalence of upset feelings and screaming was linked primarily to this issue. Not only did Benjamin become physically stuck on mechanical objects, but his thoughts would remain on them even in their absence, and his conversations were often circular and repetitive; Benjamin couldn't stop rehashing the topic of household machinery. We had to try something new.

After our first visit with the psychiatrist, I started Benjamin on the medication that had been prescribed and within a few weeks, I was getting negative feedback from school. Benjamin had reportedly entered "a new phase," seeming out of control and with an increased level of aggression and intentional misbehavior. I had kept Benjamin's teachers "blind" to our medication trial in order to avoid a placebo effect, and what they observed in Benjamin was clearly a negative change. By the time I had weaned Benjamin off the drug, giving his body time to clear it out of his system, spring break had come and gone.

The next medication trial happened in April, with similar negative results, and May was halfway over before Benjamin's "real" personality reemerged. After catching a terrible flu and then going through a period of recovery, Benjamin had become a joy to be around. He hadn't experienced such a sustained period of emotional well-being for nearly a year—not since we had begun chelation therapy the previous June—and on reflection, I thought that the fever and fasting that accompanied the flu might have had a detoxifying effect. Now Benjamin was hugging me often, declaring, "I love you forever and always," and he was interested in playing and interacting.

Summer break was upon us, and Benjamin was reconnecting with Sophia. Along with our usual summer activities (going on extensive "learning walks," practicing violin, engaging in play scenarios, attending orchestra concerts and folk-dance sessions), I felt Benjamin should have one more chance at strengthening his imagination and his social/play skills in the familiar surroundings of his old preschool.

Benjamin had clearly been missing Sophia. Anticipating the summer session, he had been recalling his past times with her, saying things like, "We love Teacher Sophia—she sings a lot. Will I have both butters at snack? Cow butter and apple butter too?" Now, while playing with a group of younger children, Benjamin could relax from the pressure he had felt during his first year at elementary school, having to measure up to same-age peers. At Sophia's, he was the oldest child by far and was being looked up to as somewhat of a leader or "big brother" by the others—an entirely new and positive experience for Benjamin.

We had caught a toad and had kept it in a terrarium for a few days of observation. "Now it's time to let him go, Benjamin. He is getting hungry." Benjamin looked ready to cry at this, but valiantly fought back his tears. He walked around our garden, struggling to hold himself together, but after about ten minutes, the effort became too much. Benjamin huddled under a tree and began to cry, weeping as if his heart were ready to break. "His sadness is genuine; this is nothing like a tantrum," I thought, marveling at the outpouring of grief coming from Benjamin. My autistic child was finally connecting with an emotion that had heretofore been absent from his range of expressed feelings.

Midsummer's Eve had been magical: Benjamin had joined the mysterious gnome in dancing beneath the trees, clearly feeling both frightened and enchanted by the creature, but also bringing up sufficient courage to draw near and mirror the gnome. After this highpoint, Benjamin's mood remained quite buoyant, and I decided to risk a ten-day solo trip to Europe.

Rick's recall to the military had ended, he had returned to work with Northwest airlines, and I would be able to pass-travel for free. It was the chance of a lifetime, and I was going to visit relatives and to explore the Dutch and German dressage horse markets. Benjamin, meanwhile, would be in Sophia's summer school and daycare program, with my parents taking over in the evenings and during the weekends. And Rick would be home and available to Benjamin for a portion of the time as well. Everything was in place, and I embarked on my adventure, marveling at the strange sensation of being free— temporarily. A break from motherhood. What a concept.

Benjamin's positive outlook had lasted for nearly two months, but after my return from Europe, he started on a downhill slide, and I took the psychiatrist's recommendation that we try another medication. This one too caused an increase in aggression and self-stimulation, and by the time Benjamin had been weaned off it, summer break was nearly over.

Second Grade—Turning Eight Years Old   2002 - 2003
Benjamin had settled into second grade, and I had observed some terrific interactions with the other kids. At home though, Benjamin was as fixated as ever, and the psychiatrist suggested one more type of medication that might control his OCD and anxiety. This time around, Benjamin's sleep cycle became severely disrupted. He was staying awake into the wee hours of the night, and at times, I would hear him singing to himself, going through the new repertoire of songs that Vanessa had been teaching in class. Soon, Ania reported that Benjamin's eyes were falling shut in the middle of school activities; he would be fast asleep, sedated by his morning dose of medicine. So that was that. Meds were out.

Benjamin's eighth birthday was just around the corner, and we were again testing him for heavy metals. Throughout the past one-and-a-half years, his mercury levels had been rising steadily, but this time, the test came back with an alarming spike in Benjamin's toxicity: he was off the chart, with the numbers indicating *twenty times* the maximum acceptable level of mercury in his body.
The numbers were shocking, but the good thing was that Benjamin's body tissues had finally released a considerable toxic burden. Our medical team's orders were to increase the dosages of aggressive chelator, to resume hot "detox" baths, and for Benjamin to spend extended time jumping on a trampoline right after drinking water infused with a specific vitamin formula. This regimen would increase Benjamin's circulation and assist his lymphatic system in flushing his bodily tissues. Indeed, when we repeated the tests around Christmas, Benjamin's mercury level had dropped back into the "very elevated" range. We were moving in the right direction.

Our beloved cat, Mandarin, who had been such a steady presence in Benjamin's day-to-day life, died suddenly and unexpectedly of kidney failure.

I was devastated, and for days, found myself leaking tears at the oddest moments. Benjamin, on the other hand, seemed to be feeling nothing at all.

Baffled at his blasé reaction and also at his disregard of my own expressions of grief, I wondered whether Benjamin was subconsciously repressing his feelings, or whether his autism prevented him from relating to the situation and interpreting it properly. I didn't know what to think. Just in this past year, there had been a few outstanding instances where Benjamin had expressed genuine sorrow, and there had been other times where Benjamin had acted exceptionally sensitive and aware.

I thought back to our first year of therapy and remembered introducing the labels for feelings using the Moody Bear puzzle. I had discovered Benjamin's hyper-reactivity to the bear's unhappy face and, since he had been intolerant of anything referencing sorrow, had developed a habit of keeping such feelings in check, expressing them only in privacy.

"Sadness is the shadow that makes happiness glow brighter in contrast, bringing greater depth to our experiences," I thought, contemplating the current situation. "Benjamin's emotional palette is missing an essential range of colors, and life is nudging me to resume work on this. From now on, I'll allow Benjamin to see sadness when it comes up in me rather than protecting him from it. I will offer him explanations, and we can discuss the emotion as it appears in stories as well."

The U.S. military's war against terrorism was raging, and a pressing situation had developed in Iraq. As the economic stability of the airlines plummeted, increasing numbers of pilots were being furloughed, starting with those who had the least amount of seniority. This unfortunately included Rick, and by Thanksgiving, he had returned to military duty in Washington D.C. This time, we anticipated that Rick would be absent into the summer months. It would be another long stint of separation—more than half a year.

On the home front, Benjamin and I were engaged in our own little winter war of opposing energies, with Benjamin's autism-driven behaviors maintaining the upper hand. Benjamin was the embodiment of resistance as he constantly evaded my attempts to engage him. He would run away, become obsessively stuck, or purposely try to push my buttons.

Benjamin was also becoming increasingly overrun by physical tics. His body often produced a nervous cacophony of jerks, head shakes, elbow twitches, foot taps, excessive eye-blinks, compulsive itching and rubbing motions, fingernail chewing, and occasional, annoying sound production—hoots and squeals would emanate from oddly contorted lips. "What is going on here?" I wondered. "Benjamin has experienced various tics in the past, but this is like a crescendo into full-blown Tourette's syndrome."

I made an appointment at Children's Hospital in Denver for Benjamin to undergo a sleep-deprived EEG test, wondering whether this might give me insight into his current problems. In the end, the test ruled out any clear seizure activity, and the supervising doctor agreed that Benjamin was exhibiting symptoms of Tourette's although he had no helpful suggestions for me other than to try psychiatric medications. "Been there, done that," I thought, feeling disheartened. All I could think of now was to keep Benjamin busy and to hope that the tics would be a passing phase, as they had been before.

A particularly heavy snow fall had caused school to be cancelled, and I dived into working with Benjamin. I treasured such days since, during the school week, Benjamin was usually too tired to do much work with me. Weekends alone didn't provide enough time for keeping up with the skill-building activities that I deemed necessary. "He needs me to jump from one thing to another," I now decided, taking into consideration the excessive attention-deficit that Benjamin was experiencing these days. "There's no point in fighting his ADD. Better to work *with* it."

As we practiced violin, I instated frequent breaks, introducing quick little movement poems, or working on some dance steps or coordination exercises to refresh Benjamin's mind. The many interruptions of the violin session made me feel discombobulated but seemed to suit Benjamin well, and I was pleased with his productivity.

Eventually, I let Benjamin bounce around on his gymno-ball while I told him about a new project idea. I pulled out a booklet of large, blank pages. "We are going to make a 'journal of special memories'," I explained. "You can tell me things, and we will write them up, just like Opal Whiteley did when she was your age. Then you can make drawings to go along." I had read out loud from Opal's diary entries, and Benjamin had loved the poetic, nature-based observations. He perked up at my new idea.

So now, as Benjamin continued bouncing, I engaged him in conversation. "Benjamin, tell me about…" I began, encouraging Benjamin to recount a recent meaningful event. My probing questions helped him come up with cohesive statements, and I began "scribing," writing down whatever he was telling me. "Do you remember…? Can you tell me more? How did you feel when…?"

Soon, Benjamin had come up with enough material to make a little story. Together, we edited the scribed rough draft and then, after lightly tracing some lines onto the journal-book's blank pages, I handed Benjamin a colored pencil. "Use your very best handwriting," I reminded him, and then supervised as Benjamin copied down the story. The next step would be an illustration, and then we would create a colorful border for the finished journal entry.

We worked on the Benjamin's first memory-story in stages, and after several days of hard work, it had been completed, turning out beautifully. "Benjamin, you can be truly proud," I praised, gazing at the first two pages of colorful writing and drawing. "We will keep adding to this and someday, it will be a real treasure."

(Note: To see samples of Benjamin's journal entries, see our blog—it is easily accessed through our website *www.benjaminbreakingbarriers.com*)

Benjamin had a team of two para-pros who alternated in helping him at school, and one of the women was interested in the "Brain Gym" exercises I had begun trying with Benjamin. The simple little exercises were touted to balance and integrate the brain and body, and I had found a whimsically illustrated booklet which was geared towards kids, showing them how to influence their energy flow. I gave the para-pro a copy of the booklet, and she soon reported opportune moments for reminding Benjamin of individual exercises. "I get the sense that he's more focused after doing them," she told me. Benjamin was certainly enjoying the novel motions at home and was particularly receptive when I made up little songs to go along with the exercises. I was glad to have found a new strategy for putting *him* in charge of regulating his inner life and his body.

I was teaching Benjamin about word contractions. "You can make a single word by mushing two words together and dropping out some extra letters," I explained, showing him how "cannot" became "can't," and "do not" became "don't." As Benjamin wrote, copying my examples, I reminded him to keep his words between the widely spaced lines which I had drawn on his paper. "Like little ballerinas slipping off the stage," Benjamin exclaimed enthusiastically, referring to the dropped letters of the contractions. "They're making a pile at the bottom."

I had been doing a lot of crying over the past few months. Near the beginning of the school year, I had bought a horse of my own, thus fulfilling a lifelong dream, but things had gone dangerously awry. After several serious riding accidents and other dire happenings, I had decided to send the horse off for retraining and sale. I had been suffering greatly, both physically and emotionally, but there was a benefit to the situation: Benjamin had been getting regular exposure to emotional turbulence and was learning how to respond appropriately. I kept my communications open, sharing the various reasons for my feelings and coaching Benjamin on how to react.

"You can give me a hug, even if I don't ask for one. You might say, 'How can I help?' Or you can reach out a hand and ask, 'How are you feeling?' But then you must be ready to listen." Gradually, Benjamin was getting over his fear of sadness and, rather than running away or acting untouched by my feelings, he was now demonstrating the beginnings of empathy. This new capacity was showing itself at school too; Vanessa reported that Benjamin was occasionally voicing genuine caring and concern when his classmates seemed sad or upset.

(Note: The dramatic story of my first year as a horse owner actually has a happy ending. I wrote a story about it titled, *Perseverance Pays Off.* It found its way into print, and a copy can be accessed on our website *www.benjaminbreakingbarriers.com* Look for it on the *"Malva"* page.)

Now that Benjamin was becoming more accepting of sad situations, new teaching opportunities were presenting themselves. When I read out loud to him, I would sometimes get a catch in my voice if something moved me, and Benjamin would pick up that I was near tears. Although he would get a bit scared, seeing the power that a book could hold over me, he would hang in there as I managed a smile for him, gently patting my chest over my heart.

"I am feeling empathy. It's like I'm actually part of the story. The feelings of the characters are coming to me, touching my heart. Here, Benjamin, try this: put your hand over your heart as I read, and let the magic of the story come to you." After some discussion, Benjamin was willing to try and eventually, with my help, he wrote about empathy and compassion in a book report, thus solidifying his initial grasp of these important concepts.

Spring break was over, and Benjamin was auditioning to join a youth orchestra. At age eight, he had already learned the entire *Double Concerto for Two Violins* by J.S. Bach, and we were now performing the first movement for the lead conductor of Boulder's youth symphony organization. As Benjamin played, I saw him smiling and repeatedly glancing at the pretty, young woman as she sat listening. Benjamin played the last note with a dramatic vibrato and a flourish of his bow, nearly bursting with the excitement of performance.

The young woman applauded enthusiastically, inviting Benjamin to join the chamber orchestra, and after some discussion about Benjamin's needs, she agreed that I should be Benjamin's stand partner. "We have another child with autism in one of our performance groups, and her mother also sits with her, helping her out. You will fit right in," the conductor told me.

During our first rehearsal with the orchestra, my heart was full to overflowing as I watched Benjamin's thrilled response to the string sounds around him. For years, he had been listening to orchestra concerts, and now he himself was contributing to making an orchestral sound. What could be more grand and satisfying?

A few weeks later, our local newspaper ran a feature article about the youth symphony's upcoming concert, titled *Beyond Words: Music Connects Two Autistic Children to the World,* by Susan Glairon. "Right on," I thought. "That is it, expressed in a nutshell."

Now school was out, and summertime was the perfect opportunity for playing "catch up," using the school materials that had been covered during the year. (I had arranged to borrow things from Vanessa's classroom.) As always, we spent time on the nature trail in order to do academic work, and these sessions were broken up by periods of brisk walking so that Benjamin could process whatever he had just learned.

Vanessa had read various chapter books out loud to the class during first and second grade, and these long stories had been mostly beyond Benjamin's grasp. Now I was rereading the books to him, stopping often to explain, summarize, or to ask comprehension questions. I also reviewed math problems with Benjamin, referring back to the notes I had taken during the school year. Although these sessions presented a constant uphill battle—Benjamin was generally resistant to the work—I kept at it, encouraged by occasional glimpses of progress.

Once, after we had struggled through a small writing exercise, Benjamin dangled his legs from the small footbridge that we regularly commandeered as a work space. Looking up into the canopy of surrounding trees, he observed, "This is the bird-singing classroom." My little poet.

By mid-July, Benjamin's tics had escalated to the point of disrupting his violin playing. The frequent jerking of his head and elbows made control of the instrument difficult, and Benjamin was unable to focus or give me eye contact on request. Alarmed at this dramatic change, I was researching Tourette's Syndrome and deliberating whether to give psychiatric medications another chance. "But what if they only make things worse?" I worried, thinking back to our unsuccessful medication trials of the previous year and the negative side-effects that Benjamin had experienced.

"I'd better return to homeopathics. At least they're safe," I finally decided. "If Julie can't find something that works, then I'll have to risk trying more drugs. These tics need to be managed somehow."

Julie was happy to see us and, after much deliberation, decided on a thrice-daily dosage-schedule of a particular remedy. To my amazement, Benjamin began improving within the week. His tics waned, the mutual stress we had been experiencing evaporated, and we were able to enjoy the last weeks of summer vacation. There was much time spent harvesting in my mom's garden, and Benjamin delighted me by willingly following directions and staying on task.

Once, as he bent over tomato plants, being careful to pick only the completely red fruits, Benjamin observed, "The vine is the ripener for the tomatoes. Green means they need to keep going, red means stop, and yellow means, 'watch out, I'm almost ripe.'" Only a mind like Benjamin's would find parallels between a traffic light and a tomato's life.

Third Grade—Turning Nine Years Old   2003 – 2004

From the time school began, all the way through the time of his ninth birthday at the end of October, Benjamin thrived, riding on the supportive energy of the homeopathic remedy, sharing his delight in the world with both Rick and me. (Rick's return to active military duty had recently ended, and he had secured a job which allowed him to come home most evenings.)

During these months, Benjamin had been altogether balanced in his moods and filled with a sweetness that made my heart sing. His ideas and conversations were interesting and varied, and the occasional misbehaviors that cropped up were entirely within the range of "normal." And, Benjamin was actively reaching out to his classmates, trying to interact. To support this impulse, Vanessa mobilized the good will of the class in helping Benjamin to play with them. She was open and direct in asking the children to work as a community, and she promised a class ice-cream party as a motivating incentive. The timing was perfect, and the bond between Benjamin and his classmates was becoming noticeably stronger.

The third-graders were studying ancient Greece and, since Benjamin was in such a cooperative state, I invited two peers to participate in rehearsing and performing a puppet show for the class. The story I chose was *Perseus and Medusa*, and as I directed rehearsals at our house, I was thrilled at the collaborative sense which arose between Benjamin and his two friends. They were practically in each other's laps since there was so little space backstage, and they had to make their puppets interact in a believable manner within the relatively small proscenium opening that fronted the stage. I had hit upon a therapeutic team activity.

During a rehearsal break, Benjamin's two classmates expressed admiration for the old-fashioned typewriter which stood nearby. I had pulled it out of the attic for Benjamin to mess with. "Oh, typing is easy," Benjamin said, sitting down and demonstrating. "I taught myself. My mom just showed me where to start."

"This is how the machine works," Benjamin went on, answering his peer's questions. He showed them the inner mechanics and how the keyboard was organized, saying that he thought of playing the piano while typing. "And if anything breaks, there's the typewriter trick book to help me," Benjamin added, referencing the manual that had accompanied the machine. I stood by, impressed at the clear organization of Benjamin's "teaching" session. When it came to explaining mechanical things, he was really very good. Except that he tended to repeat himself.

For years, I had been explaining the subtleties of people's interactions to Benjamin. I would act as interpreter of body cues and facial expressions, and I would elaborate on the layers of meaning in what someone had said. Recently, I had also begun questioning Benjamin about the complexity of his own sensations and emotions, thus heightening his self-awareness. I hoped to call forth insight, empathy, and moral thinking.

Shortly after Benjamin's ninth birthday, an incident occurred which placed these three values in the spotlight. Benjamin had regressed to his old worn behaviors; so much so, that Vanessa decided to send him home from school for two days in a row. On the second day, a letter of apology was requested from Benjamin, and he was asked to fill in a "think about" form.

When I again picked Benjamin up at school (it wasn't yet lunch time) and read Vanessa's note of explanation, Benjamin tried to shrug off the incident. However, that evening, when Rick came home and also read the teacher's note, Benjamin's reaction was fascinating. He flushed bright red, became extremely worried, and tried to make explanations. He was trying to extract himself from possible punishment by coloring the truth slightly, but then he corrected himself. I gaped. Up until now, Benjamin had never told even a hint of a lie. His concrete understanding of language and his autistic way of thinking hadn't allowed for such deviousness.

Then Benjamin choked out, "My heart is pounding, my mouth is dry, and I'm feeling all shaky inside." I wanted to cheer at his precise awareness of inner sensations. This too was a first. Benjamin struggled to keep hold of himself, trying not to cry as his father stared silently at him with a deep frown of disapproval.

When I felt that Benjamin had stewed in his juices sufficiently, I gave him some labels. "You are worried and scared, and you are feeling guilty too; that means you know what you did was wrong. You are also feeling some embarrassment." Eventually, I took Benjamin to his desk, ready to take full advantage of this teaching opportunity. The possibility of awakening Benjamin's moral conscience was within reach.

The "think about" form was first. There were three "sentence starters" which needed to be completed:

- I was asked to fill out a "think about form" because I...
- The problem this causes is...
- Next time, I will...

Then Benjamin wrote his note of apology without my assistance:

Dear Vanessa,
I apologize for being disrespectful. I will try to be respectful next time, and for the whole day.
Sincerely, Benjamin

I approved. "Good, Benjamin, you know about respect. Now, add a postscript. Write what you'll do if you feel like being disruptive." I refused to help with this, insisting that Benjamin come up with his own strategy. He needed to be responsible and to "own" his promise. After much thinking, Benjamin wrote:

P.S. When I start to be disruptive, I will for sure take three deep breaths, and refocus, and be a student, being nice and turning on my brain.

"I am proud of you," I told him. "This is very mature. And to help you remember, I will scan this letter and we'll post a copy of it here on your desk."

As Benjamin's third-grade year progressed past Christmas time and into early spring, we visited Julie only twice in order to buoy up Benjamin's slipping behaviors. Overall, his tics had moved into the background, and when I interrupted his fixations, he got over his upsets more quickly. Socially, Benjamin kept making strides, and there was an enormous leap forward in the quality of his artwork. In orchestra, Benjamin now sat with a peer as his stand partner and, although I still assisted during rehearsals (Benjamin had terrible difficulty with keeping his eyes tracking the music), I wasn't on stage with him during concerts.

Recently, Benjamin had even displayed a flair for theater. The class had performed a play which distilled the highlights of the *Odyssey,* by Homer, and the part of Odysseus had been split between several boys. Benjamin played Odysseus in the scene where the lovely singing of enticing sirens threatened to lure the hero off his ship, except that he was firmly tied to the mast and couldn't get away. Benjamin stunned all who knew him with his clear diction, projection, expressive gestures, and overall stage presence.

I thought back to the previous year's class play where Benjamin had floated about on stage, not understanding any of what was going on, lagging behind the ensemble, eyes roaming haphazardly. The comparison between last school-year's spring play and this year's autumn performance highlighted the great mental and emotional growth that had come about during the past six months.

After three years of chelation therapy, Benjamin's blood mercury levels had finally reached the "acceptable" range. Now, the burden of ongoing blood draws and other testing was lifted from us, and I felt relief knowing that my child was no longer contaminated by a dangerous substance. Would this make a difference in regards to his autism? I didn't know. But I trusted that Benjamin's overall health would benefit.

Benjamin couldn't grasp the concept of being ignored, and since the act of ignoring is such a common social signal, I decided to give him plenty of exposure so that he might one day respond appropriately. Now, I began "ignoring" Benjamin whenever he acted in a rude manner. I would repeatedly announce, "I am ignoring you. Look, do you see how my eyes and my body are shutting you out? That means you are to step back and be quiet. If you get louder and pushier, I'll have to act like I don't hear you." I would keep coaching Benjamin as I "ignored" him, only rewarding him with my attention if he cooperated and gave me five seconds-worth of space.

One evening, my parents came over so that we could practice playing board games. At one point, Benjamin became increasingly demanding as I wrapped up a discussion with my parents, simultaneously giving Benjamin "ignoring" signals. When he didn't respond, I exclaimed, "None of us can think with the noise you're making. You are excused from playing, and I'm sending you to bed as a consequence."

Later, when I went upstairs to tuck Benjamin in, he began to cry. "I'm so lonely, why did you send me away?" Benjamin's deep sadness tugged at my heart. A new level of emotional consciousness was revealing itself, and I carefully offered a hug. Rather than striking out or yelling "leave me alone" as he would have done a few months ago, Benjamin made a request. "Don't touch my back, it makes the sadness all come again."

Indeed, his crying had renewed itself as I gently rubbed his shoulder, and so I folded my hands in my lap, just sitting with him, feeling thankful for this awakening. Benjamin was finally recognizing that a loving touch can open emotional flood gates, releasing waves of stored feelings. Perhaps someday he would be ready to move *through* his sadness, to be present with the visceral pain of the emotion, and to then let it go.

Eventually, Benjamin calmed down, but made an astute observation. "I can feel inside me that my heart is still broken—one part is over here, and the other is there…"

The school year was nearly over, and yet another round of special testing had been completed. As I chatted with the school psychologist and the special education teacher, we all agreed that Benjamin appeared much brighter than the numbers made him out to be, and that standard tests really didn't address his gifts. Nevertheless, the results did make sense overall.

Benjamin's intelligence was in the normal range, but his attention deficit and resultant slow processing time had significantly dropped his overall score. He had an above-average vocabulary and was good at reading, but, as would be expected of someone with autism, his practical comprehension of most materials was spotty.

When reading stories, Benjamin's brain wiring blocked his ability to understand different characters' viewpoints, just as was the case in real life. Likewise, he couldn't infer information, nor could he interpret social interactions between characters. Translating figurative language was a problem as well. For all these reasons, answering "open-ended questions" was nearly impossible; Benjamin needed concrete guidance about what direction his thinking should take. When it came to math, word problems were the stumbling block because of their use of language. A further difficulty was the requirement that one go through an organized process of reasoning in order to come up with an answer.

While I was making every effort to remedy Benjamin's deficits with my ongoing tutoring, I was once again faced with having to accept that Benjamin's brain was not likely to change as much as I had once hoped. "Doesn't matter," I thought, giving myself an admonitory shake. "We'll just keep working hard, tenaciously playing the ongoing game of 'catch up.' There's no reason to back off until Benjamin gets closer to adulthood."

Nevertheless, I prayed that Benjamin wouldn't suffer from a cumulative feeling of burn-out. Already, he was showing some task-specific anxiety, and he was a master at evasions since he recognized that every undertaking— whether it involved old material or new—required a great deal of effort. I had to feel sorry for him; there was almost nothing that came easily.

39

The Elementary School Years, Continued

Fourth Grade, and Fifth Grade—Twice

Fourth Grade—Turning Ten Years Old   2004 - 2005

As Benjamin moved on into fourth grade, I could see the behaviors of his peers taking on "pre-teen" leanings, with both boys and girls moving about in small packs which weren't inclusive. When we could arrange for a one-on-one hang-time, these same kids were still very accepting and helpful, but once back at school, the small-group dynamics would take over. Around this time, the first small incidents of overt teasing entered the picture, and Benjamin, not understanding what was happening, needed someone else to watch out for him.

Building on last year's discovery of theater and drama as a therapeutic avenue for Benjamin, I again gathered several peers to prepare a puppet show, this time to be performed for the school's first-grade class. I chose the Grimm's fairytale of *Snow White and Rose Red*, and asked Benjamin to take on the nasty dwarf character. Unlike the other kids who now seemed embarrassed to try on new characters, Benjamin immersed himself without self-consciousness, putting on a villainous voice and playing the dwarf with great gusto. "Benjamin's experience playing Odysseus has really opened a new door," I thought, thrilled that his enjoyment of theatrical performance hadn't been a one-time hit.

Benjamin had come up with a unique performance idea, surprising me with his independently developed concept. "Mom, last year we went on a field trip to the planetarium, and I loved the feel of hearing star music while looking into the universe," Benjamin told me. "I want to play my violin in the planetarium—it should echo and feel like outer space. Maybe I can do it for this year's field trip?" The idea pulled together many of Benjamin's current fascinations, combining them into something new and special.

Once I had gotten the "go ahead," I borrowed an electronic pick-up for Benjamin's violin, found Celtic mood music for him to perform, and practiced an accompaniment on our synthesizer keyboard, choosing a setting which matched Benjamin's conception of star music. On the special day, we were dressed in coordinating purple robes sprinkled with stars, and Benjamin felt himself transported as we played on a high stage under a nighttime dome.

The magic had originated with Benjamin's idea, and I felt honored to be there, helping him to actualize his fantasy.

Over winter break, Benjamin, Rick, and I went on our first real family vacation, flying to the island of Oahu. Rick's parents had retired there, and we had long been toying with the idea of a visit, but Benjamin hadn't been ready for the upheaval of an extended period away from our predictable home environment. Now he was ten years old and set for an adventure. The trip was a resounding success, and the door was open to future travel plans—Benjamin's horizons were broadening.

Shortly after New Year's, Benjamin was in a youth symphony rehearsal. There was a substitute conductor, and she announced that kids could sit wherever they liked on this day. I hustled Benjamin to a front seat, knowing that he would benefit from sitting right under the conductor's nose where he would be able to see and hear without distraction.

I sat nearby and, as usual, helped Benjamin to find his place in the printed music whenever the conductor stopped and then started again. After a bit, Benjamin leaned over and whispered, "Stop helping me. I want the others to think that I'm a really good player." This was the first time my son had ever given an indication that he might care about the opinion of others, and I was thrilled at the distinctly un-autistic sentiment.

Benjamin's old pattern of ignoring me and following his obsessions had returned, making much of the spring semester miserable for both of us. I felt strung out as I chased after him, having to physically redirect him as if he were a much younger child. Around this time, Benjamin indicated that he wasn't happy with himself either. "I feel like I need more appointments to find out what's wrong," he told me one day, on the verge of tears. "I feel like something's wrong inside my brain. I try and try, but I can't make it remember things. At school, I get the giggles, and then I try breathing and feeling my feet on the ground, but it doesn't work. I can't stop."

I was impressed at his self-assessment. Such awareness was the first step towards self-control, and while Benjamin might not yet have the willpower to modulate his behaviors, at least he was recognizing the need for change. "And," I thought, "Now that Benjamin is older, perhaps we should give psychiatric medications another chance."

During the final part of the fourth-grade school year, the class was studying the Renaissance period, and they were putting on a shortened version of *The*

Tempest by Shakespeare. Benjamin was playing the small role of boatswain and, one afternoon, when I picked Benjamin up at school, his para-pro told me a cute story: "I was waiting for Benjamin to come out of the bathroom, and I called for him to hurry. *'Boatswain!'* I called, and Benjamin answered with *'Here, Master, what cheer?'* That's right out of his part in the play. It was so immediate and funny; he has really taken on that role, and I can see his confidence blooming."

Yes, indeed, theatrical activity was a perfect fit for Benjamin.

Now that school was out, I was taking Benjamin with me on my grocery shopping trips. During one of these times, we saw someone—a caregiver—pushing a wheelchair in which sat a severely disabled adult with a spastic body and twisted-looking limbs. Strange moaning sounds were coming from the woman. While I avoided staring, Benjamin stopped to look closely and then ran after me. He was greatly concerned.

"I think she can't talk. Maybe she was making sounds because she needed to be moved. She looked uncomfortable," Benjamin reported. After a few moments of thought, he surprised me by voicing a compassionate idea. "What if I could help? Could I somehow invent a machine that picks up thoughts? We could attach it to the lady's head and read her brainwaves. Then they could show up on a monitor, and others could respond." I was impressed with Benjamin's helpful intentions and his idea, particularly as his imagination was free of media influences. We still watched zero TV and almost no movies, so Benjamin hadn't been exposed to the kinds of science-fiction scenes that might spur such notions in another child.

Then Benjamin exclaimed, "She needs a thought-transfer machine. Like this." Hugging me, Benjamin pulled my head down to his level and then leaned his forehead against mine. "Can you hear what I'm thinking, Mommy? I wish you could connect your brain to mine. Then things would be easier for me."

This year, for summer break, we were taking a bold step. I was signing Benjamin up for a theater workshop focusing on Shakespearean scenes. I had discussed Benjamin's autism with the instructor, and he had expressed willingness to work with us. I would help out for the first day or so, just to get Benjamin integrated into the group, and then I would fade out my presence, only visiting occasionally to observe and take notes on things to practice at home. The goal was for Benjamin to participate without me being his shadow.

I briefed the instructor on what he might see. "Don't be put off by the spacey look that Benjamin often has," I told him. "He can shine on stage, but his learning process is slow, and he'll be showing much confusion. He cannot sit still for long, and you'll see him jump and skip around; his nervous system needs to discharge. Express high expectations, and as long as you use direct and clear language, Benjamin will be able to cooperate."

Although I had requested that Benjamin be part of a scene where he could practice interactions with other characters, his slowness in memorizing made that impracticable. Instead, Benjamin would recite the Prologue to *Romeo and Juliet*, and would additionally fit into some dances and courtly scenes with minimal speaking parts.

At the end of the two-week camp, the group put on a formal evening performance with costumes, sets, and lighting, and I was shaking in my boots with nerves, wondering how Benjamin would handle all the new sensory input. The curtain went up, and Benjamin came striding on stage, regal in a king's costume. From the moment he began speaking, I sat mesmerized. Benjamin's voice rang, his diction was crystal clear, his practiced gestures were smooth and fitting. I had drilled every nuance with him at home, and now Benjamin was putting forth with a charisma that was captivating—and not just to me. When the show was over, the teacher expressed his astonishment. "Your son was the highlight of the evening. Absolutely brilliant! I never would have guessed..."

Fifth Grade—Turning Eleven Years Old   2005 - 2006

At Benjamin's school, a new special education teacher had joined the staff, and she had started a weekly social skills group called "Lunch Bunch." She and the speech therapist would instigate casual conversations with the kids while they were eating lunch, and then there would be a planned activity. The group might discuss ways in which to handle particular social scenarios, and there might be some role playing. Various games addressed conversational skills, body language, and teamwork. Benjamin tended to tune out when it wasn't his turn to talk, and the teachers were holding him accountable. If he couldn't repeat what had just been said, he had to ask, "Say that again please." With such guidelines and practice, Benjamin was improving his conversational skills.

I had scheduled a psychiatric appointment. Benjamin's ongoing difficulties with focusing and staying on task were serious, and the little bit of homework that was now a part of fifth-grade expectations was making me acutely aware of how things might look the following year when Benjamin was to enter middle school.

Benjamin's resistance to working on academics was stronger now than it had ever been before, and his desire to escape was, as always, fueled by his preoccupation with compulsive interests. I tried to negotiate with him, suggesting compromises that would allow the pursuit of interests in exchange for working on assignments, but Benjamin remained generally unwilling; school work was so taxing that he couldn't help but dread it.

"I don't like to fight with you all the time, and I know this work is hard for you," I would tell him. "But, we do not give up, that is simply not allowed in this house. Whether you fight or cooperate, we will continue to work and make your brain grow. So it would be better for you to choose cooperation."

Benjamin and I were in constant battle with one another, and over the course of several months, the psychiatrist had Benjamin try out three different medications, all of which targeted the attention issues and the oppositional behaviors. While none of these medications worked for Benjamin's issues—indeed, they caused additional problems—there was a gentle sleep medication which helped somewhat with the insomnia Benjamin had recently begun struggling with.

Benjamin was participating in his first musical theater show at school, playing the Tin Woodman in *The Wizard of Oz*, and I was once again appreciating the therapeutic benefits of Benjamin's theater involvement. With prescribed lines and actions, Benjamin could repeatedly work on the same sequence of words and body language, and he was learning to angle his stance appropriately for relating to his peers on stage while still playing to the audience.

When working on lines, I kept asking Benjamin to swoop his voice up and down in a lively manner, counteracting his recurring tendency to talk in monotone. Since the flat "robot voice" was a pervasive issue, I had certain hand signals for cuing Benjamin, reminding him to maintain his "musical voice." His excellent ear helped him in imitating me when I demonstrated voice qualities accompanying various emotions, and I was thrilled to hear great nuance emerging as we practiced repeatedly. In this way, Benjamin was learning to access a range of emotional expression, working from the outside in.

Benjamin particularly enjoyed an acting exercise called, "The Mirror." One of us would lead while the other followed, precisely mirroring facial expressions and body movements. Without breaking the flow of movement, we would switch roles, going back and forth between leading and following. Then there would be a time where neither of us was the designated leader, and we would be tuned to one another in somewhat of a mind-meld.

The special education teacher had videotaped a Lunch Bunch session and was using this film footage as a teaching tool. The kids watched themselves on film, and the teacher pointed out aspects of behavior, body language, and conversation. Then each child identified something they liked about their interactions, and also chose something specific to work on.

Benjamin was enthralled with watching the video. He had never seen himself from the outside as someone else might perceive him, and he eventually picked up on how minimal his participation had been during the session. "Am I in trouble?" Now Benjamin's concern was blocking him from coming up with strategies for improvement.

"No, Benjamin. This is to help you learn. It's called 'getting feedback'." With assistance, Benjamin decided that he would sit facing the group, and that he would show interest in the group discussions by asking appropriate questions or making comments that were on topic. The teacher would help him track his progress on a chart, using attractive little stickers to mark Benjamin's valid contributions.

I was having a run-in with Benjamin's new youth symphony conductor. This was Benjamin's third full year of participation and, although his playing had progressed enormously, he was generally being placed near the back of the violin section.

"My feeling is that, because of his autism, you're not willing to take a chance on letting Benjamin sit closer to a leadership position," I posited. "I listened to the most recent set of chair auditions, and Benjamin's playing was hands-down more accurate and polished than all but one of the other kids in his section."

"Oh, I don't think of him as being autistic because he does so well," the conductor replied evasively, thus acknowledging Benjamin's good violin playing while also discounting the enormous amount of extra effort he had to expend in order to compete with his peers. Reading sheet music was such a difficulty that Benjamin had to essentially memorize his part to give the appearance of reading it off the page.

For the past year, Benjamin had been verbalizing his strong desire to sit at the front of the section, and I now tried to explain the importance of capitalizing on his motivation. "Insisting that Benjamin prove his 'leadership readiness' *before* being allowed to try his mettle is not going to work," I contended. "His autism prevents him from looking ultra-focused most of the time. However, when he is placed in a position that requires performance, and when he recognizes the reality of the situation, he can live up to high expectations."

I described Benjamin's recent theatrical performance achievements. "It's almost as if he needs a little bit of adrenaline in order to attain focused presence," I explained. "There is no risk to the group in trying this out, and it would be an appropriate pedagogical step; maybe we could try it for just *one* of the pieces." When the conductor refused to budge from her position, I sadly concluded that my pedagogical views were at odds with her intentions. Maybe it was time to take a break from this particular performance group.

Benjamin was experiencing an inordinate amount of stress at school. The dynamics within his class had been deteriorating for some time, and this year, Benjamin was being actively picked on and pushed around, especially during gym and out on the playground. Some kids were quite aggressive, and others were following their lead, ganging up to cause trouble. Eventually, in the months following winter break, the bullying atmosphere became intolerable and I decided to withdraw Benjamin from the class.

"For years, we have striven to develop social connections and trust between Benjamin and his classmates," I explained to the principal. "And now, this is in danger of being destroyed. We cannot stay with these kids—they have the energy of a hungry pack of wolves." The principal agreed. This particular class had been causing headaches for quite a few people, and I had grounds for complaint. "The primary reason for Benjamin's participation in school is the social aspect," I elaborated. "I could homeschool him for the academic part of things, but I really want to keep him here at school, interacting with the community."

"There would be room for Benjamin to join the fourth-grade class," the principal now suggested. "They are the mellowest group of kids I've seen in years, and the teacher has often spoken about the spirit of kindness that pervades this particular class." So that was how we resolved the problem.

Within the week, Benjamin's teachers unanimously agreed that he seemed much happier and more able to work, and that his class participation had risen significantly. Best of all, the art teacher reported on Benjamin blurting out his happy feelings right in the middle of a group painting project. He had exclaimed, "I love my new class!"

The fourth-graders were studying the Renaissance and, like Benjamin's class had done the previous year, they would be performing a cut-down version of a Shakespeare play. "We're doing *A Midsummer Night's Dream*," Benjamin's new teacher told me. "I think Benjamin would be terrific in the role of Demetrius—one of the lovers. Do you think he can manage such a large part?"

"Oh yes," I exclaimed. "I've been finding that Shakespeare's language is a perfect fit for Benjamin. The underlying meter provides a lilt which speaks to Benjamin's musicality; the rhythm carries him along and helps with his memorization."

The new role was coming to Benjamin at the perfect time; he was full of fresh enthusiasm following his release from the fifth grade class, and he was ready to try acting out passionate feelings. As Demetrius, he would be pursuing Hermia, his love-interest, and the various play scenes might open Benjamin's eyes to the interactions that played out in real life. After all, Benjamin *was* beginning to show an age-appropriate interest in girls.

The serene atmosphere that reigned amongst Benjamin's new peers was giving rise to a new confidence. Benjamin no longer felt stressed or oppressed, and now he was ready to try being a leader. "I love making paper airplanes," he confided to his new teacher. "Can I be a teacher to younger kids and show them how?" The situation was arranged, and Benjamin gave a paper airplane making workshop to the first-grade class.

"He was organized, clear with his directions, and patient," the teacher later told me. "Benjamin was a very good instructor, and I think he liked the feeling of having all the little ones looking up to him."

School was nearly out, and I had called a meeting with Benjamin's teachers and special education team. "Benjamin has been thriving with this new group of kids," I began, and then announced, "I'd like for him to spend another year in elementary school, redoing fifth grade with these same peers. This is a golden opportunity for Benjamin to be influenced by a class with a healthy social dynamic. I am certain this would have a lasting impact."

I went on to describe how Benjamin had recently been asking detailed questions about his time in Sophia's preschool. "The accuracy of his memories is astounding, and he is mulling over the heart-felt connections that he experienced at that school. The relationships he formed there truly touched his soul, and now he is trying to attain a new understanding of the remembered interactions. I can easily imagine the same thing happening in the future, with Benjamin asking questions about his last years of elementary school. There's much food for thought there." After a lengthy discussion about the pros and cons of holding Benjamin back in school, I reiterated my strong sense that the benefits would far outweigh the drawbacks.

"Your intuitive sense of what's right for Benjamin has always been very in tune," observed one teacher. The others nodded agreement. "I feel that we should honor your request. We'll be glad to have Benjamin at the school for another year." So that settled that.

Even though school was out, I kept Benjamin immersed in a world of Renaissance fantasy. I read a wonderful book to him—*King of Shadows*, by

Susan Cooper—in which a boy of Benjamin's age time-travels and becomes an actor in Shakespeare's *Globe* theater. I also began preparing Benjamin for his first real acting audition; he would be trying out for a part in Shakespeare's *Romeo and Juliet.*

Aside from teaching Benjamin several monologues, I also choreographed some fight scenes so he would have the opportunity to wield a sword in theatrical combat. I wanted to awaken some masculine awareness in Benjamin and felt that such fighting would be an appropriate will-strengthening exercise. I had consulted with a knowledgeable theater friend in order to glean the basic principles of crafting a fight and had come up with a fairly complex sequence of lunges, slashes, throws, and stabs. We now practiced these scenes in the flat meadows that bordered our usual trails, pretending that we were prince and squire, or two rogues indulging in a skirmish, repeatedly rehearsing the moves until the sequence flowed quite realistically.

By chance, I saw an advertisement soliciting performers for the Renaissance Faire that took place every summer in Larkspur, a town located several hours drive-time south of Boulder. "Wouldn't it be wonderful to join the faire and simulate time-travel for a few days?" I thought.

My creativity was sparked. I picked out a number of recorder duets for Benjamin and me to play together and arranged a collection of renaissance madrigals for two violins. We rehearsed these, and then I taught Benjamin some songs which he would sing, accompanied by my violin or recorder. Then I put together costumes for each of us, and we auditioned.

To my joy, we were invited to help entertain the crowds at the Renaissance village for one special weekend. Benjamin and I worked hard, acting as street musicians, learning how to serenade people in such a way that they wished to loosen their purse strings. Then, during our off-times, we had opportunities to appreciate the dedicated performers who were regular employees at the faire.

For Benjamin and me, the most notable entertainer was Zilch the Torysteller, a masterful comedian who could talk in "spoonerisms." Spoonerisms are named after Reverend William Archibald Spooner who was a dean at Cambridge University in England during the late 1800's. This man had a speech disability that caused him to frequently switch his consonants and turn his words around, thus creating new meanings which could be very funny or very embarrassing. For example, when praising Queen Victoria, he might have said "our queer old dean" when he really meant to say "our dear old queen." As Zilch explained, "he was citching his swansonants and wurning his turds."

Zilch would tell well-known fairytales, twisting them up into spoonerisms; listening to him, I laughed until tears ran down my face and my stomach ached.

Naturally, I bought CDs of this man's shows, and in the weeks following our faire experience, Benjamin began memorizing the stories simply by listening to them. I was astounded. Normally, Benjamin had to be drilled endlessly in order to memorize lines, but when it came to spoonerisms, it seemed that his brain had a special capacity.

I remembered how Benjamin, at the age of three, had spontaneously begun playing with spoonerisms, even though had had only begun speaking a few months earlier. Now it seemed that this "slippery" part of Benjamin's brain could be turned to an advantage. Soon, Benjamin told me that he intended to be "Zilch the Second," and he began entertaining family friends with the parroted stories. "There might be a future in that for you," I joked once, not thinking that this prediction might one day come true.

As I did each summer, I was regularly taking Benjamin to the high country for some hiking, and this year, he was finally ready to climb a high peak, reaching nearly 14,000 feet in altitude. Although Benjamin was in decent shape, he didn't have the natural toughness that so many boys his age exhibited; his autistic tendency to shy away from difficult mental tasks transferred to physically challenging tasks as well, and I had to give him little motivational talks all the way up the mountain. Finally, once we reached the summit and stood as if atop the world, I congratulated him. "Doing hard things, meeting challenges like this—that is how you grow from being a boy to being a young man," I told Benjamin, raising my hand for a high-five. He straightened his shoulders and stood a little taller, feeling suddenly proud rather than wiped-out and tired. I thought, "He got that. He truly read my meaning."

Fifth Grade, Second Time Around—Turning Twelve Years Old 2006 – 2007
Shortly after school began, with Benjamin happily returning to fifth grade with his new class, the class teacher, the special education staff, and I joined together in educating the kids about autism. (I had prepared Benjamin for this during the previous weekend, recognizing that the "right" time had arrived for allowing his "label" to become a part of our vocabulary.)

We started by discussing the idea that, in addition to our five physical senses, we also have something like a "sixth sense"—our social sense—and that for some people, this sense doesn't work as well as it should.

The teacher read from a children's book, focusing on short biographies of famous people on the autism spectrum, including Albert Einstein and Temple Grandin. She asked the class to identify strengths and then weaknesses in how these people learned and interacted with the world. This discussion segued into how Benjamin too had a different learning style, and that this was due to autism—a different kind of brain wiring.

Next was an activity which would help the kids to empathize with Benjamin's perception of his surroundings: the teacher read a list of directions that the kids were to follow in drawing a certain, as-yet-unnamed object. She purposely read much too fast, and sometimes too softly or too loudly, while the other adults in the room created extra distractions, flashing the lights on and off, running around, poking kids, talking to them.

"Now, everybody stop. How many of you were able to complete your drawings? No one? There were too many distractions, right? And how many of you felt frustrated? Most of you? Well, in some ways, you just got to experience how things can feel for Benjamin. He can't filter out distractions, and his autism makes him miss out on a lot of information—not just the school stuff, but also the things that help us in making friends and participating in group activities."

With guidance, the class came up with a list of strategies for how they would support Benjamin, helping him to socialize, to pay attention, and so on. At this time, the kids also had a chance to air their concerns, to make observations, and to ask questions, addressing the adults in the room, as well as asking Benjamin for feedback. Some kids asked whether he really wanted their help—they were making sure that Benjamin wouldn't be offended by their directing him. Through such open discussion, a pact of sorts was formed between Benjamin and his new friends, with mutual agreement on how things would proceed. Then, in the weeks that followed, the classroom teacher reinforced kids for being peer mentors to Benjamin. Their willingness as a group was truly heartwarming, and I felt profoundly thankful for the collective class spirit. Benjamin was in the right place, at the right time.

I had withdrawn Benjamin from youth symphony, and now that his practice time wasn't taken up with working on easy-to-play-but-hard-to-memorize orchestra parts, the rate of his progress into fairly advanced solo repertoire was immensely satisfying. At one point, Benjamin gave a "concert" for his new class at school, performing a virtuosic piece called *Scene de Ballet,* by C. de Beriot, with me accompanying him on the piano. When Benjamin played the final dramatic notes, the entire group of kids leapt up, applauding and cheering, giving their new buddy a heart-felt standing ovation that put tears of appreciation into my eyes. Truly, things couldn't get any better.

As winter break neared, Benjamin moved into a new phase of language comprehension. He was finally expanding beyond his autistic tendency to interpret things literally and was now making up jokes, motivated by the idea that he could make someone smile or giggle. While I still had to explain idioms whenever they came up (phrases like "hold your horses" or "don't have a cow"), Benjamin understood double-meanings easily when he was the one generating them. His love of music and nature often found their way into his invented word-plays.

"What instrument does a bird blow before he sings a song with his chorus? A pitch-peep. Get it? That's like the pitch-pipe that my choir director used when I was singing with her group. Here's another one I made up: *What is a bird's favorite card game? Go finch.* I love birds, can you tell? How about this: *What is a seagull's favorite food topping? Ghee!"* Now Benjamin was doing a perfect imitation of a seagull's piercing shriek, bouncing up and down with excitement. Benjamin had discovered an important key to social connection: mutually shared laughter and levity.

This year, during spring CSAP testing, we were trying some new strategies. Benjamin had someone to scribe for him during the reading and writing portions of the test. I also made a list of sensory activities and gave them to Benjamin's aide, requesting that numerous small breaks be interspersed into his testing periods. "Please don't wait for signs of stress—we want to prevent the anxiety attacks that he is prone to. Benjamin should stand up to stretch and breathe regularly, and he can do some brain-gym or self-massage, as well as something aerobic like jumping jacks to oxygenate his blood."

Having a scribe helped enormously since Benjamin could now focus on the content of the questions without getting bogged down by the physical act of writing. And the frequent breaks supported his need for movement and helped him to calm down when anxiety threatened.

During the last weeks of Benjamin's time in elementary school, the social confidence gained from a year's worth of peer support was in full evidence. This progress was highlighted when the class was on a retreat in the mountains and everyone was sitting around an evening campfire. Benjamin offered to tell stories and, on receiving a nod of assent, launched into the spoonerism routines that he had memorized from listening to *Zilch the Torysteller.*

Benjamin soon had his entire audience in stitches. The adults were laughing at the incongruity of a young person telling such naughty stories, and the kids were laughing because it all sounded so garbled and funny, and Benjamin was beaming, loving his time in the spotlight, not understanding the adult content hidden in his blithely parroted spoonerizing but assured of his performance prowess.

"You are a budding comedian," somebody declared, and shouts of approval went up all around. It was truly amazing to see Benjamin stepping into the role of being a bold entertainer with a generally outgoing personality—and all this in spite of his autism.

During the summer, Benjamin was again attending a two-week theater camp which would culminate in the performance of a play. I had met the directors and explained how theater was a therapeutic activity for Benjamin and that my goal was a role involving dialogue and interaction with other characters. Since Benjamin couldn't possibly learn his script in the same timeframe as the others, the directors had pre-cast him, thus giving him several extra weeks for learning lines. This had set Benjamin up for success; he would now get the maximum benefit out of camp.

When performance time rolled around, Benjamin surprised everyone by opening the show with a special solo performance. He had taught himself the ancient Polynesian skill of "poi-ball swinging" and had now created an exciting and beautiful visual treat, whirling his set of poi-swings in time to music. (The swings consisted of two beanbags, each of which had a long streamer of cloth trailing from its end-seam. Each beanbag was attached to a yard-long string, and the pair could be independently whirled around by their strings in a variety of showy patterns—that is, as long as the performer was sufficiently coordinated to keep them from colliding and getting tangled together.)

The black velvet curtains opened, the lights went up, Celtic music from *Lord of the Dance* started playing, and Benjamin began twirling his poi-swings. Soon he couldn't contain his grin; he was right with the music, the variations in his twirls were expertly choreographed, and the audience couldn't help but join in clapping with the beat. The excitement in the music and in the twirling mounted until the final chord propelled Benjamin into an explosive jump, with wild applause ensuing.

Benjamin's performance had been remarkable with his beautiful smile and radiant presence endearing him to the audience, and I was overwhelmed with pride: for the first time ever, Benjamin had prepared something with absolutely *zero* input from Mom! I was stunned at how his early childhood fixation on spinning objects had been transformed into an entertaining art.

40

The Middle School Years

The transition from elementary school into middle school was like moving from a small, cozy nest into a big flock of birds. Our neighborhood school happened to emphasize the arts (drama, dance, music, and visual arts classes were all on offer, and every student chose a particular focus); thus, the school was well suited to Benjamin's abilities and interests.

Now, for the first time, Benjamin was taking the school bus, and each morning I walked him to the stop where several other kids would be waiting. As we walked, I would brief Benjamin on the routine of saying "Hello," asking "How are you?" and then initiating a conversation. I quizzed Benjamin. "What can you talk about today? Yesterday, you mentioned your favorite animal. Now you have to find something new to say." Together, we came up with tidbits of information that Benjamin might share.

"Remember to ask questions and show your interest," I reminded Benjamin as we brainstormed some things he might ask about. "That's the best way to keep someone talking with you." Benjamin was able to practice his conversational skills each morning with a friendly girl who was generally a bit early in arriving at the bus stop, and I was excited that Benjamin seemed to be making a new friend.

As I had during elementary school, I made sure to connect with each of Benjamin's teachers, attending class with him on his first day, and then providing each teacher with an updated *Guide to Benjamin*. "Please don't hesitate to contact me as questions or problems come up," I told each teacher. "I am an 'involved' parent, and I will support you in your work with Benjamin. Please think of me as an easily available and willing resource."

Once the teachers had gotten to know Benjamin a little, I began dropping in for brief conferences, asking for feedback, and explaining how Benjamin's brain might process things differently than expected. My job as a parent was to be pro-active in educating Benjamin's teachers on how to get the best response out of their new student.

In the case of autism, the executive functions of the brain are compromised, and thus the ability to stay organized is a big issue. Fortunately, Benjamin's new school had a blanket system of organization: all students were required to have an accordion folder which contained individual folders for the papers and work done in each class. I customized Benjamin's system using differently colored folders for each class and then added two more folders labeled "**Inbox**—*homework to do"* and "**Outbox**—*completed, ready to turn in."*

Because Benjamin tended to misplace or lose things, I tied his daily planner to a string which was attached to the accordion folder. A second string was tied into the folder with a large Ziploc bag at its end containing whatever chapter book was being read during Language Arts class. Textbooks would remain in the classroom.

On the outside of the accordion folder, I posted a laminated list of expectations which reminded Benjamin to: 1) be on time; 2) turn in homework; 3) copy down assignments; 4) listen to the teacher; and 5) raise hand for questions. However, even with this much structure, Benjamin still needed individual prompting to follow his list. It might catch his eye, but that didn't mean it was catching his conscious attention.

In some of his classes, Benjamin would have a para-pro assisting him and reminding him of his "expectations" list. For those classes where he was on his own, I requested that Benjamin be seated right under each teacher's nose, as this would provide the best chance of him being able to pay attention. Additionally, such placement would facilitate unobtrusive requests from the teacher for Benjamin's focus or participation.

Within the first weeks of school, teachers had already mentioned that Benjamin tended to talk too much and at inappropriate times. I suggested that they use a "tickets system" to limit his questions, a strategy which had been successful during Benjamin's final year in elementary school. "Benjamin can wear a number of loose rubber bands on his wrist, and every time he asks a question, he must forfeit one of the bands. Once they are all gone, he can't ask anything more. You'll need to prompt him to think whether he really needs to ask, or whether it might be wiser to wait, in case a more important question comes up," I explained. "The same can go for when he just wants to make a comment. Be sure and ask him whether it's on topic. If not, and he seems to be getting agitated, try to set a time when he has permission to talk, like for one minute, right after class."

Although Benjamin often received compliments on his good manners and politeness (our years of drilling were paying dividends), he would unwittingly monopolize his teachers' time and attention. Autism was still causing him to miss the social cues that would keep him in check. Furthermore, the act of talking could in itself become a fixation, as well as being an effective means of procrastinating work.

One of the communications issues that I kept running into was that people were reluctant to use the concrete and direct style that would enable Benjamin to respond easily. "I feel too harsh or bossy," was the common sentiment.

"The autistic brain processes language differently," I would explain. "The words we use to 'soften' our communication create too much ambiguity for someone like Benjamin. If you want Benjamin to do something and you use phrases like *'do you think you could,'* or *'would you consider,'* or *'how about if,'* he won't realize that you expect compliance. Instead, he'll tend to interpret the phrases literally and think that his opinion is being solicited. So, if you have a request, state it simply: 'Benjamin, please do this now.' If you feel too bossy, remember that you can communicate kindness through your voice quality and facial expression."

Each school day, Benjamin had a "learning lab," a time to do classwork under the supervision of the special education teacher. As the school year progressed, I noticed a correlation between the amount of time spent on the school computers and the degree of Benjamin's vague and spacey behavior. Computers fed into Benjamin's fixation on technology, and in addition, the type of light coming from the computer screens was scrambling Benjamin's brain. The electro-magnetic energy of the machines couldn't be healthy either. "I'm sorry, but I can't allow Benjamin to play 'educational games' on the computer," I told the teacher.

She looked at me with dismay. Computers were such a convenient way of keeping kids busy and quiet. Like TV. And video games. And cell phone apps.

"I've spent years bringing Benjamin out of his autism and into the world of people and relationships," I explained. "However, computers and technology can so insidiously replace human interaction. As you know, many people feel the addictive effects of texting and playing computer games, and that effect is greatly multiplied for someone like Benjamin. I'm not adverse to computers per se; they're very useful tools, and now that he's in middle school, Benjamin is becoming proficient at using them. That's enough." I was swimming against the current with my request, but once Benjamin's computer time had been reduced, his behavior improved noticeably, both at school and at home.

Benjamin was again getting teased, but now the provocations were more sophisticated than they had been during elementary school. Initially, Benjamin didn't realize what was going on because he couldn't interpret the social signals coming from his tormentors. Dead-panned taunts didn't make sense to him, and he couldn't pick up on the subtext beneath honeyed words. Sarcasm, irony, lies, or emotional barbs—none of these were part of Benjamin's repertoire, and the kids that were teasing Benjamin surely got a kick out of his guileless innocence. Eventually, Benjamin began recounting certain incidences and asking me, "What does that mean? What did they want?" With a pang, I realized what was going on.

It was clearly time to teach Benjamin about self-advocacy. If he could identify when something "wasn't right," then he could go to a teacher or a counselor for help. I began probing Benjamin about his interactions at school, giving him suggestions about what to say and how to act in certain situations. Just as when learning lines for a play, Benjamin needed to practice social scripts that would help him negotiate the increasingly complex peer interactions that were happening in middle school.

He also needed to learn phrases for soliciting help such as, "Can you say that again?" "What do you mean by that?" "Can you put that in different words?" In addition, we discussed putting people at ease by giving a simple explanation. "Most people are happy to be supportive if they know what you need," I told Benjamin as we practiced yet another scripted phrase. "Try saying, 'Can you explain this situation to me? Because of autism, my brain works a bit differently than most, but I am trying to understand.'"

Benjamin was consistently late for his classes, and when he was excused for a bathroom break, he might not return to the classroom for much of the period. He would wander the hallways, seemingly forgetting that he had an objective. Having reached middle school, Benjamin was receiving considerably less para-pro support than he was eligible for (district budget cuts were cited), and this lack of assistance was making itself felt, both in and out of the classroom.

"We need a behavioral plan that can stimulate Benjamin's motivation," I thought. With the special education teacher's help and Benjamin's agreement, we created a chart with spaces for each of his teachers to check off if Benjamin was on time for class. Once he achieved promptness a certain number of times, he could choose a toy or treat from a box of rewards at the end of the week. As Benjamin became more responsible for his timeliness, the percentage of required signatures would be raised, and Benjamin would be challenged towards promptness on an increasingly regular basis.

This chart system worked fairly well, and when its power began waning, I refreshed the rewards system, enticing Benjamin to work for a really "big" thing that would be awarded at the end of the semester. Leveraging Benjamin's long-standing obsession with airplanes, we all agreed on a model aircraft which he would try to earn. As a motivational reminder, I posted a picture of it on the outside of Benjamin's time-charts folder, and by term's end, he had managed to become the proud owner of the model in question.

Just as he did at home, Benjamin needed sensory breaks at school. I brought one of our large gymno-balls for him to have in the learning lab classroom, and Benjamin would take breaks to sit on the ball, bouncing vigorously up and down for several minutes at a time. The motion was soothing and allowed him to release some of the stress associated with learning.

His other sensory supports included carrying a pair of earplugs to use for auditory overload, sunglasses and a baseball cap to shield him from the irritating fluorescent lighting, and a slanted pillow to sit on for improved posture. We also experimented with having Benjamin wear a compression shirt and with putting weights in his jacket pockets in order to keep him feeling more contained and grounded.

Benjamin had special permission to carry an Ipod with relaxing music for him to listen to. He particularly liked recordings that combined gentle music with the sounds of nature, and we uploaded one with "bilateral sound," where the music would shift from one earbud to the other in a rhythmic fashion for a particularly calming effect.

Although some kids found Benjamin an easy target for teasing, he was making social connections at school and was becoming well-liked by many of his peers. For the past year, Benjamin's autistic self-centeredness had been giving way, and his interest in being around other people was now blooming.

Benjamin was particularly eager to talk with the various adults around school, remembering details about their personal lives such as the names of their spouses, children, and grandchildren. "Everyone knows Benjamin," the principal told me. "He is a real highlight around here. His joy and excitement are so genuine—he doesn't mask his feelings in the manner of a typical teen. In this way, his autism seems almost like a gift."

Further social interactions were facilitated by Benjamin's ongoing participation in school acting classes. The kids who were drawn to acting tended to be outgoing and easily engaged in conversation, which made things easier for Benjamin. There was much opportunity for chit chat as scenes from plays were being rehearsed, and the structure of repeated work on lines and stage blocking (one's movements as a character on stage) dovetailed with the scripted dialogue work that Benjamin and I had done throughout most of his life. This feeling of familiarity engendered confidence in Benjamin, prompting him to reach out and try making friends.

Indeed, the acting teacher surprised me one day by commenting, "Benjamin is becoming quite popular, especially amongst the girls. He is gaining fans— kids will cheer for him and give him 'high fives'." Such ebullient shows of support were beginning to outweigh the continued teasing that Benjamin had to endure. Clearly, kids were recognizing and appreciating Benjamin's talents. His acting partners could see that, in spite of his frequent confusion while learning lines and blocking, by the time the curtain went up, Benjamin could be counted on to do well and to be a seamless member of the cast.

No one was aware that Benjamin's success on stage was due to countless hours of careful rehearsal outside of school. I would coach Benjamin relentlessly, drilling him on his lines and inflection, and then choreographing every nuance of expression that would help make his character come alive. No one would have guessed at the artificiality of the process because, over the course of weeks, the pastiche of gestures, vocal inflections, and facial expressions that I imposed on Benjamin became practiced and smooth, eventually seeming quite natural.

Even so, when I would attend class rehearsals to double-check blocking, I was often disappointed to see Benjamin retreating to flat and uninspired acting. He needed frequent pep-talks in order to access his energy, and even in the moments before an actual performance, I would be backstage, reminding him of key spots and expressions. Such "priming of the pump" invariably paid off, and Benjamin would perform with considerable élan, his clarity of diction and his resonant voice standing out as exceptional. The sincere compliments that were showered upon him by peers and audience members alike were Benjamin's greatest reward, and he lived for these moments of praise.

As always, academic work was causing Benjamin to struggle and me to worry. Throughout elementary school, I had managed to keep Benjamin relatively caught up in his work, but now the material was becoming more abstract, and scads of homework were being assigned. Everything was becoming harder for Benjamin to understand, and as always, he needed much extra drilling in order to retain information. Plus, after a long day at school, Benjamin needed a break from academics.

"We need to find a balance here," I thought each day as I looked through Benjamin's accordion binder and identified the most crucial homework assignments. We would work on these during breaks from violin practice. The others would be left for learning lab where the teacher would reduce the scope of the assignments. Communication was crucial, and Benjamin's planner became the site for short, handwritten notes between me and the special education teacher.

Inevitably, much of Benjamin's schoolwork remained incomplete. Even if he had spent every waking hour doing homework, Benjamin still wouldn't have been able to finish; his processing time was simply too slow, and his ability to focus was too spotty. Benjamin was bright, sometimes even brilliant, but he had a hard time harnessing his abilities to serve him academically.

I was putting considerable effort into maintaining a relationship with each of Benjamin's teachers. Knowing how overloaded teachers are, I wasn't about to sit back and trust that Benjamin was getting the attention and help that he required. When I got the pat answer of, "Oh yeah, Benjamin is doing fine, just great," I would begin probing and, not surprisingly, would often discover that someone was taking the path of least resistance and wasn't expecting much of Benjamin. Sometimes this could be remedied through increased communication, but sometimes not. In that case, I had to make up for the deficit at home.

Getting enough para-pro support was an ongoing struggle as district budget cuts kept reducing the number of hours and personnel that were available. Some parents would take the legal route of leveraging the school system for increased support, and sometimes they would be successful. In our case, my talents lay in the area of teaching and helping my child, and so I chose to spend my time in this way rather than involving myself in a legal headache that would take me away from Benjamin.

Besides, getting another para-pro wasn't always the answer. One time, when a teacher pressured the administration on Benjamin's behalf because she couldn't bear to see him going downhill without support, we did in fact get an additional helper. Unlike in elementary school where things had been much more individualized, the middle-school scene didn't allow for that. The new helper didn't have a knack for the job, and the teacher eventually admitted that directing the para was nearly more work than trying to keep Benjamin on task.

Luckily, most of the paras at school were extraordinarily caring and talented individuals, and they developed excellent rapport with Benjamin. Per my request, they also kept me "in the loop" by writing me notes and occasionally phoning. The squeaky wheel would get the grease.

Much as I wished for Benjamin to keep up with his classes, I wouldn't sacrifice his hard-won musical skills by cutting back on our home practice sessions. And, Benjamin's participation in acting class was his life-line to having a niche at school; if we didn't keep putting in the extra hours of scene preparation, he would lose this crucial foothold on peer recognition, along with the attendant happiness and satisfaction.

However, on Saturdays and Sundays, I would collect all the skipped work from the school week, shove it into a backpack along with snacks, and then spend much of the day on the trails with Benjamin, alternating between walking and doing homework.

While walking, I would drill Benjamin on his play scripts and gave him strategies for memorization. I would identify cue words and mnemonic patterns to trigger his memory, and then make up a distinct motion to go along with each spoken cue. I would also create a color-coded outline of these same cues, thus reducing a lengthy script down to a small "cheat sheet." This skeleton of cue words provided a visual structure which allowed Benjamin to remain mentally organized when speaking the full lines of text imbued with emotion. I was strengthening Benjamin's memory by combining three primary sources of feedback: visual, auditory, and movement-based.

When, at intervals, we sat down on flat rocks or in soft grassy spots, we would focus on written homework. I frequently began with math, drilling those skills which had given Benjamin the most trouble during the week. I kept after him, thinking that math was a little bit like practicing daily scales and arpeggios on the violin. "Solving math problems will organize your brain, making it strong and flexible," I would say while writing out a series of problems based on the homework, thus providing Benjamin with the necessary extra practice.

In the case of writing assignments, I would help organize Benjamin's thoughts by giving him "sentence starters," writing out the first several words of a sentence and then asking him to continue. This simple strategy was quite effective.

For reading comprehension, I would read out loud from the assigned texts and chapter books, paraphrasing or summarizing, as well as engaging Benjamin in discussions about content and asking him to write a few notes. We also had some workbooks which specifically targeted reading comprehension, and I would have Benjamin work on these while I sat by, assisting him only when necessary. He desperately needed opportunities to work independently, but there were few areas of learning where I could step back and still keep him going. Sometimes I would get audiobooks for him which he would listen to while following along in the printed text. This was very effective for keeping Benjamin on task, but the downside was that his comprehension level tended to go down without the discussions.

Often, I would be gritting my teeth, unable to fathom that Benjamin couldn't recall certain things that had transpired just minutes or seconds earlier. For example, he might come up with an answer to a certain question, but if I asked that same question a short while later in order to review the information, Benjamin might not even understand the question, much less give me an answer to it.

This was one of the frustrating mysteries of his autistic brain, and it happened as much during our violin practices as during our academic work sessions. For example, after Benjamin had played a certain musical scale and had taken a momentary breather, I would ask him to repeat the scale at a faster tempo. Benjamin would stare at me blankly as I prompted him to remember. "Which scale did you just play? Play it again for me." Try as he would, Benjamin would be unable to comply. Similarly, when using sheet music while practicing a particular spot, Benjamin would be unable to locate the relevant spot on the page within seconds of looking elsewhere. His visual memory seemed wiped clean by his attention deficit.

On the other hand, there were times where his mind seemed like a steel trap for both aural and visual information: he would recall trivia and details of things buried in the past. He might recount a song or poem from his earliest preschool years, or ask me an obscure question about a story we had read during elementary school.

Thinking about Benjamin's brain, I imagined a maze of neurons with innumerable dead-ends, with various treasure alcoves nested within the mess. Or, I thought of a computer riddled with loose connections which might, or might not, respond to vigorous manual jiggling. In spite of the ongoing "repair work" that our years of therapy had achieved, Benjamin's learning processes remained complicated and unpredictable.

As in years past, I was requiring Benjamin to transform his obsessions into something useful. He had long been fixated on making signs, and now he offered to make professional-looking signs for various classroom doors at school. He got special permission to use the laminating machine and created a slew of excellent "products." The hardest part was ending the project. Benjamin kept finding new possibilities, and most staff members were reluctant to say, "No, that's enough now." This frustrated me. How could saying "no" be so hard? Benjamin was uniformly respectful of his teachers and would comply if he felt the decisive conviction of someone "putting their foot down."

Benjamin also found an outlet for his obsession with paper airplanes and for his desire to be an "events planner." He instigated various teacher sponsored paper-airplane contests, appropriately connecting the activity with science class discussions of physics principles.

Another successful "fixation transformation" involved the school's intercom system which had long enthralled Benjamin. For years, he had dreamed of talking into the loudspeaker during morning announcements. Now, spurred on by discussions in science class, Benjamin came up with a series of "environmental bulletins" designed to raise awareness about endangered animals, global warming, and conservation issues—topics of great interest to him. With Benjamin acting as broadcaster, these bulletins became a regular part of morning announcements. Throughout his three years at middle school,

Benjamin researched and wrote these reports under his own steam with very little guidance from me, and I was enormously pleased with the outcome. When Benjamin had a burning interest in something, and when the impulse to action came from within, he could do amazing work.

One of the science teachers had a menagerie of animals living in his classroom, and kids were allowed to borrow these over the weekend. Benjamin, with his love of birds, had formed an immediate attachment to Rudi, an Amazon orange-wing parrot. This bird had been caught in the wild nearly thirty years ago and, although unable to imitate human speech, he was a master imitator of various mechanical sounds.

Rudi became a regular visitor to our house, spending lengthy vacation periods with us even after Benjamin had entered high school. Aside from Rudi's repertoire of phone-ringing sounds, microwave beeps, parrot squawks, and sweet little peeping noises, the parrot would imitate me when I laughed. This giggly laugh was indistinguishable from my own and invariably engendered great hilarity from both Benjamin and me. Rudi was a great source of joy to us.

As Benjamin became increasingly attached to Rudi, we heard about a researcher who had proved that African Grey parrots were capable of more advanced thought processes than those required for rote imitation. Irene Pepperberg's research was a breakthrough in establishing the possibilities of animal intelligence, and her memoire about working with a parrot named Alex had just been published.

I purchased a copy of *Alex and Me* and began reading. Alex had lived to become thirty years old, and throughout his lifetime, he had undergone one-on-one schooling/training on a daily basis. For an average of eight hours per day, Ms. Pepperberg and her lab assistants had interacted with Alex, administering many carefully structured learning programs with the amazing result that Alex had learned to think and reason, making it possible for him to both count and spell.

Motivational rewards and occasional reprimands were integral to Alex's behavioral program, and his intelligence had developed far beyond mere imitation. No one had thought this possible for a bird-brain to achieve, but the constant stimulation had allowed Alex's brain to develop in amazing ways.

I had to smile at the parallels between Alex and Benjamin. My boy's brain had likewise developed far beyond anyone's expectations. We too had worked all day long, every day, and we were not done yet.

Benjamin was beginning to set up "hang-times" with new school friends, initiating phone calls and using a cheat sheet of cue words for his conversation;

these outlines were particularly useful when leaving messages on answering machines. As various pretty and talented girls came over for hour-long get-togethers, I would eavesdrop from afar, marveling at how well Benjamin was handling himself. He would keep appropriate conversation going, moving from one activity to the next gracefully, and generally keeping his focus. I began to realize that Benjamin's attention-deficit mind could actually be a boon. It allowed him to jump from one topic to the next, to come up with fun facts and interesting trivia, and to thus amuse his companions and keep things lively. After these hang-times were over though, Benjamin would often be quite fatigued. Maintaining his concentration throughout an hour of socializing took a lot of effort.

Socially, Benjamin was blooming, but in other areas of his life, he seemed less capable of self-direction than ever. I was determined that he learn to stand on his own two feet, and I would regularly back off of our learning program, allowing things to slide, encouraging Benjamin to "catch" himself and take over, to apply himself.

It wasn't happenin'.

Much as Benjamin loved being involved in music, drama, and dance, he couldn't seem to move beyond being my puppet. If I stopped asking him to practice violin with me, he wouldn't even think to pick up the instrument, and I wasn't ready to let that go for more than a few experimental days. We had worked too long and hard on achieving real skill.

I doggedly worked at getting Benjamin to think for himself. Watching the minutes tick away, waiting for his focus to filter in out of the clouds was excruciating, and I couldn't help worrying about Benjamin's future, wondering how things would look if he couldn't surmount his absentmindedness.

Benjamin's seventh-grade P.E. teacher had the dual role of teaching health class, and late in the spring semester, she asked Benjamin whether he might come in and speak to her group about living with autism. It would be an impromptu sort of presentation, with Benjamin talking about his challenges and then answering questions. Benjamin was immediately willing. "That'll be sort of like the 'talk backs' we do after drama performances," he told the teacher. "I like that kind of thing."

I was unable to attend Benjamin's little presentation since I was working as the choral director at another middle school, but later, when I checked in with the teacher, she told me that Benjamin had impressed the class with his openness, his confidence, and his ability to articulate some of his issues. He had done it all independently, with no special "prepping" from me. Little did

I know that this casual foray into autism advocacy would be like a seedling planted in fertile soil, and that three years later, Benjamin would begin giving formal presentations on autism for large audiences.

At the end of his seventh-grade year, Benjamin conceived of a grand personal goal. "I've already figured out how to play our guitar, and now I want to buy a banjo," he told me. "I love the happy sound of it."

"You can work in Oma and Opa's garden all summer long to earn the necessary money," I told Benjamin, excited that he was sufficiently motivated to agree with this plan. This was the perfect opportunity for teaching Benjamin a bit about real-world finances and about sticking with a job, even if it became tedious or uncomfortable. Indeed, Benjamin managed well, keeping time sheets and adding up his earnings until the target sum had been reached. Then I took him to the music store to pick out his new instrument and a method book. Benjamin would be teaching himself to play that banjo, thus building independence.

As Benjamin turned fifteen (with eighth grade well underway), I noted his growing capacity for identifying and discussing his needs. For example, he once told me, "Some paras just give answers, but Carla makes me work—more like you do. That's what I need." Another time, when I was helping him with homework, he exclaimed in frustration. "My brain feels like a jeep that just won't go. It feels like something is grinding inside, and I can't make the wheels turn."

I empathized, but explained that he needed to keep trying a bit longer. I watched Benjamin's struggle as he tried to bring himself to focus—the barrier in his brain was palpable—and with my prodding, he kept working until his attention settled and he began comprehending the work. I could practically *see* the bulldozer breaking through the mental block. "There, you see?" I praised, "You really can do it. You are getting stronger, you just need to keep trying."

Benjamin agreed. "*Never give up.* That's what President Obama said when we watched his speech for school kids. I like mottos, especially that one."

Benjamin still had a tendency to bounce around, to make jerky motions with his arms and torso, and to flip his fingers, particularly when he got excited about something. He was also growing like a weed. "I think it's time to start up some regular bodywork again," I told Benjamin as I made appointments with a massage therapist and a rolfer. Benjamin needed to release the muscle tension that his growth and self-stimulatory motions were causing, and I also hoped that the sessions would enhance his body awareness, possibly allowing him an increased level of self-control.

Around this time, we also tried a brain integration therapy called Crossinology which had been quite helpful to someone we knew. This technique had some research backing its effectiveness, and thus I was able to secure a special autism support grant to cover the considerable expense. However, as with so many of the therapies we had tried through the years, Benjamin reaped very little benefit. "That's how it is," I thought. "There's simply no way of knowing what will help in any particular case of autism."

Although Benjamin enjoyed gym class, he was unable to understand how team games worked. He couldn't recognize the floor patterns that were formed by the players, and he didn't understand the actions that were unfolding as a game progressed. His floaty attention kept him from following a ball as it was passed from person to person, and there was no way for us to work on this skill alone at home. It required a team.

However, I *could* help Benjamin with awareness of how a space might be divided. I decided to choreograph a dance for him to help him visualize "lines" of choreography. To this end, I used thick colorful strings, laying out curvy paths of travel on the floor. The dance piece also involved Benjamin's "partnering" a silk scarf, manipulating it as he danced to piano music by Chopin. Wafting the silk in a prescribed manner would help him tune in to the three-dimensional space around him. Simultaneously, he would be attending to the floor pattern.

Benjamin still had trouble with imitating movements and with remembering their sequences, and so, just as I had done when he was very little, I broke down each dance move into its smallest increments, drilling Benjamin over and over again over the course of many weeks. Finally, the two-minute solo dance came together, and Benjamin performed it as part of the school dance recital. His piece was unique amongst the many hip-hop and jazz pieces, and he was rewarded when people remembered the performance months later. Benjamin was *different*. In a good way.

With me as his driving force, Benjamin had been happily performing in one capacity or another with increasing frequency. He was singing boy-soprano solos at various churches, was involved with musical theater shows, had garnered the male-lead role of Benedick in Shakespeare's *Much Ado About Nothing*, and had joined the advanced level Boulder Youth Symphony after a three year hiatus from playing in an orchestra.

However, during the last semester of Benjamin's eighth-grade year, things took a dramatic downturn. It was as if the hormonal turbulence associated with adolescence had finally caught up to him and was now wreaking havoc with the autistic aspects of his brain. Benjamin began having episodes of heightened anxiety and began chewing the insides of his cheeks until they were raw and his face was swollen. Ocular migraines entered the picture. And bouts of exceeding agitation were becoming frequent.

At first, when I asked Benjamin to describe what was bothering him, he refused to talk. Eventually however, he admitted to having unspeakable thoughts and impulses. He was afraid to describe them because that would be like letting the cat out of the bag—putting words to his inner experiences might give them the power to take over completely. Tearfully, Benjamin explained, "They make me feel like being violent, even though I am *not* a violent person."

With further careful conversation and me asking indirect questions, Benjamin indicated that the thoughts were like a nightmarish tangle of repetitive loops that wouldn't let him go. They were ever present and, although he could often keep them "in the background," Benjamin felt persecuted by them. "I feel like life isn't worth living anymore," Benjamin finally burst out, hiding his tearstained face in his arms.

"Oh, my God," I thought, staring at my son. "What's to be done? What if he gets rash and acts on that impulse?" I wasn't sure whether to consider this a depressive episode since Benjamin wasn't continually "down"; indeed, he had seemed quite happy just a few hours earlier. No, the hormonal rollercoaster was more likely taking him on an extreme ride. However, help was definitely called for, and Benjamin would benefit from discussing his new issues with someone other than me.

"How about an appointment with Dr. R? It's been a few years since you've seen him." Since Benjamin liked his psychiatrist, he agreed, on the condition that I would do most of the talking. "And you can visit with your school psychologist too, you know." Benjamin had already developed a friendship with this man, and he looked relieved at the idea of asking this trusted individual for helpful suggestions.

As Benjamin's new difficulties burgeoned, it came time to declare which classes he intended to take on entering high school. Benjamin would be starting ninth grade in the fall, and I had been attending various transition meetings, trying to formulate a strategy for making Benjamin's high school time a manageable and successful experience.

I had always set expectations sky-high, and even though Benjamin had progressed enormously in response, I now realized that his autism wasn't likely to fade away. Indeed, some of Benjamin's autistic issues were as much of a problem *now* as they had been when he was three years old and, with the new level of personal drama happening in his life, I became tense just *thinking* about getting him into a college degree program.

I was all for keeping Benjamin's options open, but as I perused the prerequisites for attending an institution of higher learning, my heart sank. Just getting through the basic graduation requirements of high school would be a struggle. I thought back to the many hoops I had jumped through in my schooling, working my way through one requirement or degree after another until I had finished my doctorate. I had taken this hoop-jumping for granted; it wasn't a problem for me. But Benjamin? Such an approach would be impossible.

No, it was time to put a long-term plan in place that would support Benjamin's needs. After much discussion with various teachers, counselors, and special education staff, I came up with a viable strategy. Since Benjamin needed so much extra time in his academic learning, we would spread his classes out over five-and-a-half years, and he would take some courses during summer school sessions as well. Legally, Benjamin could attend high school up through the semester that he turned twenty-one years of age.

Benjamin was agreeable with this plan, recognizing that he couldn't handle the pressure of a full load of academics. Besides, he was excited about being in the school's outstanding choir program for the duration of these years, and he also looked forward to having room in his schedule for fun classes like dance, fitness, acting, and cooking. In addition, there was the possibility of attending the district's tech center, and we were considering courses in urban agriculture and greenhouse management. Such classes were more hands-on and practical, and would suit Benjamin's learning style better than the traditional school setting.

During his last semester of eighth grade, Benjamin regularly visited the school psychologist, and he often brought home little 3 x 5 index cards with something special written on them: a motto, a short poem, a meditation. To Benjamin, these cards were like little gifts, and he took them seriously, memorizing their content and reciting the lines under his breath when he felt emotionally vulnerable.

Near the end of the term, I checked in with the psychologist who told me, "Benjamin is remarkably good at describing what's going on inside, even though he's not effectively able to change it." Shuffling through his notes, he pulled out a paper and read to me. "In describing his mind, Benjamin said that it's *like a woodpecker and also like a caged tiger: there's the relentless pecking away, drilling on a subject, and also the restless feeling of being caught, of being an animal that can't get out of its trap.'* He also made the comment that his intrusive thoughts feel like an infestation of pine beetles in his brain. Your son is so poetic in his pain. His perceptions are uncommon— not what I generally hear from kids his age." I nodded, deeply touched by

Benjamin's words. Benjamin's autism could truly be seen as both a gift and a curse. The hard part was not losing sight of the "gift."

A new volunteer mentoring program had just been established at school, and I was talking to the program administrator. She had met Benjamin during his first-grade year in elementary school and had never forgotten him. "I saw Benjamin the other day," she told me. "He asked me about my kids, and, get this—he remembered their names. How is that possible, after all these years?" She shook her head in wonder and then went on. "With the latest district budget cuts, Benjamin will have even less support than anticipated as he moves into high school. This mentoring program could help fill the gap a little; Benjamin would have a mature role model meeting with him weekly at the high school, providing steady, predictable friendship."

I was enthusiastic at the prospect and even more so when I heard that there was a young man, a graduate student at the university, who might be just the right match for Benjamin. With Rick's job taking him out of town so frequently, Benjamin still had less male influence in his life than I would have liked.

A few days later, Benjamin and I met with the potential mentor. Steve had a calm, steady air of responsibility, and as we chatted, it turned out that he had recently married, and that both he and his wife spoke fluent German. "That's the icing on the cake," I exclaimed. "When you guys get together, you can encourage Benjamin to practice his German a little. He's sometimes resistant with me, but it's different when someone outside the family talks with him." This was a serendipitous match indeed.

Benjamin's bouts of anxiety and agitation had been steadily increasing throughout his last semester of middle school. Once summer vacation began and the predictable routine of school was no longer in place, his initial cheek-chewing tic exploded into a horrifying display of other bodily tics and ever lengthening obsessive-compulsive rituals. "Let's work together. That'll distract you and help your brain out of its rut," I would say, holding up Benjamin's violin or a play script, knowing that our session together would be torturous if the tics didn't die down. There was no predicting when they would take over, and the various psychiatric medications we had tried throughout the past months were not helping.

During acute periods, Benjamin would wake up at night, howling like a wild animal as nightmares of obsessive tics pursued him. I would be torn out of sleep by Benjamin's screams of agony; the timbre of his newly dropped voice, which was now a resonant baritone, sounded like he was being murdered. Heart pounding, I would run to his room and sit by him, trying to calm him, stroking his forehead and back, offering him sips of water. Benjamin, his breath ragged, would be gasping. "They're like weird patterns, eating me alive. I'm afraid of going back to sleep." Not that he could have done so, even if he had wanted to. The physical tics that invariably arose from these dreams would keep him awake for hours, regardless of his exhaustion. Naturally, the next day would be impossible as Benjamin, suffering from sleep-deprivation, became even less resistant to the whims of his rogue brain chemistry. It was heartbreaking to watch, and I felt utterly powerless; nothing I tried made any difference whatsoever.

There were a few weeks in July where the tics laid relatively low, and Benjamin was motivated to make some independent forays into various parts of Boulder, taking the city bus. I was thrilled at this new development and at Benjamin's uncanny ability to work the bus system without assistance.

During one of these outings, I got a call from him on his cell phone. "Hey mom, I'm on the bus returning from Denver. I changed my mind about going to the north-Boulder trail heads and decided to check out Denver's light-rail system instead. Now I'm almost home."

"Holy mackerel," I exclaimed. Benjamin had had an adventure, based on sheer curiosity with no extensive planning, and he was even getting home around the time we had agreed on. "Benjamin is like a teenager with a new car, except that his wheels are on a bus," I thought, thrilled at the show of independent competence. "It's probably good that he didn't ask my permission; I'd have been concerned about unsavory characters he might run into without picking up clues that would help him out of harm's way. But, *all's well that ends well*."

August had arrived, and Benjamin was in musical theater camp. When I peeked in on rehearsals, I would often find him sitting alone, chewing his cheek, rocking, staring into nothingness as the rest of the cast was busy rehearsing. "You're part of the ensemble, go join in, this is supposed to be fun for you," I would whisper to him, and Benjamin would float onto the stage, still looking somewhat vacant. Somehow, at the end of the two-week camp, he made it through the opening night performance with a glowing smile, singing in the ensemble, and loving his short solo moment. At the performance the following night however, I was crushed. Benjamin couldn't stop squinting into the bright stage lights, and he looked sedated, sluggishly following the actions of the ensemble actor in front of him. "This is it, we've reached the end," I thought, feeling agonized both for Benjamin and for his cohorts on stage. "Now that Benjamin is older, expectations are going up. The high school musicals are like professional productions, and there's no way Benjamin will be allowed to participate with this kind of thing going on."

I wanted to cry. Only the year before, I had been entertaining high hopes as Benjamin shone in his various performances. Now there would be no further outlet for Benjamin's acting, even though it was therapeutic for him and gave him something to strive for. The proper support system just wasn't there.

41

High School

High school had begun, and Benjamin was thrilled, primarily because he was seeing many of the friends who had graduated from middle school a year before him. The school was enormous, over 2,000 students, and Benjamin seemed to like the beehive-busy feeling in the school's halls and lobbies. The highlight of each day for him was the freshman choir class. Several social events had been scheduled right at the beginning of the year, and Benjamin, with his love for special occasions and a party atmosphere, was eager to attend these, regardless of whether his friends would be present or not. I admired his boldness; most kids his age wouldn't want to go alone like that.

While Benjamin was generally having fun in his transition to high school, I was sweating it. Now grades would "count" and go on a permanent transcript, and I lived in fear of Benjamin's receiving below-passing marks. I had already sent each teacher a copy of my updated *Guide to Benjamin*, preparing them for a bright young man whose special needs would make it extremely difficult to keep up with regular academic performance standards. Now I was trying coordinate with teachers in regards to how assignments might be adjusted and/ or reduced.

The catch-22, of course, was that Benjamin actually required *more,* not less, practice in order to comprehend and assimilate materials. Yet, there weren't enough hours in the day to get through even half of what was being assigned. For example, the math modification had Benjamin doing every other problem, and we slaved over these assignments, but Benjamin was quickly falling behind due to lack of sufficient drill. Even though I had done some pre-teaching of algebra during the past year, this head-start only carried Benjamin through the first few weeks of class.

Frustrated, I lamented the recent cuts that had eliminated a slowed-down math class where one semester's material would have been stretched out over the course of an entire year. Surely there were many kids who would have benefitted from such a class, not just special-needs students like Benjamin. These same cuts had eliminated para-pro support as well, and I spent many hours each week, emailing teachers, trying to figure out their systems and expectations, educating them about Benjamin's needs, and attempting to keep track of Benjamin's belongings which were disappearing regularly, having been forgotten in one location or another.

Each day, after Benjamin returned from school, I would spend time digging through his accordion folder, trying to figure out what the homework was; no one was monitoring Benjamin to be sure the assignments were written down. Next, I would study the math book in order to refresh my memory of high school algebra—I didn't want to teach the wrong material—and then we would finally sit down and start the homework. "This is insane," I would think, gritting my teeth and uttering a bitter laugh. "It would be easier for me to volunteer as a para at the school and to just attend class with Benjamin." Not that I was going to do it; Benjamin had to stop depending so much on his "mom-safety-net."

After the initial weeks of school, the pace became unsustainable as assignments piled up. Some teachers, on observing Benjamin's apparent brightness, couldn't come to grips with the degree of his daily challenges. They were convinced that Benjamin simply had to learn accountability and that things would begin to "click" once he was used to the routine of high school. "He just needs to apply himself and become a little more responsible and independent."

Right. Sure. But focused application and independence were amongst Benjamin's areas of greatest weakness. Part of why his homework took so long to complete was because I kept pushing him to think for himself, to be somewhat independent. And if any teacher spent individual time with Benjamin, they too would eventually realize that he was slow in processing things even when he did understand them. They would also recognize that his acute ADD was preventing him from being as responsible as he would like to be. Plus, there were the tics and the OCD rituals. Benjamin's initial euphoria about the excitement and fun of high school had suppressed some of his symptoms, but as homework created an increasing level of stress, his episodes began impacting him again. Too often, I was hearing the horrifying phrases, "Life isn't worth living. Everything is ruined for me...I can't overcome this." Now, we were trying further psychiatric medications and the latest one was sedating Benjamin, making him fall asleep in class.

Finally, after six weeks of struggle, something wonderful occurred. Unexpected funding allowed the school to re-hire its para-pros. Benjamin and I finally had the support we so desperately needed. And joy of joys, the woman assigned to Benjamin was extraordinary. "She does things like you do, mom," Benjamin told me. "She knows how to make me work better, and I can feel her heart. She's warm, even though she's strict with me." Thank heavens.

Benjamin had turned sixteen at the end of October, and by the end of his first semester in high school, he was in anguish due to escalating episodes of tics and OCD rituals. The stress of finals week had put Benjamin over the edge, and the episodes were becoming increasingly scary as new, self-injurious impulses compounded the already out-of-control behaviors.

By the time spring came around, we had tried and abandoned nine psychiatric medications, and I had received occasional alarming calls from school staff. At times, the agitation and hyperventilation that could accompany Benjamin's episodes made it look like he was starting a seizure. Other times, he couldn't get himself out of the building, becoming stuck in hallways or on stairs. Even if someone accompanied him outside, Benjamin couldn't combat his compulsion to return to the "stuck" site within the building.

Strategies like having him carry a cell phone with a preprogrammed "help" number didn't work since, when having an episode, Benjamin wouldn't have the presence of mind to call anyone. Besides that, the cell phone itself had become a source of obsessive fixation that could keep Benjamin rooted to the spot, unable to move his feet as he repeatedly pulled out his phone and then pocketed it again. Since constant supervision wasn't feasible, there were scary moments when Benjamin became a danger to himself. For example, he reported dashing across the street without looking because that was the only way he could force himself to move beyond the curb. Apparently, he had nearly gotten run over by a car during one of these times.

Even the activities that usually gave Benjamin joy and relief could not stand up to his issues. He could no longer go on bike rides because he couldn't keep his mind on safety. Spending time with favorite friends was no guarantee of distraction either, and Benjamin would sequester himself in various bathrooms throughout the school, compulsively washing his hands as he tried to hide his problems from peers. Orchestra rehearsals were no longer enjoyable as tic attacks would keep Benjamin from focusing on the music; he often appeared unable to play his part, even though he had practiced plenty and knew the music. The times leading up to youth symphony concerts were also becoming an agony: Benjamin could barely make it onstage due to his tics, although, once in his seat with me beside him, the performance energy would take over, and he would play well. The same issues were happening before school choir concerts. Most of the time, life was an unpredictable hell.

In order to rule out possible seizure activity in his brain, I took Benjamin to the hospital for a sleep-deprived EEG, just as I had done when he was eight years old. Throughout the appointment, Benjamin was suffering terribly from tics which made it difficult to get a good reading from the myriad electrodes connected to his head. In the end, however, the neurologist called us to report no unusual findings. I then began scheduling regular visits with an osteopath, signed Benjamin up for forty sessions in a hyperbaric oxygen chamber (hard sided), started him on a series of EEG neurofeedback appointments, and tried brain-spotting therapy with him, all to no avail.

We were still doing medication trials as well, and finally we hit upon a medication that seemed to take the edge off for Benjamin, allowing him to become a little bit more relaxed and tolerant of my "interfering" with his tics. However, as school ended and we moved into summer break, the effects of the medication began wearing off, and we found that increasing the dosage only sedated Benjamin into sleep. Fortunately, this drug could be used on an as-needed basis, and that was how we eventually began managing the worst of Benjamin's episodes, with varying degrees of success.

School had resumed, Benjamin was now in tenth grade, and he would soon be turning seventeen years old. Mentally and emotionally, he was fragile, and his teachers recognized that putting on the pressure would achieve nothing but a breakdown. Per my request, they came to accept that whatever Benjamin could manage at school would have to be "good enough," and that he wouldn't be able to do homework outside of school hours. Benjamin himself asked to be exempted from most computer assignments since, whenever he spent much time on the machines, he could feel his thoughts spiraling into fixation, propelling him into obsessive behaviors. He also found himself stammering and having difficulty finishing sentences as his mind looped back over previously spoken words. "It's like when you listen to a CD that's been scratched, and it skips or keeps getting stuck," he would tell me.

At home, I too was careful with Benjamin, gauging his capacity for limited violin or voice sessions, and otherwise allowing him to spend most of each afternoon eating, lying down, or bouncing on his gymno-ball, a motion which clearly soothed his nervous system. With a renewed attitude of acceptance, I was stepping back and giving Benjamin space, feeling that we had arrived at a tipping point. He was nearly an adult now, and it was time to realistically assess which direction his future might take. Clearly, the level of recovery that I had always hoped for was not going to happen, and I needed to create a new definition of success which would resonate with reality.

To start with, I needed to let go of the goal that Benjamin attend college right after high school and that he attain a traditional degree. Certainly, he might take individual college courses if they were of true interest to him, but he couldn't be expected to take scads of required classes as would be standard with a prescribed degree format. Most likely, Benjamin would benefit from signing up for classes offered within the community and from joining clubs or other social groups in order to extend his learning beyond high school.

Now, what about an eventual job? What was Benjamin truly suited for?

What scenarios would maximize his strengths while also accommodating his myriad challenges? Probably, a patchwork of varied tasks would best fit Benjamin's attention-deficit style of interacting with the world. He was certainly not cut out for a "steady job" or heavy responsibilities. As I mulled this over, I considered Benjamin's personality, identifying key traits that might lead to satisfying work.

In essence, his soul was filled with music and nature, he loved being social and performing for large audiences, and he had a deeply caring side to him that needed an outlet. In fact, during the past year, Benjamin had begun regularly visiting an elderly family friend, knowing that she was lonely. Benjamin would read out loud to her, and he would help her when she needed to go shopping or take the bus. Sometimes, Benjamin would ask for her grocery list and would go to a nearby store on his own, enjoying the feel of helping while also being independent. As long as Benjamin wasn't having a bad spell with his tics, he was an excellent home companion, and perhaps this could become a paying job one day.

As I considered apprenticeships or trade schools which might suit Benjamin's nature, I kept drawing a blank. There wasn't yet any drive or interest coming from him, and all the things I had thought of so far didn't really fit. However, beginning in Benjamin's junior year, he would be enrolled in an urban agriculture class, to be followed by a greenhouse management course. These classes would dovetail into Benjamin's lifelong experiences with my parents' garden and might lead us to some answers.

Music and acting? These would be lifelong loves for Benjamin, but he couldn't compete in a professional setting. And what about his knack for entertaining people and making them laugh? Benjamin was known throughout his high school for telling jokes and spoonerism stories, and he brightened many people's days in spite of his own depressing difficulties. He had even entertained at several large parties, causing great hilarity with the mind-bendingly funny routines that he had memorized. Perhaps he could one day capitalize on this ability.

As I meditated on Benjamin's talents and on how to draw out his natural charisma, an idea came to me. We would create an educational and inspiring presentation about living with autism, and this would be Benjamin's outlet for performing on his own terms while also contributing something valuable to the community. What could be better?

I would start off the presentation, briefly introducing our journey with autism. Then Benjamin would take over, speaking for a full half-hour. He would use a script for support, and while he was speaking, I would project power-point slides containing a variety of evocative photos and other visuals. Benjamin could even tell some jokes for comic relief. Following the presentation, Benjamin would perform his poi-swing routine; this would be a source of energy and joy for him and would have an equally rousing effect on his audiences. Then we would field questions from the audience, both of us providing our differing perspectives on living with autism. It was a perfect plan, and when I presented it to Benjamin, he was immediately charged up at the thought of becoming a public speaker.

Coming home from school a few days later, Benjamin announced, "Mom, I talked with the librarian at school, and he was totally enthusiastic about me giving a presentation. We worked out a date and a time, and I'm going to invite all my friends and even people that we know outside of school. I've got permission."

Benjamin's debut as a public speaker was successful beyond anything I had imagined. On April 17, 2012, hordes of students and adults converged in the spacious school library to hear what Benjamin had to say. Approximately 120 people were able to squeeze into the presentation space, and another seventy or so had to be turned away at the doors since there was no more room. There was laughter in all the right places, and there were tears too—Benjamin's story and his courage in telling it were deeply touching, reaching the hearts of his listeners.

Audience feedback made it immediately clear that we were providing more than an education on autism. We were inspiring people to face their own life challenges with renewed determination and perseverance, and our underlying message of hope and hard work was engendering widespread resonance. The silver lining that rimmed our dark autism cloud suddenly seemed luminous indeed.

We had fresh, positive energy to share, and autism would be our springboard.

Epilogue

As I sit at home writing this, the morning sun is streaming in the window, and Benjamin is off at his summer gardening job on the other side of town where, twice per week, he spends half the day planting, weeding, and harvesting along with fifty other youths who have earned their spots working for a community agriculture initiative called *Cultiva*.

Three afternoons per week, Benjamin is in rehearsal with *Tapestry*, a newly formed theater group which pairs special-needs actors with typical peers as their mentors and understudies. This year, they are producing the musical *Annie* (in its reduced "junior" version), and Benjamin has the male-lead role of Daddy Warbucks. Of course, learning the part involves much time outside of rehearsals, and I drill Benjamin on his lines and acting as I have always done.

At home, Benjamin is polishing up his spoonerism routines with the idea that he might start up a small party entertainment business. He has told these stories at numerous gatherings already, making quite a splash with the somewhat naughty and highly amusing tales.

With my help, Benjamin is learning yet another violin concerto and is also practicing his singing, memorizing the bass part of an *a capella* vocal quartet. He'll begin rehearsing this quartet with several of his choir friends once school resumes. (This coming year, Benjamin will be a senior. After that, he will be considered a "super-senior" and will continue with classes until he turns twenty-one years old, the district's age limit for special-needs students attending high school.)

Benjamin continues visiting his elderly friend who is now in a nursing home, reading out loud to her and keeping her company. He is also active in contacting various friends and setting up fun things to do—folk-dancing, hiking, going to special events, and so on. As has always been the case, Benjamin reaches out and makes these get-togethers happen, knowing that if he doesn't, the phone won't necessarily be ringing for him.

And our autism presentations? Since his debut, Benjamin has spoken for "standing room only" crowds at universities and colleges and has been featured in several news articles and on TV. He has also presented at high schools and community organizations, at the Colorado Department of Education, and for SEAC (Special Education Advisory Council). He was recognized by the Autism Society of Colorado with their "Compassionate Youth of the Year" award, and was the featured entertainer at the ASC's inaugural "Walk With Autism" fundraiser. He has been invited to speak for the CAGT conference (Colorado Association for Gifted and Talented), and also for the Autism National Committee conference. Further speaking engagements are in the works.

Benjamin continues his struggles with autism, tics, OCD, and ADD, and with his inability to handle pressure or to do things quickly. However, the sense of devastating disability that pervaded Benjamin's freshman and sophomore years of high school has gradually lessened over the past year.

I believe that most of the change is due to the new gut-healing diet that Benjamin has been on since early last summer. He has always had mild gut issues (common in persons with autism), and the various dietary interventions which we pursued over the years did not resolved the gut problems. The so-called GAPS diet primarily involves cutting out all carbohydrates and processed sugars, focusing instead on animal proteins and fats which have many gut-building properties. Vegetables and fruits, nuts and seeds, raw honey, and various plant oils are gradually added to the diet, depending on the individuals' tolerance of these foods. The basic premise of GAPS is that, by healing the gut, the body's immune system and detoxifying mechanisms begin working properly, which allows brain functioning to improve.

The GAPS protocol for healing the digestive system is outlined in a book by Natasha Campbell-McBride called *Gut and Psychology Syndrome*. However, the basic approach may need customizing, depending on individual response, and I recommend finding a practitioner with experience to help in this. In Benjamin's case, we discovered that he had an extreme sensitivity to most foods. The more we cut back on food groups in order to unburden his digestive system, the worse things seemed to get. It seemed that his body was finally being given the space to express its opinion loud and clear, and the message was: "I can't tolerate *anything*—except for animal meats, animal fats, and egg yolks." If I ignored the evidence and tried adding a half teaspoon of something mild like banana or cooked apple to a single meal, Benjamin would experience violent diarrhea within twelve hours. In the end, I had no choice but to listen to his body if I didn't want to make him sick.

So, here is what happened: for over a month, Benjamin' diet was limited to volumes of freshly cooked chicken broth and various freshly prepared meats which resulted in his gut becoming stabilized. Then I began an extremely conservative schedule of adding certain cooked vegetables, fruits, and probiotic foods to the broth and meat. As dictated by Benjamin's gut reactions, I was only able to build up *one food at a time*, initially at the rate of *1/8 teaspoon* every two or three days, increasing in quarter teaspoon increments as tolerance developed. It was an excruciatingly slow process, and I kept meticulous charts tracking the foods, Benjamin's gut reactions, and his autism/tic/OCD symptoms.

Now, a full year after beginning this process, I can say that it has been worth it, frustrating as it was in its initial stages. Benjamin has built up tolerance to a considerable array of foods, both cooked and raw, and his gut issues are consistently under control. The frequency of tic and OCD episodes has definitely been diminishing, even though he still has times of great suffering. In the large scheme of things, one year of healing isn't much, and it is clear that Benjamin's gut has quite a ways to go. However, his diet will continue to expand over the course of years, and Benjamin's sense of well-being will surely increase as healing continues.

In addition to following the GAPS diet, Benjamin has been visiting a homeopathic practitioner who has experience with "Cease Therapy." This newly developed branch of homeopathy involves a special protocol of administering detoxifying remedies, and Benjamin has been feeling the positive effects of this approach.

Benjamin has also gotten better at applying self-regulating strategies, and the most helpful one to date has been "EFT tapping" (Emotional Freedom Technique). Various energy meridians are stimulated by gently tapping them while simultaneously verbalizing positive affirmations. (Several useful EFT sites can be found on the internet.) Benjamin has also found great comfort in certain eurythmy exercises taught to him by a family friend with a lifetime's experience in therapeutic applications of eurythmy.

Clearly, there is hope for more progress in the future, and I maintain faith that the right people and situations will enter Benjamin's life at the right time. As we reach out, sharing our story and putting forth positive energy, we are gratified by the heartfelt resonance that comes to us from the many people we meet.

If you would like to read about Benjamin's junior year in high school and want to join in keeping up with Benjamin's latest doings, please "like" us on Facebook and subscribe to our free blog; we post photos and/or Benjamin's artwork with each entry. Both can be accessed by Googling *Benjamin Breaking Barriers* or by going to our website. To find out about scheduled autism presentations, to view a short demo-video of Benjamin, and to keep up on new product development, please check our website: *www.benjaminbreakingbarriers.com*

All the best to you, and please join us in breaking barriers!

Appendix

Index of Benjamin's Therapies, Games, Exercises

Shaping an autistic person's thinking and actions with behavioral therapy can open the door to a meaningful and satisfying life; the disabling aspects of autism can be alleviated to varying degrees, and the strengths and positive differences of the person can be fostered. When skill and creativity are combined with genuine caring, behavioral therapy becomes more than a recipe; it provides structure when teaching the complex skills involved in language, social interaction, and meaningful activity. Benjamin's story demonstrates how I imbued my behavioral work with heart and soul so that my son might grow up with the greatest chance at finding joy in life.

An outline of Benjamin's behavioral programs is omitted here; my primary resources for these were *Let Me Hear Your Voice,* by C. Maurice, and *Behavioral Interventions for Young Children With Autism: A Manual for Parents and Professionals*, edited by C. Maurice, with G. Green and S. Luce.

Below is an index of the primary issues and interventions that became relevant in my work with Benjamin. Please keep in mind that teaching/learning can be a messy process and that one keeps returning to even the most basic skills, refreshing and refurbishing them, expanding on skills which have already been developed, and building up new possibilities for thinking, feeling, and acting.

Getting Started:
- Underlying **attitude/philosophy**: foster joy in learning, build intrinsic motivation
- Tune in to subtle **communication**, find what **motivates** a connection, take advantage of **natural settings**
- Develop **eye contact**, **turn-taking**, and **imitation skills**
- **Reduce language** to bare bones, essential words
- **Reduce sensory overload** and shape **tantrum behaviors, phobias**
- Work with **emotional/spiritual energy**, invite **inspiration**
- Be sensitive and flexible when **facilitating**/shadowing; monitor your communication style
- Allow **assimilation** time
- Recognize the **individual's** particular talents, strengths/weaknesses
- Take **notes**—track progress, analyze issues, process your own feelings

Language/Communication:
subtle signals 8
pointing 3, 12, 26, 171
reduced language 10, 11

Working with Personal Energy & Visualization: (continued)
acting as facilitator/shadow 77, 92, 96, 113, 127, 138, 155, 164-165, 166, 171, 209, 284, 285, 309, 326
inviting inspiration/using intuition 97, 98, 105, 120, 159-160, 164, 178, 183, 314
using imagery 59, 89, 139, 155, 164, 224, 293-294
maintaining a "vision" for the present/future 89, 106, 134, 143, 159-160, 163, 164, 235, 293

Motivation/Rewards:
willpower 16, 43, 44, 51, 53, 60, 79, 84, 97, 159, 176, 177, 178, 188, 248, 271, 263, 283
intrinsic motivation 31, 33, 35, 44, 98-99, 245,
rewards 12, 23, 24, 25, 42, 52, 56, 75, 95, 122, 151-152, 166-167, 177, 178, 192, 209, 289, 302, 323
working *with* a disability vs. *against* it 84, 97, 122, 123, 175, 283, 298
fixations; expanding/transforming these 87-88, 90, 130, 148-149, 175, 179-180, 188-189, 190, 195, 196, 206, 209, 210-211, 214, 221, 241, 251, 258-259, 265, 270, 272, 307-308

Music as Therapy:
music as a means for connecting emotionally 9, 24, 33, 35, 45, 54, 72, 77, 87, 88, 123, 128, 137-138, 142, 167, 176, 268, 292
movement with music 9, 17, 18, 28, 36, 37, 55, 57, 68, 155, 213, 246
singing for language development 68, 70, 75-76, 86, 253, 266
learning a musical instrument 35, 40, 76-77, 79, 94, 103, 180, 191, 201-202, 243
music to facilitate task-completion 154, 160, 161, 165, 167, 202, 252-253
music as a social activity 143-144, 224, 237, 258, 268, 272, 300, 317, 332

The Arts as Therapy:
music (see separate section)
drawing 64-65, 150, 174, 203, 245, 251, 255-256, 263
painting 33, 92, 164, 176, 205, 213
dance/expressive movement 36-37, 55, 202, 219, 246, 271, 263, 298, 332
theater 178-179, 304-305, 307, 309-310, 311, 313-314, 315, 319, 324-325, 336-337, 344
puppetry 80, 147-148, 168, 235, 237, 249, 264, 302, 305, 307,
poetry 75, 104, 132-133, 144, 147-148, 155, 185, 191, 207, 218, 233, 263, 292
storytelling/stories as teaching tools 80, 85, 97, 142-143, 167, 204, 210, 212, 213, 237-238, 245-246, 262, 264, 267-268, 272

Basic Game Skills:
sorting 83, 140
matching 36, 40, 83-84, 91, 98, 112
auditory/visual recall 141, 167, 242
following directions 141, 191
using clues/guessing 91, 118-119, 168
searching/retrieving 110, 168, 191, 206
playing games with others 182, 187, 211, 235

Daily Life:
tantrums/phobias 11, 28-29, 60, 138, 148, 177, 193, 241, 274, 280
feeding 2, 161
dressing 161
toilet training 73
transitions 93, 148, 168, 247
picture schedules 151, 168-169, 173,
shaping self-stimulatory/injurious behaviors 89, 110-111, 163, 206, 211, 257
preparing for upcoming situations 128, 132, 168, 226, 235, 277
boundaries/consequences 116, 157, 177, 179, 188-189, 190, 191, 192, 193, 229-230, 243, 245, 248, 250, 257, 267, 278, 283, 329
negotiating/compromising 177, 221, 283
clear expectations/saying "no" 177, 188, 211, 221, 267, 271, 310
developing independence 159-160, 161, 165, 166, 174, 177-178, 188, 248, 265-266, 331, 336
self-awareness/control 185, 189, 192, 224, 245, 250, 299, 303-304, 308, 331, 334, 346
responsibility/chores 162, 203, 213-214, 238, 265-266
manners 155, 321
work ethic 331
"rules for living" 231, 228, 254, 263, 275, 276, 277, 279, 290
conscience/moral thinking 253, 258, 261-262, 303-304
dealing with bullying/teasing 96, 114, 124, 199, 307, 313, 322-333, 324
parent as advocate 123-124, 274, 309-310, 312, 320, 326, 339
self-advocacy 185, 323, 330-331, 342-343, 344

Other Considerations:
viewpoints on autism/the autistic brain 25, 26, 29, 30, 43-44, 59, 65, 75, 82-83, 84, 87, 94, 132, 144, 156-157, 163, 165, 169, 181, 182, 183, 185, 306, 320, 322, 323, 327-328, 329, 332
the autism label 153, 158, 288, 316

Other Considerations: (continued)
developmental stages 43, 73, 84, 87, 116-117, 144, 154, 156-157, 163, 171, 174, 176, 179, 181, 185, 188, 199, 212, 217, 228, 242, 251
assimilation time 35, 51, 97, 170
special talents/splinter skills 59, 70, 150, 156, 181, 186, 190, 201-202, 222, 245, 266, 342
unusual insightfulness 159, 229, 250-251, 255, 260, 279-280, 282, 292, 293-294, 299, 302, 305, 309, 331, 334
connecting with nature/animals 47, 48, 56, 60, 62, 102, 121, 135, 136-137, 143, 148-149, 174, 203, 219-220, 223, 295
influence of weather 51, 96, 105, 128, 174, 208
Waldorf education 15-16, 43, 49, 78, 284
celebrations/rhythm of the year 71, 75, 80, 85, 87-88, 89, 99-100, 110, 123, 132-134, 160, 168, 172, 178, 185, 187, 198, 206, 218, 232-233, 236, 270, 281, 289, 290-291, 295

Sensory Integration:
massage/body brushing 7, 41, 88
compression/weight 17, 57, 107, 204, 207, 211, 247
bouncing, rolling, rocking, spinning, swinging 9, 17-18, 20, 42, 46, 56-57, 87-88, 201, 213, 227
balancing, climbing, strength/coordination 19, 20, 32, 47, 50, 58, 78, 114, 202, 220, 226, 319
olfactory and tactile stimulation 20, 28, 32, 34, 41, 48, 58, 98, 192, 205
eye/hand coordination/handcrafts 19, 30, 39-40, 46, 77-78, 109, 146, 163, 171, 189, 203, 205, 237
water play/swimming 33, 40-41, 55, 60, 148, 191, 206-207, 211, 220-221, 227, 249
therapy pets 20, 95-96, 165, 203, 210, 277
horseback riding 62-63, 131-132, 245, 273
gardening 116, 158, 203, 261
walking, strenuous hiking 47, 121, 135, 136-137, 143, 219, 220, 260, 316, 295, 301, 326
sensing personal space/larger spaces 207, 246, 332
"brain gym" 299, 318
bilateral sound recordings 324

Biochemical Issues:
diet/nutrition 7, 39, 107, 117, 149
medical testing for 107-108, 117, 185
lead abatement 69

Biochemical Issues: (continued)
chelation therapy 278-279, 281, 282, 290, 295, 296, 305
liver functioning/gut issues 278, 345-346

Therapeutic Modalities in Benjamin's Life:
behavioral therapy 21-22, 120-123, 123, 126-127, 128
homeopathy 15-16, 21, 52, 53, 56, 62, 84, 88, 109, 158, 174, 188, 212, 217, 301-302
cranio-sacral therapy 15, 21, 35, 37, 53, 59, 70, 100, 110, 117, 178
sensory integration (see separate section)
chirophonetics 42, 44, 58, 88, 114
eurythmy 104, 128, 165, 346
psychiatric medications 294, 296, 298, 301, 310-311, 335, 339-340, 341
Crossinology/brain integration 332
osteopathic treatment/rolfing/massage 331
HBOT (hyperbatic oxygen treatments—hard-sided chamber) 340
EEG biofeedback 341
brain spotting 341
EFT tapping (Emotional Freedom Technique) 346
"Cease" therapy (homeopathic detox) 346
GAPS diet (Gut and Psychology Syndrome) 345-346

General School Concepts:
- Be an **involved parent**: cultivate relationships with teachers/administrators; open communication is key
- Provide copies of *Teacher's Guide to My Child* and update this as the years go by: outline strengths/weaknesses; identify quirks/emotional triggers; effective strategies/cues; expectations;
- **Flexibility/Teamwork**: parent's/teacher's willingness to learn from each other *and from the child*
- Think outside the box: parents/teachers **collaborate** so that taught materials are meaningful
- Maintain **balance**: build on child's **strengths** even while remediating difficulties
- Be aware of personal **energy/intentions** and the power of unconditional love
- Maintain a **vision** of what is possible: aim high, have faith (but don't ignore the day-to-day needs and realities)
- **Scaffolding:** provide layers of support and withdraw incrementally as student works towards independence

General School Concepts: (continued)
- **Strategize:** use concrete language; picture schedules; sensory breaks; behavior charts; adjust assignments to take advantage of student's interests/motivations;
- **Appreciate "neuro-diversity":** different perspectives make the world a richer place

School Strategies:

Discussion Questions
for classroom use and reading groups

Benjamin has spent a lifetime learning skills that most people take for granted. Have you ever had a hard time learning something that others seem to find easy? How did that feel? What thoughts went through your mind? Did you feel different or excluded?

Benjamin has experienced various difficulties with developing speech and being able to express himself verbally. Think of a time when you had something to say, but it came out wrong, or you couldn't find the words to express yourself. How did that feel? How did it affect your interaction?

Motivation is a key issue with autism, as is repeatedly illustrated by Benjamin's story. What motivates you in different circumstances? When are your motivations internally driven by desire, and when do you depend on external rewards to accomplish something? What happens when you are lacking in motivation? How do you feel, and what is the result?

Fixations can be a major hindrance to a person with autism. Have you ever experienced an "earworm"—a song that keeps repeating itself in your mind? Have you ever obsessed on a particular thought? How do you feel when this occurs? How does it affect your thinking and actions?

The arts—and music in particular—have been a lifeline for Benjamin, both as a means for expression and as a ticket into social interaction. They have also facilitated much of his therapy. What role do the arts play in your life? In what capacity do they support your emotional, mental, and physical health? If the arts were cut out of your life, what impact would that have?

Benjamin has, at various times, had difficulty dealing with sadness—both within himself and when others display the emotion. Have you known people who seem to shut down emotionally? How do you feel in response? How do you interpret their behavior?

Benjamin's autism causes him to create rituals that might help in controlling/ managing himself and/or the world around him, thus creating a perception of safety/predictability. What rituals do you engage in? How do you calm yourself? How much predictability do you need in order to feel secure?

Benjamin was teased and bullied at school. Can you think of ways to prevent such behavior? Have you ever exhibited such behavior to someone who is different? If you have children of your own, how might you help them learn compassion and kindness? How can an appreciation for differences be developed?

Benjamin wears his heart upon his sleeve, and this is partly due to his autism—he isn't capable of playing "mind games". Have you known someone to be completely transparent about their feelings—particularly positive ones? When is this a gift? When can it cause problems? Think of a time when you were young and felt great joy. As you grow older, do you find your expressions of joy changing? Do you ever hide or suppress your joy? If so, why?

Benjamin derives great joy and satisfaction from performing, and he loves the "high" feeling that comes from being on stage. When you engage in an activity you love, do you experience magical moments? How is this state of mind different from ordinary day-to-day consciousness?

Four major areas of a person's life are impacted by autism: language; social skills; sensory/motor functions; interests. Do you know anyone who exhibits autistic traits? Would you treat them differently if you knew they had a diagnosis? Does "labeling" someone affect your perception of them? What are the advantages and disadvantages of having a label?

The disabling aspects of autism can distract one from recognizing the affected person's strengths. Imagine every aspect of your life being run according to your weaknesses. How would others perceive you? How would you feel and act in response?

Autism causes difficulties with picking up on the subtle clues of communication. Consider the layers of subtext and body language contained in a conversation. What happens when someone doesn't "get" implied information? What feelings arise for each side when misunderstanding or lack of comprehension occurs? How might you change your style of communication when interacting with someone who has autism?

There is as much variance between people on the autism spectrum as there is between "neurotypicals". Certain traits and behaviors are hallmarks of autism, but these manifest on a continuum from mild to severe. Do you know anyone with autism? Discuss the similarities and differences between the various persons with autism known to your discussion group.

Benjamin's mother has repeatedly looked for life's "silver lining" and has made the best of a difficult situation. If you approached your life in this manner, what might change? Can you take something you consider a liability (a weakness or problem) and turn it around so it becomes an advantage? What are your sources of strength and inspiration? Is there an element of acceptance that might facilitate your process?

Nowadays, persons with physical disabilities have access to wheelchair ramps, curb cuts, and other physical supports. With autism, the disability affects thinking and behavior in ways that aren't always readily recognizable as being autism-driven. For example, someone with autism might come across as acting purposefully anti-social, as unreasonable, or as immature (i.e. child tantrums). Can you brainstorm ways in which autism can be accommodated—in schools, the work-place, in restaurants and other public facilities? How might sensory challenges be accommodated in public spaces (for example, a quiet calming-area with dimmed lights)?

Educating people about autism is a vital first step towards building understanding and compassion. Now that you have read Benjamin's story, how can you help with this? Beyond education, how might our attitudes/actions as a society shift in order to better accommodate the growing population of persons with autism?

Resources

People often ask me to recommend books or resources that resonate with my life philosophy and my way of working with Benjamin. Please see our website *www.benjaminbreakingbarriers.com* for a listing of favorite books, news articles, web links, movies, and other resources. The list is a "living document," an *Addendum* that gets updated as new things come to my attention; it doesn't strive to be comprehensive, but it does reflect my values and aesthetics when approaching pedagogical issues, autism therapy, and life in general.

In this book, various children's titles are mentioned in passing, and these are included in the website *Addendum*. The listing below is limited to materials specifically referenced in the text.

Baldwin, Rahima. *You Are Your Child's First Teacher.* California: Celestial Arts, 1989.

Ballinger, Erich. *The Learning Gym: Fun-to-Do Activities for Success at School.* California: Educational Kinesiology Foundation, 1996.

Berger, Barbara Helen. *The Jewel Heart.* New York: The Putnam and Gosset Group, 1994.

Bockemühl, Wera. *Unser Jahreskreis.* Germany: Emil Fink Verlag, 1960's.

Campbell-McBride, Natasha. *Gut and Psychology Syndrome.* England: Medinform Publishing, 2010.

Cooper, Susan. *The King of Shadows.* New York: Margaret K. McElderry Books, 1999.

Curtiss, Arline. *In the Company of Bears.* Illustrated by Barbara Stone. California: Oldcastle Publishing, 1994.

Diestel, Hedwig. *Kindertag.* Stuttgart, Germany: Verlag Freies Geistesleben GmbH, 1967.

Fairman, Eric. *Path of Discovery: a Program of a Waldorf Grade School Teacher.* Australia: Eric Fairman, 1996.

Foster, Nancy, editor. *Let Us Form A Ring: an Acorn Hill Anthology of Songs, Verses, and Stories for Children.* Maryland: Acorn Hill Children's Center, 1989.

Freymuth, Malva. *Mental Practice and Imagery for Musicians: a Practical Guide for Optimizing Practice Time, Enhancing Performance, and Preventing Injury.* Colorado: Integrated Musician's Press, 1999.

Garff, Marianne. *Es Plaudert der Bach.* Switzerland: Verlag Die Pforte, 1976.

Glairon, Susan. "Beyond Words: Music Connects Two Autistic Children to the World." *The Daily Camera* 4 May 2003: D1. Print.

Grandin, Temple. *Thinking In Pictures: and Other Reports From My Life With Autism.* New York: Knopf Doubleday Publishing Group, 1996.

Kaufman, Barry Neil. *Son Rise: The Miracle Continues.* California: H. J. Kramer, Inc., 1994.

Klin, Ami, Warren Jones, Robert Schultz, and Fred Volkmar. "The Enactive Mind, or From Actions to Cognition: Lessons From Autism." *Philosophical Transactions of the Royal Society B* (January 20, 2003): 345-360. http://www. ncbi.nlm.nih.gov/pmc/articles/PMC1693114/pdf/12639332.pdf

Maurice, Catherine. *Let Me Hear Your Voice: A Family's Triumph Over Autism.* New York: Fawcett Columbine, 1993.

Maurice, Catherine, Gina Green, and Stephen C. Luce. *Behavioral Interventions for Young Children With Autism: A Manual for Parents and Professionals.* Texas: Pro-Ed Publishers, 1996.

Pepperberg, Irene. *Alex and Me: How a Scientist and a Parrot Discovered a Hidden World of Animal Intelligence—and Formed a Deep Bond In the Process.* New York: Harper Collins Publishers, 2009.

Reagan, Lisa. "What About Mercury? Getting Thimerosal Out of Vaccines." Mothering Magazine (March/April 2001): 40-55.

Roberts, Monty. *The Man Who Listens To Horses: The Story of a Real-Life Horse Whisperer.* New York: The Ballantine Publishing Group, 1996.

Rosemond, John. *Six-Point Plan for Raising Happy, Healthy Children.* New York: Andrews and McMeel, 1989.

Shaw, William. *Biological Treatments for Autism and PDD.* Kansas: Great Plains Laboratory, 1998.

The Complete Grimm's Fairy Tales. Based on translation by Margaret Hunt. Commentary by Padraic Colum and Joseph Campbell. New York: Random House, Inc., 1972.

The Complete Tales of Beatrix Potter: The 23 Original Peter Rabbit Books. England: The Penguin Group, 1989.

Whiteley, Opal. *The Diary of Opal Whiteley.* Tennessee: September Productions, Inc., 1995. (Originally published as *The Story of Opal: The Journal of an Understanding Heart,* in the Atlantic Monthly Press, 1920.)

About the Author

MALVA FREYMUTH TARASEWICZ is first and foremost a mother—her son Benjamin has long been the focus of her creative energies. Now, Benjamin is a young adult with a talent for public speaking, and Malva has teamed up with him, creating presentations about living with autism which educate while also inspiring others to overcome their personal challenges.

In addition, Malva pursues activities as a professional musician, as a writer, and as an equestrienne competing in upper-level dressage. Malva lives in Boulder with her family, appreciates the beauty of nature that surrounds her home, and revels in the expanding adventure that is *Benjamin Breaking Barriers*. Please visit our website *www.benjaminbreakingbarriers.com*

To follow Benjamin's story, visit our blog, *Benjamin Breaking Barriers*, which picks up where this book leaves off, and watch our YouTube videos as well. Looking for photos of Benjamin? You'll find them on the blog and on our Facebook page, also named—you guessed it—*Benjamin Breaking Barriers*.

This book is available as an ebook.

To contact the author, visit
www.benjaminbreakingbarriers.com.

Coming soon: *Benjamin Breaking Barriers* presentation on DVD.